C. H. Spurgeon's Autobiography

The Life of the Great Baptist Preacher

Compiled from his diary, letters, records and sermons

By the wife of

Charles Haddon Spurgeon

Volume One – 1834 - 1854

Published by Pantianos Classics

ISBN-13: 9781979135191

First published in 1897

Contents

Chapter One - Introduction

Biographies are generally interesting if they are biographies; that is to say, if the events of the person's life are truly told; but I think that the most interesting biography to any man is his own life.... It would have been impossible for me to quote the experiences of other men if they had not been bold enough to record them, and I make an honest attempt to acknowledge my debt to my greater predecessors by writing down my own. Whether this arises from egotism or not, each reader shall decide according to the sweetness or acidity of his own disposition. A father is excused when he tells his sons his own life-story, and finds it the readiest way to enforce his maxims; the old soldier is forgiven when he "shoulders his crutch, and shows how fields were won;" I beg that the license which tolerates these may, on this occasion, be extended to me.

— C. H. S.

THE publication of this work carries out a plan long ago formed by Mr. Spurgeon. In the occasional intervals of comparative leisure that he was able to snatch from his busy life's labors, — and mainly in the bright sunshine at Mentone, — he recorded many of the principal incidents in his wonderful career. As each one was completed, he used joyfully to exclaim,

"There's another chapter for my Autobiography;" and had he been spared long enough, he would doubtless have given to the church and the world a full account of his life as it appeared from his own standpoint. This he has virtually done from the commencement of his public ministry, though not in the connected form in which it is now issued. His preaching was always so largely illustrated from his personal experience that his true biography is delightfully enshrined in the whole series of his Sermons, while "his own Magazine" — *The Sword and the Trowel* — was confessedly autobiographical during the entire period of his unique editorship. His many other published works abound in allusions to the Lord's gracious dealings with him, and these are now for the first time gathered together into a continuous narrative. The record is given entirely in Mr. Spurgeon's own words, except here and there where an explanatory sentence or two had to be inserted, or where letters written to him, and references made by others to the incidents he described, seem to be necessary to the completeness of the history.

Mr. Spurgeon's writings are enriched with many references to other biographies beside his own. In the year 1870, after reading Mr. Arnot's Life of Dr. James Hamilton, he wrote: — "The value of a biography depends far less upon its subject than upon its author. Milton mutilated by Ivimey, and Carey smothered by his nephew Eustace, are mournful instances of literary murder. James Hamilton has the singular good fortune to be embalmed by William Arnot, his own familiar friend and acquaintance, a spirit cast in the same fair mould, a genial genius wealthy in grace and wisdom. It were worthwhile to pray for an earlier end to one's career, if we could be sure of an Arnot to produce its record. Apples of gold in baskets of silver are precious things in an appropriate setting, the golden apple being neither dishonored by contact with a basket too homely, nor shamed by comparison with costlier metal than its own; the memorial of a good man's life should not be marred by poor writing, neither should it be overshadowed by excessive authorship." In *this* Autobiography, the subject is also the author, so the apples of gold are perfectly matched by the golden basket in which they are displayed.

In his early volume, *The Saint and his Savior,* published in 1857, Mr. Spurgeon wrote: — "Few men would dare to read their own autobiography, if all their deeds were recorded in it; few can look back upon their entire career without a blush. 'All have sinned, and come short of the glory of God.' None of us can lay claim to perfection. True, at times, a forgetful self-complacency bids us exult in the virtue of our lives; but when faithful memory awakes, how instantly she dispels the illusion! She waves her magic wand, and in the king's palaces frogs arise in multitudes; the pure rivers at her glance become blood; the whole land is creeping with loathsomeness. Where we imagined purity, lo, imperfection ariseth! The snow-wreath of satisfaction melts before the sun of truth, the nectared bowl of gratulation is embittered by sad remembrances; while, under the glass of honesty, the deformities and irregularities of a life, apparently correct, are rendered, alas! too visible.

"Let the Christian, whose hair is whitened by the sunlight of Heaven, tell his life-long story. He may have been one of the most upright and moral; but there will be one dark spot in his history, upon which he will shed the tear of penitence, because then he knew not the fear of the Lord. Let you heroic warrior of Jesus recount his deeds; but he, too, points to deep scars, the offspring of wounds received in the service of the evil one."

Speaking in the Tabernacle, many years ago, Mr. Spurgeon said: — "I used to marvel at William Huntington's *Bank of Faith,* — a strange enough book, by the way, — but I am sure I could, from my own history, write a far more remarkable *Bank of Faith* than William Huntington has penned. I have often told you, dear friends, that, if I possessed the powers of a novelist, I might write a three-volume novel concerning the events of any one day in my life, so singularly striking has my experience been. I should never need to describe things from the outside, as I should have plenty of material from within. My life seems to me like a fairy dream. I am often both amazed and dazed with its mercies and its love. How good God has been to me! I used to think that I should sing among the saints above as loudly as any, for I owe so much to the grace of God; and I said so once in a sermon, long ago, quoting those lines, —

"'*Then loudest of the crowd I'll sing,*
While Heaven's resounding mansions ring
With shouts of sovereign grace.'

"I thought that I was the greatest debtor to Divine grace, and would sing the loudest to its praise; but when I came down out of the pulpit, there was a venerable woman who said to me, 'You made a blunder in your sermon this evening.' I said, 'I daresay I made a dozen, good soul, but what was that particular one?' 'Why, you said that you would sing the loudest because you owed most to Divine grace; you are but a lad, you do not owe half as much to grace as I do at eighty years of age! I owe more to grace than you, and I will not let you sing the loudest.' I found that there was a general conspiracy among the friends that night to put me in the background, and that is where I meant to be, and wished to me; that is where those who sing the loudest, long to be, to take the lowest place, and praise most the grace of God in so doing."

In *The Sword and the Trowel* for 1869, Mr. Spurgeon turned to good account a popular superstition. He was too humble to apply to himself the closing sentences in the following paragraph; but all who read it must see how exactly it describes the abiding influence of his long and gracious ministry. He wrote: —

"Hone, in his *Year Book*, gives a letter from a correspondent in Raleigh, Nottinghamshire, which states that, many centuries since, the church and a whole village were swallowed up by an earthquake. Many villages and towns have certainly shared a similar fate, and we have never heard of them more.

"'The times have been
When the brains were out, the man would die;'

"but at Raleigh, they say, the old church bells still ring at Christmas time, deep, deep, in earth; and that it was a Christmas morning custom for the people to go out into the valley, and put their ears to the ground to listen to the mysterious chimes of the subterranean temple. This is sheer superstition; but how it illustrates the truth that those preachers, whose voices were clear and mighty for truth during life, continue to preach in their graves! Being dead, they yet speak; and whether men put their ears to their tombs or not, they cannot but hear them."

In the last sermon but one that Mr. Spurgeon ever revised, that remarkable discourse upon the text, "I shall not die, but live, and declare the works of the Lord;" he uttered these words, which have already been to a large extent fulfilled with regard to himself: — "Often, the death of a man is a kind of new birth to him; when he himself is gone physically, he spiritually survives, and from his grave there shoots up a tree of life whose leaves heal nations. O worker for God, death cannot touch thy sacred mission! Be thou content to die if the truth shall live the better because thou diest. Be thou content to die, because death may be to thee the enlargement of thine influence. Good men die as dies the seed-corn which thereby abideth not alone. When saints are apparently laid in the earth; they quit the earth, and rise and mount to Heaven-gate, and enter into immortality. No, when the sepulcher receives this mortal frame, we shall not die, but live."

The portrait, which forms the frontispiece to this volume, has never before, so far as I know, been published. It was a lover's gift to the one who was very soon to become his bride, and I recall how, in the glamour of "love's young dream," I used to gaze on the sweet boyish face, and think no angel could look half so lovely! Afterwards, the picture was enshrined in a massive oaken frame, and it occupied the place of honor on the walls of the house in the New Kent Road, where we began our life's journey together, and founded our first home. Many a time, during my husband's long absences, when fulfilling his almost ceaseless preaching engagements, has this portrait comforted me; its expression of calm confident faith strengthened my heart, and I used to think the up-raised finger pointed to the source whence I must draw consolation in my loneliness.

Something of the same soothing and sacred influence steals over me as I look at it now with tear-filled eyes; it speaks to me, even as it did in those days of long ago, and it says, "Do not fear, my beloved, God is *taking care of us both;* and though we are still separated for a little while, we shall meet again *at home* by-and-by!"

There have been many representations of my dear husband during the intervening years; — the young face changed into that of a strong, energetic man, then it grew into the semblance of one who knew sorrow and suffering, and again it changed into the grave and noble features which we remember best, because his departure has stamped them forever on the tablet of our loving heart. Throughout them all can be traced the sweet humility, the gentle kindness, the mighty faith in God which characterized his glorious and blameless life; but I think it is reserved to this early portrait to depict the intense love and unfailing devotion to his Master which was the secret of his power both with God and man.

In the early portion of the present volume, Mr. Spurgeon's reminiscences of his life at Stambourne are given at considerable length, partly because they present such a charming picture of his happy childhood at his grandfather's, but also because they are of special value to his many friends from the fact that this was the literary work upon which he was engaged just before his long and terrible illness in 1891. They also contain his inimitable description of the interest taken in him in his boyhood by Mr. Knill when at Stambourne, the remarkable prophecy uttered by that godly man over the head of the little ten-years-old lad, its literal fulfillment, and the influence of the incident itself, and the circumstances that followed it, upon the whole of his after history.

Most of the letters, written by Mr. Spurgeon, which are here published for the first time, were copied by his direction specially with a view to his Autobiography. Some of the others have been placed at my disposal by various friends; a few had been printed before. There are, doubtless, many thousands of my dear husband's letters still extant; but no useful purpose could be served by the publication of even a tithe of them. There must, however, be a very large number of the products of his pen that ought to have an enlarged ministry through the press. I shall be glad, therefore, to receive copies of special epistles of public and permanent interest; or, if the originals are lent to me, I will have them copied, and returned at once. All communications for me should be addressed,

— *Mrs. C. H. Spurgeon,*
"Westwood," Beulah Hill, Upper Norwood, London.

Chapter Two - Ancestry and Genealogy

I sing of the noble Refugee,
Who strove in a holy faith,
At the altar of his God to bow,
When the road was marked with death.
When the despot's sword and the bigot's torch
Had driven him forth to roam,
From village, and farm, and city, and town,
He sought our Island Home.
And store of wealth and a rich reward
He brought in his open hand,
For many a peaceful art he taught,
Instead of the fireman's brand.

Dr. Byles.

MR. SMILES, one of the ablest authors of our time, has produced a work upon the Huguenots, [1] which is not only intensely interesting in its style, but of the utmost importance in its subject. It should be read carefully by every states-man in Europe, especially by those who entertain a lingering love to persecution for righteousness' sake, for beyond anything else in print it illustrates the great fact that the oppression of the conscience is an injury to the State, — an injury not only to its mental and moral health, but to its material prosperity. We were not aware that our little isle, the asylum of the banished, had received so great a reward for the entertainment of the Lord's exiles. We knew that they had brought with them many of our most lucrative trades, but we had no idea of the great extent of the boon.

England must have been a poor land until, in entertaining strangers, she enter-tained angels unawares. We are certainly a very singular race; the Huguenot blood has had more to do with us than many suppose; let us hope that, by God's grace, enough of the characteristics of these good men may be found among us to keep us from drifting utterly to Rome and perdition. If England's opening her gates to receive the hunted Protestants of the Continent may be rewarded, in our day, by a revival of the brave spirit which they brought with them, it would be a blessing from the Lord's own right hand.

Many of the Flemish, Dutch, and French Protestants, driven by persecution out of their native country, found a haven of refuge in England; and, naturally, great numbers of them settled down in the Southern and Eastern Counties, though others journeyed to the Midlands, and the North and West of England, and some went as far as Scotland and Ireland. Mr. Smiles says that "Colchester became ex-ceedingly prosperous in consequence of the settlement of the Flemish artisans there. In 1609, it contained as many as 1,300 Walloons and other persons of for-eign parentage." He also mentions that, in many towns, where the refugees fixed their abode, "the artisans set up their looms, and began to work at the manufac-ture of sayes, bayes, and other kinds of cloth, which met with a ready sale." This information is very interesting to me, for in my early days in Essex I used to hear a great deal about "the bay and say industry." I daresay our fathers were poor weavers, but I had far rather be descended from one who suffered for the faith than bear the blood of all the emperors within my veins. I remember speaking with a Christian brother, who seemed right happy to tell me that he sprang of a family which came from Holland during the persecution of the Duke of Alva, and I felt a brotherhood with him in claiming a like descent from Protestant forefathers.

One namesake, and perhaps an ancestor, Job Spurgeon, of Dedham, had to suffer both in purse and in person, "for the testimony of a good conscience," as the Quaker record puts it. In 1677, a distress was levied upon him, and some of his goods were seized, because he had committed the atrocious *crime* of attending a Nonconformist meeting at Dedham! Six years later, for a similar *offense,* he and three other godly men "were required to give sureties for their good behavior, which refusing to do, they were re-committed to prison, where three of them lay upon straw about fifteen weeks in the midst of a winter remarkable for extremity of cold; but the fourth, Job Spurgeon, being so weak that he was unable to lie down, sat up in a chair the most part of that time." In my seasons of suffering, I have often pictured to myself this modern Job in Chelmsford gaol, and thanked God that I bore the same name as this persecuted Spurgeon of two hundred years ago. So far as I can make out the genealogy, it appears to me that this Essex Quaker was my great-grandfather's grandfather, and I sometimes feel the shadow of his broad brim come over my spirit. Grace is not tied to families, but yet the Lord delights to bless to a thousand generations. There is a sweet fitness in the passing on of holy loyalty from grandsire to father, and from father to son. I like to feel that I serve God "from my fathers." I can cast my eye back through four generations, and see that God has been pleased to hear the prayers of our grandfather's father, who used to supplicate with God that his children might live before Him to the last generation; and God has never deserted the house, and has been pleased to bring first one and then another to fear and love His name.

I was amused when I read that a friend in China wrote concerning my name: — "The Chinese cannot pronounce 'Spurgeon' correctly, so we call him in this quarter, 'Sze-Pah-ng,' *i.e.,* 'the successor or continuator of a hundred virtues.' The word 'hundred' in Chinese stands for an indefinite number." My godly ancestors possessed many more than a hundred virtues; and I am very grateful to God for the grace which has enabled me to be the continuator of any of them.

I notice how very particular the Holy Ghost is that a good man should not be confounded with a bad one. He says, when mentioning one of the twelve, — "Judas... not Iscariot" (John 14:22). There were two apostles of the name of Judas; the one who betrayed our Lord, and the other who wrote the Epistle of Jude, who should properly have been called Judas.

Some of us, in reading the name Judas, might have said, "Ah! it was that traitor Judas Iscariot who asked the question." But the Holy Spirit would not allow this mistake to be made. This should teach us that it is not an idle wish for us to desire that our name should be handed down to posterity untarnished. We ought all to seek to have an unblemished character; we ought to desire to have that promise fulfilled, "The memory of the just is blessed." I would not like my name to be mistaken for that of some criminal who was hanged. I would not wish to have my name written even by mistake in the calendar of infamy. However much I may now be misrepresented, it will one day be known that I have honestly striven for the glory of my Master.

My second Christian name — Haddon — has often reminded me of my godly ancestry. When I have had to endorse a great heap of checks for the College and Orphanage, I have wished that my father had not given me so many initials, and I took care that my own sons should not have the same cause for complaint, for they are simply "Charles" and "Thomas." Yet there is such a pleasing story associated with the name of "Haddon" that I am very glad it was given to me. It appears that, before my grandfather became a minister, he had several years of business life as a country shopkeeper. Amongst other things, he sold cheese, which he used to buy of a wholesale dealer in that useful article of commerce. One day, a friend, named Haddon, said to him, "Mr. Spurgeon, you should go down to the cheese fairs at Derby and Leicester, and buy what you want at first hand; you would get a much larger profit if you did so." "Oh!" replied grandfather, "I could not do that, for I have not sufficient money to spare for such a purpose." "You need not have any difficulty on that score," said the generous man; "if you tell me when the next fair is to be held, I will let you have the money, and you can pay me back when you have sold the cheese. I have such confidence in your Christian integrity, that I shall be glad to aid you in this way."

Accordingly, grandfather bought the cheese, sold them at a good profit, and went to his friend who had lent him the money. This is one of the most remarkable parts of the story. When the amount was repaid, grandfather asked how much interest was due from him; but the lender replied, "Oh, Mr. Spurgeon, that is not my way of transacting business! I had that money lying idle, and you have done me great service in putting it to such good use, so I mean to *give you five percent, for your trouble in laying it out for me;* and when the season comes round again, I want you to buy another lot of cheese on the same terms." That very singular arrangement was continued until there was no further need of the good man's help; and, afterwards, when grandfather had a son born to him, he gave him the name of "Haddon" in remembrance of his generous friend. That son was my Uncle Haddon, who, in my childhood days, used to give out the hymns at Stambourne Meeting-house; and when my father also had a son, he gave him the name of Charles HADDON Spurgeon; and now, without any wish on my part, Mr. William Olney and his friends in Bermondsey have perpetuated the name by calling their splendid mission premises "Haddon Hall." It always seems to me that this chain of circumstances is a fresh illustration of the inspired promise, "The righteous shall be in everlasting remembrance."

GENEALOGICAL TABLE,
COMPILED FROM AN ANCIENT FAMILY REGISTER.

Clement.	William.
(1797)	(1771)
John.	Thomas.
(1768)	(1774)

JAMES.
(*Born, Sept.* 29,1776)
Hannah.
(1778)
(Also 6 who died in infancy)
Sarah.
(1807.)
HADDON Rudkin.
(1808.)
"Uncle Haddon"
JOHN.
(*Born, July* 15, 1810.)
Samuel.
(1811.)
Obadiah.
(1813.)
Eliza.
(1815.)
Ann.

(1818.)
"Aunt Ann"
James.
(1820.)
Susannah.
(1823.)
15
Charles HADDON.
(*Born, June* 19, 1834)
Eliza.
James Archer.
Emily.
Louisa.
Charlotte.
Eva
Flora.
Charles.
Thomas.
(*Born, September* 20, 1856.)

Chapter Three - Happy Childhood at Stambourne

Oh, the old house at home! who does not love it, the place of our childhood, the old roof-tree, the old cottage? There is no other village in all the world half so good as that particular village! True, the gates, and styles, and posts have been altered; but, still, there is an attachment to those old houses, the old tree in the park, and the old ivy-mantled tower. It is not very picturesque, perhaps, but we love to go to see it. We like to see the haunts of our boyhood.

There is something pleasant in those old stairs where the clock used to stand; and in the room where grandmother was wont to bend her knee, and where we had family prayer. There is no place like that house after all. — C. H. S.

THIS drawing of the old Manse at Stambourne has far more charms for me than for any of my readers; but I hope that their generous kindness to the writer will cause them to be interested in it. Here my venerable grandfather lived for more than fifty years, and reared his rather numerous family. In its earlier days it must have been a very remarkable abode for a dissenting teacher; a clear evidence that either he had an estate of his own, or that those about him had large hearts and pockets. It was in all respects a gentleman's mansion of the olden times. The house has been supplanted by one which, I doubt not, is most acceptable to the excellent minister who occupies it; but to me it can never be one-half so dear as the revered old home in which I spent some of my earliest years. It is true the old parsonage had developed devotional tendencies, and seemed inclined to prostrate its venerable form, and therefore it might have fallen down of itself if it had not been removed by the builder; but, somehow, I wish it had kept up forever and ever. I could have cried, "Builders, spare that home.

Touch not a single tile, or bit of plaster;" but its hour was come, and so the earthly house was happily dissolved, to be succeeded by a more enduring fabric. The new house, as Smith told me, was "built on the same destruction." It stood near the chapel, so that the pastor was close to his work.

It looks a very noble parsonage, with its eight windows in front; but at least three, and I think four, of these were plastered up, and painted black, and then marked out in lines to imitate glass. They were not such very bad counterfeits, or the photograph would betray this. Some of us can remember the window tax, which seemed to regard light as a Latin commodity — *lux,* and therefore a luxury, and as such to be taxed. So much was paid on each aperture for the admission of light; but the minister's small income forced economy upon him, and so room after room of the manse was left in darkness, to be regarded by my childish mind with reverent awe. Over other windows were put up boards marked DAIRY, or CHEESE-ROOM, because by being labeled with these names they would escape the tribute. What a queer mind must his have been who first invented taxing the light of the sun! It was, no doubt, meant to be a fair way of estimating the size of a house, and thus getting at the wealth of the inhabitant; but, incidentally, it led occupiers of large houses to shut out the light for which they were too poor to pay.

Let us enter by the front door. We step into a spacious hall, innocent of carpet. There is a great fireplace, and over it a painting of David, and the Philistines, and Giant Goliath. The hall-floor was of brick, and carefully sprinkled with fresh sand. We see this in the country still, but not often in the minister's house. In the hall stood "the child's" rocking-horse. It was a gray horse, and could be ridden astride or side-saddle. When I visited Stambourne, in the year 1889, a man claimed to have rocked me upon it. I remembered the horse, but not the man, — so sadly do we forget the better, and remember the baser. This was the only horse that I ever enjoyed riding. Living animals are too eccentric in their movements, and the law of gravitation usually draws me from my seat upon them to a lower level; therefore I am not an inveterate lover of horseback. I can, however, testify of my Stambourne steed, that it was a horse on which even a member of Parliament might have retained his seat.

How I used to delight to stand in the hall, with the door open, and watch the rain run off the top of the door into a wash-tub! How much better to catch the overflow of the rain in a tub than to have a gutter to carry it off!

So I thought; but do not now think. What bliss to float cotton-reels in the miniature sea! How fresh and sweet that rain seemed to be! The fragrance of the water which poured down in a thunder-shower comes over me now.

Where the window is open on the right, was the best parlor. Roses generally grew about it, and bloomed *in the room* if they could find means to insert their buds between the wall and the window-frame. They generally found ample space, for nothing was quite on the square. There had evidently been a cleaning up just before my photograph was taken, for there are no roses creeping up from below. What Vandals people are when they set about clearing up either the outsides or the insides of houses! On the sacred walls of this "best parlor" hung portraits of my grandparents and uncles, and on a piece of furniture stood the fine large basin which grandfather used for what he called "baptisms." In my heart of hearts, I believe it was originally intended for a punch-bowl; but, in any case, it was a work of art, worthy of the use to which it was dedicated. This is the room which contained the marvel to which I have often referred, —

AN APPLE IN A BOTTLE.

I remember well, in my early days, seeing upon my grandmother's mantel-shelf an apple contained in a phial. This was a great wonder to me, and I tried to investigate it. My question was, "How came the apple to get inside so small a bottle?" The apple was quite as big round as the phial; by what means was it placed within it? Though it was treason to touch the treasures on the mantel-piece, I took down the bottle, and convinced my youthful mind that the apple never passed through its neck; and by means of an attempt to unscrew the bottom, I became equally certain that the apple did not enter from below. I held to the notion that by some occult means the bottle had been made in two pieces, and afterwards united in so careful a manner that no trace of the join remained. I was hardly satisfied with the theory, but as no philosopher was at hand to suggest any other hypothesis, I let the matter rest. One day, the next summer, I chanced to see upon a bough another phial, the first cousin of my old friend, within which was growing a little apple which had been passed through the neck of the bottle while it was extremely small. "Nature well known, no prodigies remain."

The grand secret was out. I did not cry, *Eureka! Eureka!* but I might have done so if I had then been versed in the Greek tongue.

This discovery of my juvenile days shall serve for an illustration at the present moment. Let us get the apples into the bottle while they are little: which, being translated, signifies, let us bring the young ones into the house of God, by means of the Sabbath-school, in the hope that, in after days, they will love the place where His honor dwelleth, and there seek and find eternal life. By our making the Sabbath dreary, many young minds may be prejudiced against religion: we would do the reverse. Sermons should not be so long and dull as to weary the young folk, or mischief will come of them; but with interesting preaching to secure attention, and loving teachers to press home the truth upon the youthful heart, we shall not have to complain of the next generation, that they have "forgotten their resting-places."

In this best parlor grandfather would usually sit on Sunday mornings, and prepare himself for preaching. I was put into the room with him that I might be quiet, and, as a rule, *The Evangelical Magazine* was given me.

This contained a portrait of a reverend divine, and one picture of a mission-station. Grandfather often requested me to be quiet, and always gave as a reason that I "had the magazine." I did not at the time perceive the full force of the argument to be derived from that fact; but no doubt my venerable relative knew more about the sedative effect of the magazine than I did. I cannot support his opinion from personal experience. Another means of stilling "the child" was much more effectual. I was warned that perhaps grandpa would not be able to preach if I distracted him, and then, — ah! then, what would happen, if poor people did not learn the way to Heaven? This made me look at the portrait and the missionary-station once more. Little did I dream that some other child would one day see my face in that wonderful Evangelical portrait-gallery.

14

When I was a very small boy, I was allowed to read the Scriptures at family prayer. Once upon a time, when reading the passage in Revelation which mentions the bottomless pit, I paused, and said, "Grandpa, what can this mean?" The answer was kind, but unsatisfactory, "Pooh, pooh, child, go on." The child, however, intended to have an explanation, and therefore selected the same chapter morning after morning, and always halted at the same verse to repeat the inquiry, hoping that by repetition he would importune the good old gentleman into a reply. The process was successful, for it is by no means the most edifying thing in the world to hear the history of the Mother of Harlots, and the beast with seven heads, every morning in the week, Sunday included, with no sort of alternation either of Psalm or Gospel; the venerable patriarch of the household therefore capitulated at discretion, with, "Well, dear, what is it that puzzles you?" Now "the child" had often seen baskets with but very frail bottoms, which in course of wear became bottomless, and allowed the fruit placed therein to drop upon the ground; here, then, was the puzzle, — if the pit aforesaid had no bottom, where would all those people fall to who dropped out at its lower end? — a puzzle which rather startled the propriety of family worship, and had to be laid aside for explanation at some more convenient season. Queries of the like simple but rather unusual stamp would frequently break up into paragraphs of a miscellaneous length the Bible-reading of the assembled family, and had there not been a world of love and license allowed to the inquisitive reader, he would very soon have been deposed from his office. As it was, the Scriptures were not very badly rendered, and were probably quite as interesting as if they had not been interspersed with original and curious inquiries.

I can remember the horror of my mind when my dear grandfather told me what his idea of "the bottomless pit" was. There is a deep pit, and the soul is falling down, — oh, how fast it is falling! There! the last ray of light at the top has disappeared, and it falls on-on-on, and so it goes on falling — on-on-on for a thousand years! "Is it not getting near the bottom yet?

Won't it stop?" No, no, the cry is, "On-on-on." "I have been falling a million years; am I not near the bottom yet?" No, you are no nearer the bottom yet; it is "the *bottomless* pit." It is on-on-on, and so the soul goes on falling perpetually into a deeper depth still, falling forever into "the bottomless pit" — on-on-on — into the pit that has no bottom! Woe, without termination, without hope of its coming to a conclusion!

In my grandfather's garden there was a fine old hedge of yew, of considerable length, which was clipped and trimmed till it made quite a wall of verdure. Behind it was a wide grass walk, which looked upon the fields; the grass was kept mown, so as to make pleasant walking. Here, ever since the old Puritanic chapel was built, godly divines had walked, and prayed, and meditated. My grandfather was wont to use it as his study. Up and down it he would walk when preparing his sermons, and always on Sabbath-days when it was fair, he had half-an-hour there before preaching.

To me, it seemed to be a perfect paradise; and being forbidden to stay there when grandfather was meditating, I viewed it with no small degree of awe.

I love to think of the green and quiet walk at this moment; but I was once shocked and even horrified by hearing a farming man remark concerning this

15

sanctum sanctorum, "It 'ud grow a many 'taturs if it wor ploughed up." What cared he for holy memories? What were meditation and contemplation to him? Is it not the chief end of man to grow potatoes, and eat them? Such, on a larger scale, would be an unconverted man's estimate of joys so elevated and refined as those of Heaven. Alphonse Karr tells a story of a servant-man who asked his master to be allowed to leave his cottage, and sleep over the stable. What was the matter with his cottage?

"Why, sir, the nightingales all around the cottage make such a 'jug, jug, jug,' at night that I cannot bear them." A man with a musical ear would be charmed with the nightingales' song, but here was a man without a musical soul who found the sweetest notes a nuisance. This is a feeble image of the incapacity of unregenerate man for the enjoyments of the world to come, and as he is incapable of enjoying them, so is he incapable of longing for them.

While my grandfather was preacher at the meeting-house, Mr. Hopkins was Rector at the church. They preached the same gospel, and without surrendering their principles, were great friends. The Bible Society held its meetings alternately in connection with the church and the meeting-house.

At times, the leading resident went to church in the morning, and to chapel in the afternoon; and, when I was a boy, I have, on Monday, gone to the Squire's to tea, with Mr. Hopkins and my grandfather. The glory of that tea-party was that we four, the three old gentlemen, and the little boy, *all ate sugared bread and butter together for a treat.* The sugar was very brown, but the young boy was very pleased, and the old boys were merry also. Yes, Stambourne had its choice pleasures!

It is pleasant to read of the harmony between these two men of God: they increased in mutual esteem as they increased in years. As Mr. Hopkins had more of the meat, and Mr. Spurgeon more of the mouths, the Rector did not forget to help his friend in divers quiet ways; such as a five-pound note for a sick daughter to go to the sea-side, and presents of comforts in illness. On one occasion, it is said that, having a joint of beef on the Rectory table, the clergyman cut it in halves, and sent his man on horseback with one half of it to the Independent Parsonage, while it was yet hot, — a kind of joke not often practiced between established and dissenting ministers.

In the front of the house, towards the left, nearly hidden by a shrub, is a very important window, for it let light into the room wherein were the oven, the mangle, and, best of all, the kneading-trough. How often have I gone to that kneading-trough; for it had a little shelf in it, and there would be placed "*something for the child!*" A bit of pastry, which was called by me, according to its size, a pig or a rabbit, which had little ears, and two currants for eyes, was carefully placed in that sacred shrine, like the manna in the ark. Dear grandmother, how much you labored to spoil that "child"!

Yet your memory is more dear to him than that of wiser folks, who did not spoil "the child." Do you now look down from your mansion above upon your petted grandson? Do you feel as if he would have been better if you had been sour and hard? Not a bit of it. Aunt Ann, who had a finger in it all, would spoil "the child" again if she had a chance. I have put in such an approach to a portrait of my grandmother as I could find: it was taken by some traveling artist who visited the district, and took off several of the family.

The dairy at the back of the house was by no means a bad place for a cheese-cake, or for a drink of cool milk. It makes one think of the hymn, —

"I have been there; and still would go."

The cupboard under the stairs, where they kept the sand for the floors, would be a real Old Curiosity Shop nowadays; but there it was, and great was the use of it to the cottagers around.

There was a sitting-room at the back of the house, where the family met for meals. In that which looks like a blank side in our picture there certainly was a window looking out upon the garden; perhaps it was a little further back than the picture goes. A very pleasant outlook there was from that window down the green garden paths, and over the hedge into the road.

When I last saw the "keeping-room", a bit of ivy had forced its way through the lath and plaster, and had been trained along the inside of the room; but in my childish days we were not so verdant. I remember a mark on the paper which had been made by the finger of one of my uncles, so they told me, when one year the flour was so bad that it turned into a paste, or pudding, inside the loaf, and could not be properly made into bread. History has before this been learned from handwritings on the wall.

The times of the old Napoleon wars, and of the Corn Laws, must often have brought straitness of bread into the household; and a failure in the yield of the little farm made itself felt in the family.

There was a mysterious jack over the fire-place, and with that fire-place itself I was very familiar; for candles were never used extravagantly in grandfather's house, and if anyone went out of the room, and took the candle with him, it was just a little darker, not very much; and if one wished to read, the fire-light was the only resort. There were mould candles now and then in the best room, but that was only on very high days and holidays. My opinion, derived from personal observation, was that all everyday candles were made of rushes and tallow.

Our young readers in London and other large towns have probably never seen a pair of snuffers, much less the flint and steel with which a light had to be painfully obtained by the help of a tinder-box and a brimstone match.

What a job on a cold raw morning to strike, and strike, and see the sparks die out because the tinder was damp! We are indeed living in an age of light when we compare our incandescent gas-burners and electric lights with the rushlights of our childhood. And yet the change is not all one way; for if we have more light, we have also more fog and smoke, at least in London. Our "keeping-room" was a very nice, large, comfortable dining-room, and it had a large store-closet at one end. You should have seen the best china! It only came out on state occasions, but it was very marvelous in "the child's" eyes.

A quaint old winding stair led to the upper chambers. The last time I occupied the best bedroom, the floor appeared anxious to go out of the window, at least, it inclined that way. There seemed to be a chirping of birds very near my pillow in the morning, and I discovered that swallows had built outside the plaster, and sparrows had found a hole which admitted them inside of it, that there they might lay their young. It is not always that one can lie in bed and study ornithology. I confess that I liked all this rural life, and the old chintz bed-furniture, and the paper round the looking-glass cut in the form of horse-chestnut leaves and dahlias, and the tottery old mansion altogether.

THE BOY AMONG THE BOOKS.

I am afraid I am amusing myself rather than my reader, and so I will not weary him with more than this one bit more of rigmarole just now. But there was one place upstairs which I cannot omit, even at the risk of being wearisome. Opening out of one of the bedrooms, there was a little chamber of which the window had been blocked up through that wretched window-duty. When the original founder of Stambourne Meeting quitted the Church of England, to form a separate congregation, he would seem to have been in possession of a fair estate, and the house was quite a noble one for those times. Before the light-excluding tax had come into operation, that little room was the minister's study and closet for prayer; and a very nice cozy room, too. In my time, it was a dark den; — but *it contained books,* and this made it a gold mine to me. Therein was fulfilled the promise, "I will give thee the treasures of darkness." Some of these were enormous folios, such as a boy could hardly lift. Here I first struck up acquaintance with the martyrs, and specially with "Old Bonner", who burned them; next, with Bunyan and his "Pilgrim"; and further on, with the great masters of Scriptural theology, with whom no moderns are worthy to be named in the same day. Even the old editions of their works, with their margins and old-fashioned notes, are precious to me. It is easy to tell a real Puritan book even by its shape and by the appearance of the type. I confess that I harbor a prejudice against nearly all new editions, and cultivate a preference for the originals, even though they wander about in sheepskins and goatskins, or are shut up in the hardest of boards. It made my eyes water, a short time ago, to see a number of these old books in the new Manse: I wonder whether some other boy will love them, and live to revive that grand old divinity which will yet be to England her balm and benison.

Out of that darkened room I fetched those old authors when I was yet a youth, and never was I happier than when in their company. Out of the present contempt, into which Puritanism has fallen, many brave hearts and true will fetch it, by the help of God, ere many years have passed. Those who have daubed up the windows will yet be surprised to see Heaven's light beaming on the old truth, and then breaking forth from it to their own confusion.

(The following incident in Mr. Spurgeon's childhood's days is here given as it was related by his "Aunt Ann" on the occasion when he visited Stambourne in the summer of 1887.

One of the members of the church at Stambourne, named Roads, was in the habit of frequenting the public-house to have his "drop of beer", and smoke his pipe, greatly to the grief of his godly pastor, who often heaved a sigh at the thought of his unhappy member's inconsistent conduct. Little Charles had doubtless noticed his grandfather's grief on this account, and laid it to heart. One day he suddenly exclaimed, in the hearing of the good old gentleman, "I'll kill old Roads, that I will!" "Hush, hush! my dear," said the good pastor, "you mustn't talk so; it's very wrong, you know, and you'll get taken up by the police, if you do anything wrong." "I shall not do anything bad; but I'll kill him though, that I will." Well, the good grandfather was puzzled, but yet perfectly sure that the child

18

would not do anything which he knew to be wrong, so he let it pass with some half-mental remark about "that strange child." Shortly after, however, the above conversation was brought to his mind by the child coming in and saying,

"I've killed old Roads; he'll never grieve my dear grandpa any more." "My dear child," said the good man, "what have you done? Where have you been?" "I haven't been doing any harm, grandpa," said the child; "I've been about the Lord's work, that's all."

Nothing more could be elicited from little Charles; but, before long, the mystery was cleared up. "Old Roads" called to see his pastor, and, with downcast looks and evident sorrow of heart, narrated the story of how he had been killed, somewhat in this fashion: — "I'm very sorry indeed, my dear pastor, to have caused you such grief and trouble. It was very wrong, I know; but I always loved you, and wouldn't have done it if I'd only thought." Encouraged by the good pastor's kindly Christian words, he went on with his story. "I was a-sitting in the public just having my pipe and mug of beer, when that child comes in, — to think an old man like me should be took to task, and reproved by a bit of a child like that! Well, he points at me with his finger, just so, and says, 'What doest thou here, Elijah? sitting with the ungodly; and you a member of a church, and breaking your pastor's heart. I'm ashamed of you! I wouldn't break my pastor's heart, I'm sure.' And then he walks away. Well, I did feel angry; but I knew it was all true, and I was guilty; so I put down my pipe, and did not touch my beer, but hurried away to a lonely spot, and cast myself down before the Lord, confessing my sin and begging for forgiveness. And I do know and believe the Lord in mercy pardoned me; and now I've come to ask you to forgive me; and I'll never grieve you any more, my dear pastor." It need not be said that the penitent was freely forgiven, and owned a brother in the Lord, and the Lord was praised for the wonderful way in which it had all come about.)

(The genuineness of the backslider's restoration is evident from the testimony of Mr. Houchin, the minister at Stambourne who succeeded Mr. Spurgeon's grandfather, and who has also ascertained from official records the correct way of spelling "Old Roads'" name. Mr. Houchin writes: —

"Thomas Roads was one of the old men of the table-pew, — an active, lively, little man, but quite illiterate, — not much above a laborer, but he kept a pony and cart, and did a little buying and selling on his own account.... I found him an earnest and zealous Christian, striving to be useful in every way possible to him; especially in the prayer-meetings and among the young people, opening his house for Christian conversation and prayer. He only lived about four years of my time, and was sustained with a cheerful confidence to the end. When near death, on my taking up the Bible to read and pray with him, he said, 'I have counted the leaves, sir.' I said,

'Why! what did you do that for?' and he replied, 'I never could read a word of it, and thought I would know how many leaves there were.' This was very pathetic, and revealed much. We had a good hope of him, and missed him greatly.")

Chapter Four - Stambourne Meeting-House.

IT was a rare old chapel. I wish it could have remained forever as I used to know it: let me see if I can sketch it with my pen. When I was a boy of twelve, I made this drawing of the back of the old meeting-house. I have been welcomed at a farmer's table on the promise of making a picture of his house. I am rather glad that this pencil memorial was preserved by my dear Aunt Ann; but I must now, forty-five years after, use the pen on the same subject.

The pulpit was glorious as "the tower of the flock." Over it hung a huge sounding-board: I used to speculate as to what would become of grandfather if it ever dropped down upon him. I thought of my Jack-in-the-box, and hoped that my dear grandpapa would never be shut down and shut up in such a fashion. At the back of the pulpit was a peg to hold the minister's hat: inside, there was room for two, for I have sat there with grandfather when quite a little boy; but I guess that two grown-up people would have found it "quite too small enough," as my Dutch friend puts it.

Just below, and in front of the pulpit, was the table-pew, wherein sat the elders of the congregation, the men of gracious "light and leading." There Uncle Haddon generally stood, and gave out the hymns and the notices; and from that semi-sacred region was raised the block of wood by which to the singers upstairs the meter of the hymn was made known, — Common, Long, or Short. There were big tomb-stones forming the bottom of this large pew, which took its name from containing *the table,* on which were spread the bread and wine on days *when they had the ordinance:* I think that was the correct phrase when our good folks intended "the communion." I don't remember hearing them style infant baptism "the ordinance"; but I suppose they thought it to be one. A few had qualms upon the question, and were baptized quietly at some Baptist Chapel.

The pews in the middle were mostly square in form, and roomy. Those on either side were aristocratic, and lined with green baize, for the most part very faded. In some cases, brass rods carried up little curtains, which made the family pew quite private, and shut out all sights but that of the grave and reverend senior who dispensed to us the Word of Life. There were flaps inside the pew so as not to lose the space where the door opened, and flaps for the poor to sit upon in the aisle outside of these pews; and when the time came to go home, there was such a lifting up and letting down of flaps, and flap-seats, within the pew, and without the pew, as one never does see in these degenerate days. A little boy on a hassock on the floor of one of these holy loose-boxes ought to have been good; and no doubt was as good there as anywhere, especially if he had a peppermint to suck, and nobody to play with.

I cannot forget the big clock which had a face outside the chapel as well as one inside. When his long body had been newly grained, he seemed a very suitable piece of furniture for a nice, clean, old-fashioned Puritan meeting-house. If I am rightly informed, the veteran time-keeper was bought by the miller, and is now upon one of his sheds. To what strange uses we may come at last!

The people were mainly real Essex: they talked of places down in "the Shires" as if they were quite foreign parts; and young fellows who went down into "the

Hundreds" were explorers of a respectable order of hardihood. They loved a good sermon, and would say, "Mr. Spurgeon, I *heard* you well this morning." I thought the good man had *preached* well, but their idea was not so much to his credit; they judged that they had *heard* him well, and there's something in the different way of putting it; at any rate, it takes from the preacher all ground of glorying in what he has done. They were a people who could and would hear the gospel, but I don't think they would have put up with anything else. They were as apt at criticism as here and there one: some of them were very wise in their remarks, and some were otherwise. Well do I remember an occasion upon which the preacher had treated "the tares" after the manner of the East, and was altogether right in so doing; but they said, "He wouldn't know a tare if he saw one. It was painful to hear a man talk so ignorant. To say that you couldn't tell wheat from tares when they were a-growing was ridiculous." The rustic critics were wrong for once; but on matters of doctrine or experience, you would have found them quite a match for you.

I do not think our folks were anything like so superstitious and weak as the peasants I came to know ten years after in Cambridgeshire. Tales of white wizards and witches were unknown to my juvenile mind; though I heard enough of them when my age was between sixteen and twenty. Then one of my best workers told me that a witch had dragged a cat down his naked back by its tail: he did not show me the marks, but he fully believed in the feline operation. We cannot forget that in the village of Hedingham, which is not more than five miles from Stambourne, a murder was committed so late as 1865, which grew out of popular belief in witchcraft. The old men I talked with, as a little child, were, I am sure, far above all such nonsense; and upon many a Biblical, or political, or ecclesiastical, or moral subject, they would have uttered great and weighty thoughts in their own savory Essex dialect.

There were, no doubt, in Stambourne a few rough fellows who did not go to any place of worship; but those who came to the meeting-house were the great majority, and the plain, practical, common-sense sermons which they heard had lifted them out of that dense superstition which still benumbs the brains of too many of the East Anglian peasantry.

THE SINGING AT STAMBOURNE MEETING-HOUSE.

The prayer-meetings during the week were always kept up; but at certain seasons of the year grandfather and a few old women were all that could be relied upon. It occurred to me, in riper years, to ask my venerated relative how the singing was maintained. "Why, grandfather," said I, "we always sang, and yet you don't know any tunes, and certainly the old ladies didn't." "Why, child," said he, "there's one Common meter tune which is all, 'Hum Ha, Hum Ha,' and I could manage that very well." "But how if it happened to be a Long or Short meter hymn?" "Why, then, I either put in more Hum Ha's, or else I left some out; but we managed to praise the Lord." Ah, shade of my dear old grandsire! your grandson is by no means more gifted as to crotchets and quavers than you were, and to this day the only solo he has ever ventured to sing is that same universally useful tune! [2] Even that he has abandoned; for audiences are growing either more intelligent or less tolerant than they used to be.

My grandfather once ventured upon publishing a volume of hymns. I never heard anyone speak in their favor, or argue that they ought to have been sung in the congregation. In that volume he promised a second, if the first should prove acceptable. We forgive him the first collection because he did not inflict another. The meaning was good, but the dear old man paid no attention to the mere triviality of rhyme. We dare not quote even a verse. It may be among the joys of Heaven for my venerated grandsire, that he can now compose and sing new songs unto the Lord. When we say we dare not quote, we do not refer to the meaning or the doctrine: in that respect, we could quote every line before the Westminster Assembly, and never fear that a solitary objection would or could be raised.

The Stambourne style of singing led me into trouble when I returned to my home. The notion had somehow entered my little head that the last line of the hymn must always be repeated, and grandfather had instilled into me as a safe rule that I must never be afraid to do what I believed to be right; so, when I went to the chapel where my parents attended, I repeated the last line whether the congregation did so or not. It required a great deal of punishment to convince me that a little boy must do what his parents think to be right; and though my grandfather made a mistake in that particular instance, I have always been grateful to him for teaching me to act according to my belief whatever the consequences might be.

I recollect, when first I left my grandfather, how grieved I was to part from him; it was the great sorrow of my little life. Grandfather seemed very sorry, too, and we had a cry together; he did not quite know what to say to me, but he said, "Now child, to-night, when the moon shines at Colchester, and you look at it, don't forget that it is the same moon your grandfather will be looking at from Stambourne;" and for years, as a child, I used to love the moon because I thought that my grandfather's eyes and my own somehow met there on the moon.

Outside the Meeting, near that long side, which was really the front, there stood a horsing-block. Ladies went up the steps, and found themselves on a platform of the same height as their horse's back. It was a commendable invention: how often have I wished for something of the sort when I have had to climb my Rosinante! To me, this horsing-block was dear for quite another reason. The grand old lime trees shed their leaves in profusion, and when these were swept up, the old chapel-keeper would ram a large quantity of them under the horsing-block. When I had pulled out about as many as fitted my size, I could creep in; and there lie hidden beyond fear of discovery. My friend, Mr. Manton Smith, has written a book called *Stray Leaves,* and another which he has entitled *More Stray Leaves;* I entered into his work before he was born. So good was the hiding-place, that it remained a marvel where "the child" could be. The child would get alone; but where he went to, his guardian angels knew, but none on earth could tell. Only a little while ago, my dear old Aunt Ann said, "But, Charles, where did you get to when you were such a little child? We used to look everywhere for you, but we never found you till you came walking in all by yourself." The horsing-block was the usual haunt when there were leaves, and an old tomb would serve at other times. No, I did not get into the grave; but it had a sort of altar tomb above it, and one of the side stones would move easily, so that I could get inside, and then by setting the slab of stone back again I was enclosed in a sort of large box where nobody would dream of looking for me. I went to the aforesaid tomb to show my aunt my hiding-place; but the raised altar was gone, and the top of it, with the name of the deceased thereon, was laid flat on the ground. Some of the side-stones, which formerly held up the memorial, were used to make door-steps when the buildings were put into their present state of repair, and the top stone was made to occupy the same space, only it lay flat upon the ground, instead of being raised some two feet above it.

Still, I remembered well the place, and what the tomb had formerly been.

How often have I listened to the good people calling me by my name! I heard their feet close to my den, but I was wicked enough still to be "lost", though the time for meals was gone. Dreaming of days to come befell me every now and then as a child, and to be quite alone was my boyish heaven.

Yet, there was a seventh heaven above that: let me but hear the foxhounds, and see the red coats of their pursuers, and I had seen the climax of delight.

When the huntsmen did come down by Stambourne woods, it was a season of delirious excitement to others besides "the child." At other times, all the women and children were solemnly working at straw-plait; but what they did when the fox went by I will not venture upon guessing, for I don't remember what I did myself. The woods at the back of the chapel had a charming mystery about them to my little soul, for who could tell but a fox was there? As a child, when asked what I would be, I usually said I was going to be a huntsman. A fine profession, truly! Many young men have the same idea of being parsons as I had of being a huntsman, — a mere childish notion that they would like the coat and the horn-blowing; the honor, the respect, the ease, — and they are probably even fools enough to think the riches of the ministry. (Ignorant beings they must be if they look for wealth in connection with the Baptist ministry.) The fascination of the preacher's office is very great to weak minds, and hence I earnestly caution all young men not to mistake whim for inspiration, and a childish preference for a call of the Holy Spirit.

I once learnt a lesson, while thus fox-hunting, which has been very useful to me as a preacher of the gospel. Ever since the day I was sent to shop with a basket, and purchased a pound of tea, a quarter-of-a-pound of mustard, and three pounds of rice, and on my way home saw a pack of hounds, and felt it necessary to follow them over hedge and ditch (as I always did when I was a boy), and found, when I reached home, that all the goods were amalgamated, — tea, mustard, and rice, — into one awful mess, I have understood the necessity of packing up my subjects in good stout parcels, bound round with the thread of my discourse; and this makes me keep to firstly, secondly, and thirdly, however unfashionable that method may now be. People will not drink mustardy tea, nor will they enjoy muddled-up sermons, in which they cannot tell head from tail, because they have neither, but are like Mr. Bright's Skye terrier, whose head and tail were both alike.

Somehow, I don't think our Sunday-school came to so very, very much. It was a great day when every child brought his own mug, and there was real cake, and tea, or milk and water, and an address; but that high festival came but once a year. Having been on one occasion pressed into the service when I was still a boy, but was in Stambourne on a visit, I felt myself a failure, and I fancied that some around me were not brilliant successes. Still, in those early times, teaching children to read, and to repeat verses of hymns, and to say the Catechism by heart, were a good beginning. Dr. Watts's Catechism, which I learned myself, is so simple, so interesting, so suggestive, that a better condensation of Scriptural knowledge will never be written; and the marvel is that such a little miracle of instruction should have been laid aside by teachers. While I am writing, one question and answer come to me with special freshness: —

"Who was Isaiah?"

"He was that prophet who spake more of Jesus Christ than all the rest."

At the distance of fifty-three years, I remember a little book which was read to me about a pious child at Colchester; I recollect Janeway's *Token for Children,* and I recall the bad conduct of some juveniles of my own age, who not only kicked up a dust, but literally kicked the teachers.

Memory makes a selection as she goes along; and in my case, the choice of things retained is so miscellaneous, that I cannot discover my own character by their guidance.

The weekday school for the very juveniles was kept by old Mrs. Burleigh, and to that fane of useful knowledge I was sent. The only thing that I remember was that I heard a good deal of her son Gabriel, and therefore asked, as a great favor, that when he came home from the town where he lived, he might come and see me. I had my desire; but after all these years, I have not got over my disappointment. To see Gabriel! I don't think I had absolutely reckoned upon the largest kind of wings; but wings certainly, or something otherwise angelic. To see only a young man, a youth in trousers, with no trace of cherubim or seraphim about him, was too much of a come-down. "What's in a name?" was a question not yet known to me; but no one will ever need to ask me now. Names are mere labels, and by no means proofs that the things are there.

To come back to the old chapel, the best point about it was the blessing which rested on the ministry carried on within. The dew of the Spirit from on high never left the ministry. Wherever my grandfather went, souls were saved under his sermons. My own beloved father, Rev. John Spurgeon, constantly reports to me fresh instances of the old gentleman's usefulness.

'When I first of all became a preacher, there were persons who said, "I heard your grandfather, and I would run my shoes off my feet any day to hear a Spurgeon." This was encouraging. Another told me that, to hear my grandfather once, made his wing-feathers grow a foot. He could mount as eagles, after being fed with such Heavenly food. "He was always so experimental," was the summing-up of one of the most devout of working-men. "You felt as if he had been inside of a man." Buildings may perish, and new shrines may succeed them; but no earthly house will accommodate a sounder or more useful ministry than that of my grandfather.

Chapter Five - A Memorable Visit to Stambourne. — Mr. Knill's Prophecy.

THE story of Mr. Knill's prophesying that I should preach the gospel in Rowland Hill's Chapel, and to the largest congregations in the world, has been regarded by many as a legend, but it was strictly true. Mr. Knill took the county of Essex in the year 1844, and traversed the region from town to town, as a deputation for the London Missionary Society. In the course of that journey, he spent a little time at Stambourne Parsonage. In his heart burned the true missionary spirit, for he sought the souls of young and old, whenever they came in his way. He was a great soul-winner, and he soon spied out the boy. He said to me, "Where do you sleep? for I want to call you up in the morning." I showed him my little room, and he took good note of it. At six o'clock he called me up. There stood in my grandfather's garden two arbors made of yew trees, cut into sugarloaf fashion. Though the old manse has given way to a new one, and the old chapel has gone also, yet the yew trees flourish as aforetime. We went into the right-hand arbor, and there, in the sweetest way, he told me of the love of Jesus, and of the blessedness of trusting in Him and loving Him in our childhood.

With many a story he preached Christ to me, and told me how good God had been to him, and then he prayed that I might know the Lord and serve Him. He knelt down in that arbor, and prayed for me with his arms about my neck. He did not seem content unless I kept with him in the interval between the services. He heard my childish talk with patient love, and repaid it with gracious instruction. On three successive days he taught me, and prayed with me; and before he had to leave, my grandfather had come back from the place where he had gone to preach, and all the family were gathered to morning prayer. Then, in the presence of them all, Mr. Knill took me on his knee, and said, "This child will one day preach the gospel, and he will preach it to great multitudes. I am persuaded that he will preach in the chapel of Rowland Hill, where (I think he said) I am now the minister." He spoke very solemnly, and called upon all present to witness what he said. Then he gave me sixpence as a reward if I would learn the hymn, —

"God moves in a mysterious way
His wonders to perform."

I was made to promise that, when I preached in Rowland Hill's Chapel, that hymn should be sung. Think of that as a promise from a child! Would it ever be other than an idle dream? Years flew by. After I had begun for some little time to preach in London, Dr. Alexander Fletcher was engaged to deliver the annual sermon to children in Surrey Chapel; but as he was taken ill, I was asked in a hurry to preach to the children in his stead.

"Yes," I replied, "I will, if you will allow the children to sing, 'God moves in a mysterious way.' I have made a promise, long ago, that so that hymn should be sung." And so it was: I preached in Rowland Hill's Chapel, and the hymn was sung. My emotions on that occasion I cannot describe, for the word of the Lord's servant was fulfilled. Still, I fancy that Surrey was not the chapel which Mr. Knill intended. How was I to go to the country chapel? All unsought by me, the minister at Wotton-under-Edge, which was Mr. Hill's summer residence, invited me to preach there. I went on the condition that the congregation should sing, "God moves in a mysterious way," — which was also done. To me it was a very wonderful thing, and I no more understood at that time how it came to pass than I understand today why the Lord should be so gracious to me. Did the words of Mr. Knill help to bring about their own fulfillment? I think so. I believed them, and looked forward to the time when I should preach the Word: I felt very powerfully that no unconverted person might dare to enter the ministry; this made me, I doubt not, all the more intent upon seeking salvation, and more hopeful of it, and when by grace enabled to cast myself upon the Savior's love, it was not long before my mouth began to speak of His redemption. How came that soberminded minister to speak thus of one into whose future God alone could see? How came it that he lived to rejoice with his young brother in the truth of all that he had spoken? We think *we* know the answer; but each reader has a right to his own: so let it rest, but not till we have marked one practical lesson. Would to God that we were all as wise as Richard Knill, and habitually sowed beside all waters! On the day of his death, in his eightieth year, David Brainerd, "the apostle of the Indians," was occupied in teaching the alphabet to an Indian child at his bedside. A friend said, "Why not rest from your labors now?"

"Because," replied the man of God, "I have prayed God to render me useful in my sphere, and He has heard my prayers; for now that I am unable to preach, He leaves me strength enough to teach this poor child his letters." To despise no opportunity of usefulness, is a leading rule with those who are wise to win souls. Mr. Knill might very naturally have left the minister's little grandson on the plea that he had other duties of more importance than praying with children, and yet who shall say that he did not effect as much by that act of humble ministry as by dozens of sermons addressed to crowded audiences? At any rate, *to me* his tenderness in considering the little one was fraught with everlasting consequences, and I must ever feel that his time was well laid out. May we do good everywhere as we have opportunity, and results will not be wanting!

Those who are curious as to further evidence of this story will find it in Mr. Birrell's biography of Richard Knill, though scarcely so fully told. No biographer was likely to know so much about it as myself; but yet the main facts are the same.

The following letter from Mr. Knill to my grandfather is very interesting, as showing how the good man thought of the matter: —

"Chester, 17th April, 1855.

"Revd. Mr. Spurgeon,

"Dear Sir,

"Perhaps you have forgotten me: but I have not forgotten my visit to you and your ancient chapel, and the fine trees which surround it, and your garden with the box and yew trees, and your dear grandson with whom I conversed, and on whose head I placed my hand, when I prayed with him in the arbor.

"Two years ago, he wrote to me, reminding me of these things, and of his warm feelings on the occasion.

"Last week I was at Leamington, and dined with a young artist, who had come from London to see his parents. His conversation was much about a popular young minister from the country, whom he had heard preach at Exeter Hall, whose name was Spurgeon. I said I knew him. 'How is it possible?' said the gentleman. I told him of my visit, and of your grandson's letter to me, and of his preaching to John Berridge's people at Waterbeach, near Cambridge. Oh, it was a fine season of interest and rejoicing! I hardly slept the following night for joy.

"A day or two afterwards I dined near Warwick with a party of friends. Their conversation was also about your grandson, not knowing that I had heard of him. Two of the party had been his hearers in London, and were very full of the subject. One of them said, 'He mentioned your praying with him at his relative's in the garden.' I have prayed much *for* him and *about* him, that God may keep him at the foot of the cross, that popularity may not puff him up.

"Will you please give me his address, as I should like to write to him? Forgive me for this intrusion. I feel much about this dear youth, very much. I have four or five of our ministers in London, and my heart goes out much after them. I have been settled in this city upwards of seven years, and have received more than four hundred members into the church. Matthew Henry's Chapel is still standing, but is in the possession of the Unitarians. Ours is an offshoot from some of Matthew's old members, who would have orthodox preaching.

"The Lord bless you and all your family! I have a distant recollection of seeing some of them at your house.

"Yours very truly,

"RICHARD KNILL."

After that, I went to preach for Mr. Knill himself, who was then at Chester.

What a meeting we had! He was preaching in the theater, and consequently I had to take his place at the footlights. His preaching in a theater took away from me all fear about preaching in buildings of doubtful use, and set me free for the campaigns in Exeter Hall and the Surrey Music Hall. How much this had to do with other theater services many know.

"God moves in a mysterious way,
His wonders to perform."

After more than forty years of the Lord's lovingkindness, I sat again in that arbor in the year 1887. No doubt it is a mere trifle for outsiders to hear about, but to me it was an overwhelming moment. In July of the year 1887, I went down to Stambourne, and walked about the place like one in a dream. The present minister of Stambourne Meeting-house, and the members of his family, including his son and his grandchildren, were in the garden, and I could not help calling them together around that arbor, while I praised the Lord for His goodness to me. One irresistible impulse was upon me: it was to pray God to bless those lads that stood around me.

Memory begat prayer. He who had blessed me, would bless others also. I wanted the lads to remember, when they grew up, my testimony of God's goodness to me. God has blessed me all my life long, and redeemed me from all evil, and I pray that He may be the God of all the young people who read this story.

The following is the letter mentioned by Mr. Knill on page 35: —

"No. 9, Union Road,

"My Dear Sir,

"I feel confident that you will pardon the liberty I take when you read the occasion of it. I have for some time wished to write to you, but could not find you out, until in the *Banner* I observed a notice of your preaching in the theater of Chester.

"Eight or nine years ago, you were traveling, as a deputation from the London Missionary Society, in the county of Essex. Among other places, you preached at the village of Stambourne. I was then a little boy staying at my grandfather's (Rev. Jas. Spurgeon). You kindly noticed me; I read at family prayer; you took me by your side, and talked to me in a very affectionate manner. You told me a tale of a little boy in Colchester; we went into an arbor in the garden, there you asked me to sing, and I joined in as well as I could. I shall never forget the way in which you tried to lead me to the Savior. Your conversation and spirit were all a father's could have been, and that one interview has made my heart yours. My eyes rejoice to see your name, and the mention of it brings up emotions of gratitude. In fact, unknown to you, a few words you then spoke have been a sort of star to my existence, and my friends look on them with half the reverence of prophecy. You meant them not perhaps to last so long, but now they are imperishable; they were to this effect, and were heard by more than one: — '*I think this little man will one day be a preacher of the gospel, and I hope a successful one. I think you will preach in Rowland Hill's Chapel; and when you do, tell the people this verse, "God moves in a mysterious way,"* etc.' You told me to learn the hymn, and said *it seemed perhaps unlikely, but Providence had wrought wonders, and you thought it would be so.* This is often mentioned by my grandfather; and somehow, though I am far enough from being superstitious, it holds me fast, and I do confidently, and yet, somehow (and paradoxically), distrustfully, look forward to the time when the whole shall come to pass.

"When sixteen and a half years old, I was persuaded to preach in the villages, having for some time been often called to address children in Sabbath Schools, and always gaining attention, perhaps from my youth as much as anything. Once started in lay-preaching around Cambridge, — where I was and am still assistant in a school, — I put my soul into the work. Having been invited to supply, for one Sabbath, the Baptist Church at Waterbeach, I did so; I was invited to continue, and have now been the minister of the congregation for one year and four months. The chapel is always full, many profess to have felt the power of Divine grace, and residents in the neighborhood say that there is a visible reform manifest; God has used things that are not, to bring to naught things that are. I preach thrice on the Sabbath; and often, indeed, almost constantly, five times in the weeknights. My salary being insufficient, I still remain in the school. Though the congregation is large, they being poor, or men of small property, are unable to do much, — though their kindness may be judged of from the fact that I have been to sixty-two different houses to dine on the Lord's-day.

Thus are your words in part realized.

"Though I do not say that your conversation did then lead to my conversion, yet the thought of what I conceived might be my position one day ever worked in me a desire to gain true religion, which even then I knew was the great essential in a minister. I long for nothing more earnestly than to serve God with all my might. My education is amply sufficient for my present station, and I have means and desires for further improvement.

"The particulars I have given are perhaps too lengthy, but you will excuse it. I could not refrain from letting you know what is no doubt more interesting to me than to you. I pray that, while standing on the polluted ground (in Chester theater), you may consecrate it in many a heart by being the means of their conversion. Your words spoken in season have been good to me; and if I am of any use in the army of the living God, I owe it in great part to you that I ever enlisted in it. I am not nineteen yet; and need, and trust I shall have, a mention in your prayers.

"With the greatest respect,

"I am,

"Yours truly,

"CHARLES SPURGEON."

"P.S. — Since you are much engaged, I shall scarcely expect a line from you; but if I should be happy enough to receive one, I shall be rejoiced."

Chapter Six - Incidents of Home and School Life

No man can write the whole of his own biography. I suppose, if the history of a man's thoughts and words could be written, scarce the world itself would contain the books, so wonderful is the tale that might be told. Of my life at home and at school, I can only give a few incidents as I am able to recall them after the lapse of forty or fifty years. One of the earliest, and one that impressed itself very deeply upon my childish mind, relates to —

MY FIRST AND LAST DEBT.

When I was a very small boy, in pinafores, and went to a woman's school, it so happened that I wanted a stick of slate pencil, and had no money to buy it with. I was afraid of being scolded for losing my pencils so often, for I was a real careless little fellow, and so did not dare to ask at home; what then was I to do? There was a little shop in the place, where nuts, and tops, and cakes, and balls were sold by old Mrs. Pearson, [3] and sometimes I had seen boys and girls get trusted by the old lady. I argued with myself that Christmas was coming, and that somebody or other would be sure to give me a penny then, and perhaps even a whole silver sixpence. I would, therefore, go into debt for a stick of slate pencil, and be sure to pay at Christmas. I did not feel easy about it, but still I screwed my courage up, and went into the shop. One farthing was the amount, and as I had never owed anything before, and my credit was good, the pencil was handed over by the kind dame, and *I was in debt.* It did not please me much, and I felt as if I had done wrong, but I little knew how soon I should smart for it.

How my father came to hear of this little stroke of business, I never knew, but some little bird or other whistled it to him, and he was very soon down upon me in right earnest. God bless him for it; he was a sensible man, and none of your children-spoilers; he did not intend to bring up his children to speculate, and play at what big rogues call financing, and therefore he knocked my getting into debt on the head at once, and no mistake. He gave me a very powerful lecture upon getting into debt, and how like it was to stealing, and upon the way in which people were ruined by it; and how a boy who would owe a farthing, might one day owe a hundred pounds, and get into prison, and bring his family into disgrace. It was a lecture, indeed; I think I can hear it now, and can feel my ears tingling at the recollection of it. Then I was marched off to the shop, like a deserter marched into barracks, crying bitterly all down the street, and feeling dreadfully ashamed, because I thought everybody knew I was in debt. The farthing was paid amid many solemn warnings, and the poor debtor was set free, like a bird let out of a cage. How sweet it felt to be out of debt! How did my little heart vow and declare that nothing should ever tempt me into debt again! It was a fine lesson, and I have never forgotten it. If all boys were inoculated with the same doctrine when they were young, it would be as good as a fortune to them, and save them wagon-loads of trouble in after life. God bless my father, say I, and send a breed of such fathers into old England to save her from being eaten up with villainy, for what with companies, and schemes, and paper-money, the nation is getting to be as rotten as touchwood! Ever since that early sickening, I have hated debt as Luther hated the Pope.

Another occurrence of those early days is rather more to my credit. Long after my own sons had grown to manhood, I recalled to my father's recollection an experience of which, until then, he had never had an explanation. My brother, as a child, suffered from weak ankles, and in consequence frequently fell down, and so got into trouble at home. At last, hoping to cure him of what father thought was only carelessness, he was threatened that he should be whipped every time he came back showing any signs of having fallen down. When I reminded my father of this regulation, he said quite triumphantly, "Yes, it was so, and he was completely cured from that time." "Ah!" I answered, "so you thought, yet it was not so, for he had many a tumble afterwards; but I always managed to wash his knees, and to brush his clothes, so as to remove all traces of his falls."

ILLUSTRATIONS FROM CHILDHOOD'S DAYS.

I recollect, when a child, seeing on the mantel-piece a stone apple, — wonderfully like an apple, too, and very well colored. I saw that apple years after, but it was no riper. It had been in favorable circumstances for softening and sweetening, if it ever would have become mellow; but I do not think, if the sun of the Equator had shone on it, or if the dews of Hermon had fallen on it, it would ever have been fit to be brought to table.

Its hard marble substance would have broken a giant's teeth. It was a hypocritical professor, a hard-hearted mocker of little children, a mere mimic of God's fruits. There are church-members who used to be unkind, covetous, censorious, bad-tempered, egotistical, everything that was hard and stony; are they so now? Have they not mellowed with the lapse of years? No; they are worse, if anything, very dogs in the house for snapping and snarling, rending and devouring; great men at hewing down the carved work of the sanctuary with their axes, or at filling up wells, and marring good pieces of land with stones. When the devil wants a stone to fling at a minister, he is sure to use one of them.

When we were small children, we had a little plot of garden-ground, and we put our seeds into it. I well recollect how, the day after I had put in my seed, I went and scraped the soil away to see if it was not growing, as I expected it would have been after a day or so at the very longest, and I thought the time amazingly long before the seed would be able to make its appearance above the ground. "That was childish," you say. I know it was, but I wish you were as childish with regard to your prayers, that you would, when you have put them in the ground, go and see if they have sprung up; and if not at once, — be not childish in refusing to wait till the appointed time comes, — always go back and see if they have begun to sprout. If you believe in prayer at all, expect God to hear you. If you do not expect, you will not have. God will not hear you unless you believe He will hear you; but if you believe He will, He will be as good as your faith.

He will never allow you to think better of Him than He is; He will come up to the mark of your thoughts, and according to your faith so shall it be done unto you.

When we used to go to school, we would draw houses, and horses, and trees on our slates, and I remember how we used to write "house" under the house, and "horse" under the horse, for some persons might have thought the horse was a house. So there are some people who need to wear a label round their necks to show that they are Christians at all, or else we might mistake them for sinners, their actions are so like those of the ungodly.

I remember once, when a lad, having a dog, which I very much prized, and some man in the street asked me to give him the dog; I thought it was pretty impudent, and I said as much. A gentleman, however, to whom I told it, said, "Now suppose the Duke of So-and-so" — who was a great man in the neighborhood, — "asked you for the dog, would you give it to him?" I answered, "I think I would." So the gentleman said, "Then you are just like all the world; you would give to those who do not need."

I have seen, when I was a boy, a juggler in the street throw up half-a-dozen balls, or knives and plates, and continue throwing and catching them, and to me it seemed marvelous; but the religious juggler beats all others hollow. He has to keep up Christianity and worldliness at the same time, and to catch two sets of balls at once. To be a freeman of Christ and a slave of the world at the same time, must need fine acting. One of these days you, Sir Juggler, will make a slip with one of the balls, and your game will be over. A man cannot always keep it up, and play so cleverly at all hours; sooner or later he fails, and then he is made a hissing and a by-word, and becomes ashamed, if any shame be left in him.

I can never forget the rushlight, which dimly illuminated the sitting-room of the old house; nor the dips, which were pretty fair when there were not too many of them to the pound; nor the mould candles, which came out only when there was a party, or some special personage was expected. Short sixes were very respectable specimens of household lights. Composites have never seemed to me to be so good as the old sort, made of pure tallow; but I daresay I may be wrong. Nevertheless, I have no liking for composites in theology, but prefer the genuine article without compromise.

31

A night-light is a delightful invention for the sick. It has supplanted the rush-light, which would frequently be set in a huge sort of tower, which, to me, as a sick child at night, used to suggest dreadful things. With its light shining through the round holes at the side, like so many ghostly eyes, it looked at me staringly; and with its round ring on the ceiling, it made me think of Nebuchadnezzar's burning fiery furnace.

Once, I thoughtlessly hung a pound of tallow candles on a clothes-horse.

This construction was moved near the fire, and the result was a mass of fat on the floor, and the cottons of the candles almost divested of tallow; — a lesson to us all not to expose certain things to a great heat, lest we dissolve them. I fear that many a man's good resolutions only need the ordinary fire of daily life to make them melt away. So, too, with fine professions, and the boastings of perfection which abound in this age of shams.

I have a distinct remembrance of a mission-room, where my father frequently preached, which was illuminated by candles in tin sconces which hung on the wall. These luminaries frequently went very dim for want of snuffing, and on one occasion an old man, who wanted to see his hymn-book, took the candle from its original place: out of his hand he made a candlestick; his finger and thumb he used as a pair of snuffers; and, finding it needful to cough, he accidentally made use of his mouth as an extinguisher. Thus the furniture of a candle was all contained in his own proper person.

We had practical fun with candles, too; for we would scoop out a turnip, cut eyes and a nose in the rind, and then put a candle inside. This could be judiciously used to amuse, but it might also be injudiciously turned to purposes of alarming youngsters and greenhorns, who ran away, under the apprehension that a ghost was visible. Other things besides turnips can be used to frighten foolish people; but it is a shame to use the light of truth with such a design.

During one of my many holidays at Stambourne, I had a varied experience which I am not likely to forget. My dear grandfather was very fond of Dr.

Watts's hymns, and my grandmother, wishing to get me to learn them, promised me a penny for each one that I should say to her perfectly. I found it an easy and pleasant method of earning money, and learned them so fast that grandmother said she must reduce the price to a halfpenny each, and afterwards to a farthing, if she did not mean to be quite ruined by her extravagance. There is no telling how low the amount per hymn might have sunk, but grandfather said that he was getting overrun with rats, and offered me a shilling a dozen for all I could kill. I found, at the time, that the occupation of rat-catching paid me better than learning hymns, but I know which employment has been the more permanently profitable to me.

No matter on what topic I am preaching, I can even now, in the middle of any sermon, quote some verse of a hymn in harmony with the subject; the hymns have remained with me, while those old rats for years have passed away, and the shillings I earned by killing them have been spent long ago.

Many memories were awakened, one day, when I opened my copy of White's *Natural History of Selborne,* and read the following inscription: —

After I had once succeeded in gaining my position at the top of the class, I was careful to retain it, except at one particular period, when I made up my mind to get right down to the bottom. My teacher could not understand my unusual stupidity, until it suddenly occurred to him that I had purposely worked my way from the head of the class, which was opposite a draughty door, down to the foot, which was next to the stove. He therefore reversed the position of the scholars, and it was not long before I had again climbed to the place of honor, where I had also the enjoyment of the heat from the fire.

(Writing to *The Christian World,* in February, 1892, Mr. R. D. Cheveley, of Harrogate, who had been a fellow-scholar with C. H. Spurgeon at Colchester, said: —

"Stockwell House, Colchester, where Charles Haddon Spurgeon was being educated from the age of eleven to fifteen [ten to fourteen], was a thoroughly good middle-class classical and commercial school. Mr. Henry Lewis, the principal, was a man whose literary attainments were of a superior order, and for years he was assisted by a very scholarly man in the person of Mr. Leeding, whose death occurred only very recently. Mr. Leeding was the classical and mathematical tutor; his teaching was very thorough, and in Charles Spurgeon he possessed a pupil of a very receptive mind, especially with Latin and Euclid. I remember well that in both of these subjects he was very advanced, so that he left Stockwell House a thoroughly well-educated youth; in fact, quite as much so as it was possible for him to attain outside the Universities.")

(In *The Sword and the Trowel,* October, 1890, Mr. Spurgeon made the following kind reference to the home-going of his old tutor: —) The Norwood papers contain the following death: — LEEDING, —

September 11, at the Academy, West Norwood, Edwin Sennit Leeding, aged 77 years.

This Mr. Leeding was usher at the school of Mr. Henry Lewis, of Colchester, in 1845, and I (C. H. Spurgeon) was one of the boys under his care. He was a teacher who really taught his pupils; and by his diligent skill I gained the foundation upon which I built in after years. He left Colchester to open a school of his own in Cambridge, and I to go, first to Maidstone, and then to Newmarket for some two years. Then we came together again; for I joined him at Cambridge to assist in his school, and in return to be helped in my studies. He has left on record that he did not think that there was need for me to go to any of the Dissenting Colleges, since I had mastered most of the subjects studied therein; and his impression that I might, while with him, have readily passed through the University if the pulpit had not come in the way. His school did not succeed, for he was not well enough to attend to it; and in after years I found my old tutor struggling at West Norwood against the difficult circumstances which Board Schools have created for private ventures. He was a good man and true, — a man of prayer, faith, and firm principle. His life was full of trials, and I have seen him greatly depressed, but he has honorably finished his course, and has gone to his reward. I have always looked to him, among the many of whom I have gathered help, as my tutor. Thus the tutor has gone home, and the scholar must not forget that in due course he will follow.

Chapter Seven - Memories of Maidstone and Newmarket

I RECOLLECT that, when I first came to London as a boy, to go to school at Maidstone, while I was sitting in the coach, ready to start, a man came along selling knives with a great number of blades. He put one in at the window, and stuck it right before my face. Why did he want to intrude on me like that? He had no business to poke a knife into my eye; but he had never studied that kind of modesty which some of us have. If he had kept that many-bladed knife in his pocket, and quietly said, "If there should be a person in the coach who would like to look at a knife with ever so many blades, I have one in my pocket," he would not have sold one in a century; but he picked me out as a likely customer, and opened the blades as if he knew that such a knife would be wonderfully fascinating to a boy going to school. That man's energy taught me a lesson which I have often turned to good account when I have been trying to induce people to "buy the truth."

I was about the age of fourteen when I was sent to a Church of England school, — now called St. Augustine's College, Maidstone. We had three clergymen who came by turns to teach us their doctrines; but, somehow or other, the pupils did not seem to get on much, for when one of them was asked by a clergyman how many sacraments there were, he said, "Seven,"

and when that was denied, he said, "Oh, sir, there is one that they take at the haltar!" upon which I could not help saying, "That's hanging, I should think," which suggestion made even the reverend gentleman smile, although, of course, I was bidden not to be so rude as to interrupt again. I am sure many of the sons of the gentry in that establishment were more ignorant of Scripture than the boys in some of our Ragged Schools.

One of the clergy was, I believe, a good man; and it is to him I owe that ray of light which sufficed to show me believers' baptism. I was usually at the head of the class, and on one occasion, when the Church of England Catechism was to be repeated, something like the following conversation took place: —

Clergyman. — What is your name?
Spurgeon. — Spurgeon, sir.
Clergyman. — No, no; what is your name?
Spurgeon. — Charles Spurgeon, sir.
Clergyman. — No, you should not behave so, for you know I only want your Christian name.
Spurgeon. — If you please, sir, I am afraid I haven't got one.
Clergyman. — Why, how is that?
Spurgeon. — Because I do not think I am a Christian.

Clergyman. — What are you, then, — a heathen?

Spurgeon. — No, sir; but we may not be heathens, and yet be without the grace of God, and so not be truly Christians.

Clergyman. — Well, well, never mind; what is your first name?

Spurgeon. — Charles.

Clergyman. — Who gave you that name?

Spurgeon. — I am sure I don't know, sir; I know no godfathers ever did anything for me, for I never had any. Likely enough, my mother and father did.

Clergyman. — Now, you should not set these boys a-laughing. Of course, I do not wish you to say the usual answer.

He seemed always to have a respect for me, and gave me The *Christian Year*, in calf, as a reward for my great proficiency in religious knowledge.

Proceeding with the Catechism, he suddenly turned to me, and said, —

Spurgeon, you were never properly baptized.

Spurgeon. — Oh, yes, sir, I was; my grandfather baptized me in the little parlor, and he is a minister, so I know he did it right!

Clergyman. — Ah, but you had neither faith nor repentance, and therefore ought not to have received baptism!

Spurgeon. — Why, sir, that has nothing to do with it! All infants ought to be baptized.

Clergyman. — How do you know that? Does not the Prayer Book say that faith and repentance are necessary before baptism? And this is so Scriptural a doctrine, that no one ought to deny it. (Here he went on to show that all the persons spoken of in the Bible as being baptized were believers; which, of course, was an easy task, and then said to me, —) Now, Charles, I shall give you till next week to find out whether the Bible does not declare faith and repentance to be necessary qualifications before baptism.

I felt sure enough of victory; for I thought that a ceremony my grandfather and father both practiced in their ministry must be right; but I could not find it, — I was beaten, — and made up my mind as to the course I would take.

Clergyman. — Well, Charles, what do you think now?

Spurgeon. — Why, sir, I think you are right; but then it applies to you as well as to me!

Clergyman. — I wanted to show you this; for this is the reason why we appoint sponsors. It is that, without faith, I had no more right than you to holy baptism; but the promise of my sponsors was accepted by the Church as an equivalent. You have no doubt seen your father, when he has no money, give a note-of-hand for it; and this is regarded as an earnest of payment, because, as an honest man, we have reason to expect he will honor the note he has given. Now, sponsors are generally good people, and in charity we accept their promise on behalf of the child. As the child cannot at the time have faith, we accept the bond that he will; which promise he fulfills at confirmation, when he takes the bond into his own hands.

Spurgeon. — Well, sir, I think it is a very bad note-of-hand.

Clergyman. — I have no time to argue that, but I believe it to be good. I will only ask you this, — Which seems to have the greater regard to Scripture, — I, as a Churchman, or your grandfather as a Dissenter? He baptizes in the very teeth of Scripture; and I do not, in my opinion, do so, for I require a promise, which I look upon as an equivalent of repentance and faith, to be rendered in future years.

Spurgeon. — Really, sir, I think you are more like right; but since it seems to be the truth that only believers should be baptized, I think you are both wrong, though you seem to treat the Bible with the greater politeness.

Clergyman. — Well, then, you confess that you were not properly baptized; and you would think it your duty, if in your power, to join with us, and have sponsors to promise on your behalf?

Spurgeon. — Oh, no! I have been baptized once, before I ought; I will wait next time till I am fit for it.

Clergyman. — (Smiling.) Ah, you are wrong; but I like to see you keep to the Word of God! Seek from Him a new heart and Divine direction, and you will see one truth after another, and very probably there will be a great change in those opinions which now seem so deeply rooted in you.

I resolved, from that moment, that if ever Divine grace should work a change in me, I would be baptized, since, as I afterwards told my friend the clergyman, "I never ought to be blamed for improper baptism, as I had nothing to do with it; the error, if any, rested with my parents and grandparents."

When at Mentone, on one occasion, I was greatly pleased to receive the following note from a lady I met there, as it enabled me to identify the esteemed clergyman who had shown himself so interested in my welfare while at Maidstone: —

"Mrs. S__ wrote me, the other day, that she had been dining out, and sat next to Canon Jeffreys, of Hawkhurst. The conversation turned upon Mr.

Spurgeon and his valuable Commentary on the Psalms. The Canon said that he once examined at some Grammar School where the boy Spurgeon was, and that he was the only boy out of, I forget how many, who could answer most of the questions. Some boys could not do *any,* while young Spurgeon did all excepting those on the Church Catechism."

It was while I was at Maidstone that I had the opportunity of attending the services of the Established Church, and therefore was able, long afterwards, to say to the students of the Pastors' College: — "There is an ecclesiastical twang which is much admired in the Establishment, a sort of steeple-in-the-throat grandeur, an aristocratic, theologic, parsonic, supernatural, infra-human mouthing of language and rolling over of words.

It maybe illustrated by the following specimen, — 'He that hath yaws to yaw, let him yaw,' which is a remarkable, if not impressive, rendering of a Scripture text. Who does not know the hallowed way of pronouncing —

'Dearly-beloved brethren, the Scripture moveth us in divers places'? It rolls in my ears now like Big Ben, coupled with boyish memories of monotonous peals of 'The Prince Albert, Albert Prince of Wales, and all the Royal Family... Amen.' Now, if a man who talks so unnaturally does *not* get bronchitis, or some other disease, I can only say that throat diseases must be very sovereignly dispensed. At the Nonconformist hobbies of utterance I have already struck a blow, and I believe it is by them that larynx and lungs become delicate, and good men succumb to silence and the grave."

36

I had a variety of experiences while at that Church school. One piece of mischief I remember to this day. There was a large jar of ammonia in a certain cupboard, and I used to lead the new boys to it, and tell them to take a good sniff, the usual result being that they would be quite overpowered. Once, when a boy fell down in a dead faint, I was really frightened, and I did not want to play the same trick on anyone else.

Perhaps I took the more liberty as the master (Mr. David Walker) was my uncle; at any rate, I was a great favorite with my aunt, and that fact helped me out of many a difficulty.

Mr. Walker's usual plan of punishing his pupils was to make the sentence bear as much resemblance as possible to the offense they had committed.

For instance, the boys had gone one night, and borrowed a boat from the river; so, the next night, they were roused from their slumbers, and made to go at once to return it to its proper place. They would probably be all the more careful not to repeat their wrong-doing when they found how much discomfort it brought to themselves.

It often happened that, when corporal punishment was to be administered, my uncle would send me out to find a cane for him. It was not a very pleasant task, and I noticed that I never once succeeded in selecting a stick which was liked by the boy who had to feel it. Either it was too thin, or too thick; and, in consequence, I was threatened by the sufferers with condign punishment if I did not do better next time. I learned from that experience never to expect God's children to like the particular rod with which they are chastened.

I greatly offended my uncle, on one occasion, by pointing out an error in an arithmetical problem he was working on the blackboard. He said that it was derogatory to his dignity to be corrected before his pupils, but I maintained that it was not right for me to let the mistake pass without mentioning it after I had detected the blunder. I think, after that incident, he judged that I could employ my time to the greatest advantage by taking my books, and studying by myself beneath an old oak-tree by the river Medway; at all events, he showed his appreciation of my mathematical progress by allowing me to make the calculations which are, I believe, still used by a certain Life Insurance Society in London.

(In the month of July, 1889, Mr. Spurgeon paid a short visit to the town of Maidstone. On the Sabbath evening after his drive into Kent, he preached at the Metropolitan Tabernacle a sermon upon Psalm 71:17, in which he said: —)

I went down, last week, to Maidstone, in Kent. It is as near as possible to the day, forty years ago, when I left the school called a "College" there. I thought that I must go down and look at the spot, and specially at a tree which stands by the river Medway. Under that tree I spent many hours, and many days, and even many weeks, reading all day long. "In school-time?"

say you. Yes, my master thought that I should do better under that tree than in the class; and he was a wise man. He gave me my book, and left me to myself; and as I stood last week under that tree, with the smoothly-flowing river at my feet, I could thank God for His mercy to me for all these forty years, and I could say, "O God, Thou hast taught me from my youth: and hitherto have I declared Thy wondrous works." There may be some young people here tonight, just come back from school, boys and girls who are just finishing their school days. I would to God that they would spend some time in holy, quiet thought about their future, about whom they will serve, who shall be their Teacher, for whom they will become teachers, and how the life which has now become more public than before shall be spent.

As I stood there, last week, I could not help praising God that, not long after I left that school, He led me to faith in Christ, and to rest in Him, and find eternal life; and I could not but thank God that I went to that school for twelve months. It was a Church of England school. I had never seen anything of Church of Englandism till that time; but there was a turning in my life, through being there, to which I owe my being here. The Church of England Catechism has in it, as some of you may remember, this question, "What is required of persons to be baptized?" and the answer I was taught to give, and did give, was, "Repentance, whereby they forsake sin; and faith, whereby they steadfastly believe the promises of God made to them in that sacrament." I looked that answer up in the Bible, and I found it to be strictly correct as far as repentance and faith are concerned; and of course, when I afterwards became a Christian, I also became a Baptist; and here I am, and it is due to the Church of England Catechism that I am a Baptist. Having been brought up amongst Congregationalists, I had never looked at the matter in my life. I had thought myself to have been baptized as an infant; and so, when I was confronted with the question, "What is required of persons to be baptized?" and I found that repentance and faith were required, I said to myself, "Then I have not been baptized; that infant sprinkling of mine was a mistake; and please God that I ever have repentance and faith, I will be properly baptized." I did not know that there was one other person in the world who held the same opinion; for so little do Baptists make any show, or so little did they do so then, that I did not know of their existence. So I feel grateful to the Church school, and grateful to the Church Catechism, for what I learnt at Maidstone. I do not know that I have any vivid gratitude for any other question in the Catechism; but I am very thankful for that particular one, for it led me where it was never intended to lead me by those who wrote it. It led me, however, as I believe, to follow the Scriptural teaching that repentance and faith are required before there can be any true baptism.

THE YOUNG USHER'S TEACHER IN THEOLOGY.

The first lessons I ever had in theology were from an old cook in the school at Newmarket where I was an usher. She was a good old soul, and used to read *The Gospel Standard.* She liked something very sweet indeed, good strong Calvinistic doctrine; but she lived strongly as well as fed strongly. Many a time we have gone over the covenant of grace together, and talked of the personal election of the saints, their union to Christ, their final perseverance, and what vital godliness meant; and I do believe that I learnt more from her than I should have learned from any six doctors of divinity of the sort we have nowadays. There are some Christian people who taste, and see, and enjoy religion in their own souls, and who get at a deeper knowledge of it than books can ever give them, though they should search all their days. The cook at Newmarket was a godly experienced woman, from whom I learned far more than I did from the minister of the chapel we attended. I asked her once, "Why do you go to such a place?"

She replied, "Well, there is no other place of worship to which I can go." I said, "But it must be better to stay at home than to hear such stuff."

"Perhaps so," she answered; "but I like to go out to worship even if I get nothing by going. You see a hen sometimes scratching all over a heap of rubbish to try to find some corn; she does not get any, but it shows that she is looking for it, and using the means to get it, and then, too, the exercise warms her." So the old lady said that scratching over the poor sermons she heard was a blessing to her because it exercised her spiritual faculties and warmed her spirit. On another occasion I told her that I had not found a crumb in the whole sermon, and asked how she had fared. "Oh!" she answered, "I got on better to-night, for to all the preacher said, I just put in a *not,* and that turned his talk into real gospel."

(After Mr. Spurgeon was "called home," Professor J. D. Everett, F.R.S., of Queen's College, Belfast, wrote to *The Christian World:* — "In the summer of 1849, when I was not quite eighteen, I went to Newmarket to assist in a school kept by a Mr. Swindell, [4] who had been an old friend of my father's, and who had my brothers, Percy and John, as pupils. There were two other assistants, but not long after my arrival they went off, and I was left for a week or so as the sole assistant. I was then relieved of part of my duty by a lad of fifteen, who came as an articled pupil. This was Charles H. Spurgeon, and for the next three months we shared the work between us. We boarded in the house, occupied the same bedroom, took our walks together, discussed our common grievances, and were the best of friends.

He was a keen observer of men and manners, and very shrewd in his judgments. He enjoyed a joke, but was earnest, hard-working, and strictly conscientious. He had a wonderful memory for passages of oratory which he admired, and used to pour forth to me with great gusto, in our walks, long screeds from open-air addresses of a very rousing description, which he had heard delivered at Colchester Fair, by the Congregational minister, Mr. Davids. His imagination had evidently been greatly impressed by these services, at which, by-the-by, his father was selected to give out the hymns on account of the loudness of his voice, — a quality which would appear to have run in the family, but which had not at that time shown itself in my young friend. I have also heard him recite long passages from Bunyan's *Grace Abounding.* He was a delightful companion, cheerful and sympathetic; a good listener as well as a good talker. And he was not cast in a common conventional mould, but had a strong character of his own.

"As to the early history of his theological views, I can add something to what has been already published. In Mr. Swindell's household there was a faithful old servant, — a big, sturdy woman, who was well known to me and all the inmates as 'cook.' She was a woman of strong religious feelings, and a devout Calvinist. Spurgeon, when under deep religious conviction, had conversed with her, and been deeply impressed with her views of Divine truth. He explained this to me, and told me, in his own terse fashion, that it was 'cook' who had taught him his theology. I hope I am not violating his confidence in mentioning this fact. It is no discredit to the memory of a great man that he was willing to learn from the humblest sources.")

(When the above article appeared in print, Mr. Robert Mattingly, of Great Cornard, Sudbury, wrote to the same paper: —

39

"About twenty-five years ago, I became acquainted with the person referred to, Mary King by name. She was then living in cottage lodgings, facing St. Margaret's Church, Ipswich, and was a member of the Bethesda Strict Baptist Church, close by. She was a staunch Calvinist, logical, clear-headed, and had a wonderful knowledge of the Bible. I have often heard from her lips the account of her inter-course with the youthful Spurgeon, of which she was naturally not a little proud, as he had then attained the height of his marvelous popularity. Professor Everett says she was known as 'cook.' She always spoke of herself as 'housekeeper', and as the intercourse between Mr. Spurgeon and herself seemed to be quite within the order of the household, she probably occupied something more than a meni-al position. During my acquaintance with her, I learned that she had outlived all, or nearly all, of a small income (I do not remember from what source). I wrote to Mr. Spurgeon, acquainting him with the facts, and received from him a prompt reply, thanking me for my letter, sending a hearty greeting to his old friend, and with characteristic generosity he enclosed a check for £5, with a request that I would minister to her immediate necessities, pay her 5s. a week, and generally use my discretion in dispensing the amount in his behalf. This I did, and reported to Mr. Spurgeon from time to time, always receiving a fresh check when the fund in hand became exhausted, and this was continued until her death about three years later.")

(Professor Everett has kindly transcribed from his journal all the entries relat-ing to Mr. Spurgeon while at Newmarket. Most of the matters mentioned are not of general public interest, but the two following items are worthy of preservation in this volume: —

"*Monday, Sept.* 10 (1849). — In the afternoon, the missionary meeting began. Mr. Spurgeon was made chairman. [This was a meeting of the boys, in the schoolroom. I believe it was the first time Mr. Spurgeon ever made a speech. He spoke fluently.]

"*Tuesday, October* 9. — After dinner, I took Percy and four other boys to see the races. We saw the Cesarewitch, the most celebrated race at Newmarket; thirty-one horses ran. We also saw four other races. I saw quite enough to gratify my curiosity, and did not wish to stop to see any more races. Mr. Spurgeon did not go, as he thought he should be doing wrong if he went.")

Chapter Eight - A Holiday Pastime. — Essay on Popery.

I knew a lad in Christ, who adopted the principle of giving a tenth to God. When he won a money prize for an essay on a religious subject, he felt that he could not give less than one-fifth of it. He had never after that been able to deny himself the pleasure of having a fifth to give. God had wonderfully blessed that lad, and in-creased his means, and his enjoyment of the luxury of luxuries, —
the luxury of doing good. — C. H. S.

IN the library at "Westwood," very carefully preserved, is a bound volume containing 295 manuscript pages, lettered on the back, —

On the front outside cover is a red leather label, with the following words printed upon it in gold letters thus, —

ANTICHRIST AND HER BROOD;
OR,
POPERY UNMASKED.
BY
C. H. SPURGEON, AETAT. 15.

Written in the November and December of 1849, as a kind of holiday amusement, and sent to Misters Ward and Co's on occasion of a competition for a prize offered by Mr. Morley of Nottingham. Although the writer had scarcely a distant prospect of success, he received, two years after, the following note: —

Poplar London,

Dec. 23, 1851

Dear Sir,

You were one of the competitors for a prize to be awarded for an approved essay on Popery. Your paper is not deemed entitled to the premium, — but the gentleman who offered it, and who is a relative of mine, in approval of your zeal, and in the hope that you may yet employ your talents for the public good, had requested me to offer you £ 0 0 as a gratuity. If you will tell me how you wish the money to be sent, it shall be conveyed to you, and your MS. shall be returned in any way you direct, I remain Yours truly

G. Smith

On the opposite page is a *fac-simile* of Mr. Spurgeon's own account of the origin of the volume, and of its appreciation by Mr. Morley, whose Christian name is made known in the second letter from Mr. Smith, who was at that time Congregational minister at Poplar, and who, on August 16th, 1859, met the young essayist, and took part with him in the services held in connection with the laying of the first stone of the Metropolitan Tabernacle: —

"Poplar,

"Dec. 30, 1851.

"My dear Sir,

"Enclosed is an order for ____, which my brother-in-law, Mr.

Arthur Morley, of Nottingham, presents to you. I shall be obliged by your acknowledgment of the same.

"It gives me pleasure to hear of your success in preaching the gospel of Christ. God will, I trust, continue to bless you. Depend on Him, and use all the means within your reach for the cultivation and improvement of your mind.

"I remain,

"Yours truly,

"G. SMITH.

"Mr. C. Spurgeon,

"No. 9, Union Road,

"Cambridge."

A letter of the same period, written by C. H. Spurgeon to his father, gives further particulars concerning the Essay, and also explains how the writer proposed to use most of the money that had thus unexpectedly reached him. It furnishes besides an interesting glimpse of the young preacher's early services at Waterbeach, of which more will appear in a later chapter, and also of the way in which he was preparing for his great life-work: —

"Cambridge, "Dec. 31st, 1851.

"My Dear Father,

"Your Christmas letter was quite as welcome to me as [mine was]

to you — no good action is ever forgotten. I was at Waterbeach staying among my people, and so did not receive your letter till my return. I preached twice on Christmas [day] to crammed congregations, and again on Sunday quite as full. The Lord gives me favor in the eyes of the people; they come for miles, and are wondrously attentive. I am invited [to preach at Waterbeach] for six months. My reputation in Cambridge is rather great.

"This letter from Mr. Smith is an honor. I have now more money for books. When I wrote my essay on my knees in the little room upstairs, I solemnly vowed to give two tithes of anything I might gain by it to the Lord's cause. I have written, the money is come...

My MS. will arrive here shortly. Now, if you wish, I will send you... [five-sixths of the amount received] as a little present to you and dear Mother — that shall be exactly as you please — I do not know yet how much I am to pay Mr. Leeding. I have enough. Mr. L. has given me a five-pound note, which I shall not touch except for clothes. I mean to keep that money only for clothes; what I earn on Sundays is my own for books, expenses, etc. I hope I am sparing, but I have bought several books, which I could not do without. This week I have purchased a good Septuagint, which is a Greek translation of the Old Testament; you will see it mentioned by commentators. This I did for two reasons — **1.** To improve my Greek. **2.** To assist me in studying the Bible. I got it in two volumes, unbound, for 12s. 6d. — at that price it is reckoned exceedingly cheap.

"Now and then you must give me leave to preach three times, not often. I have done so about four times, I was not at all tired. I shall never do so if I have had a hard day. When I feel myself in tune and not at all tired, I may do so; but only now and then. I must say, however, I always get the best congregation in the evening, or at least just as good, for sometimes it is best *all* day: and you would not have me give up so good a place. I have prayed earnestly that prosperity and fame may not injure me, and I believe strength will be equal to my day. More than one in Waterbeach have declared themselves on the Lord's side — the church is praying hard, and they seem very united.

"I take every opportunity of improving myself, and seize every means of improvement. I have lately attended three lectures in the Town Hall to get information; I trust I do."

In order that readers may be able to form some idea of the Essay written by C. H. Spurgeon when fifteen years of age, the headings of the seventeen chapters are here given, with one chapter as a specimen of the other sixteen. That particular portion of the work was selected to show how the writer, even before his conversion, had very clear ideas as to spiritual matters. It is remarkable that he should have quoted in this part of the Essay the very passage which, a few weeks afterwards, the Lord used as the means of his salvation: "*Look unto Me, and be ye saved, all the ends of the earth.*"

ANTICHRIST AND HER BROOD; OR, POPERY UNMASKED. HEADS OF CHAPTERS.

Chapter Three - Popery, A Spiritual Darkness.

The Bible withheld. — False statement of a priest. — The Scriptures unintelligible because in an unknown tongue. — Bible burnt round the necks of heretics. — Council of Trent. — Blasphemy of its decrees. —Case in point. — Testimony of Du Moulin. — Bible Societies. — Bull of Pius VII. — Bible mystified by notes. — Bible the Word of God. —Popery unchanged. — Bishop of Nice burns Bibles in 1841. — Declaration of Popish Bishops. — Duty to read the Bible. — Sermons omitted. —Ignorance of the Priests. — Sermons nothing but ribaldry. — Immense service of Ignorance.

The three most powerful and most apparent means used by Rome to retain her power over the minds of her votaries are Ignorance, Superstition, and Persecution.

First, then, let us look at Ignorance which, though not "the mother of devotion," is certainly the favorer of superstition. This has been one of the grand agents of Popery ever since her establishment; by it, the eyes of men have been so blinded that they can scarcely discern between good and evil, and follow implicitly any guide even until they fall into the ditch of perdition.

The grossest ignorance is spiritual ignorance; and the greatest spiritual darkness is to be ignorant of the only way of salvation as it is revealed alone in the Scriptures.

The Church which withholds the Bible from its members, or takes away from them the genuine Word of God, is guilty of bringing the most dreadful famine upon the minds of men, and will be in a great measure guilty of their blood. This charge is one of the most weighty ever brought against the Church of Rome, and one which can be very easily substantiated.

The Rev. A. Scott, of Glasgow, in a letter against *The Protestant,* a controversial work published about 30 years since, says: — "I can publicly declare — without danger of being contradicted by my brethren, or censured by my superiors, — that it never was a principle of the Roman Catholic Church that the Scriptures should be withheld from the laity, and there never was any law enacted by the supreme legislative authority in the Catholic Church by which the reading of the Scriptures was prohibited. If it was indeed a principle of the Roman Catholic Church to deprive her members of the use of the Divine Word by forbidding them to read and search the Scriptures, she would indeed be cruel and unjust."

Here, then, is a distinguished Roman Catholic priest publicly disowning this great bulwark of Romanism.

We cordially agree with the rev. gentleman, that it is cruel and unjust to withhold the Bible; but we hope to be able to disprove his barefaced falsehood, and convince the world to the contrary.

The Scriptures were translated into the Latin tongue by Jerome; but that language becoming dead, and the Church neglecting to supply translations, it was only intelligible to the learned; it was not forbidden to the people, but it was of no more use to them than a scroll of hieroglyphics. This state of things continued from the eighth to the thirteenth centuries when, at the Council of Toulouse, the Scriptures were forbidden to the laity both in the Latin and vulgar tongues. We all know how violently the Pope was enraged against Wycliffe for his undertaking to translate the Scriptures into English. Had the Pope had his will, the translator and his version of the Bible would have been burnt in the same fire; indeed, it was no uncommon thing, previous to Luther's Reformation, to burn heretics with the Bible about their necks.

The reading of the Bible was understood invariably to produce heresy; and there were many who suffered death for no other crime.

In the decisions of the Council of Trent, 1564, this clause occurs: —

"Seeing it is manifest, by experience, that if the Holy Bible be permitted to be read everywhere, without difference, in the vulgar tongue, more harm than good results thence, through the rashness of men, let it therefore be at the pleasure of the bishop or inquisitor, with the advice of the parish clerk or confessor, to grant the reading of the Bible, translated by Catholic authors, to those who, in their opinion, will thereby receive an increase of faith and piety. This license let them have in writing, and whoever shall presume, without permission, to read or possess such Bibles, may not receive the absolution of sins till he has returned them to the ordinary."

Abominable blasphemy! So, then, the Church of Rome permits the Almighty, under certain circumstances, to speak to His own creatures!! It *permits* fallen and miserable men sometimes to hear the Word of their Creator!

In the Bible, the Almighty addresses us as by a voice from Heaven: "Look unto Me, and be ye saved, all the ends of the earth." The Church of Rome stands by, and presumes to decide who shall and who shall not hear these words of the Almighty Savior; and if any person shall at all hear them, it is by her permission. Surely, then, this Church of Rome is that Antichrist, —

that opposing power that exalts itself above all that is called God, or that is worshipped.

To assume the power of permitting creatures to hear what God shall speak, is assuming an authority at least equal to that of God, and a right to control or regulate the manner of His communicating His will to His creatures.

We will suggest a case somewhat similar. Suppose that, in the City of London, there were a number of traitors who had openly rebelled against the Queen; and that she, out of her gracious disposition, and aversion to destroy those traitors, should issue a proclamation promising a free pardon to those who would submit themselves to the authority of the laws. Now suppose that the Lord Mayor and Aldermen were to sit in Council, and consider whether or not they would permit this proclamation to be published in London; and suppose that they should even come to a resolution to *permit* this proclamation to be published, would not this lead you strongly to suspect their loyalty for presuming to put their authority on a footing with that of the Sovereign, and presuming to "*permit*" her proclamation to be published?

God addresses His gospel to sinners as such, in order that, hearing and believing it, sinners may be saved; but the Church of Rome exercises her authority to prevent, as far as she is able, the Word of God from reaching the ears of sinners. She allows it to be addressed only to such as will "thereby receive an increase of faith and piety;" that is, to persons who are already faithful and pious in some degree. Thus, she proves herself to be in league with Satan, for the purpose of keeping men under the bondage of sin to the everlasting ruin of their souls.

But, to return to history, the learned and excellent Du Moulin, a French Protestant divine of the seventeenth century, says, "That the people may be blinded and deceived without understanding so much, the Pope hath wrested the Scriptures out of their hands, and taken order that they should not be translated into a known tongue. Within these few years, the Scriptures were no more known to the people than the Alcoran; there were only some Latin Bibles in monasteries and clergymen's houses."

In 1824, Pope Leo XII styles the Scriptures in the vulgar tongue,

"Poisonous Pastures," and exhorts the clergy to turn the flock away from them. In a Bull of Pope Pius VII, against Bible Societies, in 1816, he says:

— "We have been truly shocked by this most crafty device by which the very foundations of religion are undermined. The Bible printed by heretics is to be numbered among other prohibited books, conformably to the rules of the Index; for it is evident, from experience, that the Holy Scriptures, when circulated in the vulgar tongue, have through the temerity of men produced more harm than benefit. It is therefore necessary that no versions of the Bible in the vulgar tongue be permitted except such as are approved by the Apostolic see, or published with annotations extracted from the writings of the fathers of the Church."

Here, then, it is declared that the circulation and reading of the Scriptures undermine the foundations of religion, which is certainly true if Popery be the only true religion. There is another Church, however, which has its foundations laid more firmly than the Church of Rome; this is the Church of Christ, which em-

45

braces the Scriptures as its best ally, and finds in them nothing but what is in harmony with itself.

The Church of Rome is afraid to trust the Bible alone, because it destroys the foundations of its religion. If the Scriptures were given to the people simply as they are, Romanism would never be able to stand against them; it would soon be known that Rome is the very Antichrist. She therefore mystifies the Word of God by means of the words of men; she puts her own perversions side by side with Scripture; and declares that, as she alone can interpret them, whatever is said to be the meaning of them must really be so.

Is it not now proved that Popery withholds the Bible from the people? It may serve as an illustration of the character of Popery if we bear in mind the statement of the priest who declared that it never was a principle of Romanism to deny the Scriptures to the people. Popery is a system of lies; she will deny or assert, just as it suits her purpose. However, we will readily believe his assertion that, in denying the Scriptures to the people, Popery is "cruel and unjust."

But many Papists will endeavor to justify this prohibition of the Scriptures, and say that it is not the will of God that His Book should be read by common people. Such men, when they hear it said that the Bible contains a complete revelation of the Divine will for the salvation of our fallen race, and is a proclamation of grace and pardon to the very chief of sinners, will exclaim, "What nonsense!" Such was actually the case in a celebrated discussion at Glasgow. But we will leave them to laugh and jeer; we know that it is the only Book which can cheer the penitent; it is God's Word, and that alone upon which a trembling sinner dares to rely. But what argument can be of avail with those who reject truth, who despise the very essence of truth? Some among them have said, "How do you know that the Bible is the Word of God?"

Among other reasons which will readily suggest themselves, one alone will suffice. Every Christian knows, experimentally, that the Bible is the Word of God. When a sinner becomes seriously concerned about his character, state, and prospects, if he reads the Bible, he finds at first that it is all against him. By the holy law of God he is convicted and condemned; and he is conscious of a power and dignity in the Word of condemnation that makes him feel that it is the Word of God. There is a power in the Word that proves it Divine; and he who has once experienced its influence will never doubt its truth.

All the Popish arguments do but prove that they love darkness rather than light. The Bible is a light unto our feet, and a lamp unto our path. Man by nature is blind, he runs the downward road with alacrity, he sees not the end; he would still continue to follow the road which leadeth to destruction had not God, in His infinite mercy, given him a sure guide to bring him from this treacherous way to the straight and narrow path, which leads to His right hand.

Popery could never have been what it is if men had been allowed to read the Bible; the light of truth would have been too strong for her; she would have perished prematurely. What an awful account will her great men have to give in, of the blood of thousands perishing for lack of knowledge!

But you will say, "Popery is changed now; surely, she is much improved."

She has not yielded a point more than she could help! The true spirit of Popery is not allowed to develop itself in Protestant countries. Here, in England, it would seem that the Catholic is under little restraint. The Bible is printed for his use in England, though always with explanatory notes as if it could not be trusted alone. But on the Continent of Europe, and in other parts of the world, the system has full scope. In Rome, very few of the people know what you mean by a Bible.

In 1841, the Bishop of Nice burnt all the French Bibles he could collect.

Can any more flagitious wickedness be conceived than for a creature of the dust, invested with the holy character of a bishop of the living God, and a minister of Jesus, to dare, with sacrilegious hands, to cast into the flames the blessed Book of God, inspired by the Holy Ghost? In the great dread day of judgment, what excuse will this apostate Church and her Bible-burning priesthood have to prefer before the heart-searching God in justification of these things?

Dr. Doyle, an Irish Roman Catholic bishop, when asked whether he had ever seen a translation of the Scriptures in the language of Portugal, where he was brought up, answered, "No, I have not." Dr. Murray, another bishop, did not know for a fact whether there was a Spanish version of the Bible. They both stated that they would refuse the Sacrament to any person who should persist in reading the Bible. The reading of the Scriptures, then, is still condemned by the Romish Church, in opposition to the Word of God, which says, "Seek ye out of the Book of the Lord, and read" (Isaiah 34:16); "Search the Scriptures; for in them ye think ye have eternal life: and they are they which testify of Me" (John 5:39); "and take the helmet of salvation, and the sword of the Spirit, which is the Word of God" (Ephesians 6:17); and numerous other exhortations.

But this prohibition of the Bible might not have been so great an evil, if the churchmen had preached the Word of Life to the people. The first triumphs of Christianity were accomplished by the preaching of the gospel, by the mouth of the apostles, and not by the written Word; and, therefore, some amount of religious knowledge might have been communicated to the people by preaching, even in the absence of the Scriptures. But the prohibition of the Bible, together with the ignorance of the priests, soon brought the sermon into disuse, or only on special occasions were any discourses delivered.

About the beginning of the sixteenth century, "the ignorance of the priests was extreme." Numbers could not read, most only muttered mass in an unknown tongue, and read a legend on festival days; the very best seldom saw the Bible. It was held by many that the doctrines of religion were so properly expressed by the schoolmen, that there was no need to read Scripture. One of eminence was asked what were the ten commandments; he replied, "There is no such book in the library." Many doctors of the Sorbonne declared, and confirmed it by an oath, that, though they were about fifty years of age, yet they had never known what a New Testament was. Luther never saw a Bible till after he was twenty years old, and had taken a degree of arts. Carolstadt had been a doctor of divinity eight years before he read the Scriptures; and yet, when he stood for a degree in the University of Wittemberg, he obtained an honor, and it was entered in the University records that he was "*sufficientissimus.*" Pelican could not procure one Greek Testament in all Germany; the first he got was from Italy.

Who can wonder at the superstitions and errors of the Church of Rome?

When sermons were delivered, they were a collection of forced interpretations, legends fabricated on the spot, and base ribaldry. The people would have been better without them, many of these mock sermons were only calculated to excite the audience to laughter, and to furnish them with amusement for the week. Ignorance held its dark reign, with scarcely a spark of light, and must have been of immense service in the establishment of the kingdom of darkness, and the support of the dominion of Antichrist.

Chapter Nine - Early Religious Impressions

It would not be easy for some of us to recall the hour when we first heard the name of Jesus. In very infancy that sweet sound was as familiar to our ear as the hush of lullaby. Our earliest recollections are associated with the house of God, the family altar, the Holy Bible, the sacred song, and the fervent prayer. Like young Samuels, we were lighted to our rest by the lamps of the sanctuary, and were awakened by the sound of the morning hymn. Many a time has the man of God, whom a parent's hospitality has entertained, implored a blessing on our head, desiring in all sincerity that we might early call the Redeemer blessed; and to his petition a mother's earnest

"Amen" has solemnly responded. Perhaps the first song we learned to sing was concerning the children's best Friend. The first book that we began to read contained His sweet name, and many were the times when we were pressed by godly ones to think of Jesus, and to give our young hearts to Him. — C. H. S.

I WAS privileged with godly parents, watched with jealous eyes, scarcely ever permitted to mingle with questionable associates, warned not to listen to anything profane or licentious, and taught the way of God from my youth up. There came a time when the solemnities of eternity pressed upon me for a decision, and when a mother's tears and a father's supplications were offered to Heaven on my behalf. At such a time, had I not been helped by the grace of God, but had I been left alone to do violence to conscience, and to struggle against conviction, I might perhaps have been at this moment dead, buried, and doomed, having through a course of vice brought myself to my grave, or I might have been as earnest a ringleader amongst the ungodly as I now desire to be an eager champion for Christ and His truth.

I do speak of myself with many deep regrets of heart. I hid as it were my face from Him, and I let the years run round, — not without twinges of conscience, not without rebukes, when I knew how much I needed a Savior; not without the warnings which came from others whom I saw happy and rejoicing in Christ, while I had no share in His salvation. Still, I put it off, as others are doing, from day to day, and month to month, and thought that Christ might come in some odd hour, and when I had nothing else to do, I might think of Him whose blood could cleanse me. O my soul, I could fain smite thee now! Truly, I could lay this rod about my own heart to think that weeks and months should have rolled over my head, and I should have hid as it were my face from Christ in willful neglect of my dear Lord whose heart had bled for me.

Children are often very reticent to their parents. Often and often have I spoken with young lads about their souls, and they have told me they could not talk to their fathers upon such matters. I know it was so with me.

When I was under concern of soul, the last persons I should have elected to speak to upon religion would have been my parents, — not through want of love to them, nor absence of love on their part; but so it was. A strange feeling of diffidence pervades a seeking soul, and drives it from its friends. Yet I cannot tell how much I owe to the solemn words of my good mother. It was the custom, on Sunday evenings, while we were yet little children, for her to stay at home with us, and then we sat round the table, and read verse by verse, and she explained the Scripture to us. After that was done, then came the time of pleading; there was a little piece of Alleine's *Alarm,* or of Baxter's *Call to the Unconverted,* and this was read with pointed observations made to each of us as we sat round the table; and the question was asked, how long it would be before we would think about our state, how long before we would seek the Lord. Then came a mother's prayer, and some of the words of that prayer we shall never forget, even when our hair is gray. I remember, on one occasion, her praying thus: "Now, Lord, if my children go on in their sins, it will not be from ignorance that they perish, and my soul must bear a swift witness against them at the day of judgment if they lay not hold of Christ." That thought of a mother's bearing swift witness against me, pierced my conscience, and stirred my heart. When I was a child, if I had done anything wrong, I did not need anybody to tell me of it; I told myself of it, and I have cried myself to sleep many a time with the consciousness that I had done wrong; and when I came to know the Lord, I felt very grateful to Him because He had given me a tender conscience.

Fathers and mothers are the most natural agents for God to use in the salvation of their children. I am sure that, in my early youth, no teaching ever made such an impression upon my mind as the instruction of my mother; neither can I conceive that, to any child, there can be one who will have such influence over the young heart as the mother who has so tenderly cared for her offspring. A man with a soul so dead as not to be moved by the sacred name of "mother" is creation's blot. Never could it be possible for any man to estimate what he owes to a godly mother. Certainly I have not the powers of speech with which to set forth my valuation of the choice blessing which the Lord bestowed on me in making me the son of one who prayed *for* me, and prayed *with* me. How can I ever forget her tearful eye when she warned me to escape from the wrath to come? I thought her lips right eloquent; others might not think so, but they certainly were eloquent to me. How can I ever forget when she bowed her knee, and with her arms about my neck, prayed, "Oh, that my son might live before Thee!" Nor can her frown be effaced from my memory, — that solemn, loving frown, when she rebuked my budding iniquities; and her smiles have never faded from my recollection, — the beaming of her countenance when she rejoiced to see some good thing in me towards the Lord God of Israel.

Well do I remember hearing my father speak of an incident that greatly impressed him. He used to be frequently away from home preaching, and at one time, as he was on his way to a service, he feared that he was neglecting his own family while caring for the souls of others. He therefore turned back, and went to his home. On arriving there, he was surprised to find no one in the lower rooms of the house; but, on ascending the stairs, he heard a sound as of someone engaged in prayer. On listening at the bedroom door, he discovered that it was my mother, pleading most earnestly for the salvation of all her children, and specially praying for Charles, her first-born and strong-willed son. My father felt that he might safely go about his Master's business while his dear wife was caring so well for the spiritual interests of the boys and girls at home, so he did not disturb her, but proceeded at once to fulfill his preaching engagement.

My mother said to me, one day, "Ah, Charles! I often prayed the Lord to make you a Christian, but I never asked that you might become a Baptist."

I could not resist the temptation to reply, "Ah, mother! the Lord has answered your prayer with His usual bounty, and given you exceeding abundantly above what you asked or thought."

Up to the age of fourteen, I had not even heard of people called Baptists; and when I did hear of them, it was not at all a favorable report that was given to me concerning them. I do not suppose my parents meant me to believe that Baptists were bad people; but I certainly did think so; and I cannot help feeling that, somewhere or other, I must have heard some calumnies against them, or else how should I have had that opinion?

I remember seeing a baby sprinkled within less than an hour of its death; and I seem to hear even now the comfort which a certain good man gave to the bereaved parents, — "What a mercy the child was baptized! What a consolation it must be!" This was in an Independent family, and the words were spoken by an Independent minister.

I knew an instance of an aged minister, of the same persuasion, who sprinkled a little boy, although the father was averse to it. The child was running about in the hall of the minister's house, and his mother was looking on. He was caught up, and the pious man exclaimed, "Come along, Mrs. S — , the poor child shall not live like a heathen any longer." So the conjuration was performed, and the little boy was put into the Paedo-Baptist covenant. He was not only suffered to come, but forced to come; and, doubtless, went on his way rejoicing to think it was over.

It is said by some that children cannot understand the great mysteries of religion. We even know some Sunday-school teachers who cautiously avoid mentioning the great doctrines of the gospel, because they think the children are not prepared to receive them. Alas! the same mistake has crept into the pulpit; for it is currently believed, among a certain class of preachers, that many of the doctrines of the Word of God, although true, are not fit to be taught to the people, since they would pervert them to their own destruction. Away with such priestcraft! Whatever God has revealed ought to be preached. Whatever He has revealed, if I am not capable of understanding it, I will still believe and preach it. I do hold that there is no doctrine of the Word of God which a child, if he be capable of salvation, is not capable of receiving. I would have children taught all the great doctrines of truth without a solitary exception, that they may in their after days hold fast by them.

I can bear witness that children *can* understand the Scriptures; for I am sure that, when but a child, I could have discussed many a knotty point of controversial theology, having heard both sides of the question freely stated among my father's circle of friends. In fact, children are capable of understanding some things in early life, which we hardly understand afterwards. Children have eminently a simplicity of faith, and simplicity of faith is akin to the highest knowledge; indeed, I know not that there is much distinction between the simplicity of a child and the genius of the profoundest mind. He who receives things simply, as a child, will often have ideas which the man who is prone to make a syllogism of everything will never attain unto. If you wish to know whether children can be taught, I point you to many in our churches, and in pious families, — not prodigies, but such as we frequently see, — Timothys and Samuels, and little girls, too, who have early come to know a Savior's love. As soon as a child is capable of being lost, it is capable of being saved. As soon as a child can sin, that child can, if God's grace assist it, believe and receive the Word of God. As soon as children can learn evil, be assured that they are competent, under the teaching of the Holy Spirit, to learn good.

In the household in which I was trained, no cooking was ever done on the Sabbath; and if in the winter time something hot was brought on the table, it was a pudding prepared on the Saturday, or a few potatoes, which took but little trouble to warm. Is not this far better, far more Christian-like, than preparing a great Sunday feast, and compelling servants to slave in the kitchen? If the horse was taken out because the distance to the meeting-house was too great, or the weather too rough for walking, Christians of the good old school always gave the animal its Sabbath on the Saturday or the Monday; and as to the coachman, when they employed one, they always took care to give him time to put up the horse, that he might come in and worship with the family, and they were content to wait till he could come round for them after service, for they did not want him to lose even the Benediction.

Ought it not to be so everywhere? Our servants should be regarded as a part of the family, and we should study their comfort as well as our own, if for no other reason, certainly, because they will then study ours; but, above all, we should remember their souls, and give them every opportunity to enjoy the means of grace. How can they do this if we make the Lord's-day as much a work-day as any in the week? We are not of those who think it wicked to boil a kettle for tea on a Sunday, nor can we yield to the demands of some, that everybody, however feeble, or however distant his abode, should walk to the place of worship. To some, such a walk would be working with a vengeance, and to many an absolute deprivation of the means of grace; but, still, we must not allow unnecessary labor in or about our habitations on the Lord's-day, and must devise means to make the necessary work as light as possible. Is a hot joint preferable to a servant's soul? Is it fair to keep a girl at home merely for our own needless gratification? Especially, is this justifiable in the case of those who fare sumptuously everyday?

I recollect, when I was a boy, hearing a minister preach from this text, "Who can find a virtuous woman? for her price is far above rubies." The opening of that memorable discourse was somewhat in this fashion: —

"'Who can find a virtuous woman?' Why, anyone who chooses to look for her; and the only reason why Solomon could not find her was because he looked in the wrong place. Virtuous women kept clear of a king who had such a multitude

51

of wives. But," said the preacher, "if Solomon were here now, and were made truly wise, he would not long ask, — 'Who can find a virtuous woman?' He would join the church, and find himself at once among a band of holy women, whose adornment is a meek and quiet spirit.

If he were permitted to look in upon the Dorcas meeting, he would see many of the sort of whom he once said, 'She stretcheth out her hand to the poor; yea, she reacheth forth her hands to the needy.' If he would adjourn to the Sunday-school, he would there meet with others of whom he would say, 'She openeth her mouth with wisdom; and in her tongue is the law of kindness.' We, who serve the Lord Jesus, meet many a time with virtuous women, of each of whom we could say with the wise king, 'Her price is far above rubies.'"

The preacher of whom I have spoken, interested me by the remark, "Why above *rubies?* Why not above *diamonds?* My brethren, the diamond is but a pale and sickly stone, which needs the glare of candle-light or gas to set it off; but the ruby is a ruddy, healthy gem, which is beautiful by daylight.

Lovely is the woman whose face is full of the glow of activity in domestic life. That is the kind of woman who makes the housewife in whom the heart of her husband safely trusteth."

Whatever one may think of the correctness of the exposition, the sentiment of the preacher was sound and practical.

I have not all pleasant reminiscences of the preachers of my boyhood. I used to hear a divine who had a habit, after he had uttered about a dozen sentences, of saying, "As I have already observed," or, "I repeat what I before remarked." Well, good soul, as there was nothing particular in what he had said, the repetition only revealed the more clearly the nakedness of the land. If it was very good, and you said it forcibly, why go over it again?

And if it was a feeble affair, why exhibit it a second time? Occasionally, of course, the repetition of a few sentences may be very telling; anything may be good occasionally, and yet be very vicious as a habit. Who wonders that people do not listen the first time when they know it is all to come over again? I once heard a most esteemed minister, who mumbled sadly, compared to "a humble bee in a pitcher," — a vulgar metaphor, no doubt, but so exactly descriptive, that it brings to my mind the droning sound at this instant most distinctly, and reminds me of the parody upon Gray's *Elegy*: —

"Now fades the glimmering subject from the sight,
And all the air a sleepy stillness holds,
Save where the parson hums his droning flight,
And drowsy tinklings lull the slumb'ring folds."

What a pity that a man who from his heart delivered doctrines of undoubted value, in language the most appropriate, should commit ministerial suicide by harping on one string, when the Lord had given him an instrument of many strings to play upon! Alas! alas! for that dreary voice, it hummed and hummed, like a mill-wheel, to the same unmusical tune, whether its owner spake of Heaven or hell, eternal life or everlasting wrath. It might be, by accident, a little louder or softer, according to the length of the sentence; but its tone was still the same, a dreary waste of sound, a howling wilderness of speech in which there was no

52

possible relief, no variety, no music, nothing but horrible sameness. When the wind blows through the AEolian harp, it swells through all the chords; but the Heavenly wind, passing through some men, spends itself upon one string, and that, for the most part, the most out of tune of the whole. Grace alone could enable hearers to edify under the drum-drum-drum of some divines. I think an impartial jury would bring in a verdict of justifiable slumbering in many cases where the sound emanating from the preacher lulls to sleep by its reiterated note.

I have a very lively, or rather a deadly, recollection of a certain series of discourses on the Hebrews, which made a deep impression on my mind of the most undesirable kind. I wished frequently that the Hebrews had kept the Epistle to themselves, for it sadly bored one poor Gentile lad. By the time the seventh or eighth discourse had been delivered, only the very good people could stand it: these, of course, declared that they never heard more valuable expositions, but to those of a more carnal judgment it appeared that each sermon increased in dullness. Paul, in that Epistle, exhorts us to *suffer* the word of exhortation, and we did so. I also recollect hearing in my younger days long passages out of Daniel, which might have been exceedingly instructive to me if I had obtained the remotest conception of what they meant. I remember hearing a sermon from these words, "Who passing through the valley of Baca make it a well." Certainly, the preacher did not make his sermon a well, for it was as dry as a stick, and not worth hearing. There was nothing like cheerfulness in it; but all the way through a flood of declamation against hopeful Christians, against people going to Heaven who are not always grumbling, and murmuring, and doubting; fumbling for their evidences amidst the exercises of their own hearts, ever reading and striving to rival Job and Jeremiah in grief, taking the Lamentations as the fit expression of their own lips, troubling their poor brains, and vexing their poor hearts, and smarting, and crying, and wearying themselves with the perpetual habit of complaining against God, saying, "My stroke is heavier than my groaning."

I used to hear a minister whose preaching was, as far as I could make it out, "Do this, and do that, and do the other, and you will be saved."

According to his theory, to pray was a very easy thing; to make yourself a new heart, was a thing of a few instants, and could be done at almost any time; and I really thought that I could turn to Christ when I pleased, and that therefore I could put it off to the last part of my life, when it might be conveniently done upon a sick bed. But when the Lord gave my soul its first shakings in conviction, I soon knew better. I went to pray; I did pray, God knoweth, but it seemed to me that I did not. What, *I* approach the throne? Such a wretch as *I* lay hold on the promise? *I* venture to hope that God could look on me? It seemed impossible. A tear, a groan, and sometimes not so much as that, an "Ah!" a "Would that!" a "But," — the lip could not utter more. It was prayer, but it did not seem so then. Oh, how hard is prevailing prayer to a poor God-provoking sinner! Where was the power to lay hold on God's strength, or wrestle with the angel?

Certainly not in me, for I was weak as water, and sometimes hard as the nether millstone.

Once, under a powerful sermon, my heart shook within me, and was dissolved in the midst of my bowels; I thought I would seek the Lord, and I bowed my knee, and wrestled, and poured out my heart before Him. Again I ventured within His sanctuary to hear His Word, hoping that in some favored hour He would send a precious promise to my consolation; but, ah! that wretched afternoon, I heard a sermon wherein Christ was not; I had no longer any hope. I would have sipped at that fountain, but I was driven away; I felt that I would have believed in Christ, and I longed and sighed for Him. But, ah! that dreadful sermon, and those terrible things that were uttered; my poor soul knew not what was truth, or what was error; but I thought the man was surely preaching the truth, and I was driven back. I dared not go, I could not believe, I could not lay hold on Christ; I was shut out, if no one else was.

Chapter Ten - "Through Much Tribulation."

My heart was fallow, and covered with weeds; but, on a certain day, the great Husbandman came, and began to plough my soul. Ten black horses were His team, and it was a sharp plowshare that He used, and the plowers made deep furrows. The ten commandments were those black horses, and the justice of God, like a plowshare, tore my spirit. I was condemned, undone, destroyed, — lost, helpless, hopeless, — I thought hell was before me. Then there came a cross-plowing, for when I went to hear the gospel, it did not comfort me; it made me wish I had a part in it, but I feared that such a boon was out of the question. The choicest promises of God frowned upon me, and His threatenings thundered at me. I prayed, but found no answer of peace. It was long with me thus. — C. H. S.

THE abundant benefit which we now reap from the deep plowing of our heart is enough of itself to reconcile us to the severity of the process.

Precious is that wine which is pressed in the winefat of conviction; pure is that gold which is dug from the mines of repentance; and bright are those pearls which are found in the caverns of deep distress. We might never have known such deep humility if the Lord had not humbled us. We had never been so separated from fleshly trusting had He not, by His rod, revealed the corruption and disease of our heart. We had never learned to comfort the feeble-minded, and confirm the weak, had He not made us ready to halt, and caused our sinew to shrink. If we have any power to console the weary, it is the result of our remembrance of what we once suffered, — for here lies our power to sympathize. If we can now look down with scorn upon the boastings of vain, self-conceited man, it is because our own vaunted strength has utterly failed us, and made us contemptible in our own eyes. If we can now plead with ardent desire for the souls of our fellow-men, and especially if we feel a more than common passion for the salvation of sinners, we must attribute it in no small degree to the fact that we have been smitten for sin, and therefore, knowing the terror of the Lord, are constrained to persuade men. The laborious pastor, the fervent minister, the ardent evangelist, the faithful teacher, the powerful intercessor, can all trace the birth of their zeal to the sufferings they endured through sin, and the knowledge they thereby attained of its evil nature. We have ever drawn the sharpest arrows from the quiver of our own experience. We find no sword-blades so true in metal as those which have been forged in the furnace of soul-trouble.

A spiritual experience which is thoroughly flavored with a deep and bitter sense of sin is of great value to him that hath had it. It is terrible in the drinking, but it is most wholesome in the bowels, and in the whole of the after-life. Possibly, much of the flimsy piety of the present day arises from the ease with which men attain to peace and joy in these evangelistic days.

We would not judge modern converts, but we certainly prefer that form of spiritual exercise which leads the soul by the way of Weeping-cross, and makes it see its blackness before assuring it that it is "clean every whit."

Too many think lightly of sin, and therefore think lightly of the Savior. He who has stood before his God, convicted and condemned, with the rope about his neck, is the man to weep for joy when he is pardoned, to hate the evil which has been forgiven him, and to live to the honor of the Redeemer by whose blood he has been cleansed. Our own experience recalls us to the period when we panted for the Lord, even for Him, our only want. Vain to us were the mere ordinances, — vain as bottles scorched by the Simoom, and drained of their waters. Vain were ceremonies, — vain as empty wells to the thirsty Arab. Vain were the delights of the flesh, — bitter as the waters of Marah, which even the parched lips of Israel refused to drink. Vain were the directions of the legal preacher, — useless as the howling of the wind to the benighted wanderer.

Vain, worse than vain, were our refuges of lies, which fell about our ears like Dagon's temple on the heads of the worshippers. One only hope we had, one sole refuge for our misery. Save where that ark floated, — North, South, East, and West was one broad expanse of troubled waters. Save where that star burned, the sky was one vast field of unmitigated darkness.

Jesus, Jesus, JESUS! He alone, He without another, had become the solitary hiding-place against the storm. As the wounded soldier, lying on the battlefield, with wounds which, like fires, consume his moisture, utters only one monotonous cry of thrilling importunity, "Water, water, water!" so did we perpetually send our prayer to Heaven, "Jesus, Thou Son of David, have mercy on me! O Jesus, come to me!"

We have, we hope, many a time enjoyed nearness to the throne of grace in prayer; but, perhaps, never did such a prayer escape our lips as that which we offered in the bitterness of our spirit when seeking the Savior. We have often poured out our hearts with greater freedom, with more delight, with stronger faith, in more eloquent language; but never, never have we cried with more vehemence of unquenchable desire, or more burning heat of insatiable longing. There was then no sleepiness or sluggishness in our devotion; we did not then need the whip of command to drive us to labors of prayer; but our soul could not be content unless with sighs and lamentations, with strong crying and tears, it gave vent to our bursting heart. Then we had no need to be dragged to our closets like oxen to the slaughter, but we flew to them like doves to their windows; and when there, we needed no pumping up of desires, but they gushed forth like a fountain of waters, although at times we felt we could scarcely find them a channel.

I remember the first time I ever sincerely prayed; but I do not recollect the words I used; surely, there were few enough words in that petition. I had often repeated a form; I had been in the habit of continually repeating it. At last, I came really to pray; and then I saw myself standing before God, in the immediate presence of the heart-searching Jehovah, and I said within myself, "I have heard of Thee by the hearing of the ear, but now mine eye seeth Thee; wherefore I abhor myself, and repent in dust and ashes." I felt like Esther when she stood before the king, faint and overcome with dread.

I was full of penitence of heart, because of His majesty and my sinfulness. I think the only words I could utter were something like these, "Oh!-Ah!"

And the only complete sentence was, "God be merciful to me, a sinner!"

The overwhelming splendor of His majesty, the greatness of His power, the severity of His justice, the immaculate character of His holiness, and all His dreadful grandeur, — these things overpowered my soul, and I fell down in utter prostration of spirit; but there was in that prayer a true and real drawing near to God.

I have not many relations in Heaven, but I have one whom I dearly love, who, I doubt not, often prayed for me, for she nursed me when I was a child, and brought me up during part of my infancy, and now she sits before the throne in glory, — suddenly called home. I fancy she looked upon her darling grandson, and as she saw him in the ways of sin, waywardness, and folly, she could not look with sorrow, for there are no tears in the eyes of glorified ones; she could not look with regret, because they cannot know such a feeling before the throne of God; but, ah! that moment when, by sovereign grace, I was constrained to pray, when all alone I bent my knee and wrestled, methinks I see her as she said, "Behold, he prayeth; behold, he prayeth." Oh! I can picture her countenance. She seemed to have two Heavens for a moment — a double bliss, a Heaven in me as well as in herself, — when she could say, "Behold, he prayeth."

I have known some who have suspended prayer through the idea that the petitions of the wicked are an abomination to the Lord, and that therefore it was but committing sin to attempt to offer their supplications. Well can I remember, when coming to Jesus myself, that for years I sought pardon, and found it not. Often, in the deep anguish of my spirit, did I stay my petitions, because I thought them hopeless; and when again the Holy Spirit drew me to the mercy-seat, a deep horror rested on me at the recollection of my repeated, but unanswered cries. I knew myself to be unworthy, and therefore I conceived that Divine justice would not allow an answer to come to me. I thought that the heavens were brass above me, and that if I cried never so earnestly, the Lord would shut out my prayer. I durst not pray, I was too guilty; and when I did dare to pray, 'twas hardly prayer, for I had no hope of being heard. "No," I said, "it is presumption; I must not plead with Him;" and when, at times, I would have prayed, I could not; something choked all utterance, and the spirit could only lament, and long, and pant, and sigh to be able to pray.

Yet I recollect, even as a child, God hearing my prayer. I cannot tell what it was about, it may have been concerning a mere trifle; but to me, as a child, it was as important as the greatest prayer that Solomon ever offered for himself, and God heard that prayer, and it was thus early established in my mind that the Lord was God. And afterwards, when I came really to know Him, — for, like the child Samuel, I did not then know the Lord, I only felt after Him in prayer, — afterwards, when I came to cry to Him intelligently, I had this prayer answered, and that petition granted, and many a time since then — I am only telling what any who know the Lord could also say, — many a time since then He has answered our requests. I cannot tell all about this matter; for there is many a secret between us and our dear Lord. It would not be prudent, proper, or even possible, to mention all the answers to prayer which we have received, for there are love-passages between Christ and the soul, which never must be told, unless it be in choice company, and on rare occasions. Some of our communings with the Lord Jesus are too sacred, too spiritual, too heavenly, ever to be spoken of this side the gates of pearl; but the bulk of the Lord's replies to our petitions are such as might be written athwart the skies, that every eye might read them. It is beginning to be questioned, in many quarters, whether there is any real effect produced by prayer, except that "it excites certain pious emotions in the breasts of those who pray."

This is a pretty statement! We ought to be extremely obliged to those superior persons who allow that even so much may result from our visits to the throne of grace! I wonder they did not assert that prayer was ridiculous, or hypocritical, or immoral! Their moderation puts us under obligations! And yet I do not know: when I look again at their admission, I thank them for nothing, for they as good as call us fools. Do they think that we perform a useless exercise merely for the sake of exciting pious emotions? We must be grievous idiots if we can receive benefit from a senseless function. We are not willing to whistle to the wind for the sake of the exercise. We should not be content to go on praying to a god who could be proved to be both deaf and dumb. We have still some little common sense left, despite what our judicious friends consider to be fanaticism. We are sure that we obtain answers to prayer. Of this fact I am as certain as that I am a living man, and that I preach in the Tabernacle. I solemnly declare that I have received of the Lord that which I have asked at His hands, and I am not alone in such testimony, for I am associated with multitudes of men and women who bear witness to the same fact, and declare that they also sought the Lord by prayer and supplication, and He heard them, and delivered them out of their distresses.

Neither in the Church militant nor in the host triumphant is there one who received a new heart, and was reclaimed from sin without a wound from Jesus. The pain may have been but slight, and the healing may have been speedy; but in each case there has been a real bruise, which required a Heavenly Physician to heal. With some of us, this wounding commenced in early life; for, as soon as infancy gave place to childhood, the rod was exercised upon us. We can remember early convictions of sin, and apprehensions of the wrath of God on its account. An awakened conscience in our most tender years drove us to the throne of mercy.

Though we knew not the hand which chastened our spirit, yet did we "bear the yoke in our youth." How many were "the tender buds of hope" which we then put forth, alas! too soon to be withered by youthful lusts; how often were we scared with visions and terrified with dreams, while the reproof of a parent, the death of a playfellow, or a solemn sermon made our hearts melt within us! Truly, our goodness was but "as the morning cloud and the early dew;" but who can tell how much each of these separate woundings contributed toward that killing by the law, which proved to be the effectual work of God? In each of these arousings we discover a gracious purpose; we trace every one of these awakenings to His hand who watched over our path, determined to deliver us from our sins. The small end of that wedge, which has since been driven home, was inserted during these youthful hours of inward strife.

Let none despise the strivings of the Spirit in the hearts of the young; let not boyish anxieties and juvenile repentances be lightly regarded. He incurs a fearful amount of guilt who in the least promotes the aim of the evil one by trampling upon a tender conscience in a child. No one can guess at what age children become capable of conversion. I, at least, can bear my personal testimony to the fact that grace operates on some minds at a period almost too early for recollection. When but young in years, I felt with much sorrow the evil of sin. My bones waxed old with my roaring all the day long. Day and night God's hand was heavy upon me. I hungered for deliverance, for my soul fainted within me. I feared lest the very skies should fall upon me, and crush my guilty soul. God's law had laid hold upon me, and was showing me my sins. If I slept at night, I dreamed of the bottomless pit; and when I awoke, I seemed to feel the misery I had dreamed. Up to God's house I went; my song was but a sigh. To my chamber I retired, and there, with tears and groans, I offered up my prayer, without a hope and without a refuge, for God's law was flogging me with its ten-thonged whip, and then rubbing me with brine afterwards, so that I did shake and quiver with pain and anguish, and my soul chose strangling rather than life, for I was exceeding sorrowful.

That misery was sent for this reason, that I might then be made to cry to Jesus. Our Heavenly Father does not usually cause us to seek the Savior till He has whipped us clean out of all our confidence; He cannot make us in earnest after Heaven till He has made us feel something of the intolerable tortures of an aching conscience, which is a foretaste of hell. I remember, when I used to awake in the morning, first thing I took up was Alleine's *Alarm,* or Baxter's *Call to the Unconverted.* Oh, those books, those books! I read and devoured them when under a sense of guilt, but it was like sitting at the foot of Sinai. For five years, as a child, there was nothing before my eyes but my guilt; and though I do not hesitate to say that those who observed my life would not have seen any extraordinary sin, yet as I looked upon myself, there was not a day in which I did not commit such gross, such outrageous sins against God, that often and often have I wished I had never been born. Sickness is a terrible thing, more especially when it is accompanied with pain, when the poor body is racked to an extreme, so that the spirit fails within us, and we are dried up like a potsherd; but I bear witness that sickness, however agonizing, is nothing like the discovery of the evil of sin. I had rather pass through seven years of the most wearisome pain, and the most languishing sickness, than I would ever again pass through the terrible discovery of the evil of sin. It was my sad lot, at that time, to feel the greatness of my sin, without a discovery of the greatness of God's mercy. I had to walk through this world with more than a world upon my shoulders, and sustain a grief that as far exceeds all other griefs as a mountain exceeds a mole-hill; and I often wonder, to this day, how it was that my hand was kept from rending my own body in pieces through the awful agony which I felt when I discovered the greatness of my transgression. Yet, I had not been, openly and publicly, a greater sinner than others; but heart sins were laid bare, sins of lip and tongue were discovered, and then I knew — oh, that I may never have to learn over again in such a dreadful school this terrible lesson! — "the iniquity of Judah and of Israel is exceeding great." Before I thought upon my soul's salvation, I dreamed that my sins were very few. All my sins were dead, as I imagined, and buried in the graveyard of forgetfulness. But that trumpet of conviction, which aroused my soul to think of eternal things, sounded a resurrection-note to all my sins; and, oh, how they rose up in multitudes more countless than the sands of the sea! Now, I saw that my very thoughts were enough to damn me, that my words would sink me lower than the lowest hell; and as for my acts of sin, they now began to be a stench in my nostrils, so that I could not bear them. I thought I had rather have been a frog or a toad than have been made a man; I reckoned that the most defiled creature, the most loathsome and contemptible, was a better thing than myself, for I had so grossly and grievously sinned against Almighty God.

Through the Lord's restraining grace, and the holy influence of my early home-life, both at my father's and my grandfather's, I was kept from certain outward forms of sin in which others indulged; and, sometimes, when I began to take stock of myself, I really thought I was quite a respectable lad, and might have been half inclined to boast that I was not like other boys, — untruthful, dishonest, disobedient, swearing, Sabbath-breaking, and so on. But, all of a sudden, I met Moses, carrying in his hand the law of God; and as he looked at me, he seemed to search me through and through with his eyes of fire. He bade me read "God's Ten Words" — the ten commandments, — and as I read them, they all seemed to join in accusing and condemning me in the sight of the thrice-holy Jehovah. Then, like Daniel, "my comeliness was turned in me into corruption, and I retained no strength;" and I understood what Paul meant when he wrote,

"Now we know that what things soever the law saith, it saith to them who are under the law: that every mouth may be stopped, and all the world may become guilty before God." When I saw myself in this condition, I could say nothing in self-defense, or by way of excuse or extenuation. I confessed my transgression in solemn silence unto the Lord, but I could speak no word of self-justification, or apology, for I felt that I was verily guilty of grievous sins against the Holy One of Israel. At that time, a dreadful silence reigned within my spirit; even if I had tried to say a word in my own favor, I should have been self-condemned as a liar. I felt that Job's words might be applied to me, "If I wash myself with snow water, and make my hands never so clean; yet shalt Thou plunge me in the ditch, and mine own clothes shall abhor me. For He is not a man, as I am, that I should answer Him."

Then there came into my startled conscience the remembrance of the universality of law. I thought of what was said of the old Roman empire that, under the rule of Caesar, if a man once broke the law of Rome, the whole world was one vast prison to him, for he could not get out of the reach of the imperial power. So did it come to be in my aroused conscience. Wherever I went, the law had a demand upon my thoughts, upon my words, upon my rising, upon my resting. What

I did, and what I did not do, all came under the cognizance of the law; and then I found that this law so surrounded me that I was always running against it, I was always breaking it. I seemed as if I was a sinner, and nothing else but a sinner. If I opened my mouth, I spoke amiss. If I sat still, there was sin in my silence. I remember that, when the Spirit of God was thus dealing with me, I used to feel myself to be a sinner even when I was in the house of God. I thought that, when I sang, I was mocking the Lord with a solemn sound upon a false tongue; and if I prayed, I feared that I was sinning in my prayers, insulting Him by uttering confessions which I did not feel, and asking for mercies with a faith that was not true at all, but only another form of unbelief. At the very mention of that word conviction, I seem to hear my chains rattling anew. Was there ever a bond-slave who had more bitterness of soul than I, five years a captive in the dungeons of the law, till my youth seemed as if it would turn into premature old age, and all the buoyancy of my spirit had vanished? O God of the spirits of all men, most of all ought I to hate sin, for surely most of all have I smarted beneath the lash of Thy law!

While I was in the custody of the law, I did not take any pleasure in evil.

Alas! I did sin; but my sense of the law of God kept me back from many forms of iniquity. I have thanked God a thousand times in my life that, before my conversion, when I had ill desires, I had no opportunities of sinning; and, on the other hand, when I had the opportunities, I had no desires towards evil. When desires and opportunities come together, like the flint and the steel, they make the spark that kindles the fire; but neither the one nor the other, though they may both be dangerous, can bring about any very great amount of evil so long as they are kept apart. I could not, as others did, plunge into profligacy, or indulge in any of the grosser vices, for that law had me well in hand. I sinned enough without acting like that.

Oh, I used to tremble to put one foot before another, for fear I should do wrong! I felt that my old sins seemed to be so many, that it were well to die rather than commit anymore. I could not rest while in the grip of the law. If I wanted to sleep awhile, or to be a little indifferent and careless, some one or other of those ten commandments roughly aroused me, and looking on me with a frowning face, said, "You have broken me." I thought that I would do some good works; but, somehow, the law always broke my good works in the making. I fancied that, if my tears flowed freely, I might make some recompense for my wrong-doing; but the law held up the looking-glass, and I soon saw my face all smeared and made more unhandsome by my tears.

The law seemed also to blight all my hopes with its stern sentence, "Cursed is every one that continueth not in all things which are written in the book of the law to do them." Only too well did I know that I had not continued in all those things, so I saw myself accursed, turn which way I might. If I had not committed one sin, that made no difference if I had committed another; I was under the curse. What if I had never blasphemed God with my tongue? Yet, if I had coveted, I had broken the law. He who breaks a chain might say, "I did not break that link, and the other link." No, but if you break one link, you have broken the chain. Ah, me; how I seemed shut up then! I had offended against the justice of God; I was impure and polluted; and I used to say, "If God does not send me to hell, He ought to do it." I sat in judgment upon myself, and pronounced the sentence that I felt would be just. I could not have gone to Heaven with my sin unpardoned, even if I had had the offer to do it, for I knew that it would not be right that I should do so, and I justified God in my own conscience while I condemned myself. The law would not even let me despair. If I thought I would give up all desire to do right, and just go and drown my conscience in sin, the law said, "No, you cannot do that; there is no rest for you in sinning. You know the law too well to be able to sin in the blindness of a seared conscience." So the law worried and troubled me at all points; it shut me up as in an iron cage, and every way of escape was effectually blocked up.

One of the things that shut me up dreadfully was, when I knew the spirituality of the law. If the law said, "Thou shalt not commit adultery," I said to myself, "Well, I have never committed adultery." Then the law, as interpreted by Christ, said, "Whosoever looketh on a woman to lust after her hath committed adultery with her already in his heart." The law said,

"Thou shalt not steal," and I said, "Well, I never stole anything;" but then I found that even the desire to possess what was not my own, was guilt. The spirituality of the law astounded me; what hope could I have of eluding such a law as this which every way surrounded me with an atmosphere from which I could not possibly escape?

Then I remembered that, even if I kept the law perfectly, and kept it for ten, twenty, or thirty years, without a fault, yet if, at the end of that time, I should break it, I must suffer its dread penalty. Those words spoken by the Lord to the prophet Ezekiel came to my mind: "If he trust to his own righteousness, and commit iniquity, all his righteousnesses shall not be remembered; but for his iniquity that he hath committed, he shall die for it."

So I saw that I was, indeed, "kept under the law, shut up." I had hoped to escape this way, or that way, or some other way. Was I not "christened"

When I was a child? Had I not been taken to a place of worship? Had I not been brought up to say my prayers regularly? Had I not been an honest, upright, moral youth? Was all this nothing? "Nothing," said the law, as it drew its sword of fire: "Cursed is every one that continueth not in all things which are written in the book of the law to do them." So there was no rest for my spirit, nay, not even for a moment. What was I to do? I was in the hands of one who showed no mercy whatever, for Moses never said, "Mercy." The law has nothing to do with mercy. That comes from another mouth, and under another dispensation. But before faith came, I was "kept under the law, shut up unto the faith which should afterwards be revealed."

I am bold to say that, if a man be destitute of the grace of God, his works are only works of slavery; he feels forced to do them. I know, before I came into the liberty of the children of God, if I went to God's house, I went because I thought I must do it; if I prayed, it was because I feared some misfortune would happen in the day if I did not; if I ever thanked God for a mercy, it was because I thought I should not get another if I were not thankful; if I performed a righteous deed, it was with the hope that very likely God would reward me at last, and I should be winning a crown in Heaven. I was a poor slave, a mere Gibeonite, hewing wood and drawing water! If I could have left off doing it, I should have loved to do so. If

I could have had my will, there would have been no chapel-going for me, no religion for me, — I would have lived in the world, and followed the ways of Satan, if I could have done as I pleased. As for righteousness, it was slavery; sin would have been my liberty. Yet, truth to tell, of all bondage and slavery in this world, there is none more horrible than the bondage of sin. Tell me of Israel in Egypt, unsupplied with straw, yet preparing the full tale of bricks; tell me of the negro beneath the lash of his cruel task-master, and I confess it is a bondage fearful to be borne; but there is one far worse, — the bondage of a convinced sinner when he is brought to feel the burden of his guilt; the bondage of a man when once his sins are baying him, like hounds about a weary stag; the bondage of a man when the burden of sin is on his shoulder, — a burden too heavy for his soul to bear, — a burden which will sink him in the depths of everlasting torment, unless he doth escape from it. Methinks I see such a person. He hath ne'er a smile upon his face; dark clouds have gathered on his brow; solemn and serious he stands; his very words are sighs; his songs are groans; his smiles are tears; and when he seems most happy, hot drops of grief roll in burning showers, scalding furrows on his cheek. Ask him *what he is,* and he tells you he is "a wretch undone." Ask him *how he is,* and he confesses that he is "misery incarnate." Ask him *what he shall be,* and he says, "I shall be lost in hell for ever; there is no hope for me." Such is the poor convinced sinner under bondage. Such have I been in my days, and I declare that, of all bondage, this is the most painful, — the bondage of the law, the bondage of corruption.

My impression is, that this is the history of all the people of God, more or less. We are not all alike in every respect. We differ greatly in certain particulars; yet the main features of all the children of God will be found to be the same, and their Christian experience will resemble that of the other members of the Lord's family. I do not say that all have felt the apprehension of coming judgment as I did; but this is how it came to me. I knew that I was guilty, I knew that I had offended God, I knew that I had transgressed against light and knowledge, and I did not know when God might call me to account: but I did know this, when I awoke in the morning, the first thought I had was that I had to deal with a justly-angry God, who might suddenly require my soul of me. Often, during the day, when I had a little time for quiet meditation, a great depression of spirit would come upon me because I felt that sin, — *sin,* — SIN had outlawed me from my God. I wondered that the earth bore up such a sinner as I was, and that the heavens did not fall and crush me, and the stars in their courses did not fight against such a wretch as I felt myself to be. Then, indeed, did I seem as if I should go down to the pit, and I had perpetually to endure the tortures of the never-dying worm of conscience that was gnawing at my heart. I went to the house of God, and heard what I supposed was the gospel, but it was no gospel to me. My soul abhorred all manner of meat; I could not lay hold upon a promise, or indulge a well-grounded hope of salvation. If anyone had asked me what would become of me, I must have answered, "I am going down to the pit." If anyone had entreated me to hope that mercy might come to me, I should have refused to entertain such a hope. I used to feel that I was in the condemned cell. In that dungeon, the man writes bitter things against himself; he feels absolutely sure that the wrath of God abideth on him; he wonders the stones beneath his feet do not open a grave to swallow him up; he is astonished that the walls of the prison do not compress and crush him into nothingness; he marvels that he has his breath, or that the blood in his veins does not turn into rivers of flame. His spirit is in a dreadful state; he not only feels that he shall be lost, but he thinks it is going to happen now. The condemned cell in Newgate, I am told, is just in such a corner that the criminal can hear the putting-up of the scaffold. Well do I remember hearing my scaffold built, and the sound of the hammer of the law as piece after piece was put together! It appeared as if I heard the noise of the crowd of men and devils who would witness my eternal execution, all of them howling and yelling out their accursed things against my spirit. Then there was a big bell that tolled out the hours, and I thought that very soon the last moment would arrive, and I must mount the fatal scaffold to be cast away forever. Oh, that condemned cell! Next to Tophet, there can be no state more wretched than that of a man who is brought there!

When I was for many a month in this state, I used to read the Bible through, and the threatenings were all printed in capitals, but the promises were in such small type I could not for a long time make them out; and when I did read them, I did not believe they were mine; but the threatenings were all my own. "There," said I, "when it says, 'He that believeth not shall be damned,' that means me!" But when it said, "He is able also to save them to the uttermost that come unto God by Him," then I thought I was shut out. When I read, "He found no place of repentance, though he sought it carefully with tears;" I thought, "Ah! that is myself again." And when I read, "That which beareth thorns and briers is rejected, and is nigh unto cursing; whose end is to be burned;" "Ah!" I said, "that describes me to the very letter." And when I heard the Master say, "Cut it down; why cumbereth it the ground?" "Ah!" thought I, "that is my text; He will have me down before long, and not let me cumber the ground any more." But when I read, "Ho! every one that thirsteth; come ye to the waters;" I said, "That does not belong to me, I am sure." And when I read, "Come unto Me, all ye that labor and are heavy laden, and I will give you rest;" I said, "That belongs to my brother, to my sister," or those I knew round about me; for they were all "heavy laden," I thought, but I was not; and though, God knoweth, I would weep, and cry, and lament till my heart was breaking within me, if any man had asked me whether I sorrowed for sin, I should have told him, "No, I never had any true sorrow for sin."

"Well, do you not feel the burden of sin?" "No!" "But you really are a convinced sinner?" "No," I should have said, "I am not." Is it not strange that poor sinners, when they are coming to Christ, are so much in the dark that they cannot see their own hands? They are so blind that they cannot see themselves; and though the Holy Spirit has been pleased to work in them, and give them godly fear and a tender conscience, they will stand up, and declare that they have not those blessings, and that in them there is not any good thing, and that God has not looked on them nor loved them.

I speak what I do know, and not what I have learned by report, when I say that there is a chamber in the experience of some men where the temptations of the devil exceed all belief. Read John Bunyan's *Grace Abounding*, if you would understand what I mean. The devil tempted him, he says, to doubt the existence of God, the truth of Scripture, the manhood of Christ, then His Deity; and once, he says, he tempted him to say things which he will never write, lest he should pollute others. Ah! I recollect a dark hour with myself when I, who do not remember to have even heard a blasphemy in my youth, much less to have uttered one, found rushing through my mind an almost infinite number of curses and blasphemies against the Most High God. I specially recall a certain narrow and crooked lane, in a country town, along which I was walking, one day, while I was seeking the Savior. On a sudden, it seemed as if the floodgates of hell had been opened; my head became a very pandemonium; ten thousand evil spirits seemed to be holding carnival within my brain; and I held my mouth lest I should give utterance to the words of blasphemy that were poured into my ears. Things I had never heard or thought of before came rushing impetuously into my mind, and I could scarcely withstand their influence. It was the devil throwing me down and tearing me. These things sorely beset: me; for half-an-hour together, the most fearful imprecations would dash through my brain. Oh, how I groaned and cried before God! That temptation passed away; but ere many days, it was renewed again; and when I was in prayer, or when I was reading the Bible, these blasphemous thoughts would pour in upon me more than at any other time. I consulted with an aged godly man about it. He said to me, "Oh, all this many of the people of God have proved before you! But," he asked, "do you hate these thoughts?" "I do," I truly answered. "Then," said he, "they are not yours; serve them as the old parish officers used to do with vagrants, whip them, and send them on to their own parish. So," said he, "do with those evil thoughts. Groan over them, repent of them, and send them on to the devil, the father of them, to whom they belong, for they are not yours."

I have never been thoroughly an unbeliever but once, and that was not before I knew the need of a Savior, but after it. It was just when I wanted Christ, and panted after Him, that, on a sudden, the thought crossed my mind — which I abhorred but could not conquer, — that there was no God, no Christ, no Heaven, no hell; that all my prayers were but a farce, and that I might as well have whistled to the winds or spoken to the howling waves. Ah! I remember how my ship drifted along through that sea of fire, loosened from the anchor of my faith which I had received from my fathers. I no longer moored myself hard by the coasts of Revelation; I said to reason, "Be thou my captain;" I said to my own brain, "Be thou my rudder;" and I started on my mad voyage. Thank God, it is all over now; but I will tell you its brief history. It was one hurried sailing over the tempestuous ocean of free thought. I went on, and as I went, the skies began to darken; but to make up for that deficiency, the waters were gleaming with coruscations of brilliancy. I saw sparks flying upwards that pleased me, and I felt, "If this be free thought, it is a happy thing." My thoughts seemed gems, and I scattered stars with both my hands; but anon, instead of these coruscations of glory, I saw grim fiends, fierce and horrible, start up from the waters; and as I dashed on, they gnashed their teeth, and grinned upon me; they seized the prow of my ship, and dragged me on, while I, in part, gloried at the rapidity of my motion, but yet shuddered at the terrific rate with which I passed the old landmarks of my faith. I went to the very verge of the dreary realms of unbelief. I went to the very bottom of the sea of infidelity. As I hurried forward at an awful speed, I began to doubt if there were a world. I doubted everything, until at last the devil defeated himself by making me doubt my own existence. I thought I was an idea floating in the nothingness of vacuity; then, startled with that thought, and feeling that I was substantial flesh and blood after all, I saw that God was, and Christ was, and Heaven was, and hell was, and that all these things were absolute truths. The very extravagance of the doubt proved its absurdity, and there came a voice which said, "And can this doubt be true?" Then I awoke from that death-dream which, God knows, might have damned my soul, and ruined my body, if I had not awoke. When I arose, faith took the helm; from that moment, I doubted not. Faith steered me back; faith cried, "Away, away!" I cast my anchor on Calvary; I lifted my eye to God; and here I am alive, and out of hell.

Therefore, I speak what I do know. I have sailed that perilous voyage; I have come safe to land. Ask me again to be an infidel! No; I have tried it; it was sweet at first, but bitter afterwards. Now, lashed to God's gospel more firmly than ever, standing as on a rock of adamant, I defy the arguments of hell to move me, for "I know whom I have believed, and am persuaded that He is able to keep that which I have committed unto Him." I should not be astonished if many others, who now believe, have also been upon the very borders of atheism, and have doubted almost everything. It is when Satan finds the heart tender that he tries to stamp his own impress of infidelity upon the soul; but, blessed be God, he never accomplishes it in the sinner who is truly coming to Christ! Now, whenever I hear the skeptic's stale attacks upon the Word of God, I smile within myself, and think, "Why, you simpleton! how can you urge such trifling objections? I have felt, in the contentions of my own unbelief, ten times greater difficulties.' We who have contended with horses are not to be wearied by footmen. Gordon Cumming and other lion-killers are not to be scared by wild cats, nor will those who have stood foot to foot with Satan resign the field to pretentious skeptics, or any other of the evil one's inferior servants.

I do think it often proves a great blessing to a man that he had a terrible conflict, a desperate encounter, a hard-fought engagement in passing from the empire of Satan into the kingdom of God's dear Son. Sooner or later, each saved man will have his hand-to-hand fight with the prince of darkness; and, as a general rule, it is a great mercy to have it over at the outset of one's career, and to be able afterwards to feel, "Whatever comes upon me, I never can suffer as I suffered when I was seeking Christ.

Whatever staggering doubt, or hideous blasphemy, or ghastly insinuations, even of suicide itself, may assail my feeble heart, they cannot outdo the horror of great darkness through which my spirit passed when I was struggling after a Savior." I do not say that it is desirable that we should have this painful ordeal, much less that we should seek it as an evidence of regeneration; but when we have passed through it victoriously, we may so use it that it may be a perpetual armory to us. If we can now defy all doubts and fears that come, because they cannot be so potent as those which already, in the name of Jesus Christ our Savior, we have overthrown, shall we not use that fact for ourselves, and can we not equally well use it for others? Full often have I found it good, when I have talked with a young convert in deep distress about his sin, to tell him something more of his anxious plight than he knew how to express; and he has wondered where I found it, though he would not have wondered if he had known where I had been, and how much deeper in the mire than he.

When he has talked about some horrible thought that he has had, with regard to the impossibility of his own salvation, I have said, "Why, I have thought that a thousand times, and yet have overcome it through the help of God's Spirit!" I know that a man's own experience is one of the very best weapons he can use in fighting with evil in other men's hearts. Often, their misery and despondency, aggravated, as it commonly is, by a feeling of solitariness, will be greatly relieved before it is effectually driven out when they find that a brother has suffered the same, and yet has been able to overcome. Do I show him how precious the Savior is to my soul? He glorifies God in me. Right soon will he look into the same dear face and be lightened; and then he will magnify the Lord with me, and we shall exalt His name together.

Multitudes of persons are sailing in what they think to be the good ship of self-righteousness: they are expecting that they shall get to Heaven in her.

But she never did carry a soul safely into the fair Haven yet, and she never will. Self-righteousness is as rapid a road to ruin as outward sin itself. We may as certainly destroy ourselves by opposing the righteousness of Christ as by transgressing the law of God. Self-righteousness is as much an insult to God as blasphemy is, and God will never accept it, neither shall any soul enter Heaven by it. Yet this vessel manages to keep on her way against all the opposition of Scripture; for, often, men have a soft South wind blowing, and things go easily with them, and they believe that through their own doings they shall assuredly find the Port of Peace. I am glad, therefore, when some terrible tempest overtakes this vessel; and when men's hopes through their own doings and their own feelings are utterly wrecked. I rejoice when the old ship parts timber from timber, when she goes aground and breaks to pieces, and men find safety in some other way; for whatever seeming safety they may have today will only delude them. It must end in destruction, and it is therefore a thousand mercies when they find it out soon enough to get a better hope of being saved than this, which will certainly deceive them. I recollect very well when that terrific Euroclydon blew on my vessel. It was as good a ship as any others have, although I have no doubt they would vindicate their own. Her sails needed mending, and here and there she wanted a little touch of paint; but, for all that, she was sea-worthy, and fit to be registered "A1 at Lloyd's," and entered in the first class, — at least, so I thought. The storm blew over her, and she went to pieces, and I bless God that she did, for I should have been kept on board to this very minute if I had not been washed off. I tried to cling to the old hulk to the last plank, but I was obliged to give it up, and look somewhere else for help and safety.

Before I came to Christ, I said to myself, "It surely cannot be that, if I believe in Jesus, just as I am, I shall be saved? I must feel something; I must do something." I could pour scorn upon myself to think of some of the good resolutions I made! I blew them up, like children with their pipes and their soap, and fine bubbles they were, reflecting all the colors of the rainbow! But a touch, and they dissolved. They were good for nothing, — poor stuff to build eternal hopes upon. Oh, that working for salvation!

What slavery it was, but what small results it produced! I was a spinner and weaver of the poorest sort, yet I dreamed that I should be able by my own spinning to make a garment to cover myself withal. This was the trade of father Adam and mother Eve when they first lost their innocence; "they sewed fig leaves together, and made themselves aprons." It is a very laborious business, and has worn out the lives of many with bitter bondage, but its worst feature is that the Lord has declared concerning all who follow this self-righteous craft, "Their webs shall not become garments, neither shall they cover themselves with their works."

Oh, the many times that I have wished the preacher would tell me something to *do* that I might be saved! Gladly would I have done it, if it had been possible. If he had said, "Take off your shoes and stockings, and run to John o' Groat's," I would not even have gone home first, but would have started off that very night, that I might win salvation. How often have I thought that, if he had said, "Bare your back to the scourge, and take fifty lashes;" I would have said, "Here I am! Come along with your whip, and beat as hard as you please, so long as I can obtain peace and rest, and get rid of my sin." Yet that simplest of all matters — believing in Christ crucified, accepting His finished salvation, being nothing, and letting Him be everything, doing nothing but trusting to what He has done, — I could not get a hold of it. Once I thought there was salvation in good works, and I labored hard, and strove diligently to preserve a character for integrity and uprightness; but when the Spirit of God came into my heart, "sin revived, and I died." That which I thought had been good, proved to be evil; wherein I fancied I had been holy, I found myself to be unholy. I discovered that my very best actions were sinful, that my tears :needed to be wept over, and that my very prayers needed God's forgiveness. I discovered that I was seeking after salvation by the works of the law, that I was doing all my good works from a selfish motive, namely, to save myself, and therefore they could not be acceptable to God. I found out that I could not be saved by good works for two very good reasons; first, I had not got any, and secondly, if I had any, they could not save me. After that, I thought, surely salvation might be obtained, partly by reformation, and partly by trusting in Christ; so I labored hard again, and thought, if I added a few prayers here and there, a few tears of penitence, and a few vows of improvement, all would be well. But after fagging on for many a weary day, like a poor blind horse toiling round the mill, I found I had gone no farther, for there was still the curse of God hanging over me, and there was still an aching void in my heart, which the world could never fill, — a void of distress and care, for I was sorely troubled because I could not attain unto the rest which my soul desired.

What a struggle that was which my young heart waged against sin! When God the Holy Ghost first quickened me, little did I know of the precious blood which has put my sins away, and drowned them in the depths forever. But I did know this, that I could not remain as I was; that I could not rest happy unless I became something better, something purer than I was; and, oh, how my spirit cried to God with groanings, — I say it without any exaggeration, — groanings that could not be uttered! and, oh, how I sought, in my poor dark way, to overcome first one sin and then another, and so to do battle, in God's strength, against the enemies that assailed me, and not, thank God, altogether without success, though still the battle had been lost unless He had come who is the Overcomer of sin and the Deliverer of His people, and had put the hosts to flight. I tried a long time to improve myself, but I never did make much of it; I found I had a devil within me when I began, and I had ten devils when I left off. Instead of becoming better, I became worse; I had now got the devil of self-righteousness, of self-trust, and self-conceit, and many others that had come and taken up their lodging within my heart. While I was busy sweeping my house, and garnishing it, behold, the one I sought to get rid of, who had only gone for a little season, returned, and brought with him seven other spirits more wicked than himself, and they entered in and dwelt there. Then I labored to believe. It is a strange way of putting it, yet so it was. When I wished to believe, I found I could not. It seemed to me that the way to Heaven by Christ's righteousness was as difficult as by my own, and that I could as soon get to Heaven by Sinai as by Calvary. I could do nothing, I could neither repent nor believe. I fainted with despair, feeling as if I must be lost despite the gospel, and be forever driven from Jehovah's presence, even though Christ had died.

I must confess that I never would have been saved if I could have helped it.

As long as ever I could, I rebelled, and revolted, and struggled against God. When He would have me pray, I would not pray: when He would have me listen to the sound of the ministry, I would not. And when I heard, and the tear rolled down my cheek, I wiped it away, and defied Him to melt my heart. There came an election sermon; but that did not please me.

There came a law sermon, showing me my powerlessness; but I did not believe it, I thought it was the whim of some old experimental Christian, some dogma of ancient times that would not suit men now. Then there came another sermon, concerning death and sin; but I did not believe I was dead, for I thought I was alive enough, and could repent and make myself right by-and-by. Then there came a strong exhortation sermon; but I felt I could set my house in order when I liked, as well as I could do it at once.

So did I continually trust in my self-sufficiency. When my heart was a little touched, I tried to divert it with sinful pleasures; and would not then have been saved, until God gave me the effectual blow, and I was obliged to submit to that irresistible effort of His grace. It conquered my depraved will, and made me bow myself before His gracious scepter. When the Lord really brought me to myself, He sent one great shot which shivered me to pieces; and, lo, I found myself utterly defenseless. I thought I was more mighty than the angels, and could accomplish all things; but I found myself less than nothing.

Jesus said to Zaccheus, "Make haste, and *come down.*" Can I not remember when He also told me to come down? One of the first steps I had to take was to go right down from my good works; and, oh, what a fall was that! Then I stood upon my own self-sufficiency, and Christ said, "Come down! I have pulled you down from your good works, and now I will pull you down from your self-sufficiency." So I had another fall, and I felt sure I had gained the bottom, but again Christ said, "Come down!" and He made me come down till I fell on some point at which I felt I was yet salvable. But still the command was, "Down, sir! come down further yet."

And down I came until, in despair, I had to let go every bough of the tree of my hopes, and then I said, "I can do nothing; I am ruined." The waters were wrapped round my head, and I was shut out from the light of day, and thought myself a stranger from the commonwealth of Israel. But Christ said, "Come down lower yet, sir! thou hast too much pride to be saved."

Then I was brought down to see my corruption, my wickedness, my filthiness, for God always humbles the sinner whom He means to save.

While I was in this state, trying to make myself believe, a voice whispered,

"Vain man, vain man, if thou wouldst believe, come and see!" Then the Holy Spirit led me by the hand to a solitary place, and while I stood there, suddenly there appeared before me One upon His cross. I looked up; I had then no faith. I saw His eyes suffused with tears, and the blood still flowing; I saw His enemies about Him, hunting Him to His grave; I marked His miseries unutterable; I heard the groaning which cannot be described; and as I looked up, He opened His eyes, and said to me, "The Son of man is come to seek and to save that which was lost." Yet I needed more than that gracious word. The general call of the gospel is like the sheet lightning we sometimes see on a summer's evening, — beautiful, grand, — but who ever heard of anything being struck by it? But the special call is the forked flash from heaven; it strikes somewhere. It is the arrow shot in between the joints of the harness. The call which saves is like that of Jesus, when He said, "Mary," and she said unto Him, "Rabboni." Can I not recollect the hour when He whispered my name, when He said in mine ear, "Come unto Me"! That was an effectual call; there was no resisting it. I know I laughed at religion; I despised, I abhorred it; but oh, that call! I would not come.

But Christ said, "Thou shalt come. 'All that the Father giveth Me shall come to Me.'" "Lord, I will not." "But thou shalt," said Jesus. I have gone up to God's house, sometimes, almost with a resolution that I would not listen, but listen I must. Oh, how the Word came into my soul! Was there any power of resistance remaining in me? No; I was thrown down; each bone seemed to be broken. I began to think there never would be a trace of anything built up in my heart. What a trench was dug in my soul! Out went my supposed merits! What a heap of rubbish! Out went my knowledge, my good resolves, and my self-sufficiency! By-and-by, out went all my strength. When this digging-out was completed, the ditch was so deep that, as I went down into it, it seemed like my grave. Such a grief it was for me to know my own sinfulness, that it did not seem possible that this could help my upbuilding in comfort and salvation. Yet, so it is, that if the Lord means to build high, He always digs deep; and if He means to give great grace, He gives deep consciousness of need of it. Long before I began with Christ, He had begun with me; but when I began with Him, it was, as the law-writers say, "*In forma pauperis,*" after the style of a wretched mendicant, — a pauper who had nothing of his own, and looked to Christ for everything. I know, when I first cast my eye to His dear cross, and rested in Him, I had not any merit of my own, it was all demerit. I was not deserving, except that I felt I was hell-deserving: I had not even a shade of virtue that I could confide in. It was all over with me. I had come to an extremity. I could not have found a farthing's worth of goodness in myself if I had been melted down. I seemed to be all rottenness, a dunghill of corruption, nothing better, but something a great deal worse. I could truly join with Paul at that time, and say that my own righteousnesses were dung; he used a strong expression, but I do not suppose he felt it to be strong enough: "I count them but dung, that I may win Christ, and be found in Him."

I do not know what may be the peculiarity of my constitution, but I have always loved safe things. I have not, that I know of, one grain of speculation in my nature. Safe things — things that I can see to be made of rock, and that will bear the test of time, — I lay hold of with avidity. I was reasoning thus in my boyish spirit: — Scripture tells me that he that believeth in Christ shall never perish. Then, if I believe in Jesus, I shall be safe for time and for eternity, too. There will be no fear of my ever being in hell; I shall run no risk as to my eternal state, that will be secure forever. I shall have the certainty that, when my eyes are closed in death, I shall see the face of Christ, and behold Him in glory. Whenever I heard the doctrine of the final preservation of the saints preached, my mouth used to water to be a child of God. When I used to hear the old saints sing that hymn of Toplady's, which begins, —

"A debtor to mercy alone,
Of covenant mercy I sing;
Nor fear, with Thy righteousness on,
My person and offering to bring;" —

I thought I should never be able to sing it myself, it was too high doctrine, too sweet, too consoling; but when they came to the climax, in the last verse, —

"My name from the palms of His hands
Eternity will not erase;
Impressed on His heart it remains
In marks of indelible grace:
Yes, I to the end shall endure,
As sure as the earnest is given;
More happy, but not more secure,
The glorified spirits in Heaven;" —

my heart was as if it would leap out of my body, and I would cry to God,

"Oh, that I had a part and lot in such a salvation as that!" I distinctly remember having a meditation something like this: — "Now I should not like to be a thief, or a murderer, or an unclean person." I had such a training that I had an abhorrence of sin of every sort. "And yet," I thought to myself, "I may even be hanged; there is no reason why I should not turn out a thief;" because I recollected there were some of my schoolfellows, older than I was, who had already become proficient in dishonesty; and I thought, "Why may not I?" No one can tell the rapture of my spirit, when I thought I saw in my Bible the doctrine that, if I gave my heart to Christ, He would keep me from sin, and preserve me as long as I lived. I was not quite certain whether that truth was revealed in the Bible, though I thought so; but I remember, when I heard the minister of some small "Hyper" chapel utter the same doctrine, my heart was full of rapture; I panted after that kind of gospel. "Oh!" I thought, "if God would but love me, if I might but know myself to be His!" For the enchanting part of it was that, if I were so loved, He would keep me to the

70

end. That made me so in love with the gospel that, boy as I was, knowing nothing savingly about the truth, I was all the more earnest in desiring to be saved, because, if saved, God would never turn me out of doors. That made the gospel very precious to me; so that, when the Holy Spirit showed me my guilt, and led me to seek the Savior, that doctrine was like a bright star to my spirit. The Bible seemed to me to be full of this truth, "If you trust Christ, He will save you from all evil; He will keep you in a life of integrity and holiness while here, and He will bring you safe to Heaven at the last." I felt that I could not trust man, for I had seen some of the very best wandering far from the truth; if I trusted Christ, it was not a chance as to whether I should get to Heaven, but a certainty; and I learned that, if I rested all my weight upon Him, He would keep me, for I found it written, "The righteous shall hold on his way, and he that hath clean hands shall wax stronger and stronger."

I found the apostle saying, "He which hath begun a good work in you will perform it," and such-like expressions. "Why," I reasoned, "I have found an Insurance Office, and a good one, too; I will insure my soul in it; I will go to Jesus as I am, for He bids me do so; I will trust myself with Him." If I had listened to the Arminian theory, I should never have been converted, for it never had any charms for me. A Savior who casts away His people, a God who leaves His children to perish, is not worthy of my worship; and a salvation which does not save outright is neither worth preaching nor worth listening to.

I recollect the time when I was afraid that Jesus would never save me, but I used to feel in my heart that, even if He did not, I must love Him for what He had done for other poor sinners. It seemed to me, as I read the wondrous story of His life and death, that if He refused me, I would still lie at His feet, and say, "Thou mayest spurn me, but Thou art a blessed Christ for all that; and if Thou dost curse me, yet I can only say to Thee that I well deserve it at Thy hands. Do what Thou wilt with me; but Thou didst save the dying thief, and Thou didst save her out of whom Thou didst cast seven devils, and if Thou dost not deign to save me, yet Thou art a blessed Christ, and I cannot rail at Thee, or find fault with Thee, but I lie down at Thy feet, and worship Thee." I could not help saying, once, that, even if He damned me, I would love God because He was so gracious to others. One text of Scripture especially cheered me; I lived upon it for months. I felt the weight of sin, and I did not know the Savior; I feared God would blast me with His wrath, and smite me with His hot displeasure! From chapel to chapel I went to hear the Word preached, but never a gospel sentence did I hear; but this one text preserved me from what I believe I should have been driven to, — the commission of suicide through grief and sorrow. It was this sweet word, "Whosoever shall call upon the name of the Lord shall be saved." Well, I thought, I cannot believe on Christ as I could wish, I cannot find pardon; but I know I call upon His name, I know I pray, ay, and pray with groans, and tears, and sighs, day and night; and if I am ever lost, I will plead that promise, "O God, Thou saidst, Whosoever shall call upon My name shall be saved! I did call; wilt Thou cast me away? I did plead Thy promise; I did lift up my heart in prayer; canst Thou be just, and yet condemn the sinner who did really call upon Thy name?"

My heart was greatly impressed by something which I heard my mother say. I had been some years seeking Christ, and I could not believe that He would save me. She said she had heard many people swear and blaspheme God, but one thing she had never known, — she had never heard a man say he had sought Christ, and Christ had rejected him. "And," she added, "I do not believe that God would permit any man to live to say that." I thought that I could say it; I thought I had sought Him, and He had cast me away, and I determined that I would say it; even if it destroyed my soul, I would speak what I thought was the truth. But I said to myself, "I will try once more;" and I went to the Master, with nothing of my own, casting myself simply on His mercy; and I believed that He died for me, and now, blessed be His holy name, I never shall be able to say that He has cast me away! As the result of personal experience, I can add my own testimony to that of my mother. I have heard many wicked things in my life, — I also have heard men swear and blaspheme God, till I have trembled; but there is one thing I never did hear a man say yet, and I think God would scarcely permit any man to utter such a lie; I never knew even a drunken man say,

"I sincerely sought God with full purpose of heart, yet He has not heard me, and will not answer me, but has cast me away." I scarcely think it possible, although I know that men can be almost infinitely wicked, that any man could utter such an abominable falsehood as that. At any rate, I can say I have never heard it.

Chapter Eleven - The Great Change. — Conversion.

I have heard men tell the story of their conversion, and of their spiritual life, in such a way that my heart hath loathed them and their story, too, for they have told of their sins as if they did boast in the greatness of their crime, and they have mentioned the love of God, not with a tear of gratitude, not with the simple thanksgiving of the really humble heart, but as if they as much exalted themselves as they exalted God. Oh! when we tell the story of our own conversion, I would have it done with great sorrow, remembering what we used to be, and with great joy and gratitude, remembering how little we deserve these things. I was once preaching upon conversion and salvation, and I felt within myself, as preachers often do, that it was but dry work to tell this story, and a dull, dull tale it was to me; but, on a sudden, the thought crossed my mind,

"Why, you are a poor, lost, ruined sinner yourself; tell it, tell it as you received it; begin to tell of the grace of God as you trust you feel it yourself." Why, then, my eyes began to be fountains of tears; those hearers who had nodded their heads began to brighten up, and they listened, because they were hearing something which the speaker himself felt, and which they recognized as being true to him if it was not true to them.

Can you not remember, dearly-beloved, that day of days, that best and brightest of hours, when first you saw the Lord, lost your burden, received the roll of promise, rejoiced in full salvation, and went on your way in peace? My soul can never forget that day.

Dying, all but dead, diseased, pained, chained, scourged, bound in fetters of iron, in darkness and the shadow of death, Jesus appeared unto me. My eyes looked to Him; the disease was healed, the pains removed, chains were snapped, prison doors were opened, darkness gave place to light. What delight filled my soul! — what mirth, what ecstasy, what sound of music and dancing, what soarings towards Heaven, what heights and depths of ineffable delight! Scarcely ever since then have I known joys which surpassed the rapture of that first hour. — C. H. S.

LET our lips crowd sonnets within the compass of a word; let our voice distill hours of melody into a single syllable; let our tongue utter in one letter the essence of the harmony of ages; for we write of an hour which as far excelleth all other days of our life as gold exceedeth dross. As the night of Israel's passover was a night to be remembered, a theme for bards, and an incessant fountain of grateful song, even so is the time of which we now tell, the never-to-be-forgotten hour of our emancipation from guilt, and our justification in Jesus. Other days have mingled with their fellows till, like coins worn in circulation, their image and superscription are entirely obliterated; but this day remaineth new, fresh, bright, as distinct in all its parts as if it were but yesterday struck from the mint of time. Memory shall drop from the palsied hand full many a memento which now she cherishes, but she shall never, even when she tottereth to the grave, unbind from her heart the token of the thrice-happy hour of the redemption of our spirit.

The emancipated galley-slave may forget the day which heard his broken fetters rattle on the ground; the pardoned traitor may fail to remember the moment when the ax of the headsman was averted by a pardon; and the long-despairing mariner may not recollect the moment when a friendly hand snatched him from the hungry deep; but O hour of forgiven sin, moment of perfect pardon, our soul shall never forget thee while within her life and being find an immortality! Each day of our life hath had its attendant angel; but on this day, like Jacob at Mahanaim, hosts of angels met us. The sun hath risen every morning, but on that eventful morn he had the light of seven days. As the days of Heaven upon earth, as the years of immortality, as the ages of glory, as the bliss of Heaven, so were the hours of that thrice-happy day. Rapture divine, and ecstasy inexpressible, filled our soul. Fear, distress, and grief, with all their train of woes, fled hastily away; and in their place joys came without number.

When I was in the hand of the Holy Spirit, under conviction of sin, I had a clear and sharp sense of the justice of God. Sin, whatever it might be to other people, became to me an intolerable burden. It was not so much that I feared hell, as that I feared sin; and all the while, I had upon my mind a deep concern for the honor of God's name, and the integrity of His moral government. I felt that it would not satisfy my conscience if I could be forgiven unjustly. But then there came the question, — "How could God be just, and yet justify me who had been so guilty?" I was worried and wearied with this question; neither could I see any answer to it. Certainly, I could never have invented an answer which would have satisfied my conscience. The doctrine of the atonement is to my mind one of the surest proofs of the Divine inspiration of Holy Scripture. Who would or could have thought of the just Ruler dying for the unjust rebel? This is no teaching of human mythology, or dream of poetical imagination. This method of expiation is only known among men because it is a fact: fiction could not have devised it. God Himself ordained it; it is not a matter which could have been imagined.

I had heard of the plan of salvation by the sacrifice of Jesus from my youth up; but I did not know anymore about it in my innermost soul than if I had been born and bred a Hottentot. The light was there, but I was blind: it was of necessity that the Lord Himself should make the matter plain to me. It came to me as a new revelation, as fresh as if I had never read in Scripture that Jesus was declared to be the propitiation for sins that God might be just. I believe it will have to come as a revelation to every newborn child of God whenever he sees it; I mean that glorious doctrine of the substitution of the Lord Jesus. I came to understand that salvation was possible through vicarious sacrifice; and that provision had been made in the first constitution and arrangement of things for such a substitution. I was made to see that He who is the Son of God, co-equal, and co-eternal with the Father, had of old been made the covenant Head of a chosen people, that He might in that capacity suffer for them and save them. Inasmuch as our fall was not at the first a personal one, for we fell in our federal representative, the first Adam, it became possible for us to be recovered by a second Representative, even by Him who has undertaken to be the covenant Head of His people, so as to be their second Adam. I saw that, ere I actually sinned, I had fallen by my first father's sin; and I rejoiced that, therefore, it became possible in point of law for me to rise by a second Head and Representative. The fall by Adam left a loophole of escape; another Adam could undo the ruin wrought by the first.

When I was anxious about the possibility of a just God pardoning me, I understood and saw by faith that He who is the Son of God became man, and in His own blessed person bore my sin in His own body on the tree. I saw that the chastisement of my peace was laid on Him, and that with His stripes I was healed. It was because the Son of God, supremely glorious in His matchless person, undertook to vindicate the law by bearing the sentence due to me, that therefore God was able to pass by my sin. My sole hope for Heaven lies in the full atonement made upon Calvary's cross for the ungodly. On that I firmly rely. I have not the shadow of a hope anywhere else. Personally, I could never have overcome my own sinfulness. I tried and failed. My evil propensities were too many for me, till, in the belief that Christ died for me, I cast my guilty soul on Him, and then I received a conquering principle by which I overcame my sinful self.

The doctrine of the cross can be used to slay sin, even as the old warriors used their huge two-handed swords, and mowed down their foes at every stroke. There is nothing like faith in the sinners' Friend: it overcomes all evil. If Christ has died for me, ungodly as I am, without strength as I am, then I cannot live in sin any longer, but must arouse myself to love and serve Him who hath redeemed me. I cannot trifle with the evil which slew my best Friend. I must be holy for His sake. How can I live in sin when He has died to save me from it?

There was a day, as I took my walks abroad, when I came hard by a spot forever engraven upon my memory, for there I saw this Friend, my best, my only Friend, murdered. I stooped down in sad affright, and looked at Him. I saw that His hands had been pierced with rough iron nails, and His feet had been rent in the same way. There was misery in His dead countenance so terrible that I scarcely dared to look upon it. His body was emaciated with hunger, His back was red with bloody scourges, and His brow had a circle of wounds about it: clearly could one see that these had been pierced by thorns. I shuddered, for I had known this Friend full well.

He never had a fault; He was the purest of the pure, the holiest of the holy.

Who could have injured Him? For He never injured any man: all His life long He "went about doing good;" He had healed the sick, He had fed the hungry, He had raised the dead: for which of these works did they kill Him? He had never breathed out anything else but love; and as I looked into the poor sorrowful face, so full of agony, and yet so full of love, I wondered who could have been a wretch so vile as to pierce hands like His. I said within myself, "Where can these traitors live? Who are these that could have smitten such an One as this?" Had they murdered an Oppressor, we might have forgiven them; had they slain one who had indulged in vice or villainy, it might have been his desert; had it been a murderer and a rebel, or one who had committed sedition, we would have said, "Bury his corpse: justice has at last given him his due." But when Thou wast slain, my best, my only-beloved, where lodged the traitors? Let me seize them, and they shall be put to death. If there be torments that I can devise, surely they shall endure them all. Oh! what jealousy; what revenge I felt! If I might but find these murderers, what would I not do with them! And as I looked upon that corpse, I heard a foot-step, and wondered where it was. I listened, and I clearly perceived that the murderer was close at hand. It was dark, and I groped about to find him. I found that, somehow or other, wherever I put out my hand, I could not meet with him, for he was nearer to me than my hand would go. At last I put my hand upon my breast. "I have thee now," said I; for lo! he was in my own heart; the murderer was hiding within my own bosom, dwelling in the recesses of my inmost soul. Ah! then I wept indeed, that I, in the very presence of my murdered Master, should be harboring the murderer; and I felt myself most guilty while I bowed over His corpse, and sang that plaintive hymn, —

"'*Twas you, my sins, my cruel sins,*
His chief tormentors were;
Each of my crimes became a nail,
And unbelief the spear."

Amid the rabble rout which hounded the Redeemer to His doom, there were some gracious souls whose bitter anguish sought vent in wailing and lamentations, — fit music to accompany that march of woe. When my soul can, in imagination, see the Savior bearing His cross to Calvary, she joins the godly women, and weeps with them; for, indeed, there is true cause for grief, — cause lying deeper than those mourning women thought. They bewailed innocence maltreated, goodness persecuted, love bleeding, meekness about to die; but my heart has a deeper and more bitter cause to mourn. My sins were the scourges which lacerated those blessed shoulders, and crowned with thorns those bleeding brows: my sins cried, "Crucify Him! Crucify Him!" and laid the cross upon His gracious shoulders. His being led forth to die is sorrow enough for one eternity; but my having been His murderer, is more, infinitely more grief than one poor fountain of tears can express.

Why those women loved and wept, it were not hard to guess; but they could not have had greater reasons for love and grief than my heart has.

Nain's widow saw her son restored; but I myself have been raised to newness of life. Peter's wife's mother was cured of the fever; but I of the greater plague of sin. Out of Magdalene seven devils were cast; but a whole legion out of me. Mary and Martha were favored with visits from Him; but He dwells with me. His mother bare His body; but He is formed in me, "the hope of glory." In nothing behind the holy women in debt, let me not be behind them in gratitude or sorrow.

> *"Love and grief my heart dividing,*
> *With my tears His feet I'll lave;*
> *Constant still in heart abiding,*
> *Weep for Him who died to save."*

William Huntingdon says, in his autobiography, that one of the sharpest sensations of pain that he felt, after he had been quickened by Divine grace, was this, "He felt such pity for God." I do not know that I ever met with the expression elsewhere, but it is a very striking one; although I might prefer to say that I have sympathy with God, and grief that He should be treated so ill. Ah, there are many men that are forgotten, that are despised, and that are trampled on by their fellows; but there never was a man who was so despised as the everlasting God has been! Many a man has been slandered and abused, but never was man abused as God has been. Many have been treated cruelly and ungratefully, but never was one treated as our God has been. I, too, once despised Him. He knocked at the door of my heart, and I refused to open it. He came to me, times without number, morning by morning, and night by night; He checked me in my conscience, and spoke to me by His Spirit, and when, at last, the thunders of the law prevailed in my conscience, I thought that Christ was cruel and unkind. Oh, I can never forgive myself that I should have thought so ill of Him! But what a loving reception did I have when I went to Him! I thought He would smite me, but His hand was not clenched in anger, but opened wide in mercy. I thought full sure that His eyes would dart lightning-flashes of wrath upon me; but, instead thereof, they were full of tears. He fell upon my neck, and kissed me; He took off my rags, and did clothe me with His righteousness, and caused my soul to sing aloud for joy; while in the house of my heart, and in the house of His Church, there was music and dancing, because His son that He had lost was found, and he that had been dead was made alive again.

There is a power in God's gospel beyond all description. Once I, like Mazeppa, lashed to the wild horse of my lust, bound hand and foot, incapable of resistance, was galloping on with hell's wolves behind me, howling for my body and my soul as their just and lawful prey. There came a mighty hand which stopped that wild horse, cut my bands, set me down, and brought me into liberty. Is there power in the gospel? Ay, there is, and he who has felt it must acknowledge it. There was a time when I lived in the strong old castle of my sins, and rested in my own works. There came a trumpeter to the door, and bade me open it. I with anger chid him from the porch, and said he ne'er should enter. Then there came a goodly Personage, with loving countenance; His hands were marked with scars where nails had been driven, and His feet had nail-prints, too. He lifted up His cross, using it as a hammer; at the first blow, the gate of my prejudice shook; at the second, it trembled more; at the third, down it fell, and in He came; and He said, "Arise, and stand upon thy feet, for I have loved thee with an everlasting love." The gospel a thing of power! Ah! that it is. It always wears the dew of its youth; it glitters with morning's freshness, its strength and its glory abide forever. I have felt its power in my own heart; I have the witness of the Spirit within my spirit, and I know it is a thing of might, because it has conquered me, and bowed me down.

"His free grace alone, from the first to the last,
Hath won my affections, and bound my soul fast."

In my conversion, the very point lay in making the discovery that I had nothing to do but to look to Christ, and I should be saved. I believe that I had been a very good, attentive hearer; my own impression about myself was that nobody ever listened much better than I did. For years, as a child, I tried to learn the way of salvation; and either I did not hear it set forth, which I think cannot quite have been the case, or else I was spiritually blind and deaf, and could not see it and could not hear it; but the good news that I was, as a sinner, to look away from myself to Christ, as much startled me, and came as fresh to me, as any news I ever heard in my life. Had I never read my Bible? Yes, and read it earnestly. Had I never been taught by Christian people? Yes, I had, by mother, and father, and others. Had I not heard the gospel? Yes, I think I had; and yet, somehow, it was like a new revelation to me that I was to "believe and live." I confess to have been tutored in piety, put into my cradle by prayerful hands, and lulled to sleep by songs concerning Jesus; but after having heard the gospel continually, with line upon line, precept upon precept, here much and there much, yet, when the Word of the Lord came to me with power, it was as new as if I had lived among the unvisited tribes of Central Africa, and had never heard the tidings of the cleansing fountain filled with blood, drawn from the Savior's veins.

When, for the first time, I received the gospel to my soul's salvation, I thought that I had never really heard it before, and I began to think that the preachers to whom I had listened had not truly preached it. But, on looking back, I am inclined to believe that I had heard the gospel fully preached many hundreds of times before, and that this was the difference, — that I then heard it as though I heard it not; and when I did hear it, the message may not have been anymore clear in itself than it had been at former times, but the power of the Holy Spirit was present to open my ear, and to guide the message to my heart. I have no doubt that I heard, scores of times, such texts as these, — "He that believeth and is baptized shall be saved;"

"Look unto Me, and be ye saved, all the ends of the earth;" "As Moses lifted up the serpent in the wilderness, even so must the Son of man be lifted up: that whosoever believeth in Him should not perish, but have everlasting life;" yet I had no intelligent idea of what faith meant. When I first discovered what faith really was, and exercised it, — for with me these two things came together, I believed as soon as ever I knew what believing meant, — then I thought I had never before heard that truth preached. But, now, I am persuaded that the light often shone on my eyes, but I was blind, and therefore I thought that the light had never come there. The light was shining all the while, but there was no power to receive it; the eyeball of the soul was not sensitive to the Divine beams.

I could not believe that it was possible that *my* sins could be forgiven. I do not know why, but I seemed to be the odd person in the world. When the catalogue was made out, it appeared to me that, for some reason, I must have been left out. If God had saved me, and not the world, I should have wondered indeed; but if He had saved all the world except me, that would have seemed to me to be but right. And now, being saved by grace, I cannot help saying, "I am indeed a brand plucked out of the fire!" I believe that some of us who were kept by God a long while before we found Him, love Him better perhaps than we should have done if we had received Him directly; and we can preach better to others, we can speak more of His lovingkindness and tender mercy. John Bunyan could not have written as he did if he had not been dragged about by the devil for many years. I love that picture of dear old Christian. I know, when I first read *The Pilgrim's Progress,* and saw in it the woodcut of Christian carrying the burden on his back, I felt so interested in the poor fellow, that I thought I should jump with joy when, after he had carried his heavy load so long, he at last got rid of it; and that was how I felt when the burden of guilt, which I had borne so long, was forever rolled away from my shoulders and my heart.

I can recollect when, like the poor dove sent out by Noah from his hand, I flew over the wide expanse of waters, and hoped to find some place where I might rest my wearied wing. Up towards the North I flew; and my eye looked keenly through the mist and darkness, if perhaps it might find some floating substance on which my soul might rest its foot, but it found nothing. Again it turned its wing, and flapped it, but not so rapidly as before, across that deep water that knew no shore; but still there was no rest. The raven had found its resting-place upon a floating body, and was feeding itself upon the carrion of some drowned man's carcass; but my poor soul found no rest. I flew on; I fancied I saw a ship sailing out at sea; it was the ship of the law; and I thought I would put my feet on its canvas, or rest myself on its cordage for a time, and find some refuge. But, ah! it was an airy phantom, on which I could not rest; for my foot had no right to rest on the law; I had not kept it, and the soul that keepeth it not, must die.

At last I saw the bark *Christ Jesus,* — that happy ark; and I thought I would fly thither; but my poor wing was weary, I could fly no further, and down I sank; but, as providence would have it, when my wings were flagging, and I was falling into the flood to be drowned, just below me was the roof of the ark, and I saw a hand put out from it, and One took hold of me, and said, "I have loved thee with an everlasting love, therefore I have not delivered the soul of My turtle-dove unto the multitude of the wicked; come in, come in!" Then I found that I had in my mouth an olive leaf of peace with God, and peace with man, plucked off by Jesus' mighty power.

Once, God preached to me by a similitude in the depth of winter. The earth had been black, and there was scarcely a green thing or a flower to be seen. As I looked across the fields, there was nothing but barrenness, — bare hedges and leafless trees, and black, black earth, wherever I gazed. On a sudden, God spake, and unlocked the treasures of the snow, and white flakes descended until there was no blackness to be seen, and all was one sheet of dazzling whiteness. It was at the time that I was seeking the Savior, and not long before I found Him; and I remember well that sermon which I saw before me in the snow: "Come now, and let us reason together, saith the Lord: though your sins be as scarlet, they shall be as white as snow; though they be red like crimson, they shall be as wool."

Personally, I have to bless God for many good books; I thank Him for Dr. Doddridge's *Rise and Progress of Religion in the Soul;* for Baxter's *Call to the Un-converted;* for Alleine's *Alarm to Sinners;* and for James's *Anxious Enquirer;* but my gratitude most of all is due to God, not for books, but for the preached Word, — and that too addressed to me by a poor, uneducated man, a man who had never received any training for the ministry, and probably will never be heard of in this life, a man engaged in business, no doubt of a humble kind, during the week, but who had just enough of grace to say on the Sabbath, "Look unto Me, and be ye saved, all the ends of the earth." The books were good, but the man was better.

The revealed Word awakened me; but it was the preached Word that saved me; and I must ever attach peculiar value to the *hearing of the truth,* for by it I received the joy and peace in which my soul delights. While under concern of soul, I resolved that I would attend all the places of worship in the town where I lived, in order that I might find out the way of salvation. I was willing to do any-thing, and be anything, if God would only forgive my sin. I set off, determined to go round to all the chapels, and I did go to every place of worship; but for a long time I went in vain. I do not, however, blame the ministers. One man preached Divine Sovereignty; I could hear him with pleasure, but what was that sublime truth to a poor sinner who wished to know what he must do to be saved? There was another admirable man who always preached about the law; but what was the use of plowing up ground that needed to be sown? Another was a practical preacher. I heard him, but it was very much like a commanding officer teaching the maneuvers of war to a set of men without feet. What could I do? All his ex-hortations were lost on me. I knew it was said,

"Believe on the Lord Jesus Christ, and thou shalt be saved;" but I did not know what it was to believe on Christ. These good men all preached truths suited to many in their congregations who were spiritually-minded people; but what I wanted to know was, — "How can I get my sins forgiven?" — and they never told me that. I desired to hear how a poor sinner, under a sense of sin, might find peace with God; and when I went, I heard a sermon on, "Be not deceived, God is not mocked," which cut me up still worse; but did not bring me into rest. I went again, another day, and the text was something about the glories of the right-eous; nothing for poor me! I was like a dog under the table, not allowed to eat of the children's food. I went time after time, and I can honestly say that I do not know that I ever went without prayer to God, and I am sure there was not a more attentive hearer than myself in all the place, for I panted and longed to under-stand how I might be saved.

I sometimes think I might have been in darkness and despair until now had it not been for the goodness of God in sending a snowstorm, one Sunday morning, while I was going to a certain place of worship. When I could go no further, I turned down a side street, and came to a little Primitive Methodist Chapel. In that chapel there may have been a dozen or fifteen people. I had heard of the Primitive Methodists, how they sang so loudly that they made people's heads ache; but that did not matter to me. I wanted to know how I might be saved, and if they could tell me that, I did not care how much they made my head ache. The minister did not come that morning; he was snowed up, I suppose. At last, a very thin-looking man, [5] a shoemaker, or tailor, or something of that sort, went up into the pulpit to preach. Now, it is well that preachers should be instructed; but this man was really stupid. He was obliged to stick to his text, for the simple reason that he had little else to say. The text was, —

"LOOK UNTO ME, AND BE YE SAVED, ALL THE ENDS OF THE EARTH."

He did not even pronounce the words rightly, but that did not matter.

There was, I thought, a glimpse of hope for me in that text. The preacher began thus: — "My dear friends, this is a very simple text indeed. It says,

'Look.' Now lookin' don't take a deal of pains. It ain't liftin' your foot or your finger; it is just, 'Look.' Well, a man needn't go to College to learn to look. You may be the biggest fool, and yet you can look. A man needn't be worth a thousand a year to be able to look. Anyone can look; even a child can look. But then the text says, 'Look unto *Me*.' Ay!" said he, in broad Essex, "many on ye are lookin' to yourselves, but it's no use lookin' there.

You'll never find any comfort in yourselves. Some look to God the Father.

No, look to Him by-and-by. Jesus Christ says, 'Look unto *Me*.' Some on ye say, 'We must wait for the Spirit's workin'.' You have no business with that just now. Look to *Christ*. The text says, 'Look unto *Me*.'"

Then the good man followed up his text in this way: — "Look unto Me; I am sweatin' great drops of blood. Look unto Me; I am hangin' on the cross. Look unto Me; I am dead and buried. Look unto Me; I rise again.

Look unto Me; I ascend to Heaven. Look unto Me; I am sittin' at the Father's right hand. O poor sinner, look unto Me! look unto Me!"

When he had gone to about that length, and managed to spin out ten minutes or so, he was at the end of his tether. Then he looked at me under the gallery, and I daresay, with so few present, he knew me to be a stranger. Just fixing his eyes on me, as if he knew all my heart, he said, "Young man, you look very miserable." Well, I did; but I had not been accustomed to have remarks made from the pulpit on my personal appearance before. However, it was a good blow, struck right home. He continued, "and you always will be miserable — miserable in life, and miserable in death, — if you don't obey my text; but if you obey now, this moment, you will be saved." Then, lifting up his hands, he shouted, as only a Primitive Methodist could do, "Young man, look to Jesus Christ. Look!

Look! Look! You have nothin' to do but to look and live." I saw at once the way of salvation. I know not what else he said, — I did not take much notice of it, — I was so possessed with that one thought. Like as when the brazen serpent was lifted up, the people only looked and were healed, so it was with me. I had been waiting to do fifty things, but when I heard that word, "Look!" what a charming word it seemed to me! Oh! I looked until I could almost have looked my eyes away. There and then the cloud was gone, the darkness had rolled away, and that moment I saw the sun; and I could have risen that instant, and sung with the most enthusiastic of them, of the precious blood of Christ, and the simple faith which looks alone to Him. Oh, that somebody had told me this before, "Trust Christ, and you shall be saved." Yet it was, no doubt, all wisely ordered, and now I can say, —

"E'er since by faith I saw the stream
Thy flowing wounds supply,
Redeeming love has been my theme,
And shall be till I die."

I do from my soul confess that I never was satisfied till I came to Christ; when I was yet a child, I had far more wretchedness than ever I have now; I will even add, more weariness, more care, more heartache than I know at this day. I may be singular in this confession, but I make it, and know it to be the truth. Since that dear hour when my soul cast itself on Jesus, I have found solid joy and peace; but before that, all those supposed gaieties of early youth, all the imagined ease and joy of boyhood, were but vanity and vexation of spirit to me. That happy day, when I found the Savior, and learned to cling to His dear feet, was a day never to be forgotten by me. An obscure child, unknown, unheard of, I listened to the Word of God; and that precious text led me to the cross of Christ. I can testify that the joy of that day was utterly indescribable. I could have leaped, I could have danced; there was no expression, however fanatical, which would have been out of keeping with the joy of my spirit at that hour. Many days of Christian experience have passed since then, but there has never been one which has had the full exhilaration, the sparkling delight which that first day had. I thought I could have sprung from the seat on which I sat, and have called out with the wildest of those Methodist brethren who were present, "I am forgiven! I am forgiven! A monument of grace! A sinner saved by blood!" My spirit saw its chains broken to pieces, I felt that I was an emancipated soul, an heir of Heaven, a forgiven one, accepted in Christ Jesus, plucked out of the miry clay and out of the horrible pit, with my feet set upon a rock, and my goings established. I thought I could dance all the way home. I could understand what John Bunyan meant, when he declared he wanted to tell the crows on the plowed land all about his conversion. He was too full to hold, he felt he must tell somebody.

It is not everyone who can remember the very day and hour of his deliverance; but, as Richard Knill said, "At such a time of the day, clang went every harp in Heaven, for Richard Knill was born again," it was e'en so with me. [6] The clock of mercy struck in Heaven the hour and moment of my emancipation, for the time had come. Between half-past ten o'clock, when I entered that chapel, and half-past twelve o'clock, when I was back again at home, what a change had taken place in me! I had passed from darkness into marvelous light, from death to life. Simply by looking to Jesus, I had been delivered from despair, and I was brought into such a joyous state of mind that, when they saw me at home, they said to me,

"Something wonderful has happened to you;" and I was eager to tell them all about it. Oh! there was joy in the household that day, when all heard that the eldest son had found the Savior, and knew himself to be forgiven, — bliss compared with which all earth's joys are less than nothing and vanity. Yes, I had looked to Jesus as I was, and found in Him my Savior.

Thus had the eternal purpose of Jehovah decreed it; and as, the moment before, there was none more wretched than I was, so, within that second, there was none more joyous. It took no longer time than does the lightning-flash; it was done, and never has it been undone. I looked, and lived, and leaped in joyful liberty as I beheld my sin punished upon the great Substitute, and put away forever. I looked unto Him, as He bled upon that tree; His eyes darted a glance of love unutterable into my spirit, and in a moment, I was saved. [7] Looking unto Him, the bruises that my soul had suffered were healed, the gaping wounds were cured, the broken bones rejoiced, the rags that had covered me were all removed, my spirit was white as the spotless snows of the far-off North; I had melody within my spirit, for I was saved, washed, cleansed, forgiven, through Him that did hang upon the tree. My Master, I cannot understand how Thou couldst stoop Thine awful head to such a death as the death of the cross, — how Thou couldst take from Thy brow the coronet of stars which from old eternity had shone resplendent there; but how Thou shouldst permit the thorn-crown to gird Thy temples, astonishes me far more. That Thou shouldst cast away the mantle of Thy glory, the azure of Thine everlasting empire, I cannot comprehend; but how Thou shouldst have become veiled in the ignominious purple for awhile, and then be mocked by impious men, who bowed to Thee as a pretended king; and how Thou shouldst be stripped naked to Thy shame, without a single covering, and die a felon's death; — this is still more incomprehensible. But the marvel is that Thou shouldst have suffered all this for *me*! Truly, Thy love to me is wonderful, passing the love of women! Was ever grief like Thine? Was ever love like Thine, that could open the flood-gates of such grief? Was ever love so mighty as to become the fount from which such an ocean of grief could come rolling down?

There was never anything so true to me as those bleeding hands, and that thorn-crowned head. Home, friends, health, wealth, comforts — all lost their luster that day when He appeared, just as stars are hidden by the light of the sun. He was the only Lord and Giver of life's best bliss, the one well of living water springing up unto everlasting life. As I saw Jesus on His cross before me, and as I mused upon His sufferings and death, methought I saw Him cast a look of love upon me; and then I looked at Him, and cried, —

"Jesu, lover of my soul,
Let me to Thy bosom fly."

He said, "Come," and I flew to Him, and clasped Him; and when He let me go again, I wondered where my burden was. It was gone! There, in the sepulcher, it lay, and I felt light as air; like a winged sylph, I could fly over mountains of trouble and despair; and oh! what liberty and joy I had! I could leap with ecstasy, for I had much forgiven, and I was freed from sin.

With the spouse in the Canticles, I could say, "*I found Him;*" I, a lad, found the Lord of glory; I, a slave to sin, found the great Deliverer; I, the child of darkness, found the Light of life; I, the uttermost of the lost, found my Savior and my God; I, widowed and desolate, found my Friend, my Beloved, my Husband. Oh, how I wondered that *I* should be pardoned! It was not the pardon that I wondered at so much; the wonder was that it should come to *me.* I marveled that He should be able to pardon such sins as mine, such crimes, so numerous and so black; and that, after such an accusing conscience, He should have power to still every wave within my spirit, and make my soul like the surface of a river, undisturbed, quiet, and at ease. It mattered not to me whether the day itself was gloomy or bright, I had found Christ; that was enough for me. He was my Savior, He was my all; and I can heartily say, that one day of pardoned sin was a sufficient recompense for the whole five years of conviction. I have to bless God for every terror that ever scared me by night, and for every foreboding that alarmed me by day. It has made me happier ever since; for now, if there be a trouble weighing upon my soul, I thank God it is not such a burden as that which bowed me to the very earth, and made me creep upon the ground, like a beast, by reason of heavy distress and affliction. I know I never can again suffer what I have suffered; I never can, except I be sent to hell, know more of agony than I have known; and now, that ease, that joy and peace in believing, that "no condemnation" which belongs to me as a child of God, is made doubly sweet and inexpressibly precious, by the recollection of my past days of sorrow and grief. Blessed be Thou, O God, forever, who by those black days, like a dreary winter, hast made these summer days all the fairer and the sweeter! I need not walk through the earth fearful of every shadow, and afraid of every man I meet, for sin is washed away; my spirit is no more guilty; it is pure, it is holy. The frown of God no longer resteth upon me; but my Father smiles, I see His eyes, they are glancing love; I hear His voice, — it is full of sweetness. I am forgiven, I am forgiven, I am forgiven!

When I look back upon it, I can see one reason why the Word was blessed to me as I heard it preached in that Primitive Methodist Chapel at Colchester; I had been up betimes crying to God for the blessing. As a lad, when I was seeking the Savior, I used to rise with the sun, that I might get time to read gracious books, and to seek the Lord. I can recall the kind of pleas I used when I took my arguments, and came before the throne of grace: "Lord, save me; it will glorify Thy grace to save such a sinner as I am! Lord, save me, else I am lost to all eternity; do not let me perish, Lord!

Save me, O Lord, for Jesus died! By His agony and bloody sweat, by His cross and passion, save me!" I often proved that the early morning was the best part of the day; I liked those prayers of which the psalmist said, "In the morning shall my prayer prevent Thee."

The Holy Spirit, who enabled me to believe, gave me peace through believing. I felt as sure that I was forgiven as before I felt sure of condemnation. I had been certain of my condemnation because the Word of God declared it, and my conscience bore witness to it; but when the Lord justified me, I was made equally certain by the same witnesses. The Word of the Lord in the Scripture saith, "He that believeth on Him is not condemned," and my conscience bore witness that I believed, and that God in pardoning me was just. Thus I had the witness of the Holy Spirit and also of my own conscience, and these two agreed in one. That great and excellent man, Dr. Johnson, used to hold the opinion that no man ever could know that he was pardoned, — that there was no such thing as assurance of faith. Perhaps, if Dr. Johnson had studied his Bible a little more, and had had a little more of the enlightenment of the Spirit, he, too, might have come to know his own pardon. Certainly, he was no very reliable judge of theology, anymore than he was of porcelain, which he once attempted to make, and never succeeded. I think both in theology and porcelain his opinion is of very little value.

How can a man know that he is pardoned? There is a text which says,

"Believe on the Lord Jesus Christ, and thou shalt be saved." I believe on the Lord Jesus Christ; is it irrational to believe that I am saved? "He that believeth on the Son hath everlasting life," saith Christ, in John's Gospel. I believe on Christ; am I absurd in believing that I have eternal life? I find the apostle Paul speaking by the Holy Ghost, and saying, "There is therefore now no condemnation to them that are in Christ Jesus. Being justified by faith, we have peace with God." If I know that my trust is fixed on Jesus only, and that I have faith in Him, were it not ten thousand times more absurd for me not to be at peace, than for me to be filled with joy unspeakable? It is but taking God at His Word, when the soul knows, as a necessary consequence of its faith, that it is saved. I took Jesus as my Savior, and I was saved; and I can tell the reason why I took Him for my Savior. To my own humiliation, I must confess that I did it because I could not help it; I was shut up to it. That stern law-work had hammered me into such a condition that, if there had been fifty other saviors, I could not have thought of them, — I was driven to this One. I wanted a Divine Savior, I wanted One who was made a curse for me, to expiate my guilt. I wanted One who had died, for I deserved to die. I wanted One who had risen again, who was able by His life to make me live. I wanted the exact Savior that stood before me in the Word, revealed to my heart; and I could not help having Him. I could realize then the language of Ruth-erford when, being full of love to Christ, once upon a time, in the dungeon of Ab-erdeen, he said, "O my Lord, if there were a broad hell betwixt me and Thee, if I could not get at Thee except by wading through it, I would not think twice, but I would go through it all, if I might but embrace Thee, and call Thee mine!" Oh, how I loved Him! Passing all loves except His own, was that love which I felt for Him then. If, beside the door of the place in which I met with Him, there had been a stake of blazing faggots, I would have stood upon them without chains, glad to give my flesh, and blood, and bones, to be ashes that should testify my love to Him. Had He asked me then to give all my substance to the poor, I would have given all, and thought myself to be amazingly rich in having beggared myself for His name's sake. Had He commanded me then to preach in the midst of all His foes, I could have said, —

"There's not a lamb in all Thy flock
I would disdain to feed,
There's not a foe, before whose face
I'd fear Thy cause to plead."

Has Jesus saved *me?* I dare not speak with any hesitation here; I *know* He has.

His Word is true, therefore I *am* saved. My evidence that I am saved does not lie in the fact that I preach, or that I do this or that. All my hope lies in this, that Jesus Christ came to save sinners. I am a sinner, I trust Him, then He came to save me, and I am saved; I live habitually in the enjoyment of this blessed fact, and it is long since I have doubted the truth of it, for I have His own Word to sustain my faith. It is a very surprising thing, — a thing to be marveled at most of all by those who enjoy it. I know that it is to me even to this day the greatest wonder that I ever heard of, that God should ever justify *me.* I feel myself to be a lump of unworthiness, a mass of corruption, and a heap of sin, apart from His almighty love; yet I know, by a full assurance, that I am justified by faith which is in Christ

Jesus, and treated as if I had been perfectly just, and made an heir of God and a joint-heir with Christ; though by nature I must take my place among the most sinful. I, who am altogether undeserving, am treated as if I had been deserving. I am loved with as much love as if I had always been godly, whereas aforetime I was ungodly.

I have always considered, with Luther and Calvin, that the sum and substance of the gospel lies in that word *Substitution,* — Christ standing in the stead of man. If I understand the gospel, it is this: I deserve to be lost forever; the only reason why I should not be damned is, that Christ was punished in my stead, and there is no need to execute a sentence twice for sin. On the other hand, I know I cannot enter Heaven unless I have a perfect righteousness; I am absolutely certain I shall never have one of my own, for I find I sin everyday; but then Christ had a perfect righteousness, and He said, "There, poor sinner, take My garment, and put it on; you shall stand before God as if you were Christ, and I will stand before God as if I had been the sinner; I will suffer in the sinner's stead, and you shall be rewarded for works which you did not do, but which I did for you." I find it very convenient everyday to come to Christ as a sinner, as I came at the first. "You are no saint," says the devil. Well, if I am not, I am a sinner, and Jesus Christ came into the world to save sinners. Sink or swim, I go to Him; other hope I have none. By looking to Him, I received all the faith which inspired me with confidence in His grace; and the word that first drew my soul — "Look unto Me," — still rings its clarion note in my ears.

There I once found conversion, and there I shall ever find refreshing and renewal. Let me bear my personal testimony of what I have seen, what my own ears have heard, and my own heart has tasted. First, Christ is the only-begotten of the Father. He is Divine to me, if He be human to all the world besides.

He has done that for me which none but a God could do. He has subdued my stubborn will, melted a heart of adamant, broken a chain of steel, opened the gates of brass, and snapped the bars of iron. He hath turned for me my mourning into laughter, and my desolation into joy; He hath led my captivity captive, and made my heart rejoice with joy unspeakable, and full of glory. Let others think as they will of Him, to me He must ever be the only-begotten of the Father: blessed be His holy name!

"Oh, that I could now adore Him,
Like the Heavenly host above,
Who for ever bow before Him,
And unceasing sing His love!
Happy songsters!
When shall I your chorus join?"

Again, I bear my testimony that He is full of grace. Ah, had He not been, I should never have beheld His glory. I was full of sin to overflowing. I was condemned already, because I believed not upon Him. He drew me when I wanted not to come, and though I struggled hard, He continued still to draw; and when at last I came to His mercy-seat, all trembling like a condemned culprit, He said, "Thy sins, which are many, are all forgiven thee: be of good cheer." Let others despise Him; but I bear witness that He is full of grace.

Finally, I bear my witness that He is full of truth. True have His promises been; not one has failed. I have often doubted Him, for that I blush; He has never failed me, in this I must rejoice. His promises have been yea and amen. I do but speak the testimony of every believer in Christ, though I put it thus personally to make it the more forcible. I bear witness that never servant had such a Master as I have; never brother had such a Kinsman as He has been to me; never spouse had such a Husband as Christ has been to my soul; never sinner a better Savior; never soldier a better Captain; never mourner a better Comforter than Christ hath been to my spirit. I want none beside Him. In life, He is my life; and in death, He shall be the death of death; in poverty, Christ is my riches; in sickness, He makes my bed; in darkness, He is my Star; and in brightness, He is my Sun. By faith I understand that the blessed Son of God redeemed my soul with His own heart's blood; and by sweet experience I know that He raised me up from the pit of dark despair, and set my feet on the rock. He died for me. This is the root of every satisfaction I have. He put all my transgressions away. He cleansed me with His precious blood; He covered me with His perfect righteousness; He wrapped me up in His own virtues. He has promised to keep me, while I abide in this world, from its temptations and snares; and when I depart from this world, He has already prepared for me a mansion in the Heaven of unfading bliss, and a crown of everlasting joy that shall never, never fade away. To me, then, the days or years of my mortal sojourn on this earth are of little moment. Nor is the manner of my decease of much consequence. Should foemen sentence me to martyrdom, or physicians declare that I must soon depart this life, it is all alike, —

"A few more rolling suns at most
Shall land me on fair Canaan's coast."

What more can I wish than that, while my brief term on earth shall last, I should be the servant of Him who became the Servant of servants for me? I can say, concerning Christ's religion, if I had to die like a dog, and had no hope whatever of immortality, if I wanted to lead a happy life, let me serve my God with all my heart; let me be a follower of Jesus, and walk in His footsteps. If there were no hereafter, I would still prefer to be a Christian, and the humblest Christian minister, to being a king or an emperor, for I am persuaded there are more delights in Christ, yea, more joy in one glimpse of His face than is to be found in all the praises of this harlot-world, and in all the delights which it can yield to us in its sunniest and brightest days. And I am persuaded that what He has been till now, He will be to the end; and where He hath begun a good work, He will carry it on.

In the religion of Jesus Christ, there are clusters even on earth too heavy for one man to carry; there are fruits that have been found so rich that even angel lips have never been sweetened with more luscious wine; there are joys to be had here so fair that even cates ambrosial and the nectared wine of Paradise can scarcely excel the sweets of satisfaction that are to be found in the earthly banquets of the Lord. I have seen hundreds and thousands who have given their hearts to Jesus, but I never did see one who said he was disappointed with Him, I never met with one who said Jesus Christ was less than He was declared to be. When first my eyes beheld Him, when the burden slipped from off my heavy-laden shoulders, and I was free from condemnation, I thought that all the preachers I had ever heard had not half preached, they had not told half the beauty of my Lord and Master. So good! so generous! so gracious! so willing to forgive!

It seemed to me as if they had almost slandered Him; they painted His likeness, doubtless, as well as they could, but it was a mere smudge compared with the matchless beauties of His face. All who have ever seen Him will say the same. I go back to my home, many a time, mourning that I cannot preach my Master even as I myself know Him, and what I know of Him is very little compared with the matchlessness of His grace. Would that I knew more of Him, and that I could tell it out better!

Chapter Twelve - Letters to Father and Mother, January to June, 1850.

A man's private letters often let you into the secrets of his heart.
Read Rutherford's letters and you see the man at once; or those of Kirk White, or Newton. A man's writing-desk should be used to make his biography. — **C. H. S.**

"Newmarket,
"January 30th, 1850.

"My Dear Father,

"I am most happy and comfortable, I could not be more so whilst sojourning on earth, 'like a pilgrim or a stranger, as all my fathers were.' There are but four boarders, and about twelve day-boys. I have a nice little mathematical class, and have quite as much time for study as I had before. I can get good religious conversations with Mr. Swindell, which is what I most need. Oh, how unprofitable has my past life been! Oh, that I should have been so long time blind to those celestial wonders, which now I can in a measure behold! Who can refrain from speaking of the marvelous love of Jesus which, I hope, has opened mine eyes! Now I see Him, I can firmly trust to Him for my eternal salvation. Yet soon I doubt again; then I am sorrowful; again faith appears, and I become confident of my interest in Him. I feel now as if I could do everything, and give up everything for Christ, and then I know it would be nothing in comparison with His love. I am hopeless of ever making anything like a return. How sweet is prayer! I would be always engaged in it. How beautiful is the Bible! I never loved it so before; it seems to me as necessary food. I feel that I have not one particle of spiritual life in me but what the Spirit placed there. I feel that I cannot live if He depart; I tremble and fear lest I should grieve Him. I dread lest sloth or pride should overcome me, and I should dishonor the gospel by neglect of prayer, or the Scriptures, or by sinning against God. Truly, that will be a happy place where we shall get rid of sin and this depraved, corrupt nature. When I look at the horrible pit and the hole from which I have been digged, I tremble lest I should fall into it, and yet rejoice that I am on the King's highway. I hope you will forgive me for taking up so much space about myself; but at present my thoughts are most about it.

"From the Scriptures, is it not apparent that, immediately upon receiving the Lord Jesus, it is a part of duty openly to profess Him?

I firmly believe and consider that baptism is the command of Christ, and shall not feel quite comfortable if I do not receive it. I am unworthy of such things, but so am I unworthy of Jesu's love. I hope I have received the blessing of the one, and think I ought to take the other also.

"My very best love to you and my dear Mother; I seem to love you more than ever, because you love my Lord Jesus. I hope yourself, dear Mother, Archer, Eliza, Emily, Louisa, and Lottie, are well; love to all...

"May we all, after this fighting life is over, meet in —

"'That Kingdom of immense delight,
Where health, and peace, and joy unite,
Where undeclining pleasures rise,
And every wish hath full supplies;'

and while you are here, may the blessings of the gospel abound toward you, and may we as a family be all devoted to the Lord!

May all blessings be upon us, and may —

"I ever remain,

"Your dutiful and affectionate son,

"CHAS. H. SPURGEON."

"Newmarket,

"Feb. 19th, 1850.

"My Dear Mother,

"I hope the long space between my letters will be excused, as I assure you I am fully occupied. I read French exercises every night with Mr. Swindell, — Monsr. Perret comes once every week for an hour. I have 33 houses at present where I leave tracts, — I happened to take a district formerly supplied by Mrs. Andrews, who last lived in this house, and Miss Anna Swindell. Next Wednesday, — I mean tomorrow, — I am to go to a meeting of the tract-distributors. They have been at a standstill, and hope now to start afresh. On Thursday, Mr. Simpson intends coming to talk with me upon the most important of all subjects. Oh, how I wish that I could do something for Christ! Tract-distribution is so pleasant and easy that it is a nothing, — nothing in itself, much less when it is compared with the amazing debt of gratitude I owe.

"I have written to grandfather, and have received a very nice letter.

I have been in the miry Slough of Despond; he sends me strong consolation, but is that what I want? Ought I not rather to be reproved for my deadness and coldness? I pray as if I did not pray, hear as if I did not hear, and read as if I did not read, — such is my deadness and coldness. I had a glorious revival on Saturday and Sunday. When I can do anything, I am not quite so dead. Oh, what a horrid state! It seems as if no real child of God could ever look so coldly on, and think so little of, the love of Jesus, and His glorious atonement. Why is not my heart always warm? Is it not because of my own sins? I fear lest this deadness be but the prelude to death, — spiritual death. I have still a sense of my own weakness, nothingness, and utter inability to do anything in and of myself, — I pray God that I may never lose it, — I am sure I must if left to myself, and then, when I am cut off from Him, in whom my great strength lieth, I shall be taken by the Philistines in my own wicked heart, and have mine eyes forever closed to all spiritual good. Pray for me, O my dear Father and Mother! Oh, that Jesus would pray for me! Then I shall be delivered, and everlastingly saved. I should like to be always reading my Bible, and be daily gaining greater insight into it *by the help of the Spirit.* I can get but very little time, as Mr. S. pushes me on in Greek and French. "I have come to a resolution that, by God's help, I will profess the name of Jesus as soon as possible if I may be admitted into His Church on earth. It is an honor, — no difficulty, — grandfather encourages me to do so, and I hope to do so both as a duty and privilege. I trust that I shall then feel that the bonds of the Lord are upon me, and have a more powerful sense of my duty to walk circum-spectly. Conscience has convinced me that it is a duty to be buried with Christ in baptism, although I am sure it constitutes no part of salvation. I am very glad that you have no objection to my doing so. Mr. Swindell is a Baptist.

"You must have been terribly frightened when the chimney fell down, what a mercy that none were hurt! There was a great deal of damage here from the wind. My cold is about the same as it was at home, it has been worse. I take all the care I can, I suppose it will go away soon. How are all the little ones? Give my love to them, and to Archer and Eliza. How does Archer get on? Accept my best love for yourself and Father. I hope you are well,

"And remain,

"Your affectionate son,
"CHARLES HADDON SPURGEON."

"Newmarket,

"March 12th, 1850.

"My Dear Father,

"Many thanks to you for your kind, instructive, and unexpected letter... My very best love to dear Mother; I hope she will soon be better.

"At our last church-meeting, I was proposed. No one has been to see me yet. I hope that now I may be doubly circumspect, and doubly prayerful. How could a Christian live happily, or live at all, if he had not the assurance that his life is in Christ, and his support, the Lord's undertaking? I am sure I would not have dared to take this great decisive step were it not that I am assured that Omnipotence will be my support, and the Shepherd of Israel my constant Protector.

Prayer is to me now what the sucking of the milk was to me in my infancy. Alt-hough I do not always feel the same relish for it, yet I am sure I cannot live with-out it.

"'*When by sin overwhelm'd, shame covers my face,*
I look unto Jesus, who saves by His grace;
I call on His name from the gulf of despair,
And He plucks me from hell in answer to prayer.
Prayer, sweet prayer!
Be it ever so feeble, there's nothing like prayer.'

"Even the Slough of Despond can be passed by the supports of prayer and faith. Blessed be the name of the Lord, despondency has vanished, like a mist, before the Sun of righteousness, who has shone into my heart! 'Truly, God is good to

Israel.' In the blackest darkness, I resolved that, if I never had another ray of comfort, and even if I was everlastingly lost, yet I would love Jesus, and endeavor to run in the way of His commandments: from the time that I was enabled thus to resolve, all these clouds have fled. If they return, I fear not to meet them in the strength of the Beloved. One trial to me is that I have nothing to give up for Christ, nothing wherein to show my love to Him. What I *can* do, is *little;* and what I Do do, is less. The tempter says, 'You don't leave anything for Christ; you only follow Him to be saved by it. Where are your evidences?' Then I tell him that I have given up my self-righteousness, and he says, 'Yes, but not till you saw it was filthy rags!' All I have to answer is, that my sufficiency is not of myself.

("Thursday afternoon.)

"I have just now received a very nice note from my dear Mother.

Many thanks to you for the P.O. order. I do not know what money obligations are imposed upon members; I must do as you tell me.

(Here a piece of the letter has been cut out.)

"I am glad brother and sister are better. Again my best love to you all.

"I am,

"Dear Father,

"Your affectionate son,

"CHARLES."

"Newmarket,

"April 6th, 1850.

"My Dear Father,

"You will be pleased to hear that, last Thursday night, I was admitted as a member. Oh, that I may henceforth live more for the glory of Him, by whom I feel assured that I shall be everlastingly saved! Owing to my scruples on account of baptism, I did not sit down at the Lord's table, and cannot in conscience do so until I am baptized. To one who does not see the necessity of baptism, it is perfectly right and proper to partake of this blessed privilege; but were *I* to do so, I conceive would be to tumble over the wall, since I feel persuaded it is Christ's appointed way of professing Him. I am sure this is the only view which I have of baptism. I detest the idea that I can do a single thing towards my own salvation. I trust that I feel sufficiently the corruption of my own heart to know that, instead of doing one iota to forward my own salvation, my old corrupt heart would impede it, were it not that my Redeemer is mighty, and works as He pleases.

"Since last Thursday, I have been unwell in body, but I may say that my soul has been almost in Heaven. I have been able to see my title clear, and to know and believe that, sooner than one of God's little ones shall perish, God Himself will *cease to be,* Satan will conquer the King of kings, and Jesus will no longer be the Savior of the elect. Doubts and fears may soon assail me, but I will not dread to meet them if my Father has so ordained it; He knows best. Were I never to have another visit of grace, and be always doubting from now until the day of my death, yet 'the foundation of the Lord standeth sure, having this seal, the Lord knoweth them that are His.' I see now the secret, how it was that you were enabled to bear up under all your late trials. This faith is far more than any of us deserve; all beyond hell is mercy, but this is a mighty one. Were it not all of sovereign, electing, almighty grace, I, for one, could never hope to be saved. God says,

'*You shall,*' and not all the devils in hell, let loose upon a real Christian, can stop the workings of God's sovereign grace, for in due time the Christian cries, '*I will.*'

Oh, how little love have I for One who has thus promised to save me by so great a salvation, and who will certainly perform His promise!

"I trust that the Lord is working among my tract people, and blessing my little effort. I have had most interesting and encouraging conversation with many of them. Oh, that I could see but one sinner constrained to come to Jesus! How I long for the time when it may please God to make me, like you, my Father, a successful preacher of the gospel! I almost envy you your exalted privilege. May the dew of Hermon and the increase of the Spirit rest upon your labors! Your unworthy son tries to pray for you and his Mother, that grace and peace may be with you. Oh, that the God of mercy would incline Archer's heart to Him, and make him a partaker of His grace! Ask him if he will believe me when I say that one drop of the pleasure of religion is worth ten thousand oceans of the pleasures of the unconverted, and then ask him if he is not willing to prove the fact by experience. Give my love to my dear Mother....

"As Mr. Cantlow's baptizing season will come round this month, I have humbly to beg your consent, as I will not act against your will, and should very much like to commune next month. I have no doubt of your permission. We are all one in Christ Jesus; forms and ceremonies, I trust, will not make us divided...

"With my best love and hopes that you are all well,

"I remain,

"Your affectionate son,

"Not only as to the flesh, but in the faith,

"CHARLES HADDON SPURGEON."

"Newmarket,

"April 20th.

"My Dear Mother,

"I have every morning looked for a letter from Father, I long for an answer; it is now a month since I have had one from him. Do, if you please, send me either permission or refusal to be baptized; I have been kept in painful suspense. This is the 20th, and Mr. Cantlow's baptizing day is to be the latter end of the month; I think, next week. I should be so sorry to lose another Ordinance Sunday; and with my present convictions, I hope I shall never so violate my conscience as to sit down unbaptized. When requested, I assured the members at the church-meeting that I would never do so.

"I often think of you poor starving creatures, following Mr.____

for the bony rhetoric and oratory which he gives you. What a mercy that you are not dependent upon him for spiritual comfort! I hope you will soon give up following that empty cloud without rain, that type-and-shadow preacher, for I don't think there is much substance. But, my dear Mother, why do you not go and hear my friend, Mr. Langford? He is an open-communion Baptist, and I have no doubt will receive you without baptism. Perhaps his preaching may be blest to Archer, Eliza, and my sisters, as well as to myself; would it not be worth giving up a little difference of persuasion for? God can save whom He will, when He will, and where He will, but I think Mr.____'s Mount Sinai roarings are the last things to do it, to all human appearance.

91

"I think I might date this letter from a place in the Enchanted Ground, with the warm air of Beulah blowing upon me. One drop of the pleasures I have felt is worth a life of agony. I am afraid of becoming satisfied with this world.

"My very best love to yourself, dear Father, Eliza, Archer, Emily, Louisa, and Lottie. I hope you are well. I am very much better; thanks for the prescription; and with my love to you again,

"I remain,

"Dear Mother,

"Your affectionate son,

"CHARLES."

"*P.S.* — If baptized, it will be in an open river; go in just as I am, with some others... I trust the good confession before many witnesses will be a bond betwixt me and my Master, my Savior, and my King."

"Newmarket,

"May 1st, 1850.

"My Dear Mother,

"Many very happy returns of your Birthday! In this instance, my wish will certainly be realized, for in Heaven you are sure to have an eternity of happy days. May you, in your coming years, live beneath the sweet smiles of the God of peace; may joy and singing attend your footsteps to a blissful haven of rest and tranquillity!

Your birthday will now be doubly memorable, for on the third of May, the boy for whom you have so often prayed, the boy of hopes and fears, your firstborn, will join the visible Church of the redeemed on earth, and will bind himself doubly to the Lord his God, by open profession. You, my Mother, have been the great means in God's hand of rendering me what I hope I am. Your kind, warning Sabbath-evening addresses were too deeply settled on my heart to be forgotten. You, by God's blessing, prepared the way for the preached Word, and for that holy book, *The Rise and Progress.*

If I have any courage, if I feel prepared to follow my Savior, not only into the water, but should He call me, even into the fire, I love you as the preacher to my heart of such courage, as my praying, watching Mother. Impossible, I think it is, that I should ever cease to love you, or you to love me, yet not nearly so impossible as that the Lord our Father should cease to love either of us, be we ever so doubtful of it, or ever so disobedient. I hope you may one day have cause to rejoice, should you see me, the unworthy instrument of God, preaching to others, — yet have I vowed in the strength of my only Strength, in the name of my Beloved, to devote myself for ever to His cause. Do you not think it would be a bad beginning were I, knowing it to be my duty to be baptized, to shrink from it?

If you are now as happy as I am, I can wish no more than that you may continue so. I am the happiest creature, I think, upon this globe.

"I hope you have enjoyed your visit, and that it will help much to establish your health. I dare not ask you to write, for I know you are always so busy that it is quite a task to you. I hope my letter did not pain you, dear Mother; my best love to you, be assured that I would not do anything to grieve you, and I am sure that I remain,

"Your affectionate son,

"CHARLES HADDON."

"Mr. and Mrs. Swindell's respects to you and dear Father."

"Newmarket Academy,
"June 11th, 1850.

"My Dear Mother,

"Many thanks to you for your valuable letter. Your notes are so few and far between, and are such a trouble to you, that one now and then is quite a treasure.

"Truly, indeed, I have much for which to bless the Lord, when I contemplate His Divine Sovereignty, and see that my salvation is entirely of His free electing love. He has chosen me to be one of His vessels of mercy; and, despite all opposition from without and from within, He will surely accomplish His own work. I have more than sufficient to induce me to give up myself entirely to Him who has bought me and purchased me with an everlasting redemption. I am now enabled to rely upon His precious promises, and to feel that I am as safe, though not so holy, as the greatest saint in Heaven.

"I have had two opportunities of addressing the Sunday-school children, and have endeavored to do so as a dying being to dying beings. I am bound to Newmarket by holy bonds. I have 70 people whom I regularly visit on Saturday. I do not give a tract, and go away; but I sit down, and endeavor to draw their attention to spiritual realities. I have great reason to believe the Lord is working, — the people are so kind, and so pleased to see me. I cannot bear to leave them. We are so feeble here that the weakest cannot be spared. We have a pretty good attendance at prayer-meetings; but so few praying men, that I am constantly called upon...

"One of our Deacons, Mr.___, is constantly inviting me to his house he is rather an Arminian; but so are the majority of Newmarket Christians. Grandfather has written to me; he does not blame me for being a Baptist, but hopes I shall not be one of the tight-laced, strict-communion sort. In that, we are agreed. I certainly think we ought to forget such things in others when we come to the Lord's table. I can, and hope I shall be, charitable to unbaptized Christians, though I think they are mistaken. It is not a great matter; men will differ; we ought both to follow our own consciences, and let others do the same. I think the time would be better spent in talking upon vital godliness than in disputing about forms. I trust the Lord is weaning me daily from all self-dependence, and teaching me to look at myself as less than nothing.

I know that I am perfectly dead without Him; it is His work; I am confident that He will accomplish it, and that I shall see the face of my Beloved in His own house in glory.

"My enemies are many, and they hate me with cruel hatred, yet with Jehovah Jesus on my side, why should I fear? I will march on in His almighty strength to certain conquest and victory. I am so glad that Sarah, too, is called, that two of us in one household at one time should thus openly profess the Savior's name. We are brother and sister in the Lord; may our Father often give each of us the refreshing visits of His grace! I feel as if I could say with Paul,

'Would that I were even accursed, so that my brethren according to the flesh might be saved!' What a joy if God should prove that they are redeemed ones included in the covenant of grace! I long to see your face, and let my heart beat with yours, whilst we talk of the glorious things pertaining to eternal life. My best love to you and Father; may the Angel of the covenant dwell with you, and enchant you by the visions of His grace! Love to Eliza, Archer (many happy returns to him), Emily, Lottie, and Louisa; may they become members of the church in our house! I am very glad you are so well. I am so, but hard at work for the Examination, so allow me to remain,

"Your most affectionate son,

"CHARLES."

"Master H___ shall be attended to; be ye always ready for every good work. I have no time, but it shall be done."

Chapter Thirteen - Diary, April to June, 1850.

I have sometimes said, when I have become the prey of doubting thoughts, "Well, now, I dare not doubt whether there be a God, for I can look back in my Diary, and say, 'On such a day, in the depths of trouble, I bent my knee to God, and or ever I had risen from my knees, the answer was given me.'" — C. H. S.

INTRODUCTION, BY MRS. C. H. SPURGEON.

NOT very long after our marriage, my husband brought to me, one day, a small clasped book, and putting it into my hand with a grave and serious air, he said, "That book contains a record of some of my past spiritual experiences, wifie; take care of it, but I never want to see it again." He never did, and to me also it was a sealed book, for I did not dare to open it; and it has lain, unrevealed, for certainly forty years since the day I first saw it. But now, with reverent hands, I take it from its hiding-place, and, as I look upon the boyish handwriting, and begin to read the thoughts of my dear one's heart in the bygone years, I wonder whether I *can* undertake the duty of transcription, whether my eyes will see through the tears which must come, and my fingers will hold the pen without much trembling, and my heart, which loved him so well, will be able to thank God that the past *is past,* and the struggles and sorrows of earth are forever forgotten in the ecstasies of eternal glory. Lord, strengthen and help me!

The contents of the little book prove to be a continuous Diary of nearly three months' duration, commencing April 6th, 1850, and ending on June 20th in the same year. As its pages cover the season of baptism, and the young convert's first efforts in service for the Lord, it is full of deep interest and pathos to all who afterward knew and loved the great preacher. I feel that I am justified in at last revealing the long-kept secret of the book, for a perusal of its soul-confessions and holy resolutions can only redound to the glory of God, and show how He was leading His young servant by a way which he knew not. And I believe God would have me do this.

The words of the dear boy of sixteen are very touching when read in the light of his subsequent marvelous career. As the trunk and branches of the future tree may, in some cases, be seen faintly outlined in the fruit it bears, so we can here discern something of the form and beauty of the fair character which the Lord was preparing for a glorious service.

How marked is his *humility,* even though he must have felt within him the stirrings and throes of the wonderful powers which were afterwards developed. "Forgive me, Lord," he says, in one place, "if I have ever had high thoughts of myself," — so early did the Master implant the precious seeds of that rare grace of meekness, which adorned his after life. After each youthful effort at public exhortation, whether it be engaging in prayer, or addressing Sunday-school children, he seems to be surprised at his own success, and intensely anxious to be kept from pride and self-glory, again and again confessing his own utter weakness, and pleading for God-given strength. What deep foundations were laid in this chosen soul, upon what massive pillars of truth and doctrine did God construct the spiritual consciousness of the man who was to do so great a work in the world for his Master! He was truly a "building fitly framed together," and he grew into "a holy temple in the Lord," "a habitation of God through the Spirit."

So young in years, when he wrote these thoughts, yet so old in grace, and possessing an experience in spiritual matters richer and broader than most Christians attain to at an advanced age! How plainly revealed in these pages are the workings and teachings of the Divine Spirit, and how equally clear are the docility, and earnestness, and humility of the pupil! Many of the sentences in the Diary are strangely prophetic of his future position and work, — notably these two, — "Make me Thy faithful servant, O my God; may I honor Thee in my day and generation, and be consecrated for ever to Thy service!" And again, "Make me to be an eminent servant of Thine, and to be blessed with the power to serve Thee, like Thy great servant Paul!"

In these breathings, too, we see where the secret of his great strength lay.

He believed and trusted God absolutely, and his faith was honored in a Godlike fashion. Deeply realizing his own weakness, he rested with child-like and complete dependence on his Lord. And God carried him, as a father bears his little one in his arms; and God's Spirit dwelt in him, to teach him all things. His *whole heart* was given to God and His service, God's promises were verities to him; and as "He abideth faithful, He cannot deny Himself," it was with both hands that He heaped gifts and grace upon His dear servant until the time came to receive him into glory.

Perhaps, of greatest price among the precious things which this little book reveals, is the beloved author's personal and intense love to the Lord Jesus.

He lived in His embrace; like the apostle John, his head leaned on Jesu's bosom. The endearing terms used in the Diary, *and never discontinued,* were not empty words; they were the overflowings of the love of God shed abroad in his heart by the Holy Ghost. One of the last things he said to me at Mentone, before unconsciousness had sealed his dear lips, was this, *"O wifie, I have had such a blessed time with my Lord!" And it was always so, the Savior was as real to him as if his eyes could look upon Him, and it was his delight to dwell in the very presence of God, in his daily, hourly life.*

Full of a sweet pain has been the task I set myself to write out these details of my dear one's life for three short months; but if anyone shall be the gainer by it, through being drawn nearer to God, and having clearer views of Divine truth, I shall deem the pain a pleasure, and the sorrow will bring me joy.

Saved men and women date from the dawn of their true life; not from their first birthday, but from the day wherein they were born again. Their calendar has been altered and amended by a deed of Divine grace. — ***C. H. S.***

THE DIARY.
1850.

Born,
January 6, 1850.
Admitted to Fellowship,
April 4, 1850
Baptized,
May 3, 1850
Communed first,
May 5, 1850
Commenced as S. S. Teacher,
May 5, 1850
Joined Church at Cambridge,
Oct. 2, 1850

CONSECRATION.

O great and unsearchable God, who knowest my heart, and triest all my ways; with a humble dependence upon the support of Thy Holy Spirit, I yield up myself to Thee; as Thy own reasonable sacrifice, I return to Thee Thine own. I would be forever, unreservedly, perpetually Thine; whilst I am on earth, I would serve Thee; and may I enjoy Thee and praise Thee forever! Amen.

February 1, 1850.

CHARLES HADDON SPURGEON.
1850, — A BLESSED YEAR OF JUBILEE.

April 6. — I have had a blessed day of refreshing from the Lord, and from the glory of His face. Went round my Station District, and had a talk with several people. I trust the Lord is working here. Had some serious thoughts about baptism. "The Lord is my strength and my song; He also is become my salvation."

April 7. — Not well; the body bears the soul down. Heard Mr. S. from Genesis 22:8; could not take it into heart, headache would not let me.

Arminianism does not suit me now. If I were long to be so heavy as I now am, I could scarcely live. Evening, could not attend to the sermon; was happier without it. I feasted all the time on —

> *"When I soar to worlds unknown,*
> *See Thee on Thy judgment throne,*
> *Rock of Ages! cleft for me,*
> *I shall hide myself in Thee."*

Cannot think how Mr. S. could say that Esau, he trusted, was converted, when the Lord says, "Esau have I *hated*."

April 8. — Walked out after breakfast, never saw more plainly the sovereignty of God's will. He has called me; I feel sure that He will carry me to glory. Not well. O God of grace, take me home when Thou pleasest!

It is, "Mercy, mercy, mercy," from first to last.

April 9. — Happy again today; if such days continue, earth and Heaven will be but one; — but what have I written? I know I have sinned this day; in Heaven, I cannot. Oh, to be holy, to be like God! I trust I shall be one day. O glorious hour, O blest abode, when I am near, and like my God.

Jesus, how can I e'er forget Thee, Thou life of my delights? Hold Thou me by Thy free Spirit, and pour down upon me more love to Thee! Can hardly pray, yet, O my God, remember A____! Oh, that I could do more for God! "By grace ye are saved."

April 10. — Much better in health. All more than hell, is mercy. How small is my sphere, yet what a great Being condescended to fix my state before I had a being! All things are ordered by God. Blessed be His name, though He slay me, yet will I trust in Him. Sin is all cleansed by Jesu's blood.

Doubts and fears will soon come. "Desire of my soul," prepare me to meet them. The Lord's presence has not departed yet; had I the tongue of an archangel, I could not praise Him enough for this. I hope all is well at home with my dear mother; I must expect the cross soon. "He that taketh not his cross, and followeth after Me, is not worthy of Me."

April 11. — Have had sweet thoughts upon, "I am the good Shepherd, and know My sheep, and am known of Mine." How can one of His sheep be lost if He knows all His own?

I have read today of the iniquities of some in high places. Father, forgive them, and grant that Thy name may not be blasphemed through them! O my Beloved, sooner may I perish everlastingly than thus dishonor Thee, Thou sole desire of my heart! Heard Mr. S. from Psalm 68:18-20. I love to hear him give all the honor of our salvation to God. Shepherd of Israel, guide Thy flock into all truth! Quicken me, and make me love Thee more and more!

April 12. — Earthly things have engaged too much of my thoughts this day. I have not been able to fix my attention entirely upon my Savior. Yet, even yet, the Lord has not hidden His face from me. Though tempted, I am not cast down; tried, but not overcome; truly it is of the Lord's sovereign mercy. I would desire again this day to make a fresh application to the sin-atoning blood of Jesus to cleanse away my sins. O God, do Thou keep me down, and then I need fear no fall! O visit Zion, and preserve Thy Church; let her yet shine forth in glory! April showers have been coming down today; the Lord does not forget His promises. Jesus took my heart: "or ever I was aware, my soul made me like the chariots of Ammi-nadib." "Tell me, O Thou whom my soul loveth, where Thou feedest, where Thou makest Thy flock to rest at noon;" I would be ever with Thee, O my spotless, fairest Beloved! Daily meet me, for Thy embrace is Heaven; sanctify me, prepare me, help me to bring forth fruit, and to be Thine forever!

April 13. — Did not feel so tired at the end of this week; one reason is, that every day has been Sunday with me. Blessed be the Shepherd, I walk now beside the still waters. What events are transpiring in the world!

Things are quite at a crisis in the Church of England. I love my little work; Lord, be with me! "O the depth of the riches both of the wisdom and knowledge of God!" Trust in Him, my soul; follow hard after Him.

April 14. — Heard Mr. S., this morning, from 3 John 4, — the great subject of justification by faith. Who could dare to hope of going to Heaven, if works are the price? I could not; it would be like offering me a possession in the sun, if I could jump up to it, and take it in my hand!

Afternoon, — some of last Sunday over again. Esau does not give us a very interesting sermon. Evening subject was, Decision. I am quite encouraged. Hope I shall soon have an answer from home upon baptism.

"Through floods and flames, if Jesus lead,
I'll follow where He goes."

I would not desert Him in any one point, but keep close to Him.

April 15. — Quite well today, and tolerably happy. First day of the races. O God, Thou makest me to differ! Had a nice prayer-meeting. "Also unto Thee, O Lord, belongeth mercy." What else have I to trust to? Mr. P. came in this evening, and talked till past eleven, so that I lost some of the time I should have spent in devotion.

"What various hindrances we meet
In coming to a mercy-seat!
Yet who that knows the worth of prayer,
But wishes to be often there?"

April 16. — This evening, the friends at the Hythe will be assembled. Grant Thy gracious blessing! Read of the land Beulah. I have been there, and that, too, before coming to Giant Despair. Comfort we must not always have, or I am afraid I should go to sleep. I am now getting drowsy in spirit.

Strong Deliverer, keep my eyes open! My soul seems to long after the flesh-pots of Egypt, and that after eating Heavenly manna; help and forgive me, O my Savior!

April 17. — Read some of "Fuller upon Antinomianism." My God, what a gulf is near me! I think I can say that I hate this religion; I would desire to love God, and to be as holy as my Father-God Himself. There is a little cloud betwixt me and my Sun of righteousness, but I doubt not that He still shines upon me. He has not left me. I am a living miracle, a walking wonder of grace that I am alive at all; much more, following on. May I from this time live nearer to Him, and honor His name more!

April 18. — I trust the cloud has burst. I have seen some few gleams of sunshine today. I will walk on in His strength, whether it be through clouds or not. Went to chapel, very few there. I have been enabled to renew my strength; may I now run in the ways of the Lord! I begin to wonder why father has not written; he has good reason, no doubt. Lord, strengthen Thy people, and revive Thy Church by Thine enlivening grace!

April 19. — I do not live near enough to God. I have to lament my coldness and indifference in the ways of the Lord. O God of restoring grace, visit Thy servant in the midst of the days! I will trust Him, I cannot doubt His power or His love.

"Yes, I love Thee and adore,
O for grace to love Thee more!"

I shall yet have another visit, and see again His smiling face. "Whatsoever ye shall ask the Father in My name, He will give it you."

April 20. — Went round with my tracts; could not feel the Spirit of the Lord upon me. I seemed to have a clog upon my feet and my tongue. I have richly deserved this, for I have not prayed, or studied my Bible as I ought. I confess mine iniquity, and my sin is ever before me. Mercy! it is all mercy! Wash me anew, O Savior, in Thy sin-atoning blood!

"Firm as the earth Thy gospel stands,
My Lord, my hope, my trust."

I cannot perish if God protects me. I can do nothing. Weak and sinful worm am I.

April 21. — This morning, Mr. S. preached from 2 Thessalonians 3:3. This is the great hope of a Christian, the main comfort of my life, — the Lord will do it. Afternoon, Matthew 9:22. Here again it is the Savior's working; earthly physicians could not do it. Blessed art Thou, O God, for this great salvation! Evening, 3 John 4. I am not very much interested with these twice-preached sermons. On the whole, I have enjoyed much this day; — little have I deserved it, nay, not at all. No merit in me, I am sure; vilest of the vile, for so long shutting mine eyes to this great salvation and glorious state of God's people.

April 22. — The Lord has not forsaken me. Went this evening to the prayer-meeting; engaged in prayer. Why should I fear to speak of my only Friend? I shall not be timid another time, I hope the Lord has helped me in this; He will in other things. The spirit is more brisk today, more soaring, and more enchanted with that Savior who is the life of all my joy. Faith is the precious gift of God, and love is His gift; it is all of God from first to last.

April 23. — My prayer is in some measure answered; I trust the work has again revived. No desert is there in me; 'tis all of mercy, I must acknowledge. I feel that I am dependent on the Lord for all, for growing grace, and for living grace. I have my daily supply, and sure enough, I do not have two days' portion at a time. 'Tis a mercy to feel one's own dependence, and to be able to trust the Lord for all. Sing, O my soul, sing, for the Lord has redeemed thee, thou art safe!

April 24. — Letter from Mr. Cantlow. Baptism on Thursday week. God help me to live worthy of Him, and that my open confession of Him may make me more diligent! Letter from Mr. Leeding better than I had thought.

Truly, O Lord, my lot is in pleasant places, and I have a goodly heritage. I am to do as I please about baptism. Never do I lose anything by zeal for the truth, and close walk with my Savior; rather, I gain everything. Lord, Thou art my life; guide me, and allot my portion on this earth according to Thine own wisdom and love!

April 25. — Went to Burwell. Heard the examination of the children.

Education is indeed a talent from the Lord. What a weight of responsibility rests upon me! I trust I shall one day employ this more to His honor. A letter from father; in truth, he is rather hard upon me. When I followed my conscience, and did not presumptuously break through the fences of the Lord about His Church, I might have expected this. My business is to follow my Savior, and not to

99

pick out smooth paths for myself. If in any measure I have walked worthily, I would desire to give all the glory to the great Author of my salvation. I now feel so bold that, if the devil were to reproach me, I could answer him. Lord, I would ascribe it all to Thee, that I have not yet turned back, and that no enemies have yet made me to quail with terror! Onward may I press, with Heaven itself in view, trusting my salvation entirely in the hands of my Jesus, my lifts, my all in all!

April 26. — How my father's fears lest I should *trust* to baptism stir up my soul! My God, Thou knowest that I hate such a thought! No, I know that, could I from this day be as holy as God Himself, yet I could not atone for past sin. I have had a pretty good day. Fear, Mistrust, and Timorous are yet at sword's length. May I be Valiant-for-Truth, and live and die in my Master's glorious war!

April 27. — Fear, begone! Doubts, fall back! In the name of the Lord of hosts I would set up my banner. Come on, ye demons of the pit, my Captain is more than a match for you; in His name, armed with His weapons, and in His strength, I dare defy you all. How glorious 'twould be to die by the side of such a Leader! I am a worm, and no man, a vanity, a nothing; yet hath He set His love upon me, and why should I tremble or fear? I have been round with my tracts; may the good seed prosper, and take root! I have again to lament that I do not live so near to God as I ought. Blessed be the name of the Lord for that measure of grace which He has given me; I can trust Him for the rest.

April 28. — Mr. S. addressed us both morning and evening from John 1:5.

I could not fix upon the subject, so as to see the train of his thought.

Afternoon, how I did rejoice when I brought a man to chapel, and a boy to the Sunday-school! It is the Lord! By this encouragement, in Thy strength, I pledge myself to live yet more for Thee, to fight more constantly, and to work harder. Hold Thou me up! Support me, for I can do nothing. The Lord has been with me today, though my heart has not been in such transports as heretofore. I will follow through shade as well as sunshine.

Savior, dwell with me; Thine I am, help me to serve Thee, and adore Thee, world without end!

April 29. — Went to prayer-meeting. Thought upon Matthew 8:20. When I have the presence of the Lord, nothing is a hardship to me. I would love to lodge with my Master, and to endure all things for Him. Let not my first love chill. I have no fire within to keep it alight, Thou alone canst do this, my Lord and my God. I would anew devote myself to Thee, and glory only in Thy cross, and in Thy shame.

April 30. — Another month has passed, time rolls away, I am nearer home.

This month has brought me much holy enjoyment, much privilege; how little I have done when compared with what Jesus has done for me! What a slothful servant am I of so good a Master! Roll on, ye months; bring joy or sorrow as ye will, if God be with me, all is mine! How much like Vanity Fair is this place (Newmarket)! It is crowded with visitors; I saw two engines required to take them to London. Lord, give me strength, like the engine, to go straight on, guided by Thee, my great Conductor!

May 1. — Another month now dawns upon me. I have lived through one, I will bless the Lord for it, and trust Him for this also. Help me to live more to Thy glory, and to honor Thee in my daily walk and conversation. The time of my baptism approaches. May I die to the world, and live alone for Thee! I would serve Thee, O Lord; but I feel a weight, a law working against this law, and holding me in partial bondage; let Thy grace break every fetter that withholds my heart from Thee!

May 2. — Went to the lecture, very few there, not enough for a church-meeting. Lord, revive Thy Church in Newmarket! A far happier day than I deserve, I have been able to soar a little, and see the Canaan which I desire,

— though with a feeble eye. Tomorrow will be a solemn day. I have been enabled more than usual to pour out my heart in prayer. I need support now, and I feel that I shall have it. How safe are all God's people! not one of the least of them can be lost, the oath and promise of the Lord cannot be broken. 'Tis a sin to think that God, a God of truth, will ever desert His people; it is a shame, a blasphemy. "Fear thou not, for I am with thee; be not dismayed, for I am thy God." "I will never leave thee, nor forsake thee."

May 3. — My mother's birthday. May the sun of heaven shine upon her, and revive her, even as it has done upon the natural world this day! Started with Mr. Cantlow at eleven, reached Isleham at one o'clock. In the afternoon, I was privileged to follow my Lord, and to be buried with Him in baptism. Blest pool! Sweet emblem of my death to all the world! May I, henceforward, live alone for Jesus! Accept my body and soul as a poor sacrifice, tie me unto Thee; in Thy strength I now devote myself to Thy service forever; never may I shrink from owning Thy name!

"Witness, ye men and angels now,
If I forsake the Lord!"

I vow to glory alone in Jesus and His cross, and to spend my life in the extension of His cause, in whatsoever way He pleases. I desire to be sincere in this solemn profession, having but one object in view, and that to glorify God. Blessing upon Thy name that Thou hast supported me through the day; it is Thy strength alone that could do this. Thou hast, —

Thou wilt. Thou hast enabled me to profess Thee, help me now to honor Thee, and carry out my profession, and live the life of Christ on earth!

May 4. — Reached Newmarket at 9; feel high in spirit, have been round with my tracts; help me to serve Thee, O my Lord! There is a report in the church that Mr. S. and I have been on the heath. Mr. A. told me of it very gruffly. Mr. H. will not commune because so many have been to the races.

My Master knows, I have no need to tell Him I am innocent. Though I be cast out and rejected of the disciples, the Lord will not cast off one of His chosen. I can, in this respect, wash my hands in innocency.

May 5. — A third, but very strong sermon, from John 1:5. How ought the people of God to be a peculiar people, zealous for good works! Lord, help me to honor Thee! This afternoon, partook of the Lord's supper; a royal feast for me, worthy of a King's son. Mr. S. addressed me before all the people. Sunday-school for the first time, and went visiting the people with friend M. I quite like my new work. Teachers' prayer-meeting after evening service, from 8 to 9; five of us engaged in prayer. Went to Mr. B.'s to supper, talked with young C., stopped to family prayer, past 10 o'clock! I have been too excited today, amidst the busy whirl of constant action, to feel myself so solid as I could wish. Rock of Ages, bind me to Thyself! I can feel the bad law working yet. All is of God, He will perform His promise.

> *"His honor is engaged to save*
> *The meanest of His sheep."*

May 6. — Went to prayer-meeting. Missionary meeting in the afternoon, upon the glory of Christ's kingdom. "He must reign." Savior, come and extend Thy kingdom over all the world, sway Thy scepter over all hearts!

Make me Thy temple, and honor me by making me an instrument of good in Thy hands! Lord, save me from pride and from sloth, my two great enemies; keep me, oh, keep and preserve me! I am an erring sheep. It is in Thy power that I trust, upon Thy strength I rely; I am less than nothing, hold me by Thine own right hand!

May 7. — I have again to confess my lukewarmness; I fear I am losing my first love. Coldness and deadness seem to be natural to me; I have no inward warmth, it all comes from the Sun of righteousness, by rich, free, and sovereign grace. What a mercy that I have not been altogether frozen to death, and left to perish in my sinful distance from God! Lord, help me to follow Thee, and may Thy right hand uphold me! Strength, O Lord, I need! I would not fear, but trust in Thine omnipotence.

May 8. — Teachers' business meeting. Too much joking and levity to agree with my notions of what a Sunday-school teacher should be. Lord, keep me from the evil of the world, let me not be led away; but if these are Thy people, help me to serve Thee better than they, and to be more like my Master! O my God, keep me ever near to Thee, help me to live more to Thy glory, and to honor Thee more than I have hitherto done, to live alone for Thee, and to spend and be spent in Thy service! Preserve, perfect, keep, and bless me!

> *"Keep me, oh, keep me, King of kings,*
> *Beneath Thine own almighty wings!"*

May 9. — Prayer-meeting. Mr. S. has resigned. Well, we have a better Pastor, who cannot, who will not leave us. Truly, I have sunk very low; my lamp seems going out in obscurity. Lord, fan it, keep it burning yet! I know that I can never perish; yet be pleased, my God, to visit me again, to revive and uphold me, so that I may honor Thee more; make me to be an eminent servant of Thine, and to be blessed with the power to serve Thee, like Thy great servant Paul!

May 10. — Blessed be the name of the Lord, He has not left His servant, or turned away from His chosen! Though I have often sinned, and neglected the sweet privilege of prayer, yet He hath not deserted me. Had a letter from Mr. L. I hope that the Lord will bless him, and give him many souls as seals for his hire. I wonder how they are at home. Time flies away.

Seasons come and go. Lord, grant me Thy Holy Spirit to enable me to improve each moment! I am "bought with a price."

May 11. — Went round my district. I trust the Lord is moving upon the face of this people. It is Thy work, O Lord; accomplish it! I feel encouraged to go on in the ways of the Lord, and still to spend my spare time in His service. Prosper Thou the work of my hands! My own soul is encouraged, my life is revived, and I hope soon to enjoy the presence of the Lord.

May 12. — One of the days of the Son of man, — happy day when Sabbath shall never end! Went to Sunday-school at 9, stayed till service at 10:30, out at 12:15; Sunday-school at 1:45, service 3 till 4, visiting till 5.

The day has thus been closely occupied. The morning's discourse was upon 1 Corinthians 4:7. Truly, I have nothing which I have not received; I can boast of no inherent righteousness. Had the Lord not chosen me, I should not have chosen Him. Grace! Grace! Grace! 'Tis all of grace. I can do nothing, I am less than nothing; yet what a difference, — once a slave of hell, now the son of the God of Heaven! Help me to walk worthy of my lofty and exalted vocation! Afternoon, Psalm 48:14, "This God is *my* God for ever and ever; HE WILL be *my* Guide even unto death." I can wish for no better Guide, or more lasting Friend; He shall lead me in His own way.

Lord, permit me not to choose the road, allow me not to wander into By-path meadow; rather carry me straight to glory! Evening, Acts 17:11. The Word of God is my chart. Lord, give me more of Berean nobility; grant me Thy grace to search the Scriptures, and to become wise unto life eternal!

Thine is the gift, I cannot do it without Thee. Again would I give myself anew to Thee; bind Thou the sacrifice with cords, even to the horns of Thine altar! Let me not go away from Thee; hold me firmly in Thy gracious arms! Let Thine omnipotence be my protection, Thy wisdom my direction, Thy grace my salvation. "Lord, I believe; help Thou mine unbelief!"

May 13. — A day of great, unmerited mercy. Happiness cannot exist here without some cloy. How sweet the joys of religion, of communion with God! Letter from home. All well. I thank Thee, Father, for such good tidings; bless me, even me also, O my Father! I would devote myself to Thee; it is my highest privilege to be able to give myself to Thee. Thy service is the greatest pleasure, the most untiring delight; I would, more than ever, wear Thy livery, be known as Thy servant, and become one of Thy peculiar people.

May 14. — In the evening, enjoyed an ecstasy of delight. I seemed transported, and able to fly beyond the bounds of this poor atom of an earth. Spiritual realities were present to view, while the flesh, like Abraham's servant, tarried at the foot of the mountain. How much do I owe; how little good do I deserve, yea, none at all!

"Let Thy grace, Lord, like a fetter,
Bind my wandering heart to Thee!"

Blessed be Thy name forevermore! Bless the Lord, O my soul; follow hard after Him, love and serve Him!

May 15. — How feeble I am! I am not able to keep myself near to God. I am compelled to acknowledge my own deadness. I confess how greatly I have strayed from Thee, Thou great Fountain of living waters; but, —

"Since I've not forgot Thy law,
Restore Thy wandering sheep."

Revive me in the midst of the years, and make Thy face to shine upon me!

How much do I deserve eternal damnation! But salvation is not of desert, but of free grace. This is the plank whereon I hope to float to glory, when this world shall be a wreck, and perish in the vast abyss.

May 16. — Went to chapel. Sermon on Psalm 23:3. How much do I need this restoration! If the Lord does not do it, I cannot. "Turn out Thine enemy and mine." I would be passive, submitting to Thy sovereign will; Thou wilt do what is right. Lord, keep me; I will wait Thy time of revival; teach me both to work and wait, expecting and hoping that Thou wilt soon come, and restore unto me the joy of Thy salvation! I am in a low condition, yet I am eternally safe. He will lead me.

May 17. — It is now a fortnight since my baptism. How solemnly have I devoted myself to Thee! I would now repeat my vows, and again solemnly devote myself to Thee.

"Witness, ye men and angels now,
If I forsake the Lord."

In His strength I can do all things. Thou hast sworn to save, and death and hell cannot thwart Thine everlasting purpose. Hold me! Thou hast blessed me, Thou alone canst do it. If Thou dost not save, I must perish. Thou wilt not leave me, Thou hast showed me a portion of the glory of Thy face.

May 18. — Station District. When I first set out, I was all but dumb concerning spiritual things. Soon I felt the working of the Lord in some degree. Blessed be His holy name forever and ever, and let all the redeemed say, Amen! His is the power. Beloved, Thine is enduring beauty!

Thou art glorious to behold. Give me more of the entrancing visions of Thy face, the looks of Thy love, and more constant communion with Thee!

Lord, move Thou upon the earth, and bring in Thine elect from among the condemned sinners of the world!

May 19. — Went to the Sunday-school. Mr. S. preached, this morning, from 2 Corinthians 3:6-8. How glorious is the ministration of life, how beautiful the tables of stone, when enclosed in the blessed ark of the covenant! Afternoon, Ezekiel 36:27. Evening, "What is truth?" As to interest, the sermons today have been a failure. Addressed the children upon Prayer. Went visiting with Mr. M., six fresh children. Evening at Mr. B.'s. Engaged in prayer at his family altar. Today has been a sunny day with me. The Lord has visited me from on high. Rejoice, O my soul, leap for joy, renew thy strength; run, run, in the name of the Lord! He is with me, He has been with me. Weakness He has made strength! Mighty to save, Thou shalt have all my noblest songs! Let Thy grace constrain me to love Thee, and live for Thee! I am buried with my Lord and Savior; may I be crucified to the world, and die daily! How sure is it that Thy yoke is easy, and Thy burden is light! I can do all things through Christ Jesus.

May 20. — Went to the prayer-meeting, and engaged in prayer. How inexhaustible is the source from whence my life proceeds! How boundless the store from whence my provision comes! I must be saved, for Omnipotence has undertaken it. Another glorious day, another visit of His reviving grace, blessed be the name of the Lord! The service of the Lord were a happy service, even if such enjoyment as this was the only reward.

How sweet are the visits of His grace, sweeter than honey and the honeycomb!

May 21. — Glorious day, happy were all like this! Oh, the safety of a Christian, as sure, but not so blest, as any saint in Heaven! Lord, how can I leave Thee? To whom, or whither should I go? Thou center of my love, all glorious names in one, Thou brightest, sweetest, fairest One, that eyes have seen or angels known, I trust to Thee for salvation; without Thee, I can do nothing. I am utter weakness, Thou must do it all, or I shall perish! Love of loves, all love excelling, fix my wandering heart on Thee!

May 22. — My weakness is my greatest strength, for then I trust alone on Jesus, when I feel my own dependence. I am an earthen vessel, I have been among the pots of the unregenerate; make me now a vessel for Thy use!

Thy blood is my trust, I am washed; who shall now blacken me so as not to leave me spotless at the last? Joy, joy unspeakable, rapture divine, I fly beyond the bounds of earth, my Husband folds me in His arms, I am His, and He is mine, my glorious Prince, Redeemer, Love!

May 23. — Went to chapel, very few there. "He restoreth my soul." The same subject again! How true is this, how has He revived me! Short, but glorious, are the days of my refreshing, — worthy of years of sorrow and distress. O my Beloved, did my way lie over the embers of hell all my life, didst Thou but show Thyself, I would rush through the fire to meet Thee! I have not been quite so ecstatic as for some days past. I am the Lord's forever, how much do I owe to Him! My Advocate, brother, Husband, let not my first love chill and grow cold! Keep me and preserve in Thy hands!

May 24. — A day of undeserved joy. I am not altogether banished from the presence of the Lord. Though He slay me, I cannot but trust Him, since I have had such tokens of His love. Lord, when in darkness and distress, when my head is bowed down, then return unto Thy servant to encourage and support him! Forever, oh, forever, lashed to the Ark, and safe from the floods, I shall get at last upon the *terra firma* of glory! Oh, let me not dishonor Thee! Never may I bring a disgrace upon the cause of Christ!

Keep me, and I shall be infinitely safe, and rest securely.

May 25. — Free grace, sovereign love, eternal security are my safeguards; what shall keep me from consecrating all to Thee, even to the last drop of my blood? Went to my district with tracts, a woman gave me 24 new ones.

I fear Mr. T. is doing much harm by telling the people that the Lord's supper will save them. Work, Lord, work! Thou hast encouraged me; may I not be disappointed! "Bless the Lord, O my soul." The Covenant is my trust, the agreement signed between my Elder brother and the Almighty standeth sure. "None shall pluck them out of My hand."

May 26. — Went round for the children. Sunday-school in the morning.

Mr. S. preached from, "All these things are against me." Stayed in the chapel the dinner-time, had a sweet season of prayer and communion with God. Afternoon,

Jacob's consecration of himself at Bethel. I would give myself in the same manner to Thee, my best-loved King. Evening subject, Paul's great labors. Oh, could I emulate such a man, I should be the greatest on this earth!

May 27. — Life of my soul, forgive me when I am so blind as to look upon an earthly object, and forget Thine own Divine beauties! Oh, for a love as strong as death, fierce as hell, and lasting as eternity!

May 28. — Thou hast hedged me about with thorns so that I cannot get out; this is my comfort. What name can I devise for Thee, O Beloved, equal to Thy desert? All beauties joined in one perfection, "Thou art all fair, my Love, there is no spot in Thee." Thou didst die for me, and shall not I live for Thee? What a love is that of Jesus to me, surpassing knowledge! I can do nothing in return, but give Thee my worthless self.

What! shall I dare to doubt Thy love? Can I conceive that Thou wilt leave me? Yes, I may sin so as to distrust Thee; but Thou wilt never let me go.

No thief can steal away Thy precious purchase; never, never, can I be lost.

Redeemed and purchased; then, how can I be snatched away? How is my soul a battlefield between the corruptions of nature and the principle of grace! They tear up the earth of my soul with the trampling of their armies; but I cannot be destroyed.

May 29. — To the Lord belongeth strength, He has given me my portion.

He putteth His treasure in earthen vessels. How happy am I to be one of His chosen, His elect, in whom His soul delighteth! But I do not live up to my Heavenly calling; I could not at all without the Lord, He has helped, —

He will help, — this is my comfort. His everlasting promises are my rest, my bread, my support. Make me Thy faithful servant, O my God; may I honor Thee in my day and generation, and be consecrated forever to Thy service!

May 30. — The stormy commotion has somewhat passed away; the sun is still shining, though a cloud may pass between. I desire more constant communion with God. Went to church-meeting, had some nice cheering conversation with old Mrs. A. Two candidates proposed; we shall have no Ordinance next Sunday. The Lord can and will feed us without it. He has kept me, and He will. The strife in my soul is now hushed, peace returns as a river upon the dry places.

May 31. — Weakness am I in every point, I cannot keep myself in the least. Forgive me that I have tried it! I would now come, naked, stripped, exhausted, dead. I would cry, "Lash me tighter, firmer, to Thy free-grace raft of life!" Mercy is all I ask for, — continued mercy. Those whom He once loves, He loves to the end; He has once loved me, I am now secure.

May the live coal within be shown to the world by the burning flames of love to Thee! May that love burn up the stubble and sin!

June 1. — A new month; time soon glides away. How much more ought I to do this month than last! Desire of my heart, keep me nearer to Thy bosom this month! Went to South District. Talked with a woman who says there are contradictions in the Bible. Some good may be doing. He that can work, will work; and who shall hinder Him? In the Lord's time it shall be accomplished; His time is best. Arise, O Sun of righteousness, why should this people lie in darkness?

June 2. — Heard Mr. J. the first part of the day. Numbers 21:4.

Interesting, but rather too weak. Afternoon, Revelation 19:12. Many crowns indeed does my Lord deserve; crowns of glory shall be around His sacred, blessed head. Evening, 1 John 5:4. Strong meat; the Lord has sent the manna down this evening. "Overcometh the world!" Glorious victory, amazing conquest, triumph Divine; and shall I, with such a promise, dare to doubt the power of God to keep, and guide, and preserve me?

Had a large class at Sunday-school, gave an address upon Death, — the dreadful sword hanging by a single hair above the head of the ungodly.

Had tea at Mr. B's, and combated with him for what I consider "the form of sound words." Prayer-meeting after evening service. Seven present, six of us engaged in prayer. Bless the Sunday-school, great King! honor thy Master, O my soul; live *for* Him, live *in* Him! I am a prince; ought I not to be a good soldier, and fight for my Lord? Give me, lend me a sword, O

God, and strength to wield it; let my foes and Thine be as furious as lions, Thy sword shall destroy them!

June 3. — Prayer-meeting, engaged in prayer. Lord, when shall Thy set time to favor Zion come? When shall Thine elect be gathered in? "Who shall separate us from the love of Christ?" Forever, yes, forever, safe.

Rejoice, rejoice, O my soul, and let thy joy constrain thee to work more earnestly and more zealously for Him! Redeemed and purchased, I am not my own. Letter from grandfather. How glad I am he does not differ!

June 4. — I have had evidence this day of the changeableness of all mortal things. How little does it matter to me, so that my eternal inheritance is secure! Lord, help me now to mount my watch-tower against pride and sloth! Keep me always upon the look-out, lest an enemy should come unawares; forgive me, if I have ever had high thoughts of myself! Thou makest me to feel my weakness in every part; may I now trust and rely upon the arm of Omnipotence, the mercies of the Lord! Give strength, Lord, strength!

June 5. — Awake, my soul, record the mercies of the Lord!

> **"He justly claims a song from me,**
> **His lovingkindness, O how free!"**

Mercy, I breathe Another's air, I am a tenant of this earth at my Master's will; sovereign grace has kept me hitherto, upon sovereign grace I now rely. What sweet moments have I had in answer to prayer; blessed be the Lord for His rich mercy thus bestowed upon me! I would now live in close communion with my King, and feast upon the riches of His love.

June 6. — Prayer-meeting. Mr. S. spoke to us upon the Babylonian Captivity. Teachers' meeting after the service. What a want of spirituality and vital godliness! O Lord, give me *life;* increase the vital spark, fan it to a flame! I can never perish, yet would I keep upon my watch-tower, for my enemies are many, and they hate me with cruel hatred. Help me to hate sin, and pride and sloth! I live only as Thou givest me life. I have not one atom of life of my own, I must perish if Thou desert me for one moment.

June 7. — How manifold are Thy mercies toward me, O Lord! When I think of the great salvation which has been worked out for me, and remember that Heaven is secure, it seems too good to be true. Yet do I now believe Thy promise; may I now be entirely Thine, Thy glory my only aim! Could I but be like Paul, how honored should I be! Happy is the man whom Thou teachest, O Lord! I am happy; how can I be otherwise, since my Beloved has looked upon me, and I have seen His glorious face?

June 8. — Could not burn with zeal as oft I have done. When, Lord, wilt Thou arise, and let Thy power be known and felt? How sweet to flap my wings to Heaven, with others following me; then lay my crown beneath His feet, and call Him Lord of all! He is deserving of all honor and praise; dominion and power are His due, and He shall have them. Many honors on His ever-blessed head! Worthy is the Lamb who has died for me. All glorious is my Beloved.

June 9. — Mr. S. preached. Acts 16:19. Did not hear to profit. Afternoon, "Who is this that cometh up from the wilderness, leaning upon her Beloved?" Did not hear enough about *the Beloved.* Evening, "Prepare to meet Thy God." Oh, what a mercy to be prepared!

> *"So whene'er the signal's given,*
> *Us from earth to call away,*
> *Borne on angels' wings to Heaven,*
> *Glad the summons to obey,*
> *We shall surely*
> *Reign with Christ in endless day!"*

Felt rather hurt by Mr. C., he does not act quite rightly; but I hereby forgive him. I desire to look alone to Jesus, and regard His glory only. I am too proud, I am weak in every point; keep me, for I have no strength! I would look up to Thee, — the Strong, — for strength. I am Thine, keep me!

June 10. — Letter from dear mother. Mr. S. made her his text at the prayer-meeting. Engaged in prayer. Have not been able to be much in private prayer today. The joy of my Lord, however, is not gone. I can yet trust in the God of my salvation. If I ever forget Thee, let my right hand forget her fellow. What! has He done so much for me, and shall I ever leave Him? No, —

> *"While a breath, a pulse remains,*
> *I will remember Thee!"*

June 11. — Prayer seems like labor to me, the chariot wheels drag heavily; yet they are not taken off. I will still rely upon almighty strength; and, helpless, throw myself into the arms of my Redeemer. "Leave, ah, leave me not alone!" "I will never leave Thee." I shall yet walk the golden street of the New Jerusalem, I shall yet see His beauteous face. He loved me before the foundations of the earth, before I was created or called by grace.

June 12. — The Lord is my Helper, He shall plead my cause. I would desire to record the gratitude I feel for the sparing mercies of the Lord, but especially for His great grace in electing me, by the sovereign councils of His love, to be one of His redeemed ones. What! shall I not live for Him, shall I keep back a single particle of my heart, and of myself, from my charming Redeemer, my King, Husband, brother, Friend? No; oh, give me strength to say, "I will never dishonor Thee"!

June 13. — Dangers are around me, Satan stands in the way; I have no hope but in the Lord, no safety but in keeping straight on in the Heavenly road. In the Lord Jehovah is everlasting strength, and inexhaustible mines of eternal love are mine; the Lord reserves them for His chosen people.

Went to prayer-meeting. Tried to address my Lord in prayer. Come, my Beloved, Thou art ever mine; leave me not, O do not forsake me, my King, my Savior! Saved everlastingly!

June 14. — Examination. Mr. M. gave me 10s. for the Missionary Society.

I would thank the Lord for thus opening his hand to do good. Gave a Missionary speech. Lord, keep Thy servant low and humble at Thy feet!

How prone am I to pride and vain-glory! Keep me always mindful that I have nothing which I have not received; 'tis grace, free, sovereign grace that has made me to differ. Why should I be chosen an elect vessel? Not that I deserve it, I am sure; but it is rich love.

June 15. — Went round my S. District, and divided my stock amongst the people, and now, Lord, I desire to commend them to Thy keeping; look upon them with pity, let them not be as sheep without a shepherd! Let Thy work go on and prosper among this people! I can do nothing; how is it that I have lived so long in my spiritual life? It is by sovereign power I stand, by Omnipotence I shall be supported. "My grace is sufficient for thee." I trust in Him; He will perfect His own work.

June 16. — Old Mr. W. preached; could not hear him, he spoke so low.

Was set upon by him and Mr. S. Lord, help me to take firm hold of the truth, and never yield an inch! Addressed the Sunday-school children. Oh, may I be kept humble! Pride dwells in my heart. I am now to leave Newmarket; perhaps, forever. What a scene of changes is this world! How blest to have a house above the skies, eternal in the Heavens!

June 17. — Left Newmarket at 6. Reached Stambourne about 12.

Grandfather quite well. I have had journeying mercies today. This life is a journey; I know that I shall one day reach the blessed end, in bliss, unfading bliss. What can I write equal to the theme of sovereign grace? It is a miracle, a perfect miracle, that God should so love man as to die for him, and to choose him before the foundation of the world.

June 19. — My birthday. Sixteen years have I lived upon this earth, and yet I am only — scarcely six months old! I am very young in grace. Yet how much time have I wasted, dead in trespasses and sins, without life, without God, in the world! What a mercy that I did not perish in my sin!

How glorious is my calling, how exalted my election, born of the Lord, — regenerate! Help me more than ever to walk worthily, as becomes a saint!

June 20. — Truly my lot is cast in pleasant places, and I have a goodly heritage. I can love religion now in the sunshine; may I love it and prize it under all circumstances!

(The continuous Diary thus abruptly closes, giving only the brief intimation that the dear writer goes immediately to Cambridge, as usher in Mr. Leeding's school. There remain but three or four fragmentary entries during the ensuing months, — or years, — but these serve to show the young soldier still busy at his drill, loyal to his Lord's colors, and already bravely fighting that "good fight of faith," which ceased not till his Captain called him from the battlefield, to receive the victor's reward in glory. As every word of his is precious in these days, I transcribe the four succeeding paragraphs, though unable to ascertain the dates when they were written. — S. S.)

Storms have raged around me; yet, blessed be my Father's name, I have now some peace! "But more the treacherous calm I dread, than tempests breaking overhead." Let me not be left even here; let Thy grace still flow into my heart! O Lord, my King, reign in me, and be glorified by me! May it please Thee to dwell in such a bramble-bush as I am, so that, though burning, I may not be consumed! Ordered in all things and sure is the everlasting covenant of redeeming love. Forever settled and eternally complete in Him is my salvation. May it be completed in myself, and may I grow up to be a man in Christ Jesus, a perfect man, prepared for the inheritance of the saints in light! Oh, that my spirituality may be revived!

My matchless Immanuel, let me see once more Thy face in the temple of my heart! May I know the joy, and have the faith of God's elect; may I rejoice in free and sovereign grace, saving me from the guilt and power of sin! Grace is a glorious theme, above the loftiest flights of the most soaring angel, or the most exalted conceptions of one of the joint-heirs with Jesus.

All power is God's, and all is engaged to protect and preserve me. Let me have my daily-grace, peace and comfort, zeal and love, give me some work, and give me strength to do it to Thy glory!

Heard Mr. C., of Bumpstead. Morning, "What doest thou here, Elijah?"

Afternoon, "I am the door." Went to the prayer-meeting before and after chapel, engaged in prayer, read the hymns, and addressed the children.

What an honor it is to be but a door-keeper in the house of the Lord! Oh, to be humble, and to be always at the feet of Jesus! Then should I grow more in grace, and increase in the knowledge of the Lord. The Lord is able to keep me from falling, and He will, for He has promised never to leave one of His called children.

Fair Day. — Spoke to Mr. R. How can a child of God go there? "Vanity of vanities, all is vanity." Forgive him, Lord, for so forgetting his high calling! I, too, should be there, but for the grace of God. I have the seeds of all evil in my own heart; pride is yet my darling sin, I cannot shake it off.

Awake, O my Lord, against the mighty, for I shall die by his hand if Thou do not help me, and lead me on to triumph! Leave me, ye vain thoughts! I have nothing but what I have received; it is the Lord's goodness that I even have my reason.

How could I live without prayer when troubles come? How blessed to carry them to the throne! I will now say that the Lord heareth prayer, for He hath removed from me that which I feared. But, oh! could I feel the presence of the Lord as in days gone by, how joyful! Could I enjoy His face, and feast upon His love, then would it be a sort of Heaven below the skies. Yes, Thou art mine, my Savior and my King; I am bound to Thee by love, by Thine own dying love, not mine! Fairest of beings, best-beloved, come, let me yet see Thy smiling face!

Chapter Fourteen - A Good Confession. — Baptism.

I REMEMBER the difficulty that I had, when I was converted, and wished to join the Christian Church in the place where I lived (Newmarket). I called upon the minister four successive days before I could see him; each time there was some obstacle in the way of an interview; and as I could not see him, I wrote and told him that I would go down to the church-meeting, and propose myself as a member. He looked upon me as a strange character, but I meant what I said; for I felt that I could not be happy without fellowship with the people of God. I wanted to be wherever they were; and if anybody ridiculed them, I wished to be ridiculed with them; and if people had an ugly name for them, I wanted to be called by that ugly name; for I felt that, unless I suffered with Christ in His humiliation, I could not expect to reign with Him in His glory.

When I had been accepted as a member of the Congregational Church at Newmarket, I was invited to the communion table, although I had not been baptized. I refused, because it did not appear to me to be according to the New Testament order: "Then they that gladly received his word were baptized: and the same day there were added unto them about three thousand souls. And they continued steadfastly in the apostles' doctrine and fellowship, and in breaking of bread, and in prayers." I waited until I could go to the Lord's table as one who had believed, and who had been baptized. I had attended the house of God with my father, and my grandfather; but I thought, when I read the Scriptures, that it was my business to judge for myself. I knew that my father and my grandfather took little children in their arms, put a few drops of water on their faces, and said they were baptized; but I could not see anything in my Bible about babes being baptized. I learned a little Greek; but I could not discover that the word "baptize" meant to sprinkle; so I said to myself, "They are good men, yet they may be wrong; and though I love and revere them, that is no reason why I should imitate them." And they acknowledged, when they knew of my honest conviction, that it was quite right for me to act according to my conscience. I consider the "baptism" of an unconscious infant is just as foolish as the "baptism" of a ship or a bell; for there is as much Scripture for the one as for the other. Therefore I left my relations, and became what I am today, a Baptist, so-called, but I hope a great deal more a Christian than a Baptist. Many a man will go to chapel, because his grandmother did. Well, she was a good old soul; but I do not see that she ought to influence your judgment. "That does not signify," says one, "I do not like to leave the church of my fathers." No more do I; for I would rather belong to the same denomination as my father, I would not willfully differ from any of my friends, or leave their sect and denomination; but I must let God be above my parents. Though our parents are at the very top of our hearts, and we love: them, and reverence them, and in all other matters render them strict obedience, yet, with regard to religion, to our own Master we stand or fall, and we claim to have the right of judging for ourselves as men, and then we think it our duty, having judged, to carry out our conscientious convictions.

I once met a man who had been forty years a Christian, and believed it to be his duty to be baptized; but when I spoke to him about it, he said, "He that believeth shall not make haste." After forty years' delay, he talked about not making haste. I quoted to him another passage, "I made haste, and delayed not to keep Thy commandments," and showed him what the meaning of his misapplied passage was. A person who was present when John Gill preached his very *first* sermon at Kettering, also heard him deliver his *last* in London, more than fifty years after. *After his death,* she joined the church over which he had presided, relating, at some length, a truly interesting experience, which gave universal pleasure to all who heard it. Her name was Mary Bailey, and it is to be hoped that none will imitate her by postponing the confession of their faith in Jesus for so long a time.

She lived half a century in disobedience to her Lord, and even when she avowed His name it must have caused her deep regret that she had lingered so long in neglect of the Redeemer's ordinance.

When I was a boy of fifteen, I believed in the Lord Jesus, was baptized, and joined the Church of Christ; and nothing upon earth would please me more than to hear of other boys having been led to do the same. I have never been sorry for what I did then; no, not even once. I have had plenty of time to think it over, and many temptations to try some other course; and if I had found out that I had been deceived, or that I had blundered, I would have made a change before now, and would do my best to prevent others from falling into the same delusion. The day I gave myself up to the Lord Jesus, to be His servant, was the very best day of my life; then I began to be safe and to be happy; then I found out the secret of living, and had a worthy object for my life's exertions, and an unfailing comfort for life's troubles. Because I would wish every boy, who reads these lines, to have a bright eye, a light tread, a joyful heart, and overflowing spirits, I therefore plead with him to consider whether he will not follow my example, for I speak from experience, and know what I say.

Once, as I stood musing at a window, I saw a fly upon it, and made a brush with my hand to catch it. When I opened my hand, the fly was not inside, but still in the same place on the glass. Scarcely thinking what I did, I made another rush with my hand, and thought I had captured the insect, but with the same result, — there was the creature, quietly retaining his place in spite of me. *It was on the other side of the glass;* and when I saw that it was so, I smiled at my own folly. Those who attempt to find pleasure while out of Christ, will experience a like failure, for they are seeking on the wrong side of the glass. When we are on the side of Jesus, and, having believed in Him, are cleansed and forgiven, then our pursuit of joy will be successful; but till then we shall labor in vain, and spend our strength for naught.

Baptism is the mark of distinction between the Church and the world. It very beautifully sets forth the death of the baptized person to the world.

Professedly, he is no longer of the world; he is buried to it, and he rises again to a new life. No symbol could be more significant. In the immersion of a believer, there seems to me to be a wondrous setting forth of the burial of the Christian to all the world in the burial of Christ Jesus. It is the crossing of the Rubicon. If Caesar crosses the Rubicon, there will never be peace between him and the Senate again. He draws his sword, and he throws away his scabbard. Such is the act of baptism to the believer. It is the burning of the boats: it is as much as to say, "I cannot come back again to you; I am dead to you; and to prove that I am, I am absolutely buried to you; I have nothing more to do with the world; I am Christ's, and Christ's for ever." Then, the Lord's supper: how beautifully that ordinance sets forth the distinction of the believer from the world in his life and that by which his life is nourished. He eats the flesh of Christ, and drinks His blood. Both these ordinances bring a cross with them to some degree, especially the first. I was noting, when reading the life of good Andrew Fuller, that, after he had been baptized, some of the young men in the village were wont to mock him, asking him how he liked being dipped, and such like questions which are common enough nowadays. I could but notice that the scoff of a hundred years ago is just the scoff of today.

This is the way of salvation, — worship, prayer, faith, profession, — and the profession, if men would be obedient, if they would follow the Bible, must be done in Christ's way, by a baptism in water, in the name of the Father, and of the Son, and of the Holy Ghost. God requireth this; and though men are saved without any baptism, and multitudes fly to Heaven who are never plunged in the stream; though baptism is not saving, yet, if men would be saved, they must not be disobedient. And inasmuch as God gives the command, it is mine to enforce it. Jesus said to His disciples, "Go ye therefore, and preach the gospel to every creature: he that believeth, and is immersed, shall be saved; he that believeth not shall be damned." The Church of England Prayer-book approves dipping. It only says, if children be weak, they are to be sprinkled; and it is marvelous how many weakly children there have been born lately. The dear little ones are so tender, that a few drops suffice instead of the dipping which their own Church endorses. I would that all churchmen were better churchmen; if they would be more consistent with their own articles of faith, they would be more consistent with Scripture; and if they were a little more consistent with some of the rubrics of their own Church, they would be a little more consistent with themselves. I became a Baptist through reading the New Testament, — especially in the Greek, — and was strengthened in my resolve by a perusal of the Church of England Catechism, which declared as necessary to baptism, repentance and the forsaking of sin.

Mr. Doddridge has recommended a solemn covenant between the soul and God, to be signed and sealed with due deliberation and most fervent prayer. Many of the most eminent of the saints have adopted this excellent method of devoting themselves in very deed unto the Lord, and have reaped no little benefit from the re-perusal of that solemn document when they have afresh renewed the act of dedication. I conceive that burial with Christ in baptism is a far more Scriptural and expressive sign of dedication; but I am not inclined to deny my brethren the liberty of confirming that act by the other, if it seem good unto them, as I myself did soon after my conversion. According to my reading of Holy Scripture, the believer in Christ should be buried with Him in baptism, and so enter upon his open Christian life. I therefore cast about to find a Baptist minister, and I failed to discover one nearer than Isleham, in the Fen country, where resided a certain Mr. W. W. Cantlow. My parents wished me to follow my own convictions, Mr. Cantlow arranged to baptize me, and my employer gave me a day's holiday for the purpose.

I can never forget the 3rd of May, 1850; it was my mother's birthday, and I myself was within a few weeks of being sixteen years of age. I was up early, to have a couple of hours for quiet prayer and dedication to God.

Then I had some eight miles to walk, to reach the spot where I was to be immersed into the Triune Name according to the sacred command. What a walk it was! What thoughts and prayers thronged my soul during that morning's journey! It was by no means a warm day, and therefore all the better for the two or three hours of quiet foot-travel which I enjoyed. The sight of Mr. Cantlow's smiling face was a full reward for that country tramp. I think I see the good man now, and the white ashes of the peat-fire by which we stood and talked together about the solemn exercise which lay before us. We went together to the Ferry, for the Isleham friends had not degenerated to indoor immersion in a bath made by the art of man, but used the ampler baptistery of the flowing river. Isleham Ferry, on the River Lark, is a very quiet spot, half-a-mile from the village, and rarely disturbed by traffic at any time of the year. The river itself is a beautiful stream, dividing Cambridgeshire from Suffolk, and is dear to local anglers. The navigation of this little River Lark is possible between Bury St. Edmund's and the sea at Lynn; but at Isleham it is more in its infancy.

The ferry-house, hidden in the picture (on page 147) by the trees, is freely opened for the convenience of minister and candidates at a baptizing.

Where the barge is hauled up for repairs, the preacher takes his stand, when the baptizing is on a weekday, and there are few spectators present.

But on Lord's-day, when great numbers are attracted, the preacher, standing in a barge moored mid-stream, speaks the Word to the crowds on both sides of the river. This can be done the more easily, as the river is not very wide. Where three persons can be seen standing, is the usual place for entering the water. The right depth, with sure footing, may soon be found, and so the delightful service proceeds in the gently-flowing stream. No accident or disorder has ever marred the proceedings. In the course of seven or eight miles, the Lark serves no fewer than five Baptist churches, and they would on no account give up baptizing out of doors.

The first baptizing at Isleham is recorded thus: — "Sept. 13, 1798. John Webber, sen., John Webber, jun., William Brown, John Wibrow, and Mary Gunstone were baptized by Mr. Fuller, of Kettering, at Isleham Ferry."

To me, there seemed to be a great concourse on that weekday. Dressed, I believe, in a jacket, with a boy's turn-down collar, I attended the service previous to the ordinance; but all remembrance of it has gone from me: my thoughts were in the water, sometimes with my Lord in joy, and sometimes with myself in trembling awe at making so public a confession. There were first to be baptized two women, — Diana Wilkinson and Eunice Fuller, — and I was asked to conduct them through the water to the minister; but this I most timidly declined. It was a new experience to me, never having seen a baptism before, and I was afraid of making some mistake. The wind blew down the river with a cutting blast, as my turn came to wade into the flood; but after I had walked a few steps, and noted the people on the ferry-boat, and in boats, and on either shore, I felt as if Heaven, and earth, and hell, might all gaze upon me; for I was not ashamed, there and then, to own myself a follower of the Lamb. My timidity was washed away; it floated down the river into the sea, and must have been devoured by the fishes, for I have never felt anything of the kind since. Baptism also loosed my tongue, and from that day it has never been quiet. I lost a thousand fears in that River Lark, and found that "in keeping His commandments there is great reward." It was a thrice-happy day to me. God be praised for the preserving goodness which allows me to write of it with delight so long afterwards!

"Many days have passed since then,
Many changes I have seen;
Yet have been upheld till now;
Who could hold me up but Thou?"

In the Isleham Vestry, in the extremely gentle and cordial companionship of the pastor, I spent a very happy evening, which I recollect was very cold, so that a peat-fire, whose white appearance I still remember, was needed to warm the room. Mr. Cantlow was for some time a missionary in Jamaica, and is mentioned three times in Hinton's *Life of Knibb.* For thirty-two years, this excellent man resided at Isleham, and was pastor of the church till age enfeebled him, and he welcomed our worthy student, Mr. Wilson, as his successor. He was great at giving the "soft answer which turneth away wrath;" he was beloved by his people, and universally respected in the village. His death serves as a landmark in my life, reminding me that the days are long past since I was generally spoken of as "the boy-preacher." One correspondent kindly trusts that I shall be *"strengthened under the infirmities of my declining years,"* which kindly wish I gratefully acknowledge.

Mr. Stevenson, in *The Rev. C. H. Spurgeon, his Life and Work,* makes it out that I joined the Baptist Church a year before I was baptized; but it was not so. I never dreamed of entering the Church except by Christ's own way; and I wish that all other believers were led to make a serious point of commencing their visible connection with the Church by the ordinance which symbolizes death to the world, burial with Christ, and resurrection to newness of life. That open stream, the crowded banks, and the solemn plunge, have never faded from my mind; but have often operated as a spur to duty, and a seal of consecration. From henceforth let no man trouble me, for He who first saved me, afterwards accepted me, — spirit, soul, and body, — as His servant, in token whereof this mortal frame was immersed beneath the wave. The outward sign has often served to bring vividly before mind and heart the spiritual meaning, and therefore is it dearly loved, for His sake who both ordained the ordinance and Himself submitted to it.

I am indebted to Mr. Wilson for the following note, which reminds me of an excellent companion I had almost forgotten: —

"Mr. W. H. Cantlow, a worthy Baptist deacon at Ipswich, well remembers, when a boy at school, walking with Mr. Spurgeon from Newmarket to Isleham, a distance of eight miles, to be at the baptism. He says: — 'I often think of the earnest talks he had with me, and always remember one remark he made, on our way to the weeknight service, about the need of obtaining spiritual food during the week, as it was so long to have to wait from one Sunday to the other.' The recollection of the service at the river-side is fondly cherished by several still living, who rejoice that they were there.

But the most precious memory of that day is the prayer-meeting in the vestry, in the evening, where Mr. Spurgeon prayed, and people wondered, and wept for joy, as they listened to the lad. One may be excused for envying those who were there. In front of the new school-room, adjoining the chapel, is the following inscription: —

THIS STONE WAS LAID ON SEPTEMBER 19TH, 1888,
BY MR. G. APTHORPE, IN MEMORY OF THE LATE
REV. W. W. CANTLOW,
WHO. WHILE PASTOR OF THE CHURCH, BAPTIZED THE
REV, C, H. SPURGEON,
AT ISLEHAM FERRY, ON MAY 3RD, 1850.

"Mr. Cantlow's grave is only a few yards off."

Mr. Wilson also explains our picture, and adds an amusing story: — "In the view of the Ferry, the chaise and cart are waiting to cross the river by the ferry-boat. One old lighter is rotting away in the water, and another lies high and dry under repair. The box is for keeping eels until they can be sent to market; and the long pole is for crossing the river in the small boat, which is also to be seen it you look for it. The late vicar of Isleham, a very solemn man, meeting a deacon of ready wit at the Ferry, began to find fault with a recent baptizing there. Said the vicar, 'I suppose this is the place where the people came crowding, the other Sunday, showing the little respect they had for the Sabbath-day.' 'There was, indeed, a great crowd,' replied the deacon, 'but they were all as still and attentive as in the house of God.' 'Is it true that the man, J. S — ,was baptized?' inquired the vicar.

'Yes, quite true,' said the deacon, 'and he seemed to be full of joy at the time.' 'What!' exclaimed the vicar, 'a man who never went to school, and cannot read a word! How much can he know about the religion he came here to profess?' 'Well,' answered the deacon, with a smile, 'very likely the poor man knows little as yet; still, he told us how he found the Savior, and became happy in His love. But,' added the deacon, 'do not you, sir, christen little children, declaring that you make them children of God, while you are perfectly aware that the children know nothing at all?' "

If any ask, — Why was I thus baptized? — I answer, because I believed it to be an ordinance of Christ, very specially joined by Him with faith in His name. "He that believeth and is baptized shall be saved." I had no superstitious idea that baptism would save me, for I was saved. I did not seek to have sin washed away by water, for I believed that my sins were forgiven me through faith in Christ Jesus. Yet I regarded baptism as the token to the believer of cleansing, the emblem of his burial with his Lord, and the outward avowal of his new birth. I did not trust in *it*; but, because I trusted in Jesus as my Savior, I felt bound to obey Him as my Lord, and follow the example which He set us in Jordan, in His own baptism. I did not fulfill the outward ordinance to join a party, and to become a Baptist, but to be a Christian after the apostolic fashion; for they, when they believed, were baptized. It is now questioned whether John Bunyan was baptized; but the same question can never be raised concerning *me.* I, who scarcely belong to any sect, am, nevertheless, by no means willing to have it doubted in time to come whether or no I followed the conviction of my heart. I read the New Testament for myself, and found believers' baptism there; and I had no mind to neglect what I saw to be the Lord's order. If others see not as I do, to their own Master they stand or fall; but for me, the perceptions of my understanding in spiritual things were the law of my life, and I hope they will always be so.

If I thought it wrong to be a Baptist, I should give it up, and become what I believed to be right. The particular doctrine adhered to by Baptists is that they acknowledge no authority unless it comes from the Word of God.

They attach no importance to the authority of the Fathers, — they care not for the authority of the mothers, — if what they say does not agree with the teaching of the Evangelists, Apostles, and Prophets, and, most of all, with the teaching of the Lord Himself. If we could find infant baptism in the Word of God, we should adopt it. It would help us out of a great difficulty, for it would take away from us that reproach which is attached to us, — that we are odd, and do not as other people do. But we have looked well through the Bible, and cannot find it, and do not believe that it is there; nor do we believe that others can find infant baptism in the Scriptures, unless they themselves first put it there.

Our forefathers were called *Ana*-baptists, because it was said by their opponents that they re-baptized those who had been already baptized. Of course, they did nothing of the kind; but they immersed, on profession of their faith, those who had previously been sprinkled as unconscious infants.

There was no ana-baptism or re-baptism there, the two things were altogether distinct. I could tell a good many stories of that kind of ana-baptism. There was one of the elders of the Tabernacle Church who was — as the word is usually understood — "baptized" four times. The first time the babe was sprinkled, he was so ill that he was only half-done, according to the ritual provided for that purpose in the Prayer-book. When he got better, he was taken to the church to be properly finished off, but the parson gave the child a girl's name instead of the one which had been selected for him. His father and mother did not like their boy running the risk of being called by the name that had been given to him, so they took him for the third time; and the clergyman then gave him his right name.

When he grew up, he was converted, and I baptized him after the Scriptural order; but the Church of England had made three attempts to baptize him, and had failed every time!

Chapter Fifteen - Experiences After Conversion

Our faith at times has to fight for its very existence. The old Adam within us rages mightily, and the new spirit within us, like a young lion, disdains to be vanquished; and so these two strong ones contend, till our spirit is full of agony. Some of us know what it is to be tempted with blasphemies we should not dare to repeat, to be vexed with horrid temptations which we have grappled with and overcome, but which have almost cost us resistance unto blood. In such inward conflicts, saints must be alone. They cannot tell their feelings to others, they would not dare; and if they did, their Own brethren would despise or upbraid them, for the most of professors would not even know what they meant. Even those who have trodden other fiery ways would not be able to sympathize in all, but would answer the poor troubled soul, "These are points in which we cannot go with you." Christ alone was tempted in all points like as we are, though without sin. No one man is tempted in all points exactly like another man, and each one has certain trials in which he must stand alone amid the rage of war, with not even a book to help him, or a biography to assist him, no man ever having gone that way before except that one Man whose trail reveals a nail-pierced foot. He alone knows all the devious paths of sorrow. Yet, even in such byways, the Lord is with us, helping us, sustaining us, and giving us grace to conquer at the close. — C. H. S.

W HEN my eyes first looked to Christ, He was a very real Christ to me; and when my burden of sin rolled from off my back, it was a real pardon and a real release from sin to me; and when that day I said for the first time,

"Jesus Christ is mine," it was a real possession of Christ to me. When I went up to the sanctuary in that early dawn of youthful piety, every song was really a psalm, and when there

was a prayer, oh, how I followed every word! It was prayer indeed! And so was it, too:. in silent quietude, when I drew near to God, it was no mockery, no routine, no matter of mere duty; it was a real talking with my Father who is in Heaven. And oh, how I loved my Savior Christ then! I would have given all I had for Him!

How I felt towards sinners that day! Lad that I was, I wanted to preach, and

"Tell to sinners round,
What a dear Savior I had found."

One of the greatest sorrows I had, when first I knew the Lord, was to think about certain persons with whom I knew right well that I had held ungodly conversations, and sundry others whom I had tempted to sin; and one of the prayers that I always offered, when I prayed for myself, was that such an one might not be lost through sins to which I had tempted him. This was the case also with George Whitefield, who never forgot those with whom, before his conversion, he used to play cards, and he had the joy of leading every one of them to the Savior.

I think about five days after I first found Christ, when my joy had been such that I could have danced for very mirth at the thought that Christ was mine, on a sudden I fell into a sad fit of despondency. I can tell now why it was so with me. When I first believed in Christ, I am not sure that I thought the devil was dead, but certainly I had a kind of notion that he was so mortally wounded that he could not disturb me. And then I also fancied that the corruption of my nature had received its death-blow. I read what Cowper said,

"Since *the dear hour that brought me to 'Thy foot,*
And cut up all my follies by the roof;"

and I really thought that the poet knew what he was saying; whereas, never did anyone blunder so terribly as Cowper did when he said that, for no man, I think, has all his follies thus cut up by the roofs. However, I fondly dreamed that mine were, I felt persuaded they would never sprout again. I was going to be perfect, — I fully calculated upon it, — and lo, I found an intruder I had not reckoned upon, an evil heart of unbelief in departing from the living God. So I went to that same Primitive Methodist Chapel where I first received peace with God, through the simple preaching of the Word. The text happened to be, "*O wretched* man that I am: who shall deliver me from the body of this death?.... There," I thought, "that's the text for me." I had just got as far as that in the week. I knew that I had put my trust in Christ, and I knew that, when I sat in that house of prayer, my faith was simply and solely fixed on the atonement of the Redeemer. But I had a weight on my mind, because I could not be as holy as I wanted to be.

I could not live without sin. When I rose in the morning, I thought I would abstain from every hard word, from every evil thought and look; and I came up to that chapel groaning because, "when I would do good, evil was present with me." The minister began by saying, "*Paul* was not a believer when he said this." Well now, I knew I was a believer, and it seemed to me from the context that Paul must have been a believer, too. (Now, I am sure he was.) The man went on to say that no child of God ever did feel any conflict within. So I took up my hat, and left the chapel, and I have very seldom attended such places since. They are very good for people who are unconverted to go to, but of very little use for children of God. That is my notion of Methodism. It is a noble thing to bring in strangers; but a terrible thing for those that are brought in to sit and feed there. It is like the parish pound, it is a good place to put sheep in when they have strayed, but there is no food inside; they had better be let out as soon as possible to find some grass. I save that that minister understood nothing of experimental divinity, or of practical heart theology, or else he would not have talked as he did. A good man he was, I do not doubt, but utterly incompetent to the task of dealing with a case like mine.

Oh, what a horror I have had of sin ever since the day when I felt its power over my soul! O sin, *sin,* I have had enough of thee! Thou didst never bring me more than a moment's seeming joy, and with it there came a deep and awful bitterness which burns within me to this day! Well do I recollect when I was the subject of excessive tenderness, — some people called it

"morbid sensibility." How I shuddered and shivered at the very thought of sin, which then appeared exceedingly sinful! The first week after I was converted to God, I felt afraid to put one foot before the other for fear I should do wrong. When I thought over the day, if there had been a failure in my temper, or if there had been a frofhy word spoken, or something done amiss, I did chasten myself sorely. Had I, at that time, known anything to be my Lord's will, I think I should not have hesitated to do it; to me it would not have mattered whether it was a fashionable thing or an unfashionable thing, if it was according to His Word. Oh, to do His will! to follow Him whithersoever He would have me go! It seemed then as though I should never, never, never be slack in keeping His commandments.

I do not know whether the experience of others agrees with mine; but I can say this, that the worst difficulty I ever met with, or I think I can ever meet with, happened a little time after my conversion to God. When I first knew the weight of sin, it was as a burden, as a labor, as a trouble; but when, the second time, —

"I asked the Lord that I might grow,
In faith, and love, and every grace;
Might more of His salvation know,
And seek more earnestly His face;"

and when He answered me by letting all my sins loose upon me, they appeared more frightful than before. I thought the Egyptians in Egypt were not half so bad as the Egyptians out of Egypt; I thought the sins I knew before, though they were cruel task-masters, were not half so much to be dreaded as those soldier-sins, armed with spears and axes, riding in iron chariots with scythes upon their axles, hastening to assault me. It is true, they did not come so near to me as heretofore; nevertheless, they occasioned me more fright even than when I was their slave. The Israelites went up harnessed, marching in their ranks, and, I doubt not, singing as they went, because they were delivered from the daily task and from the cruel bondage; but suddenly they turned their heads while they were marching, for they heard a dreadful noise behind them, a noise of chariots and of men shouting for battle; and at last, when they could really see the Egyptians, and the thick cloud of dust rising behind them, then they said that they should be destroyed, they should now fall by the hand of the enemy. I remember, after my conversion (it may not have happened to all, but it did to me), there came a time when the enemy said, "I will pursue, I will overtake, I will divide the spoil; my lust shall be satisfied upon them; I will draw my sword, my hand shall destroy them." So Satan, loth to leave a soul, pursues it hot-foot. He will have it back if he can; and often, soon after conversion, there comes a time of dreadful conflict, when the soul seems as if it could not live. "Was it because there were no graves in Egypt that the Lord brought us into this condition of temporary freedom, that we might be all the more distressed by our adversaries?" So said unbelief; but God brought His people right out by one final stroke. Miriam knew it when she took her timbrel, and went forth with the women, and answered them in the jubilant song, "*Sing* ye to the Lord, for He hath triumphed gloriously; the horse and his rider hath He thrown into the sea." I love best of all that note in the song of Moses where he says, "*The* depths have covered them." "There remained not so much as one of them." What gladness must have been in the hearts of the children of Israel when they knew that their enemies were all gone! I am sure it was so with me; for, after my conversion, being again attacked by sin, I saw the mighty stream of redeeming love roll over all my sins, and this was my song, "The   depths have covered them." "Who   shall lay anything to the charge of God's elect?

It is God that justifieth. Who is he that condemneth? It is Christ that died, yea, rather, that is risen again, who is even at the right hand of God, who also maketh intercession for us."

I was brought up, as a child, with such care that I knew but very little of foul or profane language, having scarcely ever heard a man swear. Yet do I remember times, in my earliest Christian days, when there came into my mind thoughts so evil that I clapped my hand to my mouth for fear I should be led to give utterance to them. This is one way in which Satan tortures those whom God has delivered out of his hand. Many of the choicest saints have been thus molested. Once, when

I had been grievously assailed by the tempter, I went to see my dear old grandfather. I told him about my terrible experience, and then I wound up by saying, "*Grandfather,* I am sure I cannot: be a child of God, or else I should never have such evil thoughts as these." "Nonsense, Charles," answered the good old man; "it is just because you are a Christian that you are thus tempted. These blasphemies are no children of yours; they are the devil's brats, which he delights to lay at the door of a Christian. Don't you own them as yours, give them neither house-room nor heart-room." I felt greatly comforted by what my grandfather said, especially as it confirmed what another old saint had told me when I was tempted in a similar manner while I was seeking the Savior.

A great many people make fun of that verse, —

> "*'Tis a point I long to know,*
> *Oft it causes anxious thought,*
> *Do I love the Lord, or no?*
> *Am I His, or am I not?*"

If they ever find themselves where some of us have been, they will not do so arty more. I believe it is a shallow experience that makes people always confident of what they are, and where they are, for there are times of terrible trouble, that make even the most confident child of God hardly know whether he is on his head or on his heels. It is the mariner who has done business on great waters who, in times of unusual stress and storm, reels to and fro, and staggers like a drunken man, and is at his wits' end. At such a time, if Jesus whispers that I am His, then the question is answered once for all, and my soul has received a token which it waves in the face of Satan, so that he disappears, and I can go on my way rejoicing.

I have found, in my own spiritual life, that the more rules I lay down for myself, the more sins I commit. The habit of regular morning and evening prayer is one which is indispensable to a believer's life, but the prescribing of the length of prayer, and the constrained remembrance of so many persons and subjects, may gender unto bondage, and strangle prayer rather than assist it. To say I will humble myself at such a time, and rejoice at such another season, is nearly as much an affectation as when the preacher wrote in the margin of his sermon, "*Cry* here," "*Smile* here." Why, if the man preached from his heart, he would be sure to cry in the right place, and to smile at a suitable moment; and when the spiritual life is sound, it produces prayer at the right time, and humiliation of soul and sacred joy spring forth spontaneously, apart from rules and vows. The kind of religion which makes itself to order by the Almanac, and turns out its emotions like bricks from a machine, weeping on Good Friday, and rejoicing two days afterwards, measuring its motions by the moon, is too artificial to be worthy of my imitation.

Self-examination is a very great blessing, but I have known self-examination carried on in a most unbelieving, legal, and self-righteous manner; in fact, I have so carried, it on myself. Time was when I used to think a vast deal more of marks, and signs, and evidences, for my own comfort, than I do now, for I find that I cannot be a match for the devil when I begin dealing in these things.

I am obliged to go day by day with this cry, —

"I, the chief of sinners am,
But Jesus died for me."

While I can believe the promise of God, because it is His promise, and because He is my God, and while I can trust my Savior because He is God, and therefore mighty to save, all goes well with me; but I do find, when I begin questioning myself about this and that perplexity, thus taking my eye off Christ, that all the virtue of my life seems oozing out at every pore. Any practice that detracts from faith is an evil practice, but especially that kind of self-examination which would take us away from the cross-foot, proceeds in a wrong direction.

I used, when I first knew the Savior, to try myself in a certain manner, and often did I throw stumbling-blocks in my path through it, and therefore I can warn any who are doing the same. Sometimes I would go up into my chamber, and by way of self-examination, I used to ask myself this question, — *"Am I afraid lo die?* If I should drop down dead in my room, can I say that I should joyfully close.' my eyes?" Well, it often happened that I could not honestly say so. I used to feel that death would be a very solemn thing. "Ah, then!" I said, "I have never believed in Christ, for if I had put my trust in the. Lord Jesus, I should not be afraid to die, but I should be quite confident." I do not doubt that many a person is saying, "I cannot follow Christ, because I am afraid to die; I cannot believe that Jesus Christ will save me, because the thought of death makes me tremble." Ah, poor soul, there are many of God's blessed ones, who through fear of death have been much of their lifetime subject to bondage! I know precious children of God now: I believe that, when they die, they will die triumphantly; but I know this, that the thought of death is never pleasing to them. And this is accounted for, because God has stamped on nature that law, the love of life and self-preservation; and it is natural enough that the man who has kindred and friends should scarcely like to leave behind those who are so dear. I know that, when he gets more grace, he will rejoice in the thought of death; but I do know that there are many quite safe, who will die rejoicing in Christ, who now, in the prospect of death, feel afraid of it. My aged grandfather once preached a sermon which I have not yet forgotten. He was preaching from the text, "The God of all grace," and he somewhat interested the assembly, after describing the different kinds of grace that God gave, by saying at the end of each period, "But there is one kind of grace that you do not want." After each part of his theme, there came the like sentence, "But there is one kind of grace you do not want."

And then he wound up by saying, *"You* don't want dying grace in living moments, but you shall have dying grace when you need it. When you are in the condition to require it, you shall have grace enough if you put your trust in Christ." In a party of friends, we were discussing the question whether, if the days of martyrdom should come, we were prepared to be burned. I said, *"I* must frankly tell you that, speaking as I feel to-day, I am not prepared to be burned; but I do believe that, if there were a stake at Smithfield, and I knew that I was to be burned there at one o'clock, I should have grace enough to be burned there when one o'clock came."

I was much impressed, in my younger days, by hearing a minister, blind with age, speak at the communion table, and bear witness to us who had just joined the church, that it was well for us that we had come to put our trust in a faithful God; and as the good man, with great feebleness and yet with great earnestness, said to us that he had never regretted having given himself to Christ as a boy, I felt my heart leap within me with delight that I had such a God to be my God. His testimony was such as a younger man could not have borne: he might have spoken more fluently, but the weight of those eighty years at the back of it made the old man eloquent to my young heart. For twenty years he had not seen the light of the sun. His snow-white locks hung from his brow, and floated over his shoulders, and he stood up at the table of the Lord, and thus addressed us: — "Brethren and sisters, I shall soon be taken from you; in a few more months, I shall gather up my feet in my bed, and sleep with my fathers. I have not the mind of the learned, nor the tongue of the eloquent; but I desire, before I go, to bear one public testimony to my God. Fifty and six years have I served Him, and I have never once found Him unfaithful. I can say, 'Surely goodness and mercy have followed me all the days of my life, and not one good thing hath failed of all the Lord God has promised.'" There stood the dear old man, tottering into his tomb, deprived of the light of heaven naturally, and yet having the Light of Heaven in a better sense shining into his soul; and though he could not look upon us, yet he turned towards us, and he seemed to say, "Young people, trust God in early life, for I have not to regret that I sought Him too soon. I have only to mourn that so many of my years ran to waste." There is nothing that more tends to strengthen the faith of the young believer than to hear the veteran Christian, covered with scars from the battle, testifying that the service of his Master is a happy service, and that, if he could have served any other master, he would not have done so, for His service is pleasant, and His reward everlasting joy.

In my early days, I knew a good man, who has now gone to his reward, who was the means of producing, under God, a library of useful lives. I do not mean books in paper, but books in boots! Many young men were decided for the Lord by his means, and became preachers, teachers, deacons, and other workers; and no one would wonder that it was so, if he knew the man who trained them. He was ready for every good word and work; but he gave special attention to his Bible-class, in which he set forth the gospel with clearness and zeal. Whenever any one of his young men left the country town in which he lived, he would be sure to arrange a parting interview. There was a wide spreading oak down in the fields; and there he was wont to keep an early morning appointment with John, or Thomas, or William; and that appointment very much consisted of earnest pleading with the Lord that, in going up to the great city, the young man might be kept from sin, and made useful. Under that tree several decided for the Savior. It was an impressive act, and left its influence upon them; for many men came, in after years, to see the spot, made sacred by their teacher's prayers.

Oh! how my young heart once ached in boyhood, when I first loved the Savior. I was far away from father and Mother, and all I loved, and I thought my heart would burst; for I was an usher in a school, in a place where I could meet with little sympathy or help. Well, I went to my chamber, and told my little griefs into the ears of Jesus. They were great griefs to me then, though they are nothing now. When on my knees I just whispered them into the ear of Him who had loved me with an everlasting love, oh, it was so sweet! If I had told them to others, they would have told them again; but He, my blessed Confidant, knows all my secrets, and He never tells again.

There is one verse of Scripture which, as a young believer, I used often to repeat, for it was very dear to me; it is this: "Bind the sacrifice with cords, even unto the horns of the altar." I did feel then that I was wholly Christ's.

In the marriage covenant of which the Lord speaks, when the Husband put the ring upon His bride's finger, He said to her, "Thou hast become Mine;"

and I remember when I felt upon my finger the ring of infinite, everlasting, covenant love that Christ put there. Oh, it was a joyful day, a blessed day!

Happy day, happy day, when His choice was known to me, and He fixed my choice on Him! That blessed rest of soul, which comes of a sure possession of Christ, is not to be imitated, but it is greatly to be desired. I know that some good people, who I believe will be saved, nevertheless do not attain to this sweet rest. They keep on thinking that it is something that they may get when they are very old, or when they are about to die, but they look upon the full assurance of faith, and the personal grasping of Christ, and saying, "My Beloved is mine," as something very dangerous. I began my Christian life in this happy fashion as a boy fifteen years of age; I believed fully and without hesitation in the Lord Jesus Christ; and when I went to see a good Christian woman, I was simple enough to tell her that I believed in Christ, that He was mine, and that He had saved me. I expressed myself very confidently concerning the great truth that God would ne'er forsake His people, nor leave His work undone. I was at once chid, and told that I had no right to speak so confidently, for it was presumptuous. The good woman said to me, "Ah! I don't like such assurance as that," and then she added, "I trust you are believing in Christ, — I hope so; — but I have never got. beyond a hope or a trust, and I am an old woman." Bless the old woman, she was no example for us who know whom we have believed; we ought to rise far above that groveling kind of life. The man who begins right, and the boy who begins right, and the girl. who begins right, will begin by saying, "God hath said it: 'He that believeth on Him is not condemned.' I believe on Him, therefore I am not condemned; Christ is mine."

Before my conversion, I was accustomed to read the Scriptures to admire their grandeur, to feel the charm of their history, and wonder at the majesty of their language; but I altogether missed the Lord's intent therein. But when the Spirit came with His Divine life, and quickened all the Book to my newly-enlightened soul, the inner meaning shone forth with wondrous glory. I was not in a frame of mind to judge God's Word, but I accepted it all without demur; I did not venture to sit in judgment upon my Judge, and become the reviser of the unerring God.

Whatever I found to be in His Word, I received with intense joy. From that hour, I bless; God that, being not exempt from trouble, and especially not free from a tendency to despondency which is always with me, I yet rejoice and will rejoice, and am happy, unspeakably happy in resting upon Jesus Christ. Moreover, I have found that those points of my character which were most weak have been strengthened, while strong passions have been subdued, evil propensities have been kept under, and new principles have been implanted. I am changed; I am as different from what I was as a man could be who had been annihilated, and had then been made over again.

Nor do I claim any of the credit for this change, — far from it. God has done great things for me, but He has done the same for others, and is willing to do it for any soul that seeks His face through Jesus Christ and His great atoning sacrifice.

I have known some men who were almost idiots before conversion, but they afterwards had their faculties wonderfully developed. Sonic time ago, there was a man who was so ignorant that he could not read, and he never spoke anything like grammar in his life, unless by mistake; and, moreover, he was considered to be what the people in his neighborhood called "daft."

But when he was converted, the first thing he did was to pray. He stammered out a few words, and in a little time his powers of speaking began to develop themselves. Then he thought he would like to read the Scriptures, and after long, long months of labor, he learned to read. And what was the next thing? He thought he could preach; and he did preach a little, in his own homely way, in his house. Then he thought, "I must read a few more books." And so his mind expanded, until, I believe he is at the present day a useful minister, settled in a country village, laboring for God.

An idea has long possessed the public mind, that a religious man can scarcely be a wise man. It has been the custom to talk of infidels, atheists, and deists, as men of deep thought and comprehensive intellect; and to tremble for the Christian controversialist as if he must surely fall by the hand of his enemy. But this is purely a mistake; for the gospel is the sum of wisdom, an epitome of knowledge, a treasure-house of truth, and a revelation of mysterious secrets. In it we see how justice and mercy may be married; here we behold inexorable law entirely satisfied, and sovereign love bearing away the sinner in triumph. Our meditation upon it enlarges the mind; and as it opens to our soul in successive flashes of glory, we stand astonished at the profound wisdom manifest in it. I have often said that, before I knew the gospel, I had gathered up a heterogeneous mass of all kinds of knowledge from here, there, and everywhere, — a bit of chemistry, a bit of botany, a bit of astronomy, and a bit of this, that, and the other. I put them all together, in one great confused chaos; but when I learned the gospel, I got a shelf in my head to put everything upon just where it should be. It seemed to me as if, when I had discovered Christ and Him crucified, I had found the center of the system, so that I could see every other science revolving in due order. From the earth, the planets appear to move in a very irregular manner, — they are progressive, retrograde, or stationary; but if you could get upon the sun, you would see them marching round in their constant, uniform, circular motion. So is it with knowledge. Begin with any other science you like, and truth will seem to be all awry. Begin with the science of Christ crucified, and you will begin with the sun, you will see every other science moving round it in complete harmony. The greatest mind in the world will be evolved by beginning at the right end. The old saying is, "Go from nature up to nature's God;" but it is hard work going up-hill. the best thing is to go from nature's God down to nature; and if you once get to nature's God, and believe Him, and love Him, it is surprising how easy it is to hear music in the waves, and songs in the wild whisperings of the winds, to see God everywhere, in the stones, in the rocks, in the rippling brooks, and to hear Him everywhere, in the lowing of cattle, in the rolling of thunders, and in the fury of tempests. Christ is to me the wisdom of God. I can learn everything now that I know the science of Christ crucified.

Chapter Sixteen - Defense of Calvinism

The old truth that Calvin preached, that Augustine preached, that Paul preached, is the truth that I must preach to-day, or else be false to my conscience and my God. I cannot shape the truth; I know of no such thing as paring off the rough edges of a doctrine. John Knox's gospel is my gospel. That which thundered through Scotland must thunder through England again. — C. H. S.

IT is a great thing to begin the Christian life by believing good solid doctrine. Some people have received twenty different "gospels" in as many years; how many more they will accept before they get to their journey's end, it would be difficult to predict. I thank God that He early taught me the gospel, and I have been so perfectly satisfied with it, that I do not want to know any other. Constant change of creed is sure loss. If a tree has to be taken up two or three times a year, you will not need to build a very large loft in which to store the apples. When people are always shifting their doctrinal principles, they are not likely to bring forth much fruit to the glory of God. It is good for young believers to begin with a firm hold upon those great fundamental doctrines which the Lord has taught in His Word.

Why, if I believed what some preach about the temporary, trumpery salvation which only lasts for a time, I would scarcely be at all grateful for it; but when I know that those whom God saves He saves with an everlasting salvation, when I know that He gives to them an everlasting righteousness, when I know that He settles them on an everlasting foundation of everlasting love, and that He will bring them to His everlasting kingdom, oh, then I do wonder, and I am astonished that such a blessing as this should ever have been given to me!

"Pause, my soul! adore, and wonder!
Ask, 'Oh, why such love to me?'
Grace hath put me in the number
Of the Savior's family:
Hallelujah!
Thanks, eternal thanks, to Thee

I suppose there are some persons whose minds naturally incline towards the doctrine of free-will. I can only say that mine inclines as naturally towards the doctrines of sovereign grace. Sometimes, when I see some of the worst characters in the street, I feel as if my heart must burst forth in tears of gratitude that God has never let me act as they have done! I have thought, if God had left me alone, and had not touched me by His grace, what a great sinner I should have been! I should have run to the utmost lengths of sin, dived into the very depths of evil, nor should I have stopped at any vice or folly, if God had not restrained me. I feel that I should have been a very king of sinners, if God had let me alone. I cannot understand the reason why I am saved, except upon the ground that God would have it so. I cannot, if I look ever so earnestly, discover any kind of reason in myself why I should be a partaker of Divine grace. If I am not at this moment without Christ, it is only because Christ Jesus would have His will with me, and that will was that I should be with Him where He is, and should share His glory. I can put the crown nowhere but upon the head of Him whose mighty grace has saved me from going down into the pit.

Looking back on my past life, I can see that the dawning of it all was of God; of God effectively. I took no torch with which to light the sun, but the sun enlightened me. I did not commence my spiritual life-no, I rather kicked, and struggled against the things of the Spirit: when He drew me, for a time I did not run after Him: there was a natural hatred in my soul of everything holy and good. Wooings were lost upon me-warnings were cast to the wind- thunders were despised; and as for the whispers of His love, they were rejected as being less than nothing and vanity. But, sure I am, I can say now, speaking on behalf of myself, "He only is my salvation." It was He who turned my heart, and brought me down on my knees before Him. I can in very deed, say with Doddridge and Toplady, —

"Grace taught my soul to pray,
And made my eyes o'erflow."

and coming to this moment, I can add —

"Tis grace has kept me to this day,
And will not let me go."

Well can I remember the manner in which I learned the doctrines of grace in a single instant. Born, as all of us are by nature, an Arminian, I still believed the old things I had heard continually from the pulpit, and did not see the grace of God. When I was coming to Christ, I thought I was doing it all myself, and though I sought the Lord earnestly, I had no idea the Lord was seeking me. I do not think the young convert is at first aware of this. I can recall the very day and hour when first I received those truths in my own soul-when they were, as John Bunyan says, burnt into my heart as with a hot iron, and I can recollect how I felt that I had grown on a sudden from a babe into a man-that I had made progress in Scriptural knowledge, through having found, once for all, the clue to the truth of God. One weeknight, when I was sitting in the house of God, I was not thinking much about the preacher's sermon, for I did not believe it. The thought struck me, How did you come to be a Christian? I sought the Lord. But how did you come to seek the Lord? The truth flashed across my mind in a moment- I should not have sought Him unless there had been some previous influence in my mind to make me seek Him. I prayed, thought I, but then I asked myself, How came I to pray? I was induced to pray by reading the Scriptures. How came I to read the Scriptures? I did read them, but what led me to do so? Then, in a moment, I saw that God was at the bottom of it all, and that He was the Author of my faith, and so the whole doctrine of grace opened up to me, and from that doctrine I have not departed to this day, and I desire to make this my constant confession, "I ascribe my change wholly to God."

I once attended a service where the text happened to be, "He shall choose our inheritance for us;" and the good man who occupied the pulpit was more than a little of an Arminian. Therefore, when he commenced, he said,

"This passage refers entirely to our temporal inheritance, it has nothing whatever to do with our everlasting destiny, for," said he, "we do not want Christ to choose for us in the matter of Heaven or hell. It is so plain and easy, that every man who has a grain of common sense will choose Heaven, and any person would know better than to choose hell. We have no need of any superior intelligence, or any greater Being, to choose Heaven or hell for us. It is left to our own free- will, and we have enough wisdom given us, sufficiently correct means to judge for ourselves," and therefore, as he very logically inferred, there was no necessity for Jesus Christ, or anyone, to make a choice for us. We could choose the inheritance for ourselves without any assistance. "Ah!" I thought, "but, my good brother, it may be very true that we could, but I think we should want something more than common sense before we should choose aright."

First, let me ask, must we not all of us admit an over-ruling Providence, and the appointment of Jehovah's hand, as to the means whereby we came into this world? Those men who think that, afterwards, we are left to our own free-will to choose this one or the other to direct our steps, must admit that our entrance into the world was not of our own will, but that God had then to choose for us. What circumstances were those in our power which led us to elect certain persons to be our parents? Had we anything to do with it? Did not God Himself appoint our parents, native place, and friends? Could He not have caused me to be born with the skin of the Hottentot, brought forth by a filthy mother who would nurse me in her "kraal," and teach me to bow down to Pagan gods, quite as easily as to have given me a pious mother, who would each morning and night bend her knee in prayer on my behalf? Or, might He not, if He had pleased have given me some profligate to have been my parent, from whose lips I might have early heard fearful, filthy, and obscene language? Might He not have placed me where I should have had a drunken father, who would have immured me in a very dungeon of ignorance, and brought me up in the chains of crime? Was it not God's Providence that I had so happy a lot, that both my parents were His children, and endeavored to train me up in the fear of the Lord?

John Newton used to tell a whimsical story, and laugh at it, too, of a good woman who said, in order to prove the doctrine of election, "Ah! sir, the Lord must have loved me before I was born, or else He would not have seen anything in me to love afterwards." I am sure it is true in my case; I believe the doctrine of election, because I am quite certain that, if God had not chosen me, I should never have chosen Him; and I am sure He chose me before I was born, or else He never would have chosen me afterwards; and He must have elected me for reasons unknown to me, for I never could find any reason in myself why He should have looked upon me with special love. So I am forced to accept that great Biblical doctrine. I recollect an Arminian brother telling me that he had read the Scriptures through a score or more times, and could never find the doctrine of election in them. He added that he was sure he would have done so if it had been there, for he read the Word on his knees. I said to him, "I think you read the Bible in a very uncomfortable posture, and if you had read it in your easy chair, you would have been more likely to understand it. Pray, by all means, and the more, the better, but it is a piece of superstition to think there is anything in the posture in which a man puts himself for reading: and as to reading through the Bible twenty times without having found anything about the doctrine of election, the wonder is that you found anything at all: you must have galloped through it at such a rate that you were not likely to have any intelligible idea of the meaning of the Scriptures."

If it would be marvelous to see one river leap up from the earth full-grown, what would it be to gaze upon a vast spring from which all the rivers of the earth should at once come bubbling up, a million of them born at a birth?

What a vision would it be! Who can conceive it. And yet the love of God is that fountain, from which all the rivers of mercy, which have ever gladdened our race-all the rivers of grace in time, and of glory hereafter-take their rise. My soul, stand thou at that sacred fountain-head, and adore and magnify, for ever and ever, God, even our Father, who hath loved us!

In the very beginning, when this great universe lay in the mind of God, like unborn forests in the acorn cup; long ere the echoes awoke the solitudes; before the mountains were brought forth; and long ere the light flashed through the sky, God loved His chosen creatures. Before there was any created being-when the ether was not fanned by an angel's wing, when space itself had not an existence, when there was nothing save God alone-even then, in that loneliness of Deity, and in that deep quiet and profundity, His bowels moved with love for His chosen. Their names were written on His heart, and then were they dear to His soul. Jesus loved His people before the foundation of the world-even from eternity! and when He called me by His grace, He said to me, "I have loved thee with an everlasting love: therefore with lovingkindness have I drawn thee."

Then, in the fullness of time, He purchased me with His blood; He let His heart run out in one deep gaping wound for me long ere I loved Him. Yea, when He first came to me, did I not spurn Him? When He knocked at the door, and asked for entrance, did I not drive Him away, and do despite to Ms grace? Ah, I can remember that I full often did so until, at last, by the power of His effectual grace, He said, "I must, I will come in;" and then He turned my heart, and made me love Him. But even till now I should have resisted Him, had it not been for His grace. Well, then since He purchased me when I was dead in sins, does it not follow, as a consequence necessary and logical, that He must have loved me first? Did my Savior die for me because I believed on Him? No; I was not then in existence; I had then no being. Could the Savior, therefore, have died because I had faith, when I myself was not yet born? Could that have been possible? Could that have been the origin of the Savior's love towards me? Oh! no; my Savior died for me long before I believed. "But," says someone, "He foresaw that you would have faith; and, therefore, He loved you." What did He foresee about my faith? Did He foresee that I should get that faith myself, and that I should believe on Him of myself? No; Christ could not foresee that, because no Christian man will ever say that faith came of itself without the gift and without the working of the Holy Spirit. I have met with a great many believers, and talked with them about this matter; but I never knew one who could put his hand on his heart, and say, "I believed in Jesus without the assistance of the Holy Spirit."

129

I am bound to the doctrine of the depravity of the human heart, because I find myself depraved in heart, and have daily proofs that in my flesh there dwelleth no good thing. If God enters into covenant with unfallen man, man is so insignificant a creature that it must be an act of gracious condescension on the Lord's part; but if God enters into covenant with sinful man, he is then so offensive a creature that it must be, on God's part, an act of pure, free, rich, sovereign grace. When the Lord entered into covenant with me, I am sure that it was all of grace, nothing else but grace.

When I remember what a den of unclean beasts and birds my heart was, and how strong was my unrenewed will, how obstinate and rebellious against the sovereignty of the Divine rule, I always feel inclined to take the very lowest room in my Father's house, and when I enter Heaven, it will be to go among the less than the least of all saints, and with the chief of sinners.

The late lamented Mr. Denham has put, at the foot of his portrait, a most admirable text, "Salvation is of the Lord." That is just an epitome of Calvinism; it is the sum and substance of it. If anyone should ask me what I mean by a Calvinist, I should reply, "He is one who says, Salvation is of the Lord." I cannot find in Scripture any other doctrine than this. It is the essence of the Bible. "He only is my rock and my salvation." Tell me anything contrary to this truth, and it will be a heresy; tell me a heresy, and I shall find its essence here, that it has departed from this great, this fundamental, this rock-truth, "God is my rock and my salvation." What is the heresy of Rome, but the addition of something to the perfect merits of Jesus Christ-the bringing in of the works of the flesh, to assist in our justification? And what is the heresy of Arminianism but the addition of something to the work of the Redeemer? Every heresy, if brought to the touchstone, will discover itself here. I have my own Private opinion that there is no such thing as preaching Christ and Him crucified, unless we preach what nowadays is called Calvinism. It is a nickname to call it Calvinism; Calvinism is the gospel, and nothing else. I do not believe we can preach the gospel, if we do not preach justification by faith, without works; nor unless we preach the sovereignty of God in His dispensation of grace; nor unless we exalt the electing, unchangeable, eternal, immutable, conquering love of Jehovah; nor do I think we can preach the gospel, unless we base it upon the special and particular redemption of His elect and chosen people which Christ wrought out upon the cross; nor can I comprehend a gospel which lets saints fall away after they are called, and suffers the children of God to be burned in the fires of damnation after having once believed in Jesus. Such a gospel I abhor.

"If ever it should come to pass,
That sheep of Christ might fall away,
My fickle, feeble soul, alas!
Would fall a thousand times a day"

If one dear saint of God had perished, so might all; if one of the covenant ones be lost, so may all be; and then there is no gospel promise true, but the Bible is a lie, and there is nothing in it worth my acceptance. I will be an infidel at once when I can believe that a saint of God can ever fall finally. If God hath loved me once, then He will love me for ever. God has a mastermind; He arranged everything in His gigantic intellect long before He did it; and once having settled it, He never alters it, 'This shall be done," saith He, and the iron hand of destiny marks it down, and it is brought to pass. "This is My purpose," and it stands, nor can earth or hell alter it. "This is My decree," saith He, "promulgate it, ye holy angels; rend it down from the gate of Heaven, ye devils, if ye can; but ye cannot alter the decree, it shall stand for ever." God altereth not His plans; why should He? He is Almighty, and therefore can perform His pleasure. Why should He? He is the All-wise, and therefore cannot have planned wrongly. Why should He? He is the everlasting God, and therefore cannot die before His plan is accomplished. Why should He change? Ye worthless atoms of earth, ephemera of a day, ye creeping insects upon this bay-leaf of existence, ye may change your plans, but He shall never, never change His.

Has He told me that His plan is to save me? If so, I am for ever safe.

"My name from the palms of His hands
Eternity will not erase;
Impress'd on His heart it remains,
In marks of indelible grace."

I do not know how some people, who believe that a Christian can fall from grace, manage to be happy. It must be a very commendable thing in them to be able to get through a day without despair. f I did not believe the doctrine of the final perseverance of the saints, I think I should be of all men the most miserable, because I should lack any ground of comfort. I could not say, whatever state of heart I came into, that I should be like a well- spring of water, whose stream fails not; I should rather have to take the comparison of an intermittent spring, that might stop on a sudden, or a reservoir, which I had no reason to expect would always be full. I believe that the happiest of Christians and the truest of Christians are those who never dare to doubt God, but who take His Word simply as it stands, and believe it, and ask no questions, just feeling assured that if God has said it, it will be so. I bear my willing testimony that I have no reason, nor even the shadow of a reason, to doubt my Lord, and I challenge Heaven, and earth, and hell, to bring any proof that God is untrue. From the depths of hell I call the fiends, and from this earth I call the tried and afflicted believers, and to Heaven I appeal, and challenge the long experience of the blood-washed host, and there is not to be found in the three realms a single person who can bear witness to one fact which can disprove the faithfulness of God, or weaken Ms claim to be trusted by His servants.

There are many things that may or may not happen but this I know shall happen:

"He shall present my soul,
Unblemish'd and complete,
Before the glory of His face,
With joys divinely great"

All the purposes of man have been defeated, but not the purposes of God.

The promises of man may be broken-many of them are made to be broken-but the promises of God shall all be fulfilled. He is a promise-maker, but He never was a promise- breaker; He is a promise-keeping God, and every one of His people shall prove it to be so. This is my grateful, personal confidence, "The Lord will perfect that which concerneth me"-unworthy me, lost and ruined me. He will yet save me; and —

"I, among the blood-wash'd throng,
Shall wave the palm, and wear the crown,
And shout loud victory"

I go to a land which the plough of earth hath never upturned, where it is greener than earth's best pastures, and richer than her most abundant harvests ever saw. I go to a building of more gorgeous architecture than man hath ever builded; it is not of mortal design; it is "a building of God, a house not made with hands, eternal in the Heavens." All I shall know and enjoy in Heaven, will be given to me by the Lord, and I shall say, when at last I appear before Him —

"Grace all the work shall crown
Through everlasting days;
It lays in Heaven the topmost stone,
And well deserves the praise"

I know there are some who think it necessary to their system of theology to limit the merit of the blood of Jesus: if my theological system needed such a limitation, I would cast it to the winds. I cannot, I dare not allow the thought to find a lodging in my mind, it seems so near akin to blasphemy.

In Christ's finished work I see an ocean of merit; my plummet finds no bottom, my eye discovers no shore. There must be sufficient efficacy in the blood of Christ, if God had so willed it, to have saved not only all in this world, but all in ten thousand worlds, had they transgressed their Maker's law. Once admit infinity into the matter, and limit is out of the question.

Having a Divine Person for an offering, it is not consistent to conceive of limited value; bound and measure are terms inapplicable to the Divine sacrifice. The intent of the Divine purpose fixes the application of the infinite offering, but does not change it into a finite work. Think of the numbers upon whom God has bestowed His grace already. Think of the countless hosts in Heaven: if thou wert introduced there to-day, thou wouldst find it as easy to tell the stars, or the sands of the sea, as to count the multitudes that are before the throne even now. They have come from the East, and from the West, from the North, and from the South, and they are sitting down with Abraham, and with Isaac, and with Jacob in the Kingdom of God; and beside those in Heaven, think of the saved ones on earth. Blessed be God, His elect on earth are to be counted by millions, I believe, and the days are coming, brighter days than these, when there shall be multitudes upon multitudes brought to know the Savior, and to rejoice in Him. The Father's love is not for a few only, but for an exceeding great company. "A great multitude, which no man could number," will be found in Heaven. A man can reckon up to very high figures; set to work your Newtons, your mightiest calculators, and they can count great numbers, but God and God alone can tell the multitude of His redeemed. I believe there will be more in Heaven than in hell. If anyone asks me why I think so, I answer, because Christ, in everything, is to "have the pre-eminence," and I cannot conceive how He could have the pre-eminence if there are to be more in the dominions of Satan than in Paradise. Moreover, I have never read that there is to be in hell a great multitude, which no man could number. I rejoice to know that the souls of all infants, as soon as they die, speed their way to Paradise. Think what a multitude there is of them! Then there are already in Heaven unnumbered myriads of the spirits of just men made perfect-the redeemed of all nations, and kindreds, and people, and tongues up till now; and there are better times coming, when the religion of Christ shall be universal; when —

"He shall reign from pole to pole,
With illimitable sway,"

when whole kingdoms shall bow down before Him, and nations shall be born in a day, and in the thousand years of the great millennial state there will be enough saved to make up all the deficiencies of the thousands of years that have gone before. Christ shall be Master everywhere, and His praise shall be sounded in every land. Christ shall have the pre-eminence at last; His train shall be far larger than that which shall attend the chariot of the grim monarch of hell.

Some persons love the doctrine of universal atonement because they say,

"It is so beautiful. It is a lovely idea that Christ should have died for all men; it commends itself," they say, "to the instincts of humanity; there is something in it full of joy and beauty." I admit there is, but beauty may be often associated with falsehood. There is much which I might admire in the theory of universal redemption, but I will just show what the supposition necessarily involves. If Christ on His cross intended to save every man, then He intended to save those who were lost before He died. If the doctrine be true, that He died for all men, then He died for some who were in hell before He came into this world, for doubtless there were even then myriads there who had been cast away because of their sins. Once again, if it was Christ's intention to save all men, how deplorably has He been disappointed, for we have His own testimony that there is a lake which burneth with fire and brimstone, and into that pit of woe have been cast some of the very persons who, according to the theory of universal redemption, were bought with His blood. That seems to me a conception a thousand times more repulsive than any of those consequences which are said to be associated with the Calvinistic and Christian doctrine of special and particular redemption. To think that my Savior died for men who were or are in hell, seems a supposition too horrible for me to entertain. To imagine for a moment that He was the Substitute for all the sons of men, and that God, having first punished the Substitute, afterwards punished the sinners themselves, seems to conflict with all my ideas of Divine justice.

That Christ should offer an atonement and satisfaction for the sins of all men, and that afterwards some of those very men should be punished for the sins for which Christ had already atoned, appears to me to be the most monstrous iniquity that could ever have been imputed to Saturn, to Janus, to the goddess of the Thugs, or to the most diabolical heathen deities. God forbid that we should ever think thus of Jehovah, the just and wise and good!

There is no soul living who holds more firmly to the doctrines of grace than I do, and if any man asks me whether I am ashamed to be called a Calvinist, I answer- I wish to be called nothing but a Christian; but if you ask me, do I hold the doctrinal views which were held by John Calvin, I reply, I do in the main hold them, and rejoice to avow it. But far be it from me even to imagine that Zion contains none but Calvinistic Christians within her walls, or that there are none saved who do not hold our views.

Most atrocious things have been spoken about the character and spiritual condition of John Wesley, the modern prince of Arminians. I can only say concerning him that, while I detest many of the doctrines which he preached, yet for the man himself I have a reverence second to no Wesleyan; and if there were wanted two apostles to be added to the number of the twelve, I do not believe that there could be found two men more fit to be so added than George Whitefield and John Wesley. The character of John Wesley stands beyond all imputation for self-sacrifice, zeal, holiness, and communion with God; he lived far above the ordinary level of common Christians, and was one "of whom the world was not worthy." I believe there are multitudes of men who cannot see these truths, or, at least, cannot see them in the way in which we put them, who nevertheless have received Christ as their Savior, and are as dear to the heart of the God of grace as the soundest Calvinist in or out of Heaven.

I do not think I differ from any of my Hyper-Calvinistic brethren in what I do believe, but I differ from them in what they do not believe. I do not hold any less than they do, but I hold a little more, and, I think, a little more of the truth revealed in the Scriptures. Not only are there a few cardinal doctrines, by which we can steer our ship North, South, East, or West, but as we study the Word, we shall begin to learn something about the North-west and North-east, and all else that lies between the four cardinal points.

The system of truth revealed in the Scriptures is not simply one straight line, but two; and no man will ever get a right view of the gospel until he knows how to look at the two lines at once. For instance, I read in one Book of the Bible, "The Spirit and the bride say, Come. And let him that heareth say, Come. And let him that is athirst come. And whosoever will, let him take the water of life freely." Yet I am taught, in another part of the same inspired Word, that "it is not of him that willeth, nor of him that runneth, but of God that sheweth mercy." I see, in one place, God in providence presiding over all, and yet I see, and I cannot help seeing, that man acts as he pleases, and that God has left his actions, in a great measure, to his own free-will. Now, if I were to declare that man was so free to act that there was no control of God over his actions, I should be driven very near to atheism; and if, on the other hand, I should declare that God so over-rules all things that man is not free enough to be responsible, I should be driven at once into Antinomianism or fatalism. That God predestines, and yet that man is responsible, are two facts that few can see clearly. They are believed to be inconsistent and contradictory to each other. If, then, I find taught in one part of the Bible that everything is foreordained, that is true; and if I find, in another Scripture, that man is responsible for all his actions, that is true; and it is only my folly that leads me to imagine that these two truths can ever contradict each other. I do not believe they can ever be welded into one upon any earthly anvil, but they certainly shall be one in eternity. They are two lines that are so nearly parallel, that the human mind which pursues them farthest will never discover that they converge, but they do converge, and they will meet somewhere in eternity, close to the throne of God, whence all truth doth spring.

It is often said that the doctrines we believe have a tendency to lead us to sin. I have heard it asserted most positively, that those high doctrines which we love, and which we find in the Scriptures, are licentious ones. I do not know who will have the hardihood to make that assertion, when they consider that the holiest of men have been believers in them. I ask the man who dares to say that Calvinism is a licentious religion, what he thinks of the character of Augustine, or Calvin, or Whitefield, who in successive ages were the great exponents of the system of grace; or what will he say of the Puritans, whose works are full of them? Had a man been an Arminian in those days, he would have been accounted the vilest heretic breathing, but now we are looked upon as the heretics, and they as the orthodox. We have gone back to the old school; we can trace our descent from the apostles. It is that vein of free-grace, running through the sermonizing of Baptists, which has saved us as a denomination. Were it not for that, we should not stand where we are today. We can run a golden line up to Jesus Christ Himself, through a holy succession of mighty fathers, who all held these glorious truths; and we can ask concerning them,

"Where will you find holier and better men in the world?" No doctrine is so calculated to preserve a man from sin as the doctrine of the grace of God.

Those who have called it "a licentious doctrine" did not know anything at all about it. Poor ignorant things, they little knew that their own vile stuff was the most licentious doctrine under Heaven. If they knew the grace of God in truth, they would soon see that there was no preservative from lying like a knowledge that we are elect of God from the foundation of the world. There is nothing like a belief in my eternal perseverance, and the immutability of my Father's affection, which can keep me near to Him from a motive of simple gratitude. Nothing makes a man so virtuous as belief of the truth. A lying doctrine will soon beget a lying practice. A man cannot have an erroneous belief without by-and-by having an erroneous life. I believe the one thing naturally begets the other. Of all men, those have the most disinterested piety, the sublimest reverence, the most ardent devotion, who believe that they are saved by grace, without works, through faith, and that not of themselves, it is the gift of God. Christians should take heed, and see that it always is so, lest by any means Christ should be crucified afresh, and put to an open shame.

In my early Christian days, I remember seeing a man about to enter a place of worldly amusement. Though he was a professing Christian, he was going to spend the evening in a dancing booth at the village fair, drinking and acting as other men did. I called out to him, just as he was at the entrance, "What doest thou there, Elijah?.... Why do you ask me such a question as that?" said he. I asked again, "What doest thou there, Elijah?

Art thou going in there?.... "Yes," he replied, with some sort of blush, "I am, but I can do so with impunity; I am a child of God, and I can go where I like, and yet be safe." "I could not," said I; "if I went there, I know I should commit sin. It is a place of danger, and I could not go there without great risk of sinning against God." "Ah!" said he, "I could; I have been before, and I have had some sweet thoughts there. I find it enlarges the intellect. You are narrow-minded; you do not appreciate these good things.

It is a rich treat, I assure you; I would go if I were you." "No," I said, "it would be dangerous for me; from what I hear, the name of Jesus is profaned there; and there is much said that is altogether contrary to the religion I believe. The persons who attend there are none of the best, and it will surely be said that birds of a feather flock together." "Ah, well!" he replied, "perhaps you young men had better keep away; I am a strong man, I can go;" and off he went to the place of amusement. My soul revolted from the man ever afterwards, for I felt that no child of God would ever be so wicked as to take poison in the faith that his Father would give him the antidote, or thrust himself into the fire, in the hope that he should not be burned. That man was an apple of Sodom, and I guessed that there was something rotten at the core; and I found by experience that it was so, for he was a downright sensualist even then. He wore a mask, for he was a hypocrite, and had none of the grace of God in his heart.

(This is evidently the man mentioned in the Diary, on page 146, and is quite a different person from "Old Roads" — see pages 23 and 24, — who was rebuked by "the child" for frequenting the Stambourne public-house, and who, through that rebuke, was restored to a consistent Christian life.)

Chapter Seventeen - Beginning to Serve the Lord.

"As Jesus passed forth from thence, He saw a man named Matthew, sitting at the receipt of custom, and He saith unto him, Follow Me; and he arose, and followed Him." This is a little bit of autobiography. Matthew wrote this verse about himself. I can fancy him, with his pen in his hand, writing all the rest of this Gospel; but I can imagine that, when he came to this very personal passage, he laid the pen down a minute, and wiped his eyes. He was coming to a most memorable and pathetic incident in his own life, and he recorded it with tremulous emotion. This verse reads to me so tenderly that I do not know how to communicate to you just how I feel about it. I have tried to imagine myself to be Matthew, and to have to write this story; and I am sure that, if I had not been inspired as Matthew was, I should never have done it so beautifully as he has done it, for it is so full of everything 'flint is touching, tender, timid, true, and gracious.

I know another man, not named "Matthew," but "Charles," and the Lord said to him, "Follow Me;" and he also arose, and followed Him. I do not know all that He saw when He looked upon me, I fear that He saw nothing in me but sin, and evil, and vanity; but I believe that He did say to Himself concerning me, "I see one to whom I can teach My truth, and who, when He gets a hold of it, will grip it fast, and never let it go, and one who will not be afraid to speak it wherever he is." So the

Lord saw what use He could make of me. There is an adaptation in men, even while they are unconverted, which God has put into them for their future service.

Luke was qualified to write his Gospel because he had been a physician; and Matthew was qualified to write the particular Gospel which he has left us, because he had been a publican. There may be a something about your habits of life, and about your constitution, and your condition, that will qualify you for some special niche in the Church of God in the years to come. O happy day, when Jesus shall look upon you, and call you to follow Him! Happy day, when He did look upon some of us, and saw in us what His love meant to put there, that He might make of us vessels of mercy meet for the Master's use! — C. H. S.

Do not see how our sense of oneness to Christ could ever have been perfected if we had not been permitted to work for Him. If He had been pleased to save us by His precious blood, and then leave us with nothing to do, we should have had fellowship with Christ up to a certain point, but (I speak from experience) there is no fellowship with Christ that seems to me to be so vivid,

so real to the soul, as when I try to win a soul for Him. Oh, when I come to battle with that soul's difficulties, to weep over that soul's hardness; when I begin to set the arguments of Divine mercy before it, and find myself foiled; when I am in a very agony of spirit, and feel that I could die sooner than that soul should perish; then I get to read the heart of Him whose flowing tears, and bloody sweat, and dying wounds showed how much He loved poor fallen mankind.

I think that, when I was first converted to God, if the Lord had said, "I have taken you into My house, and I am going to make use of you, and you shall be a door-mat for the saints to wipe their feet on," I should have said, "Ah, happy shall I be if I may but take the filth off their blessed feet, for I love God's people; and if I may minister to them in the slightest degree, it shall be my delight!" I know it did not come into my head, at that time, that I should be a leader in God's Israel. Ah, no; if I might but sit in the corner of His house, or be a door-keeper, it had been enough for me!

If, like the dog under the table, I might get a crumb of His mercy, were it but flavored by His hand, because He had broken it off, that was all I wanted. In that day when I surrendered myself to my Savior, I gave Him my body, my soul, my spirit; I gave Him all I had, and all I shall have for time and for eternity. I gave Him all my talents, my powers, my faculties, my eyes, my ears, my limbs, my emotions, my judgment, my whole manhood, and all that could come of it, whatever fresh capacity or new capability I might be endowed with. Were I, at this good hour, to change the note of gladness for one of sadness, it would be to wail out my penitent confession of the times and circumstances in which I have failed to observe the strict and unwavering allegiance I promised to my Lord. So far from regretting what I then did, I would fain renew my vows, and make them over again. I pray God, if I have a drop of blood in my body which is not His, to let it bleed away; and if there be one hair in my head which is not consecrated to Him, I would have it plucked out.

The very first service which my youthful heart rendered to Christ was the placing of tracts in envelopes, and then sealing them up, that I might send them, with the hope that, by choosing pertinent tracts, applicable to persons I knew, God would bless them. And I well remember taking other tracts, and distributing them in certain districts in the town of Newmarket, going from house to house, and telling, in humble language, the things of the Kingdom of God. I might have done nothing for Christ if I had not been encouraged by finding myself able to do a little. Then I sought to do something more, and from that something more, and I do not doubt that many of the servants of God have been led on to higher and nobler labors for their Lord, because they began to serve Him in the right spirit and manner. I look upon the giving away of a religious tract as only the first step, not to be compared with many another deed done for Christ; but: were it not for the first step, we: might never reach to the second; but that being attained, we are encouraged to take the next, and so, at the last, God helping us, we may be made extensively useful.

I think I never felt so much earnestness after the souls of my fellow-creatures as when I first loved the Savior's name, and though I could not preach, and never thought I should be able to testify to the multitude, I used to write texts on little scraps of paper, and drop them anywhere, that some poor creatures might pick them up, and receive them as messages of mercy to their souls. I could scarcely content myself even for five minutes without trying to do something for Christ. If I walked along the street, I must have a few tracts with me; if I went into a railway carriage, I must drop a tract out of the window; if I had a moment's leisure, I must be upon my knees or at my Bible; if I were in company, I must turn the subject of conversation to Christ, that I might serve my Master. It may be that, in the young dawn of my Christian life, I did imprudent things in order to serve the cause of Christ; but I still say, give me back that time again, with all its imprudence and with all its hastiness, if I may but have the same love to my Master, the same overwhelming influence in my spirit, making me obey my Lord's commands because it was a pleasure to me to do anything to serve my God.

How I did then delight to sit in that upper room where stars looked between the tiles, and hear the heavenly conversation which, from a miserable pallet surrounded by ragged hangings, an enfeebled saint of the Lord did hold with me! Like divers, I valued the pearl, even though the shell might be a broken one; nor did I care where I went to win it. When those creaking stairs trembled beneath my weight, when that bottomless chair afforded me uneasy rest, and when the heat and effluvia of that sick room drove my companion away, did I not feel more than doubly repaid while that friend of Jesus told me of all His love, His faithfulness, and His grace? It is frequently the case that the most despised servants of the Lord are made the chosen instruments of comforting distressed souls, and building them up in the faith.

I love to see persons of some standing in society take an interest in Sabbath-schools. One great fault in many of our churches is that the children are left for the young people to take care of; the older members, who have more wisdom, taking but very little notice of them; and very often, the wealthier members of the church stand aside as if the teaching of the poor were not (as indeed it is) the special business of the rich. I hope for the day when the mighty men of Israel shall be found helping in this great warfare against the enemy. In the United States, we have heard of presidents, judges, members of Congress, and persons in the highest positions, not condescending, — for I scorn to use such a term, — but honoring themselves by teaching little children in Sabbath-schools. He who teaches a class in a Sabbath-school has earned a good degree. I had rather receive the title of S.S.T. than M.A., B.A., or any other honor that ever was conferred by men.

There is no time for work like the first hours of the day; and there is no time for serving the Lord like the very earliest days of youth. I recollect the joy I had in the little service I was able to render to God when first I knew Him. I was engaged in a school all the week; but I had the Saturday afternoon at liberty, and though I was but a boy myself, and might rightly have used that time for rest, it was given to a tract-district, and to visiting the very poor within my reach; and the Sabbath-day was devoted to teaching a class, and later on, also to addressing the Sunday-school. When I began to teach, — was very young in grace then, — I said to the class of boys whom I was teaching, that Jesus Christ saved all those who believed in Him. One of them at once asked me the question, "Teacher, do *you* believe in Him?" I replied, "Yes, I hope I do." Then he inquired again,

"But are you not sure?" I had to think carefully what answer I should give.

The lad was not content with my repeating, "I hope so." He would have it, "*If* you have believed in Christ, you *are* saved." And I felt at that time that I could not teach effectually until I could say positively, "*I* know that it is so. I must be able to speak of what I have heard, and seen, and tasted, and handled of the good Word of life." The boy was right; there can be no true testimony except that which springs from assured conviction of our own safety and joy in the Lord. If I was ever a little dull, my scholars began to make wheels of themselves, twisting round on the forms on which they sat.

That was a very plain intimation to me that I must give them an illustration or an anecdote; and I learned to tell stories partly by being obliged to tell them. One boy, whom I had in the class, used to say to me, "*This* is very dull, teacher; can't you pitch us a yarn?" Of course he was a naughty boy, and it might be supposed that he went to the bad when he grew up, though I am not at all sure that he did; but I used to try and pitch him the yarn that he wanted, in order to get his attention again.

At one of the teachers' meetings, the suggestion was adopted that the male teachers should, in turn, give a few words of address on the lesson at the close of the teaching, alternating in so doing with the superintendent. [15]

My turn came in due course. After I had spoken, the superintendent requested me to take his place in addressing the school on the following Sabbath, and when I had done this, he asked me, as I did so well, to speak to the children each Lord's-day. But to this I demurred, not deeming it fair to the other teachers. "Well," he said, "on Sunday week, I shall expect you to give the address in my stead." The precedent thus instituted soon became a kind of usage; so that, for a time, it was usual for one of the teachers and myself to speak on alternate Sabbaths. Speedily something else followed. The older people also took to coming when I spoke; and that, ere long, in such numbers that the auditory looked more like that of a chapel than a school, — a circumstance which the old pastor, jealous of the seeming invasion of his province, did not quite like. I always spoke as best I could, after carefully preparing my subject. Though only a youth, I said,

"I think I am bound to give myself unto reading, and study, and prayer, and not to grieve the Spirit by unthought-of effusions;" and I soon found that my hearers appreciated what I said. Oh, but, how earnestly I did it all! I often think that I spoke better then than I did in later years, for I spoke so tremblingly, but my heart went with it all. And when I began to talk a little in the villages on the Sunday, and afterwards every night in the week,. I know that I used to speak then what came fresh from my heart. There was little time for gathering much from books; my chief library was the Word of God and my own experience, but I spoke out from my very soul, — no doubt with much blundering, and much weakness, and much youthful folly, but oh, with such an intense desire to bring men to Christ! I often felt that I could cheerfully lay down my life if I might but be the means of saving a poor old man, or bring a boy of my own age to the Savior's feet. I feel it a great joy to have been called to work for my Lord in the early hours of my life's day; and I hope by-and-by to be able to say, "O God, Thou hast taught me from my youth: and hitherto have I declared Thy wondrous works. Now also when I am old and grey-headed, O God, forsake me not; until I have shewed Thy strength unto this generation, and Thy power to every one that is to come." I do not think my Lord will turn His old servant off; when I get old, men may become tired of me, but He will not; He will hear my prayer, —

"Dismiss me not Thy service Lord."

I can truly say, that I never did anything which was a blessing to my fellow-creatures without feeling compelled to do it. For instance, before I thought of going to a Sabbath-school to teach, someone called, — asked me, — begged me, — prayed me to take his class. I could not refuse to go; and there I was, held hand and foot by the superintendent, and was compelled to go on. Then I was asked to address the children; I thought I could not, but I stood up, and stammered out a few words. It was the same on the first occasion when I attempted to preach to the people, — I am sure I had no wish to do it, — but there was no one else in the place who could, and the little congregation must have gone away without a single word of warning or invitation. How could I suffer it? I felt forced to address them; and so it has been with whatever I have laid my hand to. I have always felt a kind of impulse which I could not resist; but, moreover, I have felt placed by Providence in such a position that I had no wish to avoid the duty, and if I had desired it, I could not have helped myself.

I shall never forget standing by the bed-side of a youth who had been in my Sunday-school class; he had received very little good training at home, and though he was but a lad of seventeen, he became a drunkard, and drank himself to death at one debauch. I saw him, and talked to him, and tried to point him to the Savior, and heard at last the death-rattle in his throat; and as I went downstairs, I thought everybody a fool for doing anything except preparing to die. I began to look upon the men who drove the carts in the street, those who were busy at their shops, and those who were selling'

their wares, as being all foolish for attending to anything except their eternal business, and myself most of all foolish for not pointing dying sinners to a living Christ, and inviting them to trust in His precious blood.

And yet, in an hour or so, all things took their usual shape, and I began to think that I was not dying after all, and I could go away and be as unconcerned as before, — I could begin to think that men were, after all, wise in thinking of this world, and not the next; I mean not that I really thought so, but I tear I acted as if I thought so; the impression of the death-bed was so soon obliterated. It is sadly true, that even a Christian will grow by degrees so callous, that the sin which once startled him, and made his blood run cold, does not alarm him in the least. I can speak from my own experience. When first I heard an oath, I stood aghast, and knew not where to hide myself; yet now, if I hear an imprecation or blasphemy against God, though a shudder still runs through my veins, there is not that solemn feeling, that intense anguish, which I felt when first I heard such evil utterances. By degrees we get familiar with sin. I am fearful that even preaching against sin may have an injurious effect upon the preacher. I frankly confess that there is a tendency, with those of us who have to speak upon these themes, to treat them professionally, rather than to make application of them to ourselves; and thus we lose our dread of evil in some degree'., just as young doctors soon lose their tender nervousness in the dissecting-room. We are compelled in our office to see ten thousand things which at first are heart-breakers to us. In our young ministry, when we meet with hypocrisy and inconsistency, we are ready to lie down and die; but the tendency in after years is to take these terrible evils as matters of course. Worldliness, covetousness, and carnality, shock us most at the outset of our work is not this a sad sign, that even God's ministers may feel the hardening effect of sin? I daily feel that the atmosphere of earth has as much a tendency to harden my heart as to harden plaster which is newly spread upon the wall; and unless I am baptized anew with the Spirit of God, and constantly stand at the foot of the cross, reading the curse of sin in the crimson hieroglyphics of my Savior's dying agonies, I shall become as steeled and insensible as many professors already are.

Chapter Eighteen - Cambridge Life and Letters, 1850-1851.

IT was my privilege, at Cambridge, to live in a house where, at eight o'clock, every person, from the servant to the master, would have been found for half-an-hour in prayer and meditation in his or her chamber. As regularly as the time came round, that was done, just as we par took of our meals at appointed hours. If that were the rule in all households, it would be a grand thing for us. In the old Puritanic times, a servant would as often answer one who inquired for him, "Sir, my master is at prayers," as he would nowadays reply, "My master is engaged." It was then looked upon as a recognized fact that Christian men did meditate, and study the Word, and pray; and society respected the interval set apart for devotion. It is said that, in the days of Cromwell, if you had walked down Cheapside at a certain hour in the morning, you would have seen the blinds down at every house. Alas! where will you find such streets nowadays? I fear that: what was once the rule, is now the exception.

When I joined the Baptist Church at Cambridge, — one of the most respectable churches that can be found in the world, one of the most generous, one of the most intelligent, — this was a good many years ago, when I was young, — nobody spoke to me. On the Lord's-day, I sat at the communion table in a certain pew; there was one gentleman in it, and when the service was over, I said to him, "I hope you are quite well, sir?" He said, "You have the advantage of me." I answered, "I don't think I have, for you and I are brothers." "I don't quite know what you mean," said he.

"Well," I replied, "when I took the bread and wine, just now, in token of our being one in Christ, I meant it, did not you?" We were by that time in the street; he put both his hands on my shoulders, — was about sixteen years old then, — and he said, "Oh, sweet simplicity!" Then he added,

"You are quite right, my dear brother, you are quite right; come in to tea with me. I am afraid I should not have spoken to you if you had not first addressed me." I went to tea with him that evening; and when I left, he asked me to go again the next Lord's-day, so I went, and that Sabbath day he said to me, "You will come here every Sunday evening, won't you?"

That dear friend used to walk with me into the villages when I afterwards went out to preach, and he remains to this day one of the truest Christian friends I have, and often have we looked back, and laughed at the fact that I should have dared to assume that Christian fellowship was really a truth.

I remember that he said to me at the time, "I am rather glad you spoke to me, for it' you had gone to some of our deacons, I am afraid you would not have received quite as friendly a reply as I have given you."

(In August, 1850, C. H. Spurgeon went to Cambridge, to assist his old tutor, Mr. Leeding, who was conducting a private school in the University town. On page 44, Mr. Spurgeon has recorded his recollections of Mr. Leeding; the following is the tutor's account of his pupil, as furnished by him to Mr. Spurgeon for this Autobiography, in March, 1890: —

"My acquaintance with the Rev. Charles Haddon Spurgeon commenced in 1845, when I was engaged by Henry Lewis, Esq., of Colchester, having just passed the Degree Examination at St. John's College, Cambridge. I was to conduct his school for boarders and day-pupils, and it was agreed that the course of studies should be designed to ground and advance them in the course of a first-class education. Besides the usual English subjects, some began Latin and French; Spurgeon began Latin at this time. We worked together for four years, and left at the same time, he to proceed to another school (at Maidstone), and myself (who left merely because the terms of the increase of my salary were said to absorb all the profit) to return home to Cambridge, where some friends desired that I should remain, and conduct a school of my own, several pupils being ready for me. Spurgeon had made good progress with me at Colchester; in mathematical studies, he was far ahead of the rest, and generally took the first prize in the general examination.

"Before I had been many months at Cambridge, I received a letter from his father, begging me to take him as an assistant with no salary, but only to receive such help in his studies as would contribute to qualify him for public life."

(Mr. Spurgeon had preserved among his papers Mr. Leeding's reply to his father's letter; it was as follows: —

"Academy,
"Union Road,
"Cambridge,
"Aug. 6th, 1850.

"My Dear Sir,

"I hasten to reply to your most welcome letter, which I received this morning. I have more than once wished it possible that an arrangement could be made for securing your son's services in the event of an increase in my school; but my partial success has appeared to me a bar to such an engagement, for I have such an estimate of him, that I could never have started the proposal on such terms as have proceeded from you. I will readily engage to give him all the assistance in my power for the prosecution of his own studies, and his board and washing in return for his assistance.

You do me an honor, that I am perhaps unworthy of, in making this proposition when you have a premium at your option, but I must say you could not send him to anyone who feels so great an interest in and affection for him, nor to a situation where he could possibly have better opportunities for improving himself. You may, with Mrs. S., rest assured of his domestic comfort, as I am sure he will himself anticipate. I am unwilling to pledge myself at present to an engagement that shall bind me to give a salary hereafter. I am sure we shall not differ in that particular when once it necessarily occurs.

"Your offer, coming to me at this particular juncture, is a striking interposition of the Providence of God on my behalf. Through a violent cold, I have for the last fortnight been suffering from inflammation on the chest, which has rendered so much speaking extremely painful, and now at length very dangerous; so much so that I have been on the point of applying to a person in the town for his assistance. You will at once see how acceptable Charles's presence will be to me now; it will be doing me a great kindness if he can be allowed to set out as soon as possible. I will expect him on Thursday. If you intended him to travel by third class, I will gladly pay his fare from London by second, and also any expense of carriage of any part of his luggage that may require to be sent after him.

"With   many thanks for your united Christian regards and kindness,

"I am,

"Dear Sir,

"Yours faithfully,

"E. S. LEEDING."

"Mr. J. Spurgeon."

(Mr. Leeding's account of his young assistant continues: —

"After a few months' residence with me, he began preaching in two or three villages near Cambridge; he became popular among his hearers, and extended his circuit until he excited much interest among the Dissenters of Cambridge, some of whom (members of the St. Andrew's Street Baptist Church, once the scene of Rev. Robt. Hall's labors,) proposed to send him to a Dissenting College.

At the time, it seemed to me that such a foundation had been laid for his literary progress, that the advantages to be thus acquired would not repay the time occupied in such a course, and the scheme was abandoned. Soon after, some of his friends proposed that he should compete for a sizarship at St. John's College (which would have reduced the expenses of a College course £30 per annum), but it seemed to myself and others that three years (the time of College work at Cambridge), would be too long a period to expend on studies whose bearing on ministerial work is so remote as that of mathematics, and this also was abandoned. He now became more than ever intent upon preaching, — reading, besides the Greek: Testament, the Septuagint translation, Whateley's Logic, etc., and soon occupied constantly the pulpit at Waterbeach, a large village a few miles from Cambridge. It must not be omitted that the final decision as to College studies was made after what we deemed a Providential incident [16] which took place at Cambridge.")

"Cambridge,
"August 22nd, 1850.

"My Dear Father,

"I received your kind note this morning. We do not have our letters till 10 o'clock... Mr. Leeding is very much better; has been in the school... I am studying through Romans in the Greek, with Barnes, Doddridge, and Chalmers for my commentaries. Mr. Leeding gives me every attention, and I hope to progress rapidly. Our lecture tonight was on, 'Having loved His own,... He loved them unto the end.' Give my respects to all friends making inquiries. Mr. and Mrs. L. desire their kind respects to you. My love to dear Mother, Eliza, Archer, Emily, Lottie, and Louisa, and accept the same yourself. I again thank you for your kindness to me.

I will do my best with my clothes, and hope ever to be —

"Your affectionate son,

"CHARLES."

"No. 9, Union Road,
"Cambridge,
"19th Sept., '50.

"My Dear Father,

"I received your kind letter in due time. I joined the Church here at the Lord's table last Ordinance day. I shall write for my dismission; I intended to have done so before. The Baptists are by far the most respectable denomination in Cambridge; there are three Baptist Chapels, — St. Andrew's Street, where we attend, Zion Chapel, and Eden Chapel. There is a very fine Wesleyan Chapel and some others;. I teach in the Sunday-school all the afternoon Mr. Leeding takes the morning work. Last Sabbath-day we had a funeral sermon from Hebrews 6:11, 12. We have a prayer-meeting at 7 in the morning, and one after the evening service; they are precious means of grace, I trust, to my soul. How soon would the lamps go out did not our mighty Lord supply fresh oil; and' if it were not for His unshaken promise to supply our need out of the fullness of His grace, poor indeed should we be.

"Yes, where Jesus comes, He comes to reign: how I wish He would reign more in my heart; then I might hope that every atom of self, self-confidence, and self-righteousness, would be quite swept out of my soul. I am sure I long for the time when all evil affections, corrupt desires, and rebellious, doubting thoughts shall be overcome, and completely crushed beneath the Prince's feet, and my whole soul be made pure and holy. But so long as I am encaged within this house of clay, I know they will lurk about, and I must have hard fighting though the victory by grace is sure. Praying is the best fighting; nothing else will keep them down.

"I have written a letter to grandfather; I am sorry he is so poorly. He wants the promises now, and why may not young and old live upon them? They are the bread-corn of Heaven, the meat of the Kingdom; and who that has once tasted them will turn to eat husks without any sweetness and comfort in them? God's power will keep all His children; while He says to them, 'How shall ye who are dead to sin live any longer therein?' I feel persuaded that I shall never fathom the depths of my own natural depravity, nor climb to the tops of the mountains of God's eternal love. I feel constrained day by day to fall fiat down upon the promises, and leave my soul in Jesus' keeping. It is He that makes my feet move even in the slow obedience which marks them at present, and every attainment of grace must come from Him. I would go forth by prayer, like the Israelites, to gather up this Heavenly manna, and live upon free-grace.

"Add to all your great kindness and love to me, through my life, a constant remembrance of me in your prayers. I thank you for those petitions which you and dear Mother have so often sent up to the mercy-seat for me. Give my love to my sisters and brother, and accept the same for yourself and dear Mother. Hoping you are all quite well,

"I remain,

"Your obedient, affectionate son,

"CHAS. H. SPURGEON."

"Cambridge,
"October 3rd, 1850.

"My Dear Mother,

"I am generally so slack of news, that I have been ashamed to send a letter with nothing in it. I was last night admitted into membership with this church by dismission from Newmarket. May my future relation with them, whether brief or protracted, be for the glory of Jesus Christ! I am very fond of Mr. Roffe; I like his preaching very much. There is to be a baptizing this evening.... I trust that a year or two of study with Mr. Leeding will be of equal benefit to me with a College education..... I have found a great many Christian friends; last Sunday I had two invitations to tea. I went to the house of Mr. Watts, a coal merchant, and spent the time very happily. We read round with the children, and it seemed just like home-days. I have not had a letter from Stambourne, nor from Aunt, I am quite solitary.

"Mr. Roffe preached a delightful sermon from 'I will lift up mine eyes unto the hills, from whence cometh my help.' I trust I can look by faith to the hills, and confidently expect the help. I think I learn more every day of my own natural depravity and love of sin' how stupid should I be if I trusted to my own heart! If my salvation depended upon my continuance in the fervor of devotion, how soon should I perish! How joyful it is to know that Jesus will keep that which I have committed to Him, and that he will at length save every one of His redeemed ones!

"Give my best love to dear Fat. her, and accept the same yourself. I hope you are both well' give my love to Eliza, Archer, Emily, a kiss to Louisa and Lottie. I thank you for your many prayers; continue yet to plead for me, and may I ever bee

"Your affectionate son,

"CHARLES."

"No. 9, Union Road,
"Cambridge,
"Oct., 1850.

"My Dear Father,

"I have received your kind, interesting letter, and the P.O. enclosed.

Aunt ['Walker] has written to me, and with much sorrow has told me her case. Mr. W. has; promised to let me have any of his books that may be of use to me. I did not ask, but he sent that word himself Truly, the Lord putteth down one, and setteth up another, according to His ancient decrees. How blest to feel assured that Heaven's treasures never can rust, nor can any thief rob us of our inheritance!

"I went to Mr. Watts's again last Sunday; I am quite a member of the family. I am going on Friday to a party at his house with Rev.

Roffe, Rev. Keen, and Rev. Edmonds, and other friends. I anticipate much spiritual enjoyment. I would, however, look unto the Lord; for vain is the help of man. I always connect in my mind the deep depravity, and utter disease of my soul, with the all-conquering power of my blessed Lord, who will save every one of His redeemed. Mr. Roffe beautifully says, 'The Scripture says not, the believer *shall* be saved; but, he *is* saved, and has eternal life abiding in him.' Perfectly justified, and on the road to perfect sanctification, though proceeding very slowly; who shall refuse to rejoice in the Lord? Secure of an inheritance in the skies, I would desire to walk worthy of my exalted calling, and live down every calumny, and prove the error of those who speak reproachfully concerning our liberty in the Lord. How blessed to feel sure that our sins are covered! How manifold are the mercies of the Lord to me; all things work together for good] Since I am persuaded of my interest in Jesus, and can by feeble faith lay hold on Him, I will not fear what man can do unto me.....

"Give my love to dear Mother, and all others at home; accept the same yourself, with my sincere gratitude,

"From your affectionate son,

"CHAS. H. SPURGEON."

"No. 9, Union Road,
"Cambridge,
"Nov. 12th, 1850.

"My Dear Mother,

"I have just received *The Maidstone Journal,* in which you will see an advertisement of Mr. Walker's sale. In one of my late letters to Aunt (having heard you speak of her as somewhat trusting to works), I ventured, as a babe in grace, to touch upon the subject, — I trust, with becoming prudence as well as boldness. I then received a letter from Uncle, — a long one, too, — containing much good

146

and even religious advice; of course, speaking as (Oh, how I desire it!) a Christian should speak. Mixed up with it, there was a tincture of naturalism or reason, I have therefore ventured on another letter, and have, I trust, said, though feebly, what: a boy should say to a dying Uncle. False fear should never prevent us from being faithful with men walking on the confines of the grave.

Could I make religion more the business of my life, how happy should I be! I am conscious I do not live up to my duties or my privileges; and did I not feel sure that Jesus will certainly complete what He has begun, I should never think of reaching Heaven; but, by His might, I would look confidently for it.

"I have found a little work here. I have twice spoken to the Sunday-school, and am to read an Essay on some subject connected with Sunday-schools at the next meeting of the Teachers' Institute for the town. I only do so just to fill up. I have been driven to it, Mr. Watts and some others having taken their turns. I hope yet, one day, to prove myself no Antinomian, though I confess my daily sins and shortcomings; yet I would not willfully sin, and I feel some hatred to it. I desire to hate it more.

"I hope you enjoy your health, and that, with deal' Father, you have much of the marrow of the gospel as your daily meat. Give my love to all at home, and accept the same for yourself and Father. I am pursuing my studies, though I can say little about progress.

I am most happy, and quite well; and hoping to see you before many weeks,

"I remain,

"Your most affectionate son,

"CHARLES."

(The following are the letters to the Aunt and Uncle referred to in the foregoing letter; the first part of the one written to Mrs. Walker is missing: --)

"The body of Christians, of which for some little while I have been a member, is not distinguished for high standing in the world. I trust I shall never be rich, lest I should by force of additional temptation ever bring dishonor upon the name of Him with whom I have entered into solemn league and covenant. Would that, as I have been buried with Him in baptism, I might have the inward spiritual grace, and be dead to the world, but alive unto the service of the Lord!

"There has been much stir here about the late Popish Aggression,

— the clergy seem to be very anxious about it...I hope Uncle will not write to me until he is well. He is so very kind; but he may tire himself Tell him I am now studying Paine's *Elements of Mental Science* and Porter's *Lectures on Homiletics.* I cannot in Greek get further than the Testament. We have only thirteen boys.

"Accept my best love and thanks to yourself and Uncle, and permit me ever to subscribe myself,

"Your most affectionate nephew,

"C. H. SPURGEON."

"My Dear Uncle,

"Dumb men make no mischief. Your silence, and my neglect, make one think of the days when letters were costly, and not of penny postage. You have doubtless heard of me as a top-tree Antinomian.

147

I trust you know enough of me to disbelieve it. It is one object of my life to disprove the slander. I groan daily under a body of sin and corruption. Oh, for the time when I shall drop this flesh, and be free from sin! I become more and more convinced that, to attempt to be saved by a mixed covenant of works and faith is, in the words of Berridge, 'To yoke a snail with an elephant.' I desire to press forward for direction to my Master in all things; but as to trusting to my own obedience and righteousness, I should be worse than a fool, and ten times worse than a madman. Poor dependent creatures, prayer had need be our constant employment, the foot of the throne our continued dwelling-place; for the Rock of ages is our only safe Hiding-place. I rejoice in an assured knowledge by faith of my interest in Christ, and of the certainty of my eternal salvation. Yet what strivings, what conflicts, what dangers, what enemies stand in my way! The foes in my heart are so strong, that they would have killed me, and sent me to hell long ere this, had the Lord left me; but, blessed be His name, His electing, redeeming, and saving love has got fast hold of me; and who is able to pluck me out of my Father's hand? On my bended knees, I have often to cry for succor; and, bless His name, He has hitherto heard my cry.

Oh, if I did not know that all the Lord's people had soul-contention, I should give up all for lost! I rejoice that the promises left on record are meant for me, as well as for every saint of His, and as such I desire to grasp them. Let the whole earth, and even God's professing people, cast out my name as evil; my Lord and Master, He will not. I glory in the distinguishing grace of God, and will not, by the grace of God, step one inch from my principles, or think of adhering to the present fashionable sort of religion.

"Oh, could I become like holy men of past ages, — fearless of men, — holding sweet communion with God, — weaned more from the world, and enabled to fix my thoughts on spiritual things entirely!

But when I would serve God, I find my old deceitful heart full of the very essence of hell, rising up into my mouth, polluting all I say and all I do. What should I do if, like you, I were called to be engaged about things of time and sense? I fear I should be neither diligent in business, nor fervent in spirit. 'But,' (say you,) 'he keeps talking all about himself.' True, he does; he cannot help it.

Self is too much his master. I am proud of my own ignorance: and, like a toad, bloated with my own venomous pride, — proud of what I haw.' not got, and boasting when I should be bemoaning. I trust you have greater freedom from your own corruptions than I have; and in secret, social, and family prayer enjoy more blessed, sanctified liberty at the footstool of mercy.

"Rejoice! for Heaven awaits us, and all the Lord's family! The mansion is ready; the crown is made; the harp is strung; there are no willows there. May we be enabled to go on, brave as lions, and valiant for the truth and cause of King Jesus, and by the help o! the Spirit, vow eternal warfare with every sin, and rest not until the sword of the Spirit has destroyed all the enemies in our hearts! May we be enabled to trust the Lord, for He will help us; we must conquer; we cannot be lost. Lost? Impossible! For who is able to snatch us out of our Father's hand?

"May the Lord bless you exceedingly!

"Your affectionate nephew,

"C. H. SPURGEON."

"Monday.

"My Dear Mother,

"I write to acknowledge and thank you for a box from home. Dear Mother, you are indeed very kind; how I ought to bless God for such parents!.... Mr. Leeding is very much obliged to you for the ham, and Mr. Spurgeon, your son, desires to thank you for a nice cake, apples, etc. I wish you had not laid your hand on the *Key to the Bible;* for, if I had had it, I should have been delighted to have given it to my dear Mother. Perhaps I may take the credit for it now....

We have no minister yet. Mr. Leeding said, the other morning, 'I need not ask you how you are; you are always well, like some tree.'

I have been, several times, to see a lady in this town, Mother of one of our boys. She goes to church, but I have reason to think her an eminent Christian. She is all day in pain, never goes out, and can hardly sleep. She made me think of your rheumatics. She has four little children. They are rich; her husband is a good, kind sort of man, but he is not, I fear, a renewed man. She has wave upon wave. She has no one to speak to. I think it a privilege to talk to any of God's people, to comfort and console them. We do not know how many need our prayers.

"My best love, dear Mother, to you and Father.

"Your affectionate son,

"CHARLES."
"Cambridge,
"Thursday, Dec., 1850.

"Miss Caroline Louisa Spurgeon,

"Your name is so long that it will almost reach across the paper.

We have one young gentleman in our school whose name is Edward Ralph William Baxter Tweed; the boys tease him about his long name; but he is a very good boy, and that makes his name a good one. Everybody's name is pretty, if they are good people. The Duke of Tuscany has just had a little son; the little fellow was taken to the Catholic Cathedral, had some water put on his face, and then they named him-you must get Eliza to read it, — Giovanni Nepomerceno Maria Annunziata Guiseppe Giovanbaptista Ferdinando Baldassere Luigi Gonzaga Pietro Allesandro Zanobi Antonino. A pretty name to go to bed and get up with; it will be a long while before he will be able to say it all the way through! If anyone is called by the name of Christian, that is better than all these great words: it is the best name in the world, except the name of our Lord Jesus Christ. My best love to you. I hope you will enjoy yourself, and try to make others happy, too; for then you are sure to be happy yourself; whereas, if you only look out to please yourself, you will make others uncomfortable, and will not make even yourself happy. However, of course, you know that, and I need not tell you of it. A happy Christmas to you!

"Your loving brother,

"CHARLES."

(Letter addressed to Master William Cooper, one of C. H. Spurgeon's former pupils at Newmarket: —)

"9, Union Road,
"Cambridge,
"___, 1851.

"My Dear William,

"You see, by this address, that I am no longer at Mr. Swindell's, but am very comfortable here in a smaller school of about fifteen boys. I suppose you are at home, but find farming is not all play, nor perhaps altogether so profitable or pleasant as study; it is well said, 'We do not know the value of our mercies till we lose them.

"Knowing (in some humble measure, at least,) the value of religion, let me also bring it before your attention. If you give yourself time to think, you will soon remember that you must die; and if you meditate one more moment, you will recollect that you have a soul, and that soul will never die, but will live for ever; and if you die in your present state, it must live in endless torment. You are an accountable being; God, who made you, demands perfect obedience. But you must own that you have sinned; say not, 'I am not a great sinner,' for one sin only would be sufficient to sink your soul for ever in the pit of perdition. The sentence of death stands against you, and mercy alone stays its execution. Seeing now that you are in such danger, how do you think to escape? Surely you will not be content to die as you are, for you will one day find it no light matter to endure the hot displeasure of an angry God. Do you imagine that, if you live better for the future, God will forgive your past offenses? That is a mistake; see if you can find it in the Bible.

"Perhaps you intend to think about religion after you have enjoyed sin a little longer; or (but surely you are not so foolish) possibly you think that you are too young' to die. But who knows whether that future time will be afforded, and who said that you can turn to Christ just when you please? Your heart is deceitful above all things, and your natural depravity so great that you will not turn to God. Trust not, then, to resolutions made in your own strength, they are but wind; nor to yourself, who are but a broken reed; nor to your own heart, or you are a fool. There is no way of salvation but Christ; you cannot save yourself, having no power even to think one good thought; neither can your parents' love and prayers save you; none but Jesus can, He is the Savior of the helpless, and I tell you that He died for all such as feel their vileness, and come to Him for cleansing.

"You do not deserve salvation; well, there is not a jot of merit on the sinner's part mentioned in the covenant. You have nothing; you are nothing; but Christ is all, and He must be everything to you, or you will never be saved. None reach Heaven but by free-grace, and through free-grace alone. Even a faint desire after any good thing came from God, from whom you must get more, for He giveth liberally, and no poor sinner, begging at His door, was ever yet sent empty away.

"Look at the blessedness of real religion, no one is truly happy but a child of God. The believer is safe, for God has promised to preserve him; and if once you have the pearl of great price, it cannot be taken from you. The way to Heaven is faith, 'looking unto Jesus;' this faith is the gift of God, and none but those who have it know its value. Oh, may you possess it! — is the earnest prayer of —

"Yours faithfully,

"CHARLES H. SPURGEON.
"Cambridge,
"May 3, 1851.
"My Dear Mother,

150

"Many happy returns of this day, I pray for you. Another year's journey of the vast howling wilderness have you gone; you have leaned on the arm of your Beloved, and are now nearer the gates of bliss. Happy as the year has been, I trust, to you, yet I do not think you would wish to traverse it over again, or to go back one step of the way. Glorious, wondrous, has been the grace shown to all of us, as members of the mystical body of Christ, in preservation, restraint from sin, constraint to holiness, and perseverance in the Christian state. What shall a babe say to a Mother in Israel? And yet, if I might speak, I would say, 'Take this year's mercies as earnests of next year's blessings.' The God who has kept you so long, you may rest assured will never leave you. If He had not meant to do good continually to you, He would not have done it at all. His love in time past, in the past year, forbids you —

"'FORBIDS YOU to think,
He'll leave you at last in trouble to sink'

"The rapturous moments of enjoyment, the hallowed hours of communion, the blest days of sunshine in His presence, are pledges of sure, certain, infallible glory.

Mark the providences of this year; how clearly have you seen His hand in things which others esteem chance! God, who has moved the world, has exercised His own vast heart and thought for you. All your life, your spiritual life, all things have worked together for good; nothing has gone wrong, for God has directed, controlled all. 'Why sayest thou, O Jacob, and speakest, O Israel, My way is hid from the Lord, and my judgment is passed over from my God?' He who counts the hairs of our heads, and keeps us as the apple of His eye, has not forgotten you, but still loves you with an everlasting love. The mountains have not departed yet, nor the hills been removed, and till then we may have confidence that we, His own people, are secure.

"But I am writing what to you are everyday meditations. Well, dear Mother. you know where this comes from, only from your boy. Let us rejoice together; your prayers for us I know will be answered, they are sure to be, for God has said so. May God' give you a feast — honey, wine, milk, — may you be satisfied with marrow and fatness, satiated with the dainties and luxuries of religion, and rejoice exceedingly in the Lord! I remember that, a year ago, I publicly professed the name of Jesus by baptism. Pray for me, that I may not dishonor my profession, and break my solemn vow. While I look back through the year, I can see a Great Exhibition of love and grace to me, more marvelous than even that now opened in Hyde Park. Give my love to dear Father, Archer, and sisters; and accept the same doubly. I trust all are well. I have nothing the matter with me. Mr. and Mrs. L. desire respects. Many thanks for the postal order.

"I am,
'Your affectionate son,

"CHARLES H. SPURGEON."

Chapter Nineteen - "The Boy-Preacher of Fens."

MY FIRST SERMON.

I REMEMBER well the first place in which I addressed a congregation of adults, and the illustration above sets it clearly before my mind's eye. It was not my first public address by a great many, for at Newmarket, and Cambridge, and elsewhere, the Sabbath-school had afforded me ample scope for speaking the gospel; but no regular set discourse to a congregation met for Divine worship had I delivered till one eventful Sabbath evening, which found me in a cottage at Teversham, holding forth before a little assembly of humble villagers. The tale is not a new one, but it is worth telling again.

There is a Preachers' Association in Cambridge, connected with St. Andrew's Street: Chapel, once the scene of the ministry of Robert Robinson and Robert Hall. A number of worthy brethren preach the gospel in the various villages surrounding Cambridge, taking each one his turn according to plan. In my day, the presiding genius was the venerable Mr. James Vinter, whom we were wont to address as Bishop Vinter. His genial soul, warm heart, and kindly manner were enough to keep a whole fraternity stocked with love; and, accordingly, a goodly company of zealous workers belonged to the Association, and labored as true yoke-fellows. My suspicion *is,* that he not only preached himself, and helped his brethren, but that he was a sort of recruiting sergeant, and drew in young men to keep up the number of the host; at least, I can speak from personal experience as to one case.

I had, one Saturday, finished morning school, and the boys were all going home for the half-holiday, when in came the aforesaid *"Bishop"* to ask me to go over to Teversham, the next evening, for a young man was to preach there who was not much used to services, and very likely would be glad of company. That was a cunningly-devised sentence, if I remember it rightly, and I think I do, for, at: the time, in the light of that Sunday evening's revelation, I turned it over, and vastly admired its ingenuity. A request to go and preach, would have met with a decided negative; but merely to act as company to a good brother who did not like to be lonely, and perhaps might ask me to give out a hymn or to pray, was not at all a difficult matter, and the request, Understood in that fashion, was cheerfully complied with. Little did the lad know what Jonathan and David were doing when he was made to run for the arrow, and as little did I know when I was cajoled into accompanying a young man to Teversham.

My Sunday-school work was over, tea had been taken, and I set off through Barnwell, and away along the Newmarket Road, with a gentleman some few years my senior. We talked of good things, and at last I expressed my hope that he would feel the presence of God while preaching. He seemed to start, and assured me that he had never preached in his life, and could not attempt such a thing; he was looking to his young friend, Mr. Spurgeon, for that. This was a new view of the situation, and I could only reply that I was no minister; and that, even it' I had been, I was quite unprepared. My companion only repeated that *he,* in a still more emphatic sense, was not a preacher, that he would help *me* in any other part of the service, but that there would be no sermon unless I delivered one. He told me that, if I repeated one of my Sunday-school addresses, it would just suit the poor people, and would probably give them more satisfaction than the studied sermon of a learned divine. I felt that I was fairly committed to do my best. I walked along quietly, lifting up my soul to God, and it seemed to me that I could surely tell a few poor cottagers of the sweetness and love of Jesus, for I felt them in my own soul. Praying for Divine help, I resolved to make the attempt. My text should be, "*Unto* you therefore which believe He is precious," and I would trust the Lord to open my mouth in honor of His dear Son. It seemed a great risk and a serious trial; but depending upon the power of the Holy Ghost, I would at least tell out the story of the cross, and not allow the people to go home without a word.

We entered the low-pitched room of the thatched cottage, where a few simple-winded farm-laborers and their wives were gathered together; we sang, and prayed, and read the Scriptures, and then came my first sermon.

How long, or how short: it was, I cannot now remember. It was not half such a task as I had feared it would be, but I was glad to see my way to a fair conclusion, and to the giving out of the last hymn. To my own delight, I had not broken down, nor stopped short in the middle, nor been destitute of ideas, and the desired haven was in view. I made a finish, and took up the hymn-book; but, to my astonishment, an aged voice cried out, "Bless your dear heart, how old are you?" My very solemn reply' was, "You must wait till the service is over before making any such inquiries. Let us now sing." We did sing, the young preacher pronounced the benediction, and then there began a dialogue which enlarged into a warm, friendly talk, in which everybody appeared to take part. "How old are you?" was the leading question. "I am under sixty," was the reply. "Yes, and under sixteen," was the old lady's rejoinder. "Never mind my age, think of the Lord Jesus and His preciousness," was all that I could say, after promising to come again, if the gentlemen at Cambridge thought me fit to do so. Very great and profound was my awe of "the gentlemen at Cambridge" in those days.

Are there not other young men who might begin to speak for Jesus in some such lowly fashion, — young men who hitherto have been as mute as fishes? Our villages and hamlets offer fine opportunities for youthful speakers. Let them not wait till they are invited to a chapel, or have prepared a line essay, or have secured an intelligent audience. If they will go and tell out from their hearts what the Lord Jesus has done for them, they will find ready listeners. Many of our young folks want to commence their service for Christ by doing great things, and therefore do nothing at all; let none of my readers become the victims of such an unreasonable ambition. He who is willing to teach infants, or to give away tracts, and so to begin at the beginning, is far more likely to be useful than the youth who is full of affectations, and sleeps in a white necktie, who is aspiring to the ministry, and is touching up certain superior manuscripts which he hopes ere long to read from the pastor's pulpit. He who talks upon plain gospel themes in a farmer's kitchen, and is able to interest: the carter's boy and the dairymaid, has more of the minister in him than the prim little man who keeps prating about being cultured, and means by that being taught to use words which nobody can understand. To make the very poorest listen with pleasure and profit, is in itself an achievement; and beyond this, it is the best possible promise and preparation for an influential ministry. Let our younger brethren go in for cottage preaching, and plenty of it. If there is no' Lay Preachers' Association, let them work by themselves. The expense is not very great for rent, candles, and a few forms: many a young man's own pocket money would cover it all. No isolated group of houses should be left without its preaching-room, no hamlet without its evening service.

This is the lesson of the thatched cottage at Teversham.

(Preaching at the Music Hall, Royal Surrey Gardens, on Lord's-day morning, March 13th, 1859, upon the words, "Unto you therefore which believe He is precious," Mr. Spurgeon said: — This text calls to my recollection the opening of my ministry. It is about eight years since, as a lad of sixteen, I stood up for the first time in my life to preach the gospel in a cottage to a handful of poor people, who had come together for worship.

I felt my own inability to preach, but I ventured to take this text, "Unto you therefore which believe He is precious." I do not think I could have said anything upon any other text, but Christ was precious to my soul, and I was in the flush of my youthful love, and I could not be silent when a precious Jesus 'was the subject. I had but just escaped from the bondage of Egypt, I had not forgotten the broken fetter; still did I recollect those flames which seemed to burn about my path, and that devouring gulf which opened its mouth as if ready to swallow me up. With all these things fresh in my youthful heart, I could speak of His preciousness who had been my Savior, and had plucked me as a brand from the burning, and set me upon a rock, and put a new song in my mouth, and established my goings. And now, at this time, what shall I say? "What hath God wrought!" How hath the little one become a thousand, and the small one a great people! And what shall I say concerning this text but that, if the Lord Jesus was precious then, He is as precious now? And if I could declare, then, that Jesus was the object of my soul's desire, that for Him I hoped to live, and for Him I would be prepared to die, can I not say, God being my witness, that He is more precious to me this day than ever He was? In the recollection of His unparalleled mercy towards the chief of sinners, I must anew devote myself to Him, and afresh surrender my heart to Him who is my Lord and King. This remark is uttered by way of introduction, it may seem egotistical, but that I cannot help. I must give glory to God in the midst of the great congregation, and pay my vows to the Lord now in the midst of all His saints, in the midst of thee, O Jerusalem!) Considerable weight is to be given to the judgment of men and women who live near to God, and in most instances their verdict will not be a mistaken one. Yet this appeal is not final nor infallible, and is only to be estimated in proportion to the intelligence and piety of those consulted. I remember well how earnestly I was dissuaded from preaching by as godly a Christian matron as ever breathed; I endeavored to estimate, with candor and patience, the value of her opinion; but it was outweighed by the judgment of persons of wider experience. If a man be truly called of God to the ministry, I will defy him to withhold himself from it. A man who has really within him the inspiration of the Holy Ghost calling him to preach, cannot help it, — he must preach. As fire within the bones, so will that influence be until it blazes forth. Friends may check him, foes criticize him, despisers sneer at him, the man is indomitable; he must preach if he has the call of Heaven. All earth might forsake him; but he would preach to the barren mountain-tops. If he has the call of Heaven, if he had no congregation, he would preach to the rippling waterfalls, and let the brooks hear his voice. He could not be silent. He would become a voice crying in the wilderness, "Prepare ye the way of the Lord." I no more believe it possible to stop ministers than to stop the stars of heaven. I think it no more possible to make a man cease from preaching, if he is really called, than to stay some mighty cataract, by seeking, in an infant's cup, to catch the rushing torrent. The man has been moved of Heaven, who shall stop him? He has been touched of God, who shall impede him? With an eagle's wing, he must fly; who shall chain him to the earth? With a seraph's voice, he must speak; who shall seal his lips? And when a man does speak as the Spirit gives him utterance, he will feel a holy joy akin to that of Heaven; and when it is over, he wishes to be at his work again, he longs to be once more preaching. Is not the Lord's Word like a fire within *me?* Must I not speak if God has placed it there?

I was for three years a Cambridge man, though I never entered the University. I could not have obtained a degree, because I was a Nonconformist; and, moreover,' it was a better thing for me to pursue my studies under an admirable scholar and tender friend, and to preach at the same time. I was, by my tutor's own expressed verdict, considered to be sufficiently proficient in my studies to have taken a good place on the list had the way been open. "You could win in a canter," said he to me. I had, however, a better College course, for, when I first began to preach, this was my usual way of working. I was up in the morning early, praying and reading the Word; all the day, I was either teaching my scholars 'or studying theology as much as I could; then, at five in the evening, I became a traveling preacher, and went into the villages around Cambridge, to tell out what I had learned. My quiet meditation during the walk helped me to digest what I had read, and the rehearsal of my lesson in public, by preaching it to the people, fixed it on my memory. I do not mean that I ever repeated a single sentence from memory, but I thought my reading over again while on my legs, and thus worked it into my very soul; and I can bear my testimony that I never learned so much, or learned it so thoroughly, as when I used to tell out, simply and earnestly, what I had first received into my own mind and heart. I found that I derived greater benefit by proclaiming to others what.I had learned than if I had kept it all to myself.

I must have been a singular-looking youth on wet evenings, for I walked three, five, or even eight miles out and back again on my preaching work; and when it rained, I dressed myself in waterproof leggings and a mackintosh coat, and a hat with a waterproof covering, and I carried a dark lantern to show me the way across the fields. I am sure that I was greatly profited by those early services for my Lord. How many times I enjoyed preaching the gospel in a farmer's kitchen, or in a cottage, or in a barn! Perhaps many people came to hear me because I was then only a boy.

In my young days, I fear that I said many odd things, and made many blunders; but my audience was not hypercritical, and no newspaper writers dogged my heels; so I had a happy training-school, in which, by continual practice, I attained such a degree of ready speech as I now possess.

I had many adventures, and a great variety of experiences in this itinerating work. I recollect one summer's evening, when I had engaged to preach at a village not far from Waterbeach; but, before I could reach my destination, the sky darkened, and a severe thunderstorm burst over the district. Some people are terrified at lightning; but ever since I believed in the Lord Jesus Christ, I have had no fear in a storm, however severe it might be. I distinctly remember, while quite a lad, being in my uncle's house one night during a tremendous tempest. The older folks were all afraid; but I had really trusted myself with the Lord Jesus, and I did not dare to fear. The baby was upstairs, and nobody was brave enough to fetch it down because of a big window on the stairs. I went up to the bedroom, and brought the child to its Mother, and then read a Psalm, and prayed with my relatives, who were trembling in terror. There was real danger, for a stack was set on fire a short distance away; but I was as calm as in the sunshine of a summer's day, not because I was naturally courageous, but because I had unshaken confidence in my Lord. I love the lightnings, God's thunder is my delight; I never feel so well as when there is a great thunder and lightning storm. Then I feel as if I could mount up as with the wings of eagles, and my whole heart loves then to sing, —

"The God that rules on high,
And thunders when He please,
That rides upon the stormy sky,
And manages the seas.
"This awful God is ours,
Our Father and our love;
He shall send clown His Heavenly powers
To carry us above."

Men are by nature afraid of the heavens; the superstitious dread the signs in the sky, and even the bravest spirit is sometimes made to tremble when the firmament is ablaze with lightning, and the pealing thunder seems to make the vast concave of heaven to tremble and to reverberate; but I always feel ashamed to keep indoors when the thunder shakes the solid earth, and the lightnings flash like arrows from the sky. Then God is abroad, and I love to walk out in some wide space, and to look up and mark the opening gates of heaven, as the lightning reveals far beyond, and enables me to gaze into the unseen. I like to hear my Heavenly Father's voice in the thunder.

On this particular occasion, while walking to the place where I was to preach, I was enjoying the storm; but as I was passing a cottage on the road, I noticed a woman who seemed to be greatly alarmed and in sore distress because of the tempest. I did not like to pass by, and leave a fellow-creature in trouble, so I entered the house, read a few verses of Scripture, and prayed, and so comforted the woman. I then proceeded to my destination, to fulfill my engagement. On entering the village, I took off my waterproof coat, because the smooth surface appeared to reflect `the vivid flashes of lightning in a way that might alarm the timid. I found that, because of the severity of the tempest, the people were not expecting that there would be a service; so I went round from house to house, and invited them to come to the regular meeting place. This unusual method of gathering a congregation brought me many hearers; the service was held, and, at its close, I walked back to my Cambridge home.

One night, having been preaching the Word in a country village, I was walking home, all by myself, along a lonely footpath. I do not know what it was that ailed me, but I was prepared to be alarmed; when, of a surety, I saw something standing in the hedge, — ghastly, giant-like, and with outstretched arms. Surely, I thought, for once I have come across the supernatural; here is some restless spirit performing its midnight march beneath the moon, or some demon of the pit wandering abroad. I deliberated with myself a moment, and having no faith in ghosts, I plucked up courage, and determined to solve the mystery. The monster stood on the other side of a ditch, right in the hedge. I jumped the ditch, and found myself grasping an old tree, which some waggish body had taken pains to cover with whitewash, with a view to frighten simpletons. That old tree has served me a good turn full often, for I have learned from it to leap at difficulties, and find them vanish or turn to triumphs.

Frequently, in those country places, when preaching in a low-pitched building crowded with people, I have seen the candles burn dimly for want of air, — a clear indication that we were killing ourselves by inhaling an atmosphere from which the vitalizing principle had almost all gone. I have been afraid of the lights going out, and have thought it better to let the congregation depart rather sooner than usual. On one occasion, having a candle on each side of me in a small pulpit, I was somewhat vigorous, and dashed one of my luminaries from its place. It fell upon the bald head of a friend below, who looked up with an expression which I can see at this moment, and it makes me smile still. I took no more notice of the accident than to weave it into what I was saying; and I believe most of my hearers considered it to have been a striking practical illustration of the remark which accompanied it, "How soon is the glory of life dashed down!"

In my earlier days, I read, somewhere or other, in a volume of Lectures upon Homiletics, a statement which considerably alarmed me at the time: it was something to this effect: — "If any man shall find a difficulty in selecting a text, he had better at once go back to the grocer's shop, or to the plough, for he evidently has not the capacity required for a minister."

Now, as such had been very frequently my cross and burden, I inquired within myself whether I should resort to some form of secular labor, and leave the ministry; but I have not done so, for I still have the conviction that, although condemned by the sweeping judgment of the lecturer, I follow a call to which God has manifestly set His seal. I was so much in trouble of conscience through the aforesaid severe remark, that I asked my grandfather, who had been in the ministry some fifty years, whether he was ever perplexed in choosing his theme. He told me frankly that this had always been his greatest trouble, compared with which, preaching in itself was no anxiety at all. I remember the venerable man's remark, "The difficulty is not because there are not enough texts, but because there are so many, that I am in a strait betwixt them." We are something like the lover of choice flowers, who finds himself surrounded by all the beauties of the garden, with permission to select but one. How long he lingers between the rose and the lily, and how great the difficulty to prefer one among ten thousand lovely blooms! To me, still, I must admit, my text-selection is a very great embarrassment, — *embarras de richesse, as* the French say, — an embarrassment of riches;, very different from the bewilderment of poverty, — the anxiety of attending to the most pressing of so many truths, all clamoring for a hearing, so many duties all needing enforcing, and so many spiritual needs of the people all demanding supply. I confess that I frequently sit hour after hour praying and waiting for a subject, and that this is the main part of my study; much hard labor have I spent in manipulating; topics, ruminating upon points of doctrine, making skeletons out of verses, and then burying every bone of them in the catacombs of oblivion, drifting on and on over leagues of broken water, till I see the red lights, and make sail direct to the desired haven. I believe that, almost any Saturday in my life, I prepare enough outlines of Sermons, if I felt at liberty to preach them, to last me for a month, but I no more dare to use them than an honest mariner would run to shore a cargo of contraband goods.

I am always sure to have the most happy day when I get a good text in the morning from nay Master. When I have had to preach two or three sermons in a day, I have asked Him for the morning subject, and preached from it; and I have asked Him for the afternoon's topic or the evening's portion, and preached, from it, after meditating on it for my own soul's comfort, — not in the professional style of a regular sermon-maker, but feasting upon it for myself. Such simple food has clone the people far more good than if I had been a week in manufacturing a sermon, for it has come warm from the heart just after it has been received in my own soul; and therefore it has been well spoken, because well known, well tasted, and well felt. Sometimes, my texts have come to me in a very remarkable way.

While I was living at Cambridge, I had, as usual, to preach in the evening at a neighboring village, to which I had to walk. After reading and meditating all day, I could not meet with the right text. Do what I would, no response came from the sacred oracle, no light flashed from the Urim and Thummim; I prayed, I searched the Scriptures, I turned from one verse to another, but my mind would not take hold of a text; I was, as Bunyan would say, "much tumbled up and down in my thoughts." Just then, I walked to the window, and looked out. On the other side of the narrow street in which I lived, I saw a poor solitary canary bird upon the slates, surrounded by a crowd of sparrows, who were all pecking at it as if they would tear it to pieces. At that moment the verse came to my mind, "*Mine* heritage is unto me as a speckled bird, the birds round about are against her." I walked off with the greatest possible composure, considered the passage during my long and lonely walk, and preached upon the peculiar people, and the persecutions of their enemies, with freedom and ease to myself, and I believe with comfort to my rustic audience. The text was sent to me, and if the ravens did not bring it, certainly the sparrows did.

While I was living at Cambridge, I once heard Mr. Jay, of Bath, preach.

His text was, "Let your conversation be as it becometh the gospel of Christ." I remember with what dignity he preached, and yet how simply.

He made one remark which deeply impressed my youthful mind, and which I have never forgotten; it was this, "You do need a Mediator between yourselves and God, but you do not need a Mediator between yourselves and Christ; you may come to Him just as you are." Another of his striking sayings was this, "Popery is a lie, Puseyism is a lie, baptismal regeneration is a lie." I recollect also that, in the course of his sermon, Mr. Jay said that ladies were sometimes charged with dressing in too costly a fashion. He told us that he did not himself know much about that matter; but, if they would let him hear what their income was, he would tell them how many yards of silk, satin, lace, or ribbon, they could afford. My recollections of Mr. Jay were such as I would not like to lose. It usually happens that, when we listen to a venerable patriarch, such as he then was, there is all the greater weight in his words because of his age. I fancy that, if I had heard the same sermon preached by a young man, I should not have thought much of it; but there appeared all the greater depth in it because it came from an old man standing almost on the borders of the grave.

In an early part of my ministry, while but a lad, I was seized with an intense desire to hear Mr. John Angell James; and, though my finances were somewhat meager, I performed a pilgrimage to Birmingham, solely with that object in view. I heard him deliver a week-evening lecture, in his large vestry, on that precious text, "*Ye* are complete in Him." The savor of that very sweet discourse abides with me to this day, and I shall never read the passage without associating therewith the quiet but earnest utterances of that eminent man of God. Years afterwards, on being in Mr. James's company, I told him that I went all the way from Cambridge to Birmingham to hear him preach. On my mentioning the text, he replied,

"Ah! that was a Calvinistic sermon. You would enjoy that; but you would not get on with me always." I was glad also to have the opportunity of thanking him for that precious book of his, *The Anxious Enquirer,* which has been the means of bringing so many sinners to the Savior, and which I had found exceedingly helpful when I was seeking the Lord.

A CRITICAL JUNCTURE IN THE YOUNG PREACHER'S HISTORY.

"Cambridge, May 15/51.

"My Dear Father,

"My choice of return home is easily made. I hope very much you will be so kind as to let me go to the Exhibition. Mr. C__, who was at Mr. Lewis's, has just called to see me...I am going to his house to tea, he lodges with Mr. R_. I guess I feel no mercy for him; I mean, Mr. R ; a cap and gown are poor things to sell one's principles for. 32u *have not written to Mr. Leeding.* Where is Mr. Walker? I cannot write, for I know nothing of his whereabouts. We have no minister yet. We have had some excellent supplies. I am very comfortable, and I may say, happy. Were it not for my vile heart, I might rejoice'. I am the least of God's people, I am sure I am the worst. But yet I *am* one; I believe in Jesus and trust in Him, and this, I take it, is the evidence of life. I can fall into His arms, though I cannot rest on my own merits, for I have none. Jesus and Jesus alone is my defense. I know you pray for me. I think I have felt the answer to your earnest entreaties. Sometimes, I pour my heart out sweetly, freely; at another time, I can hardly bring up a petition. What a contrast, mixture, paradox I am! I hope you and dear Mother are well. Love to all.

"Your affectionate son,

"CHARLES."

(The sentence in the above letter "You have not written to Mr. Leeding," implies that an important communication from Mr. John Spurgeon was anxiously awaited at Cambridge by both tutor and pupil. When it arrived, Mr. Leeding wrote the following reply, which was the means of retaining C. H. Spurgeon at Cambridge, and so, indirectly, affected the whole of his future life: —)

"Union Road,
"Cambridge,
"June 11th, 1851.

"My Dear Sir,

"I hasten to reply to your note, which I should have been glad to have received earlier. I did not expect to part with Charles before the end of next week, but a few days are of little consequence, and you may rest assured of his leaving Cambridge by the first train on Monday next.

"As I conceive you have written with candor, I shall think myself criminal if I do not reply in the same spirit upon the subject of your son's future career. I have been thankful unceasingly for that merciful Providential arrangement that first brought him under my roof, as well for the assistance he renders me, as for the wholesome influence of his piety and general character; it will be a severe blow to me to lose him, on the latter account especially. I will gladly give him f5 per half-year for the next two half-years, when he shall have a fair addition in proportion to the increase of the school; that increase is slow at present, but I have still good hope of all the success I desire; I have had most malignant foes to contend with, but their violence has fallen on their own heads.

"With regard to Charles's improvement, I can speak with confidence as to

those points which are directed to his future life as a minister or a teacher. He has read a great deal,, and has made excellent progress in his facility in reading Latin authors; he has done well in Greek, but he had much more to do in that department, and appeared to have done nothing of service in that since he left Mr. Lewis's. You may rely on my word, as a Christian man, that he is in the clear path of mental improvement and eminence. I am positive he is in as fair a way of preparation for the ministry as he would be were he in a College with that view.

"You may make up your minds that he is safe for the ministry, and in a very few years; he has first-rate abilities, a head adequate to the investigation of the deepest points, accompanied with a fluency of utterance. He is considered a most valuable help in the Sabbath-school, and is treated with the greatest kindness by one gentleman connected with it, who often expresses the highest esteem for him, and indeed makes him his most intimate friend. That gentleman is a man of sound judgment and genuine piety, in affluent circumstances, and the father of a family; whatever lack of honor Charles may experience 'in his own country,' I can tell you he is not without honor here. He has also regularly served at preaching-stations connected with our church, and is universally acceptable.

One of the lay preachers, in whom I place the greatest confidence, has expressed to me a high opinion of him, and has authorized me to say that he has no doubt, at seasonable time, the church will properly estimate his talents for the ministry.

"I might add to this; but I judge this is sufficient to convince you that you will consult his interests by allowing him to remain here at least another year. I lay some claim to disinterestedness in this matter; if I considered his interests would be best served by his seeking for a larger salary elsewhere, I should feel it my duty to advise it. He might get a little more money, but he would have far less opportunity for self-improvement. The thought has several times occurred to me that, as he is young', and has some years before him ere he could enter the ministry, he might be able to pass through the Cambridge University course. This would be of great advantage to him as a student, and a good recommendation to him.

He might pursue the same work that I did, and pay his own expenses without costing you a shilling; if my school increases pretty well, it can be done; — a year hence will be early ,enough to decide this.

"I am, as you must perceive, anxious to retain him, as much for his sake as my own; but if you are desirous of more money than I offer for the next year, I must yield to the painful alternative of parting with him; at the same time, I am sure you will be taking a wrong step.

"Hoping yourself, Mrs. S., and your family are well,

"I remain,

"Dear Sir,

"Yours most faithfully,

"E. S. LEEDING."

"Mr. Spurgeon."

(The following letter shows that Mr. Spurgeon had his request concerning going to the Great Exhibition granted, and it also expresses his gratitude that he was shortly to return to Cambridge, though probably even he scarcely realized then how much was involved in his father's decision: —)

"Colchester,

"June 25 (1851).

"My Dear Aunt, "I enclose this in Uncle's note. Is he better? I have much enjoyed my three days in London, and am now happy at home. I am very thankful that, if spared, I am going back to Cambridge. Of my progress there, I am not ashamed; it should and might have been greater, but still it is somewhat. My faults I have not learned there, I had the same at Maidstone, and I am not at all fond of having blame thrown on the place where Providence has placed me. I am all fault, but what God's grace has made right. I am content to be evil spoken of, if I can but grow in grace and serve God. Where I have most opportunity of telling sinners the way of salvation, and of preparation for a future course of labor, I trust I shall always feel most happy. Human wisdom I desire to gain, but only in subservience and as handmaid to spiritual knowledge and Divine instruction.

"Grandfather is now with us; he preached last night on 'Cast thy burden upon the Lord, and He shall sustain thee: He shall never suffer the righteous to be moved.' A blessed thing it must be for the new-born sons of God to have such a stay in the hour of trouble; and he who, having left hi,; own righteousness, trusts alone on Jesus, has a perfect right to this promise.

"Mother is gone to old Mr. 'Merchant's 51st anniversary at Layer Breton. He is almost past preaching, and stands a monument of the unchanging love of God,

161

who, having once. loved a person, will always love him. The motto over his pulpit is, 'We preach Christ, and Him crucified.' I am sure you need all the comforts of the gospel now, and I wish I knew enough to be able to give them faithfully and successfully; that is reserved for future lessons of experience. None who rely on Jesus ,Christ will ever find their troubles too heavy; for all those who take Him as their whole Savior, He is a supporter.

May God deal kindly with you, and support you!

"Love to self and Uncle from all.

"I am,

"Your affectionate nephew,

"C. H. SPURGEON."

Chapter Twenty - First Outlines of Sermons, 1851-1852.

AMONG the many literary treasures so carefully preserved by Mr. Spurgeon, there are two sets of books containing his first brief Outlines of Sermons, and the more lengthy manuscripts which he used to prepare until the claims of his London pastorate made impossible to continue doing so any longer. Probably, by that time, he also felt that he did not need to write so fully as in his early preaching days; and, shortly afterwards, as he often told his students, the revision of his printed Sermons gave him all the advantages that he might have derived from more elaborate preparation for the pulpit.

The first volume of Outlines must have been commenced very soon after Mr. Spurgeon began to preach, for the second written in it was only the fourth discourse delivered by the youthful evangelist. The text was Revelation 21:27, and it was preached at Barton, near Cambridge, on February 9th, 1851. This fact fixes, approximately, the date of the commencement of that wonderful world-wide ministry which the Lord so long and so greatly blessed, and which He still continues most graciously to own and use. Such intense interest attaches to these early record:;, that the Autobiography would be incomplete unless it included at least a few specimens of the beloved preacher's first homiletic efforts. Mr. Spurgeon had himself intended, long ago, to publish a selection from them; in the Preface to *The New Park Street Pulpit* for 1857, he announced that he hoped shortly to issue a volume, of his earliest Sermons, while Pastor at Waterbeach, but this was prevented by the pressure of his rapidly increasing work. The Outlines are valuable, not only because of their intrinsic merits, but also as the first products of the mind and heart which afterwards yielded so many thousands of discourses to the Church and the world, for the glory of God and the good of men. It must be remembered that they were made by a youth of sixteen; literally, "the boy-preacher." At the beginning of Vol. 1. is a *textual* index, showing that the seventy-seven Outlines were based upon passages taken from fifteen Books in the Old Testament, and sixteen in the New Testament; while at the end is a *subject* index, which bears a remarkable resemblance to those which set forth the contents of every volume of the *Metropolitan Tabernacle Pulpit.* Happy preacher, who commenced, as he continued, and concluded, the ministry he "received of the Lord Jesus, to testify the gospel of the grace of God."

As indicating the character of the whole series, the first three Sermon-notes are given in the present work, together with one Outline from each of the succeeding volumes, *facsimile* reproductions of the highly-adorned title-pages of Vols. 1. and 2., and the characteristic inscriptions written by Mr. Spurgeon at the commencement and conclusion of most of the volumes.

OUTLINE 1. — ADOPTION.

"Having predestinated us unto the adoption of children by Jesus Christ to Himself according to the good pleasure of His will." —

Ephesians 1:5.

Meaning of the term. Common among Romans. Two instances in Scripture, — Moses and Esther. Adoption differs from Justification and Regeneration.

I. THE SENSE IN WHICH BELIEVERS ARE SONS OF GOD.

Not as Jesus. More so than creatures.

(i) In some things spiritual adoption agrees with civil.

1. In name and thing. **2.** To an inheritance. **3.** Voluntary on the part of the Adopter. **4.** Taking the Adopter's name. **5.** Received into the Family. **6.**

Considered as children: food, protection, clothing, education, attendance provided. **7.** Under the control of the Father.

(ii) In some things they disagree.

1. Civil adoption requires the consent of the adopted. **2.** Civil adoption was intended to provide for childless persons. **3.** In civil adoption, the adopted had something to recommend him. **4.** The nature of a son could not be given. **5.** The children did not inherit till their father's death. **6.** The Pontifex might make it void.

II. THE CAUSE OF ADOPTION.

1. The Person: God. Father. Son. Spirit.

2. The motive. free-grace, not works.

III. THE OBJECTS OF IT.

Elect sinners, not angels. All believers. not all men, but justified men.

IV. THE EXCELLENCY OF IT.

1. It is an act of surprising grace. (1 John 3:1.) Consider the persons. **2.** It exceeds all others. **3.** It makes men honorable. **4.** Brings men into the highest relations. **5.** Includes all things. **6.** Immutable and everlasting.

V. THE EFFECTS OF IT.

1. Share in the love, pity, and care of God. **2.** Access with boldness. **3.** Conformity to the image of Jesus. **4.** The Holy Spirit. **5.** Heirship.

Encouragement. Appeal to saints and sinners.

OUTLINE II. — NECESSITY OF PURITY FOR AN ENTRANCE INTO HEAVEN.

"And there shall in no wise enter into it any, thing that defileth, neither whatsoever worketh abomination, or maketh a lie: but they which arc written in the Lamb's book of life." — Revelation 21:27.

I. THE STRICTNESS OF THE LAW.... "any thing that defileth."

Satan cannot. Sin cannot. What a matter of rejoicing to Christians! How can man enter?

Not by ceremonies. Not by the law. Not by sincere obedience in part.

The heart must be purified.

All past sin forgiven. How? By free-grace.

All present sin crucified. How? By the Holy Spirit.

All future sin avoided. How? By the Spirit's help.

II. THE IMPOSSIBILITY OF ENTRANCE.... "in no wise."

God has said so. He will not allow it; nor will the angels; nor the redeemed.

A wicked man would not be happy in Heaven.

No prayers, cries, groans, strife, can get a dead, unholy sinner into Heaven.

If a man is not in, he is out for ever, no coming in, no change.

Call to enter in by faith in Jesus Christ.

OUTLINE III. — ABRAHAM JUSTIFIED BY FAITH.

"And he believed in the LORD; and He counted il to him for righteousness." — Genesis 15:6.

I. THE FACT... "he believed in the Lord."

Leaving his country. Life in Canaan. Sodom.

Isaac's birth. Promises to him. Isaac's sacrifice.

Two sorts of faith

1. Historical, or dead faith.

2. Living faith, producing works.

II. THE RESULT... "He counted it to him for righteousness."

1. Sins forgiven, — 2. Righteousness imputed, — by faith.

By it, he gained God's favor and love, Heaven, and eternal life.

These bring —

Peace. How easy lies the head that does no ill!

Love. When we are pure, we love God.

Joy. The justified person has true joy.

Comfort. All things work together for good.

Security. None can condemn, nor destroy.

III. AS ABRAHAM WAS SAVED, SO MUST WE BE.

Not by works, or Abraham would have been.

Not by ceremonies. Abram believed before circumcision.

Reasons why sinners and Christians should believe God; exhortations to faith.

OUTLINE 133. — BY FAITH JERICHO FELL.

"By faith the walls of Jericho fell down, after they were compassed about seven days." — Hebrews 11:30.

Faith is the one grand essential in salvation. It must be inwrought, or else there will be no spiritual life at first. It is necessary ewer after in numberless

ways. We cannot have knowledge of gospel doctrines without faith, nor can we lay hold on the promises without it. The graces are all dependent on faith. He loves most who believes most. He will have most zeal who has; most faith. Humility is produced by faith, and hope breathes through faith. In doing good to others, and particularly in combat with evil, let us have faith.

I. FAITH IS THE GRACE TO WHICH VICTORY IS GIVEN.

1. The other graces are not decked with laurel, lest man should steal their crowns; but faith is too tall, man cannot reach its head. Faith has less to do with man, and more to do with God than any of the other graces; for faith is looking away from self, and trusting the Eternal.

164

2. Faith gains the victory because she engages the arm of the Almighty on her behalf. She has power with Him, and therefore she prevails.

3. That man is most able to bear with humility the joy of victory who endured the conflict by faith; he will give all the glory to God.

4. other graces do wonders, but faith does impossibilities. She is the only grace that can act in certain places, and under certain circumstances. She is intended for this very purpose.

II. FAITH WINS HER VICTORIES IN GOD'S APPOINTED WAY.

1. She uses no means of her own contrivance; she waits upon God for guidance.

2. She neglects not His appointments; she is not presumptuous.

3. When she uses the means, she does not despise them. She ungirds the sword, — she follows the ark, — she hears the rams' horns.

4. She is laughed at for seeming folly; but in her turn she smiles.

5. She does her Maker's will, and she expects the blessing, but all in an orderly way. That is no faith at all which believes and does nothing. We may not expect to be saved by faith, unless that faith pushes us on to run in God's way. Whether we seek salvation, the good of our friends, the stopping of evil, or the destruction of our corruptions, let us seek it in the Divinely-appointed way.

III. FAITH WINS HER VICTORIES IN GOD'S TIME.

1. She goes round Jericho thirteen times; she expects the wall will come down at last, so round and round she goes.

2. She expects that, on the Lord's appointed day, her sins will all be overthrown, and she thinks her work well repaid when she knows this will happen. Therefore is she persevering in the conflict.

Now let us apply these thoughts —

1. *To the pulling down of Jericho in our own hearts.*

We want to slay all the old sinful inhabitants, but the lofty wall stands firm.

Let us have faith. Let us follow the ark. Let us hear the sound of the trumpets, even though they are only rams' horns. Let us go round the wall all the seven days, — that is, all the week, — all the days of our life. Let us inwardly groan, but not grumble with our lips; and soon, when the ordained day arrives, the walls will tremble, we shall shout, and our enemies will be gone.

2. *To the pulling down of Jericho in the world.*

Sin has strong and lofty towers. The Tower of Babel or Babylonish Rome, idolatry, etc., — let us yet believe that these will tumble to the earth. Let us continue our rounds as minister, Sunday-school teachers, and Christian workers. Keep the poor rams' horns going; do your duty, and one day Jesus shall reign universally.

3. *To the pulling down of Jericho in this village.*

Dagon stands fast here; but the ark of God is come. The trumpeters of God have long blown the trumpet; the rams' horns are still sounding a loud rough blast. Many are following the ark, but the time for the complete victory has not quite come. Keep on, brethren, and give a great shout, all at once, — by faith, — and down will come the mighty walls.

The Lord help us to believe His Word, and then fulfill to us His promises!

Amen, through JESUS.

(The following poem was written by Mr. Spurgeon at the time that he prepared and preached the foregoing discourse: —)

The Fall of Jericho

The day is come, the seventh morn
Is usher'd in with blast of horn;
Tremble, ye tow'rs of giant height,
This is the day of Israel's might.
Six days ye mock'd the silent band,
This hour their shout shall shake your land.
Old Jordan's floods shall hear the sound,
Yon circling hills with fear shall bound.
Thou palm — tree'd city, at thy gates
Death in grim form this moment waits;
See, hurrying on the howling blast,
That dreaded hour, thy last, thy last.
Lo, at the leader's well-known sign,
The tribes their mighty voices join,
With thund'ring noise the heavens are rent,
Down falls the crumbling battlement;
Straight to the prey each soldier goes,
The sword devours his helpless foes.
Now, impious! on your idols call;
Prostrate at Baal's altar fall.
In vain your rampart and your pride,
Which once Jehovah's power defied.
Now Israel, spare not, strike the blade
In heart of man, and breast of maid;
Spare not the old, nor young, nor gay,
Spare not, for Justice bids you slay.
Who shall describe that dreadful cry?
These ears shall hear it till they die.
Pale terror shrieks her hideous note,
War bellows from his brazen throat,
Death tears his prey with many a groan,
Nor earth itself restrains a moan.
Ho! vultures, to the banquet haste,
Here ye may feast, and glut your taste;
H o! monsters of the gloomy wood,
Here cool your tongues in seas of blood.
But, no; the flames demand the whole,
In blazing sheets they upward roll;
They fire the heavens, and cast their light
Where Gibeon pales with sad affright;
A lurid glare o'er earth is cast,
The nations stand, with dread aghast.

The shepherd on the distant plain
Thinks of old Sodom's fiery rain;
He flies a sheltering hill to find,
Nor casts one lingering look behind.
The magician scans his mystic lore,
Foretells the curse on Egypt's shore;
The Arab checks his frighted horse,
Bends his wild knee, and turns his 'course.
E'en seas remote behold the glare,
And hardy sailors raise their prayer.
Now, in dim smoke, the flames expire
That lit the city's fun'ral fire,
The glowing embers cease to burn:
Haste, patriot, fill the golden urn!
In crystal tears her dust embalm,
In distant lands, in strife or calm,
Still press the relic to thy heart,
And in the rapture lose the smart!
It must not be; her sons are dead,
They with their Mother burned or bled;
not one survives: the vip'rish race
Have perish'd with their lodging-place.
No more lascivious maidens dance,
No youths with lustful step advance,
No drunkard's bowl, no rite unclean,
No idol mysteries are seen.
A warrior stands in martial state,
And thus proclaims her changeless fate:
"Accursed city, blot her name
From mind of man, from lip of fame.
Curs'd be the man, and curs'd his race,
Who dares his house on thee to place;
He founds it on his firstborn's tomb,
And crowns it with the brother's doom."
Thus God rewards the haughty foe,
Great in their sin and overthrow.
He ever reigns immortal King;
With Israel's song the mountains ring.
Yet 'mid the justice dread, severe,
Where pity sheds no silv'ry tear,
A gleam of golden mercy strays,
And lights the scene with pleasing rays.
One house escapes, by faith secure:,
The scarlet thread a token sure,
Rahab, whose seed in future time
Should bear the virgin's Son sublime.
Thus, when the Thund'rer grasps His arms,

And fills our earth with just alarms,
His hand still shields the chosen race,
And 'midst His wrath remembers grace.

(At the end of the hundredth Outline, Mr. Spurgeon wrote: —) For this 100, I bless the Lord, for the good is His. May they be the seed of many a plant of the Lord!

(Inscription inside front cover of Volume II: —)

FINIS.

June 19. My 18th birthday. With my staff I crossed this Jordan, and now I am become two bands.

Lovingkindness runs faster than time; it outstrips me, and then waits to be gracious.

(Inscription at the end of Volume II: —)

Better is the end of life than the beginning.

Better the end of labor than the starting.

These sketches are so many proofs of the power of 'faith... By faith I got them.

They are evidences of God's love, — for oft have they come just at the moment when, had they tarried, I had been undone.

Blessed be God for making men so much His darlings as to let them speak His Word!

May it be my topmost desire to live as much to God's glory as possible; and —

"When I shall die,
'Receive me,' I'11 cry,
'For Jesus has lov'd me,
I cannot tell why.'"

In health, contentment, and peace, June 19/52, only feeling the thorns of sin and sin's effects.

OUTLINE 172. — THE CHURCH AT ANTIOCH.

"And it came to pass, that a whole year they assembled themselves with the church, and taught much people. And the disciples were called Christians first in Antioch." — Acts 11:26.

Kings are wont to chronicle their wars; mighty men expect to be made to live after death in the historic page; but though these matters have a certain amount of interest, what is it compared with the interest attaching to this inspired Book of the Acts of the Apostles? The History of England is not so important as this one portion of the Bible. It is a "Book of Martyrs," —

Stephen, Paul, and many more. It is a "Book of voyages and travels," of thrilling and permanent interest. It is Vol. 1. of "The Christian Times." It is a book of de. bates, speeches, addresses, sermons, etc.

The church at Antioch has a history so interesting that I only pray that I may be helped to make it so, as I give —

I. A BRIEF SKETCH OF THE HISTORY OF THE CHURCH IN ANTIOCH.

Certain saints, driven by persecution from Jerusalem, fled to Antioch, and commenced there their labors of love. Their names are unmentioned, but God knoweth them, and they are now receiving their reward. Let my name perish, but let Christ's name last for ever.

The Lord's hand helped them, and many believed, and turned unto the Lord. These were so pious that the church in Jerusalem heard of it, and for their further edification sent down Barnabas to labor among them. He was full of faith and the Holy Ghost, and under him the church grew so great that he went after Paul to assist him.

The saints at Antioch were a liberal people; and, by God's grace, continuing to increase, they soon had five pastors, and the Holy Ghost put it into their minds to send out, as missionaries elsewhere, two who became eminently successful. Thus, Antioch became a Mother-church to many surrounding parts. Paul and Barnabas used to return there, after their laborious missionary tours. They anchored at Antioch, as in a haven of refuge.

1. Let us note that the gospel is not of necessity a slowly-progressing affair. The first preachers were very successful, for it seems that in about two years the church at Antioch was firmly established. That church grew amazingly, then why should not ours, and why should not all others grow in similar fashion? The conversion of the world will not always go on at snail-pace, and we ought to pray that it may not in this place. O God, grant it!

2. Let us notice the principal elements of success in this case, believing them to be the same in all. There were things from *God, the ministers,* and *the people.* God in Providence shielded this Gentil Jerusalem from persecution, and gave peace to the people. He sent them faithful ministers, and with those ministers He sent His Spirit.

The ministers preached the Lord Jesus. Barnabas was a good, kind, faithful, Spirit-filled man. Paul also was a mighty preacher of the Word.

The people must have had much grace, — a close cleaving to God and to one another, — liberality and readiness to assist any work of faith, — and abundance of that jewel called "all prayer."

II. A FEW REMARKS UPON THE TITLE FIRST GAINED BY THIS CHURCH AT ANTIOCH, — "CHRISTIANS."

Perhaps the name was given as a designation by the Gentiles, gladly adopted by the disciples, and sanctioned by Divine authority. They had hitherto styled themselves "disciples," "the faithful," "the elect," "brethren." The Jews called them Nazarenes, Galileans, etc. The sect was so small that, doubtless, among the masses of the heathen, it was nondescript; but, in Antioch, the talent, the zeal, the number, the influence, and (in some cases) the wealth of the members of the new church made it needful that it should have a name. The name given is a good one, —

CHRISTIANS.

1. This intimates that there was much unity among the disciples, so that one name would apply to all. Blessed time when this unity shall return, and we shall be all gathered in one!

2. This shows that the conversation, singing, worship, preaching, etc., of these men and women must have been much about Christ; else, how would the common people know their name?

3. This shows that their life and conduct must have been according to the example of Christ; otherwise, the more knowing members of the community would have denied their right to the title.

But I also am called a Christian.

How honorable a name! Manaen, the foster-brother of Herod, was more honored in bearing this name than by his connection with an earthly prince.

Paul, at one time a learned doctor in the Pharisaic school, owns this name of Christian as his highest title. Surely, 'tis a title which an angel might almost covet. But what does this name show?

1. That I am a believer in the Divine mission of Jesus, — a believer in His official name, "*Christ.*" Let me then take care to trust in Him most implicitly, and never by my doubts dishonor Him.

2. That I am a professed imitator of the holy, harmless, undefiled, loving, generous Jesus; let me then really be so in all things.

3. That I am a lover of Jesus; 'then let my conversation and talk and meditation be concerning Him.

A Christian is one who is anointed to be a priest unto God, to offer continual prayer' and praise in the name of Jesus. Bearing the one name which the glorious army of martyrs, the great apostles of Christ, and the saints in all ages, have borne, may we honor the name of Jesus, and on our shoulder bear the cross of Jesus!

(Inscription at the end of Volume III: —)

Praise, praise, unto Him who causeth the river to run on still, — though, as some say, unfed by natural streams.

God doeth good, and all the good herein is every atom His. Bear witness, oh, paper, of my thanks for these instances of grace!

(Inscription on Title-page of Volume IV: —)

In this volume, may I have the pen of a ready writer!

(Inscription at the back of Title-page: —)

By faith, I begin this volume.

(note at the end of Outline No. 200: —)

I desire to record thanks for this second 100. May God receive glory *from* them as well as *for* them!

OUTLINE 212. — NOWISE CAST OUT.

"All that the Father giveth Me shall come to Me; and him that cometh to Me I will in no wise cast out." — John 6: 37.

Upon reading this verse, one feels inclined to break out with the angelic song, "Behold, I bring you good tidings of great joy."

Here are two sets of doctrine, the high and the low conjoined; surely, this passage will suit all, from the "Hyper" down to the Primitive.

I. THE ETERNAL "SHALL" — POSITIVE.

II. THE ETERNAL "WILL" — NEGATIVE.

I. THE POSITIVE ETERNAL "SHALL." "All that the Father giveth Me shall come to Me."

These words may be regarded as —

1. A prophecy of our Lord, the Prophet of His people.

2. A solemn oath of God the Son.

3. A triumphant boast of Jesus the Conqueror.

4. A challenge to death and hell.

In these words, He speaks like one —

1. Who knows the number of His people: "all."
2. Who regards past and present as one: "giveth."
3. Who knows His rights are good: "shall." And —
4. Who is convinced of His own power to perform what He has promised.

But this is of no comfort to us unless we can see —

1. That He has given us the Holy Spirit.
2. That we have given ourselves to Him.

If we have done so, then let us glory in these blessed words, and sing them aloud, —

"All that the Father giveth Me shall come to Me."

II. THE NEGATIVE ETERNAL "WILL." "And him that cometh to Me I will in no wise cast out."

Notice here the Speaker, — our Lord Jesus Christ. The Father has never spoken thus in His absolute character; it were an insult to try to go to Him except through Christ, when He has made His Son the only medium of access to Him.

Notice the character addressed, — not the Jew that cometh, not the king or rich man that cometh, not the good man that cometh, not the young or old, but "*him that cometh*," whosoever he may be.

Notice the words of Jesus. "I will in no wise cast out." It is very strong in the original; Christ means, "I will not, not, not," or, "I will never, never, never cast out any who come to Me." Christ will not cast them out —

1. Because of their great sins.
2. Because of their long delays.
3. Because of their trying other saviors.
4. Because of the hardness of their hearts.
5. Because of their little faith.
6. Because of their poor and dull prayers.
7. Because everyone else passes them by.

When they are once in, they are in for ever. Christ will not cast them out —

1. Because of their unbelief.
2. Because of their old corruptions.
3. Because of their backslidings.

Read, write, print, shout, —

"Him that cometh to Me I will in no wise cast out."

What is it to come to Christ? Men do not know what it is; they fancy it is to re-form themselves, to be moral, honest, good, upright, etc., etc. But it is, to trust, to believe in Jesus. "Believe on the Lord Jesus Christ, and *thou* shalt be saved."

Great Savior, I thank Thee for this text; help Thou me so to preach from it that many may come to Thee, and find eternal life!

Chapter Twenty-One - The Young Soul-Winner at Waterbeach.

Coming, one Thursday in the late autumn, from an engagement beyond Dulwich, my way lay up to the top of the Herne Hill ridge.

I came along the level out of which rises the steep hill I had to ascend. While I was on the lower ground, riding in a hansom cab, I saw a light before me, and when I came near the hill, I marked that light gradually go up the hill, leaving a train of stars behind it. This line of new-born stars remained in the form of one lamp, and then another, and another. It :reached from the foot of the hill to its summit. I did not see the lamplighter. I do not know his name, :nor his age, nor his residence; but I saw the lights which he had kindled, and these remained when he himself had gone his way. As I rode along, I thought to myself, "How earnestly do I wish that my life may be spent in lighting one soul after another with the sacred flame of eternal life! I would myself be as much as possible unseen while at my work, and would vanish into the eternal brilliance above when my work is done." — C. H. S.

DID you ever walk through a village notorious for its drunkenness and profanity? Did you ever see poor wretched beings, that once were men, standing, or rather leaning, against the posts of the ale-house, or staggering along the street? Have you ever looked into the houses of the people, and beheld them as dens of iniquity, at which your soul stood aghast? Have you ever seen the poverty, and degradation, and misery of the inhabitants, and sighed over it? "Yes," you say, "we have." But was it ever your privilege to walk through that village again, in after years, when the gospel had been preached there? It has been mine. I once knew just such a village as I have pictured, — perhaps, in some respects, one of the worst in England, — where many an illicit still was yielding its noxious liquor to a manufacturer without payment of the duty to the government, and where, in connection with that evil, all manner of riot and iniquity was rife.

There went into that village a lad, who had no great scholarship, but who was earnest: in seeking the souls of men. He began to preach there, and it pleased God to turn the whole place upside down. In a short time, the little thatched chapel was crammed, the biggest vagabonds of the village were weeping floods of tears, and those who had been the curse of the parish became its blessing. Where there had been robberies and villainies of every kind, all round the neighborhood, there were none, because the men who used to do the mischief were themselves in the house of God, rejoicing to hear of Jesus crucified. I am not telling an exaggerated story, nor a thing that 'I do not know, for it was my delight to labor for the Lord in that village. It was a pleasant thing to walk through that place, when drunkenness had almost ceased, when debauchery in the case of many was dead, when men and women went forth to labor with joyful hearts, singing the praises of the ever-living God; and when, at sunset, the humble cottager called his children together, read them some portion from the Book of Truth, and then together they bent their knees in prayer to God. I can say, with joy and happiness, that almost from one end of the village to the other, at the hour of eventide, one might have heard the voice of song coming from nearly every roof-tree, and echoing from almost every heart. I do testify, to the praise of (god's grace, that it pleased the Lord to work wonders in our midst. He showed the power of Jesu's name, and made me a witness of that gospel which can win souls, draw reluctant hearts, and mold afresh the life and conduct of sinful men and women.

(The village here referred to is, of course, WATERBEACH, where Mr. Spurgeon first preached in October, 1851, as the following letter proves:—)

"No. 9, Union Road, Cambridge,
"October 15th (1851).

"My Dear Father,

"I received your most welcome note, and beg pardon if you think me negligent in returning thanks. I have been busily employed every Lord's-day; not at home once yet, nor do I expect to be this year.

Last Sunday, I went to a place called Waterbeach, where there is an old-established church, but not able to support a minister. I have engaged to supply to the end of the month. They had, for twenty years, a minister who. went over from Cambridge in the same way as you go to Tollesbury. After that, they tried to have a minister; but as they could not keep him, he has left, and they will have to do as they used to do. There is rail there and back, and it is only six miles.

"I am glad you have such good congregations. I feel no doubt there is a great work doing there; — the fields are ripe unto the harvest, the seed you have sown has yielded plenty of green, let us hope there will be abundance of wheat. Give my love to dear Mother; you have indeed had trials. I always like to see how you bear them.

I think I shall never forget that time when Mother and all were so ill. How you were supported! How cheerful you were! You said, in a letter to me, —

"When troubles, like a gloomy cloud,
Have gathered thick, and thundered kind,
He near my side has always stood;
His lovingkindness, O how good!'

"I trust that you are all well, and that the clouds are blown away. I am quite well, I am happy to say. Where is Aunt? It is four months since I have heard any-thing from her, or about her. We have no settled minister yet, nor do we expect any. I thank you much for your sermon; it will just do for me.

"How greatly must I admire the love that could choose me to speak the gospel, and to be the happy recipient of it! I trust my greatest concern is to grow in grace, and to go onward in the blessed course. I feel jealous lest my motive should change, fearing lest I should be my own servant instead of the Lord's. How soon may we turn aside without knowing it, and begin to seek objects be-low the sacred office!

"Mr. and Mrs. L. are well, and send their respects. Grandfather has asked me to go to Stambourne, but I cannot afford to go his way.

With love to you, dear Mother, and all at home,
"I am, Your affectionate son,

"CHAS. H. SPURGEON."

(The text of Mr. Spurgeon's *first* Sermon at Waterbeach was Matthew 1. 21. This passage was also the subject of his *last* Sermon as Pastor there, and of his *first Sermon as Pastor at New -Park Street,* though a different discourse was delivered on each occasion. It is delightful to notice that JESUS was the keynote of his ministry both in Waterbeach and in London, and that not one of his many thousands of Sermons was out of harmony with that opening note.

The following is the Outline of the first Sermon at Waterbeach: —) **OUTLINE 33. — SALVATION FROM SIN.**

"Thou shalt call His name JESUS: for He shall save His people from their sins." — Matthew 1:21.

The two parts of this Salvation are Justification and Sanctification.

I. JUSTIFICATION, INCLUDING PARDON AND IMPUTATION OF RIGHTEOUSNESS.

1. Pardon, — free, perfect, instantaneous, irreversible, bringing with it deliverance from the consequences of sin, which are —

God's just displeasure.

The curse of the law.

Incapacity for Heaven.

Liability, yea, certain destination to eternal punishment.

2. Imputation of righteousness, causing a man to be regarded as holy, sinless, worthy of commendation and reward. Its accompaniments are, —

God's love. Blessing of the law.

Capacity for Heaven.

A right and title, yea, certain possession of Heaven.

This Jesus effected. As to the first, by His sufferings and death; as to the second, by His holy obedience to the law.

II. SANCTIFICATION, INCLUDING DELIVERANCE FROM SIN, AND POSITIVE HOLINESS.

1. Victory over — (1) our natural depravity, (2) the habits of sin, (3) temptations, (4) backslidings.

2. Working in us all holy affections. (1) Holy nature. (2) Holy habits. (3) Desires for holiness. (4) Progress in Divine grace.

Sanctification is unlike Justification, in that it is gradual, imperfect, progressional, never consummated but in Heaven.

This is the work of Jesus, — (1) by showing us His example and commands, (2) by the Holy Spirit.

This is the beauteous salvation Jesus gives, complete deliverance from the guilt, consequences, and effects of sin.

The choicest happiness which a mortal can know is that of doing good to a fellow-creature. To save a body from death, almost gives us Heaven upon earth. Some men boast that they have sent many souls to perdition, that they have hurled a great number of their fellows out of the world. We meet, now and then, a soldier who glories that, in battle, he struck down many foemen, that his swift and cruel sword reached the heart of a host of his enemies; but I count not that glory. If I thought I had been the means of the death of a single individual, I should scarcely rest at night, for the spirit of that murdered wretch would ever seem to be staring at me. I should remember that I had slain him, and perhaps sent his soul unshriven and unwashed into the presence of his Maker. To me, it is wonderful that men can be found to be soldiers, I say not if it be right or wrong; still, I marvel that they can follow such an occupation. I know not how, after a battle, they can wash the blood from their hands, wipe their swords, and put them by, and then lie down to slumber, and their dreams be undisturbed. If I were in their place, the tears would fall hot and scalding on my cheek at night, and the shrieks of the dying and the groans of those approaching eternity would torture mine ear. I cannot imagine how others can endure it.

To me, it would be the very portal of hell, if I knew that I had been a destroyer of my fellow-creatures.

But what bliss it is to be the instrument of saving bodies from death! Those monks on Mount St. Bernard, surely must feel happiness when they rescue men from death. The dog comes to the door, and they know what he means; he has discovered some poor weary traveler who has lain down to sleep in the snow, and is dying from cold and exhaustion. Up rise the monks from their cheerful fire, intent to act the good Samaritan to the lost one. At last they see him; they speak to him, but he answers not. They try to discover if there is breath in his body, and they fear he is dead. They take him up, and give him remedies; hastening to their hostel, they lay him by the fire, and warm and chafe him, looking into his face with kindly anxiety, as much as to say, "*Poor* creature! art thou dead?" When, at last, they perceive some heaving of the lungs, what joy is in the breast of those brethren, as they say, "*His* life is not extinct!" It would be a privilege to chafe one hand of that poor man, and so help to restore him. Or, suppose another case. A house is in flames, and in it is a woman with her children, who cannot by any means escape. In vain she attempts to come downstairs; the flames prevent her. She has lost all presence of mind, and knows not how to act. A strong man comes, and says, "*Make* way! make way! I must save that woman!" And cooled by the genial streams of benevolence, he marches through the fire. Though scorched, and almost stiffed, he gropes his way. He ascends one staircase, then another; and though the stairs totter, he places the woman beneath his arm, takes a child on his shoulder, and down he comes, twice a giant, having more might than he ever possessed before. He has jeopardized his life, and perhaps an arm may be disabled, or a limb taken away, or a sense lost, or an injury irretrievably done to his body; yet he claps his hands, and says, "*I* have saved lives from death!" The crowd in the street hail him as a man who has been the deliverer of his fellow-creatures, honoring him more than the monarch who has stormed a city, sacked a town, and murdered myriads. But, alas! the body which was saved from death to-day, may die to-morrow. not so the soul that is saved from death: it is saved everlastingly. It is saved beyond the fear of destruction. And if there be joy in the breast of a benevolent man when he saves a body from death, how much more blessed must he be when he is made the means in the hand of God of saving "*a* soul from death," and hiding a multitude of sins! It was Richard Knill, that blessed missionary of the cross to whom I am personally so deeply indebted, who said that, if there were only one unconverted person in the whole world, and if that person lived in the wilds of Siberia, and if every Christian minister and every private believer in the world had to make a pilgrimage to that spot before that soul were brought to Christ, the labor would be well expended if that one soul were so saved. This is putting the truth in a striking way, but in a way in which everyone who realizes the value of immortal souls, will heartily concur.

When I began to preach in the little thatched chapel at Waterbeach, my first concern was, Would God save any souls through me? They called me a ragged-headed boy, and I think I was just that; I know I wore a jacket.

After I had preached for some little time, I thought, "*This* gospel has saved me, but then somebody else preached it; will it save anybody else now that I preach it?" Some Sundays went over, and I used to say to the deacons,

"Have you heard of anybody finding: the Lord under my ministry? Do you know of anyone brought to Christ through my preaching?" My good old friend and deacon said, "I am sure somebody must have received the Savior; I am quite certain it is so." "Oh!" I answered, "but I want to know it, I want to prove that if is so."

How my heart leaped for joy when I heard tidings of my first convert! I could never be satisfied with a full congregation, and the kind expressions of friends: I longed to hear that hearts had been broken, that tears had been seen streaming from the eyes of penitents. How I did rejoice, as one that findeth great spoil, one Sunday afternoon, when my good deacon said to me, "God has set His seal on your ministry in this place, sir." Oh, if anybody had said to me, "Someone has left you twenty thousand pounds,"

I should not have given a snap of my fingers for it, compared with the joy which I felt when I was told that God had saved a soul through my ministry! "Who is it?" I asked. "Oh, it is a poor laboring man's wife over at such-and-such a place! She went home broken-hearted by your Sermon two or three Sundays ago, and she has been in great trouble of soul, but she has found peace, and she says she would like to speak to you." I said,

"Will you drive me over there? I must go to see her;" and early on the'.

Monday morning I was driving down to the village my deacon had mentioned, to see my first spiritual child. I have in my eye now the cottage in which she lived; believe me, it always appears picturesque. I felt like the boy who has earned his first guinea, or like a diver who has been down to the depths of the sea, and brought up a rare pearl. I prize each one whom God has given me, but I prize that Woman most. Since then, my Lord has blessed me to many thousands of souls, who have found the Savior by hearing or reading words which have come from my lips. I have' had a great many spiritual children born of the preaching of the Word, but I still think that woman was the best of the lot. At least, she did not live long enough for me to find many faults in her. After a year or two of faithful witness-bearing, she went home, to lead the way for a goodly number who have followed her. I remember wall her being received into the church, and dying, and going to Heaven. She was the first seal to my ministry, and a very precious one. No Mother was ever more full of happiness at the sight of her first-born son. Then could I have sung the song of the Virgin Mary, for my soul did magnify the Lord for remembering my low estate, and giving me the great honor to do a work for which all generations should call me blessed, for so I counted and still count the conversion of one soul.

I would rather be the means of saving a soul from death than be the greatest orator on earth. I would rather bring the poorest woman in the world to the feet of Jesus than I would be made Archbishop of Canterbury.

I would sooner pluck one single brand from the burning than explain all mysteries. To win a soul from going down into the pit, is a more glorious achievement than to be crowned in the arena of theological controversy as *Dr. Sufficientissimus;* to have: faithfully unveiled the glory of God in the face of Jesus Christ will be, in the final judgment, accounted worthier service than to have solved the problems of the religious Sphinx, or to have cut the Gordian knot of Apocalyptic difficulty. One of my happiest thoughts is that, when I die, it shall be my privilege to enter into rest in the bosom of Christ, and I know that I shall not enjoy my Heaven alone.

Thousands have already entered there, who have been drawn to Christ under my ministry. Oh! what bliss it will be to fly to Heaven, and to have a multitude of converts before and behind, and, on entering the glory, to be able to say, "Here am I, Father, and the children Thou hast given me."

A minister will never, I should think, forget his earliest converts. He lives to see hundreds begotten unto God by his means, but of these who were the children of his youth he still treasures delightful memories, for are they not his first-born, his might, and the beginning of his strength? I can recall an elderly woman who had found peace with God through my youthful ministry, and especially do I recollect her wail of woe as she told of the days of her ignorance, and the consequent godless bringing up of her children. Her words were somewhat as follows, and I write them down for the good of Mothers who labor hard out of love to their dear ones, and provide them with all necessaries for this life, but never think of the life to come: —

"Oh, sir!" said she, "I should be quite happy now, only I have one sore trouble which keeps me very low. I am so sad about my dear children. I was left with eight of them, and I worked hard at the wash-tub, and in other ways, morning, noon, and night, to find bread for them. I did feed and clothe them all, but I am sure I don't know how I did it. I had often to deny myself, both in food and clothing; and times were very hard with me.

Nobody could have slaved worse than I did, to mend, and clean, and keep a roof over our heads. I cannot blame myself for any neglect about their bodies; but as to their souls, I never cared about my own, and of course I never thought of theirs. Two of them died. I dare not think about them.

God has forgiven me, but I can't forget my sin against my poor children; I never taught them a word which could be of any use to them. The others are all alive, but there is not one of them in the least religious. How could they be when they saw how their Mother lived? It troubles me more a good deal than all the working for them ever did; for I'm afraid they are going down to destruction, and *all through their cruel Mother.*"

He. re she burst into tears, and I pitied her so much that I said I hardly thought she was *cruel,* for she was in ignorance, and would never intentionally have neglected anything that was for her children's good.

"Don't excuse me," said she, "for if I had used my common sense, I might have known that my children were not like the sheep and the horses which die, and there's an end of them. I never thought about it at all, or I might have known better; and I feel that I was a cruel Mother never to have considered their souls at all. They are all worldly, and none of them go to a place of worship, year in and year out. I never took them there, and how can I blame them? As soon as I was converted, I went down to my eldest son, who has a large family, and I told him what the Lord had done for me, and entreated him to come here With me to the services; but he said he wondered what next, and he had no time. When I pleaded hard with him, he said he was sure I meant well, but 'it was no go,' — he liked his Sunday at home too well to go to hear parsons. You know, sir, you can't bend a tree; I ought to have bent the twig when I could have done it. Oh, if I had but led him to the house of God when he was little! He would have gone then, for he loved his Mother, and so he does now, but not enough to go where I want him. So, you see, I can do nothing with my son now. I was a cruel Mother, and let the boy go into the fields, or the streets, when he should have been in the Sunday-school. Oh, that I could have my time back again, and have all my children around me as little ones, that I might teach them about my blessed Savior! They are all beyond me now. What can I do?"

She sat down and wept bitterly, and I heartily wish all unconverted Mothers could have seen her, and heard her lamentations. It was very pleasant to know that she was; herself saved, and to see in her very sorrow the evidence of her genuine repentance; but, still, the evil which she lamented was a very terrible one, and might well demand a lifetime of mourning. Young Mother, do not, as you love your babe, suffer it to grow up without Divine instruction. But you cannot teach your child if you do not know the Lord Jesus yourself. May the good Lord lead you to give your heart to Christ at once, and then help you to train your dear little ones for Heaven!

There was one woman in Waterbeach who bore among her neighbors the reputation of being a regular virago, and I was told that, sooner or later, she would give me a specimen of her tongue-music. I said, "All right; but that's a game at which two can play." I am not sure whether anybody reported to her my answer; but, not long afterwards, I was passing her gate, one morning, and there stood the lady herself; and I must say that her vigorous mode of speech fully justified all that I had heard concerning her.

The typical Billingsgate fish-woman would have been nowhere in comparison with her. I made up my mind how to act, so I smiled, and said,

"Yes, thank you; I am quite well, I hope you are the same." Then came another outburst of vituperation, pitched in a still higher key, to which I replied, still smiling, "Yes, it does look rather as if it is going to rain; I think I had better be getting on." "Bless the man!" she exclaimed, "he's as deaf as a post; what's the use of storming at him?" So I bade her, "Good morning," and I am not sure whether she ever came to the chapel to hear the "deaf" preacher who knew it was no use to give any heed to her mad ravings.

If I could have had a hope of doing her any good, I would have gone into her house, and talked with her, for I certainly went into some queer places while I was in that region.! used to think that, where my Master went, I need never be ashamed to go; and I have gone into some persons' houses, before I came to London, that I should have felt ashamed to enter if they had not invited me on a Sabbath-day. As I have stepped in there for the purpose of giving them religious advice, some have said to me, "What! going into that house?.... Yes, and quite right, too. 'The whole have no need of a physician, but they that are sick.'" I have gone after "the lost sheep of the house of Israel," and I have won their hearts because I went there, and talked to 'them of their sins. But had I stayed away, there would have been something of this spirit, "Stand by, for I am holier than you are; I cannot enter your house, because you are such an outrageous sinner."

But when I go and talk to a man, and lay my hand on his shoulder, and ask him questions, he does not mind telling out his state of mind when I am under his own roof; and when I am gone, he says, "That man is not ashamed to speak to his fellows, I like that kind of preacher."

While I was at Waterbeach, I had one man who caused me many bitter tears. When I first knew him, he was the ringleader in all that was bad; a tall, fine, big fellow, and one who could, perhaps, drink more than any man for miles around him, — a man who would curse and swear, and never knew a thought of fear. He was the terror of the neighborhood; there were many incendiary fires in the region, and most people attributed them to him. Sometimes, he would be drunk for two or three: weeks at a spell, and then he raved and raged like a madman. That man came to hear me; I recollect the sensation that went through the little chapel when he entered.

He sat there, and fell in love with me; I think that was the only conversion that he experienced, but he professed to be converted. He had, apparently, been the subject of genuine repentance, and he became outwardly quite a changed character; he gave up his drinking and his swearing, and was in many respects an exemplary individual. All the parish was astonished.

There was old Tom So-and-so weeping, and it was rumored about that he felt impressed; he began regularly to attend the chapel, and was manifestly an altered man. The public-house lost an excellent customer; he was not seen in the skittle-alley, nor was he detected in the drunken rows that were so common in the neighborhood. After a while, he ventured to come forward at the prayer-meeting; he talked about what he had experienced, what he had felt and known. I heard him pray; it was rough, rugged language, but there was such impassioned earnestness, I set him down as being a bright jewel in the Redeemer's crown. He held out six, nay, nine months he persevered in our midst. If there was rough work to be done, he would do it; if there was a Sunday-school to be maintained, six or seven miles away, he would walk there. At any risk, he would be out to help in the Lord's work; if he could but be of service to the meanest member of the Church of Christ, he rejoiced greatly. I remember seeing him tugging a barge, with perhaps a hundred people on board, whom he was drawing up to a place where I was going to preach; and he was glorying in the work, and singing as gladly and happily as any one of them. If anybody spoke a word against the Lord or His servant, he did not hesitate a moment, but knocked him over.

So he went on for a time; but, at last, the laughter to which he was exposed, the jeers and scoffs of his old companions, — though at first he bore them like a man, — became too much for him. He began to think he had been a little too fanatical, a little too earnest. He slunk up to the place of worship instead of coming boldly in; he gradually forsook the weeknight service, and then neglected the Sabbath-day; and, though often warned, and often rebuked, he returned to his old habits, and any thoughts of God or godliness that he had ever known, seemed to die away. He could again utter the blasphemer's oath; once more he could act wickedly with the profane; and he — of whom we had often boasted, and said, in our prayer-meetings, "Oh! how much is God glorified by this man's conversion! What cannot Divine grace do?" — to the confusion of us all, was to be seen sometimes drunk in our streets, and then it was thrown in our teeth, "This is one of your

Christians, is it? — one of your converts gone back again, and become as bad as he was before?" Before. I left the district, I was afraid that there was no real work of grace in him. He was a wild Red Indian sort of a man; I have heard of him taking a bird, plucking it, and eating it raw in the field. That was not the act of a Christian man, it was not one of the things that are comely, and of good repute. After I left the neighborhood, I asked after him, and I could hear nothing good of him; he became worse than he was before, if that was possible; certainly, he was no better, and seemed to be unreachable by any agency.

Among my early hearers at Waterbeach was one good old woman whom I called "Mrs. Much-afraid." I feel quite sure she has been many years in Heaven, but she was always fearing that she should never enter the gates of glory. She was very regular in her attendance at the house of God, and was a wonderfully good listener. She used to drink in the gospel; but, nevertheless, she was always doubting, and fearing, and trembling about her own spiritual condition. She had been a believer in Christ, I should think, for fifty years, yet she had always remained in that timid, fearful, anxious state. She was a kind old soul, ever ready to help her neighbors, or to speak a word to the unconverted; she seemed to me to have enough grace for two people, yet, in her own opinion, she had not half enough grace for one.

One day, when I was talking with her, she told me that she had not any hope at all; she had no faith; she believed that she was a hypocrite. I said,

"Then don't come to the chapel any more; we don't want hypocrites there.

Why do you come?" She answered, "I come because I can't stop away. I love the people of God; I love the house of God; and I love to worship God." "Well," I said, "you are an odd sort of hypocrite; you are a queer kind of unconverted woman." "Ah!" she sighed, "you may say what you please, but I have not any hope of being saved." So I said to her, "Well, next Sunday, I will let you go into the pulpit, that you may tell the people that Jesus Christ is a liar, and that you cannot trust Him." "Oh!" she cried,

"I would be torn in pieces before I would say such a thing as that. Why, He cannot lie! Every word He says is true." "Then," I asked, "why do you not believe it?" She replied, "I do believe it; but, somehow, I do not believe.' it for myself; I am afraid whether it is for me." "Have you not any hope at all?" I asked. "No," she answered; so I pulled out my purse, and I said to her, "Now, I have got £5 here, it is all the money I have; but I will give you that £5 for your hope if you will sell it." She looked at me, wondering what I meant. "Why!" she exclaimed, "I would not sell it for a thousand worlds."

She had just told me that she had not any hope of salvation, yet she would not sell it for a thousand worlds!

I fully expect to see that good old soul when I get to Heaven, and I am certain she will say to me, "Oh, dear sir, how foolish I was when I lived down there at Waterbeach! I went groaning all the way to glory when I might just as well have gone there singing. I was always troubled and afraid; but my dear Lord kept me by His grace, and brought me safely here." She died very sweetly.; it was with her as John Bunyan said it was with Miss Much-afraid, Mr. Despondency's daughter. Mr. Great-heart had much trouble with those poor pilgrims on the road to the Celestial City; for, if there was only a straw in the way, they were fearful that they would stumble over it. Yet Bunyan says, "When the time was come for them to depart, they went to the brink of the river. The last words of Mr. Despondency were, 'Farewell night, welcome day.' His daughter went through the river singing." Our Lord often makes it calm and peaceful, or even joyous and triumphant, for His departing timid ones. He puts some of His greatest saints to bed in the dark, and they wake up in the eternal light; but He frequently keeps the candle burning for Mr. Little-faith, Mr. Feeble-mind, Mr. Ready-to-halt, Mr. Despondency, and Miss Much-afraid. They go to sleep in the light, and they also wake up in the land where the Lamb is all the glory for ever and ever.

Chapter Twenty-Two - The Lord's Hand Behind The Maid's Mistake.

The life of Jonah cannot be written without God; take God out of the prophet's history, and there is no history to write. This is equally true of each one of us. Apart from God, there is no life, nor thought, nor act, nor career of any man, however lowly or how, Per high. Leave out God, and you cannot write the story of anyone's career. If you attempt it, it will be so ill-written that it shall be clearly perceived that you have tried to make bricks without straw, and that you have sought to fashion a potter's vessel without clay. I believe that, in a man's life, the great secret of strength, and holiness, and righteousness, is the acknowledgment of Goal. When a man has no fear of God before his eyes, there is no wonder that he should run to an excess of meanness, and even to an excess of riot. In proportion as the thought of God dominates the mind, we may expect to find a life that shall be true, and really worth living; but in proportion as we forget God, we shall play the fool. It is the fool who says in his heart, "No God," and it is the fool who lives and acts as if there were no God. In every godly life there is a set time for each event; and there is no need for us to ask, "Why is the white here and, the black there; why this gleam of sunlight and that roar of tempest; why here a marriage and there a funeral; why sometimes a harp and at other times a sackbut?" God knows, and it is a great blessing for us when we can leave it all in His hands. — C. H. S.

SOON after I had begun to preach the Word in the village of Waterbeach, I was strongly advised to enter Stepney, now Regents Park, College, to prepare more fully for the ministry. Knowing that solid learning is never an encumbrance, and is often a great means of usefulness, I felt inclined to avail myself of the opportunity of attaining it: although I hoped that I might be useful without a College training, I consented to the opinion of friends that I should be more useful with it. Dr. Angus, the tutor of the College, visited Cambridge, and it was arranged that we should meet at the house of Mr. Macmillan, the publisher. Thinking and praying over the matter, I entered the house exactly at the time appointed, and was shown into a room where I waited patiently a couple of hours, feeling too much impressed with my own insignificance, and the greatness of the tutor from London, to venture to ring the bell, and make inquiries as to the unreasonably long delay At last, patience having had her perfect work, and my school-engagements requiring me to attend to my duties as an usher, the bell was set in motion, and on the arrival of the servant, the waiting young man was informed that the Doctor had tarried in another room until he could stay no longer, and had ,gone off to London by train. The stupid girl had given no information to the family that anyone had called, and had been shown into the drawing-room; and, consequently, the meeting never came about, although designed by both parties. I was not a little disappointed at the moment, but have a thousand times since thanked the Lord very heartily for the strange Providence which forced my steps into another path.

Still holding to the' idea of entering the Collegiate Institution, I thought of writing and making an immediate application, but this was not to be. That afternoon, having to preach at one of the village-stations of the Cambridge Lay Preachers' Association, I walked slowly, in a meditative frame of mind, over Midsummer Common to the little wooden bridge which leads to Chesterton, and in the midst of the Common I was startled by what seemed a loud voice, but which may have been a singular illusion. Whichever it was, the impression was vivid to an intense degree; I seemed very distinctly to hear the words, "Seekest thou great things for thyself? seek them not!"

This led me to look at my position from another point of view, and to challenge my motives and intentions. I remembered the poor but loving people to whom I ministered, and the souls which had been given me in my humble charge; and, although at that time I anticipated obscurity and poverty as the result of the resolve, yet I did there and then solemnly renounce the offer of Collegiate instruction, determining to abide for a season at least with my people, and to remain preaching the Word so long as I had strength to do it. Had it not been for those words, in all probability I had never been where and what I now am. I was conscientious in my obedience to the monition, and I have never seen cause to regret it.

Waiting upon the Lord for direction will never fail to afford us timely intimation of His will; for though the ephod is no more worn by a ministering priest, the Lord still guides His people by His wisdom, and orders all their paths in love; and in times of perplexity, by ways mysterious and remarkable, He makes them to "hear a voice behind them, saying, '

This is the way, walk ye in it.'" Probably, if our hearts were more tender, we might be favored with more of these sacred monitions; but, alas!

instead thereof, we are like the horse and the mule, which have no understanding, and therefore the bit and bridle of affliction take the place of gentler means, else might that happier method be more often used, to which the psalmist alludes when he says, "*Thou* shalt guide me with Thine eye."

(The following letters give further particulars concerning the proposed College course: —)

"Cambridge,
"Feb. 24, 1852.

"My Dear Father,

"Mr. Angus, the tutor of Stepney College, preached for us on Sunday, Feb. 1. Being at my own place, I had no opportunity of seeing him, and was very surprised when, on Monday, I was told that he wanted to see me. I assure you, I never mentioned myself to him, nor to anyone, — this came quite unexpectedly. I suppose the deacons of our church, hearing of my doings at Waterbeach, had thought right to mention me to him.

"Well, I went to the place of meeting; but, by a very singular occurrence, we missed each other; he waited in the parlor, while I was shown into the drawing-room, and the servant forgot to tell him I had come.

As he was going to London, and could not wait, he wrote the enclosed."

(On the envelope containing the following letter, there is this note in Mr. Spurgeon's handwriting: —

"Sent to Mr. Watts because he is my dear friend, and Mr. A. knew he would give it: to me. Mr. Watts treats me like a son; he is well qualified to be a father: he will do anything for me, I know.")

"College,
"Tuesday, Feb. 3, 1852.

"Dear Sir,

"I am sorry that I missed seeing Mr. Spurgeon yesterday, and now write, through you, in the hope that you will lay this note before him. I cannot, of course'., in any way pledge our Committee in the matter; but if, on prayerfully considering the whole case, he apply for admission here, I can assure him of a candid, friendly consideration of his application. There is a great need of hearty, devoted ministers; and to form such, so that they may occupy important posts, and wear well, we need to 'have them thoroughly furnished, especially with Bible knowledge. I should regret for your friend to settle without thorough preparation. He may be useful in either case, but his usefulness will be very much greater, it will fill at all events a wider sphere, with preparation than without it.

"Applications must be sent to us before May, our Session beginning in September; and if Mr. S. think further of it, I shall be glad in due time to hear from him.

"Yours truly,

"JOSEPH ANGUS."

"Mr. Watts,
"Wood Merchant, etc.,
"Cambridge."

(Mr. Spurgeon's letter to his father continues: —)

"I have waited thus long because (1) I wanted to get a little more to tell you; (2) I do not want to appear to desire to go to College at your expense. I do not wish to go until I can pay for it with my own money, or until friends offer to help, because I do not want to burden you. It is said by almost all friends that I ought to go to College: I have no very great desire for it; in fact, none at all. Yet I have made it a matter of prayer, and I trust, yea, I am confident, God will guide me.

"Of course, you are my only earthly director and guide in these matters; your judgment always has been best; you must know best.

But perhaps you will allow me just to state my own opinion, not because I shall trust in it, but only that you may see my inclination.

I think, then, (with all deference to you,) that I had better not go to College yet, at least not just now, for —

"**1.** Whatever advantages are to be derived from such a course of study, I shall be more able to improve when my powers are more developed than they are at present. When I know more, I shall be more able to learn.

"**2.** Providence has thrown me into a great sphere of usefulness, —

a congregation of often 450, a loving and praying church, and an awakened audience. Many already own that the preaching has been with power from Heaven. Now, ought I to leave them?

"**3.** In a few years' time, I hope to improve my financial position, so as to be at no expense to you, or at least not for all. I should not like to know that you were burdening yourself for me. I should love to work my own way as much as possible. I know you like this feeling.

"**4.** I am not uneducated. I have many opportunities of improvement now; all I want is more time; but even that, Mr. Leeding would give me, if it were so arranged. I have plenty of practice; and do we not learn to preach by preaching? You know what my style is. I fancy it is not very College-like. Let it be never so bad, God has blessed it, and I believe He will yet more. All I do right, He does in me, and the might is of Him. I am now well off; I think as well off as anyone of my age, and I am sure quite as happy.

If I were in need, I think the people might be able to raise more for me. Now, shall I throw myself out, and trust to Providence as to whether I shall ever get another place as soon as I leave College?

"**5.** But, no; — I have said enough, — you are to judge, not 1. I leave it to God and yourself; but, still, I should like you to decide in this way. Of course, I have a will, and you now know it; but I say, '

not mine, but your will, and God's will.'

"I have just acknowledged the letter, and said that I could make no reply until I had consulted my friends. I think it might be as well, if you think so, too, to let Mr. Angus know' as much as is right of my present position, that he may be favorable toward me at any future time...

"I hope you will excuse my scrawl, for, believe me, I am fully employed. Last night, I thought of writing; but was called out to see a lying man, and I thought I dare not refuse. The people would not like to get even a hint of my leaving them. I do not know why they love me, but they do; it is the Lord's doing.

"Give my love and many thanks to dear Mother, Archer, and sisters. If at any time you think a letter from me would be useful, just hint as much, and I will write one. May God keep me, in every place, from every evil, and dwell with you, and abide with you for ever; and with my best love,

"I am,

"Dear Father,

"Your affectionate son,

"CHARLES."

(Extract from C. H. Spurgeon's letter to his father, March 9th, 1852: —)

"I have all along had an aversion to College, and nothing but a feeling that I must not consult myself, but Jesus, could have made me think of it. It appears to my friends at Cambridge that it is my duty to remain with my dear people at Waterbeach; so says the church there, unanimously, and so say three of our deacons at Cambridge."

(Letter from Deacon King to C. H. Spurgeon's father: —)

"Waterbeach,
"March 20, '52.

"Dear Sir,

"Having heard, with deep regret, of your intention of placing your son at Stepney College, I write to say that, if you were aware of all the circumstances connected with his ministry at Waterbeach, I think you would defer doing so, at least for a time.

"Allow me to say that, since his' coming, the congregation is very much increased, the aisles and vestry being often full, and many go away for want of room; there are several cases of his being made useful in awakening the careless; and although we have only known him about five months, the attachment is as strong as if we had been acquainted with him as many years; and if he were to leave us just now, it: would be the occasion of general *'Lamentation, Mourning, and Woe.'* Added to which, he has no wish to go, but rather the reverse; and his friends in Cambridge, who previously recommended his going, now hesitate, and feel disposed to alter their opinion. If you, sir, could come over, and see for yourself, you would find that this account is not exaggerated, but perhaps would be ready to exclaim, 'The hall was not told me.' That we may be Divinely directed to act as shall be most conducive to the promotion of the Redeemer's glory, in connection with the best interests of those around us,' is: the sincere desire and earnest prayer of — "Yours respectfully,

"C. King, on behalf of the Church and Congregation."

"P.S. — Our friends are very anxious that Mr. S. should continue with us at least a year. Your acceding to this would cause many devout thanksgivings to God, and we hope would be attended with lasting benefit to many amongst us. A line to this effect would much oblige."

"April 6th, 1852.

"My Dear Father,

"I am sorry that anything I said in my letter should have grieved you. It was nothing you *said* that made your letter a sad one; it was only my thoughts of leaving the people at 'Beach. I thank you most sincerely for your very kind offer, and also for your assurance that I am at perfect liberty to act as I think it is the will of God I should act. I am sure I never imagined that you would force me, — it was only my poor way of expressing myself that caused the blunder, —

and I do now most affectionately entreat forgiveness of you if I said anything that had a shadow of wrong in it, or if I have thought in any wrong manner. I have desired, all along, to act the part of a dutiful son to an affectionate parent; and if I fail, I feel sure that you and dear Mother will impute it rather to my weakness in act, than to a want of love.

"With regard to my decision, — I have said so much in my' last that more would be unnecessary. I do really think it to be my duty to continue in the place which I now occupy, — for a short time at least. I have been assured that never were more tears shed in Waterbeach, at any time, than when I only hinted at leaving. They could[not give me stronger tokens of their affection than they *did* give. One prayer went up from all,' Lord, keep him here!' I am assured by Mr. King that the' people have had ministers whom one lot were very pleased with, but there always was a party opposed; but now, though he has a good scope for observation, he has not heard one opinion contrary to me. The Lord gave me favor with the people, and I am so young that they look over many faults; I believe this is one of the facts of the case. The worst is, I am in a dangerous place; the pinnacle is not so safe as the quiet vale. I know you pray that I may be kept humble, and I know I do. Oh, if the clouds pass without rain, how sorrowful I shall feel! When I have been thinking on the many difficulties in preaching the Word, the doctrine of election has been a great comfort to me. I *do* want men to be saved, and it is my consolation that a multitude no man can number are by God's immutable decree ordained to eternal life.

So we cannot labor in vain, we must have *some;* the covenant renders that secure.

"I shall always be glad o! some of your skeletons, for though I do not want them to make me lazy, yet they give some hints when a passage does not open at once. It will be too much trouble for you to write them, but I have no doubt Archer will copy them for me..... As to my cash, I have bought a great many books lately, for my constant work requires them, and you know Mr. L. would not have many of the class of books I want. Yet I calculate on having £15 in hand at Midsummer, or by God's blessing, more. I think that (of course, I mean, if God prosper me,) I shall be able to save enough to put myself to College, and if not, if I should go, which, as you say, is not very certain, why then friends at Cambridge would help me if I could not manage it. Has taken the positive steps yet with regard to joining the church? If not, tell her, *I blush that she should blush to own her Lord.* Do not forget me in earnest prayer..... My very best love to my dear Mother. I am sure she can tell all the Mothers in the world that parents' prayers are not forgotten. I daresay you think God saved the worst first; if you do not, I do. I believe I have given you more trouble than any of the others, but I did not mean it; and I still believe that I have given you joy, too, and I hope the trouble, though not repaid, will yet be recompensed by a comfort arising from seeing me walk in the truth. Remember me to Emily.... The little ones are getting big, I suppose; my love to them, I hope they will be God's daughters.

"I remain,

"Your affectionate son,

"CHARLES."

(Part of undated letter from C. H. Spurgeon to his Mother; the first portion is missing: —)

"I need your prayers doubly at this time. I know I shall have them, and I believe I have felt the blessing of them more than once. The Lord visit you both, and bear you up in His everlasting arms!

Troubles you have had, but I believe the comforts have always kept you joyful in tribulation; cast down, but not in despair.

"Bless the Lord, I must say, for making me His son; 'tis of His own sovereign mercy, not one good thing has failed. I have felt corruptions rise, and the old man is strong, — but grace always comes in just at the critical time, and saves me from myself. The Lord keep me! I have no hope of going on well but by His power. I know that His almighty arm is all-sufficient. Get everyone you can to pray for me; a prayer is more precious than gold, it makes me rich. Lift up your' arms, like Moses; there is a great battle both in me and out of me. Jesus intercedes; sweet thought, to one who needs just such a Pleader. Jehovah-Jesus, His people's buckler, is near; an ever-present help in time of trouble; not afar off. We live in Him, He is all around us; who shall destroy His favorites, His darlings? I have had for one of my sermons, John 15:9: 'As the Father hath loved Me, so have I loved you: continue ye in My love.' Here is (1.) *Love without beginning.* God never began to love Jesus. (2.) *Love without limit.* God loves Jesus with an unbounded love. (3.) *Love without change.* God always loved Jesus alike:, equally. (4.) *Love without end.* When will God leave off loving Jesus? Even so does Jesus love you and me.

"*'The weakest saint shall win the day,*
Though death and hell obstruct the way.'

"How are all Christian friends? Love to Mr. Langford, and my best respects; tell him I desire: a special interest in his prayers. I want to feel 'less than nothing,' but this is a very great attainment. Thank Father for his letter; the Lord of hosts prosper his labors abundantly! My very best love to yourself I hope, if it is right:, that your hands are well. Kiss the little ones, and give them my love.

May they learn of Jesus! I am glad Archer gets on so well; may your ten thousand prayers for us be answered by Him that heareth prayer! Emily is stronger, I hope, ask her to think whether she loves Jesus with all her heart.

"I should very much like to know where Aunt lives. I have asked several times, but I have not learned yet. I do not expect many letters from home. Father is so much engaged, that I wonder I get so many. If you want to know any points in which I am not quite explicit enough, write and ask at any time.

My affairs are your affairs. I hope always to do that which you would approve of.

"Love to all once more, —
"From your affectionate son,

"CHARLES."

(Extract from letter from C. H. Spurgeon to his Mother, November, 1852:—)

"I am more and more glad that I never went to College. God sends such sunshine on my path, such smiles of grace, that I cannot regret if I have forfeited all my prospects for it. I am conscious that I held back from love to God and His cause, and [had *rather be poor in His service than rich in my own.* I have all that heart can wish for; yea, God giveth more than my desire. My congregation is as great and loving as ever. During all the time that I have been at Waterbeach, I have had a different house for my home every Sabbath day. Fifty-two families have thus taken me in; and I have still six other invitations not yet accepted. Talk about the people not caring for me, because they give me so little! I dare tell anybody under heaven 'tis false! They do all they can. Our anniversary passed off grandly' six were baptized; crowds on crowds stood by the river; the chapel was afterwards crammed, both to the tea and the sermon."

At this anniversary, (in 1852,) my venerable friend, Mr. Cornelius Elven, of Bury St. Edmund's, as a man of mark in that region, was requested to preach, and right well do I remember his hearty compliance with my request. I met him at the station as he alighted from a third-class carriage, which he had selected in order to put the friends to the least possible expense for his traveling. His bulk was stupendous, and one soon saw that his heart was as large as his body. There was a baptismal service in the river in connection with the anniversary, but Mr. Elven said that he could not go into the water with us, for if he got wet through, there were no garments nearer than Bury St. Edmund's that would fit him. He gave me much sage and holy advice during his visit, advice which came to me with much the same weight as Paul's words came to Timothy. [17] He bade me study hard, and mind and keep abreast of the foremost Christians in our little church; "for," said he, "if these men, either in their knowledge of Scripture, or their power to edify the people, once outstrip you, the temptation will arise among them to be dissatisfied with your ministry; and, however good they are, they will feel their superiority, and others will perceive it, too, and then your place in the church will become very difficult to hold." I felt the common sense of the observation, and the spur was useful. The sermons of the day were very homely in style, and pre-eminently practical. I remember his reading the narrative of Naaman the Syrian, and his pithy comments thereon. He seemed to have taken Matthew Henry for his model, and in the course of one of the services he gave us Henry's inimitable description of the Father receiving the prodigal, which occurs in the commentator's exposition of Luke 15. With a voice deep-toned and graciously tender, he said: — "When he was yet a great way off, his father saw him,' — here were eyes of mercy; 'and had compassion,' — here were bowels of mercy; 'and ran,' — here were feet of mercy; 'and fell on his neck,' — here were arms of mercy; 'and kissed him,' — here were lips of mercy; — it was all mercy!" But one thing above all others fixed itself upon my memory, and when I heard of the good man's departure, it came before me with great vividness; he told me anecdotes of the usefulness of addressing individuals one by one about their souls, and urged the duty upon me with great earnestness, quoting again and again from the life of a certain Harlan Page. Being busy with a thousand matters, I had never looked up the biography which he so strongly recommended; but my first thought, when I learned of his death, was, Harlan Page.

Cornelius Elven completed an honorable ministry of fifty years in his native town, and passed away amid the respectful regrets of all the inhabitants, and the deep affection of his church. He was a man of large and loving heart, with a vivacious mind, and interesting manner of 'utterance. He was not only the friend of my youth, but he also preached for me in London in after days. He used, with a merry laugh, to tell the story of a lady who came to hear me at New Park Street, but putting her head inside the door, and seeing the vast form of Cornelius Elven, she retreated, exclaiming,

"No, no; the man has too much of the flesh about him, I cannot hear him."

It was a very unjust judgment, for the dear man's great bulk was a sore affliction to him. Peace to his memory! I weave no lading Wreath for his tomb, but I catch the gleaming of that immortal crown which the Master has placed upon his brow. He was a good man, full of faith and of the Holy Ghost.

(Professor Everett has preserved the following reminiscence of this period:
"In or about 1852, I was occupying a post in a high-class school, — Mr. Thorowgood's, at Totteridge, near London, — and there being a vacancy for another assistant, I wrote, with Mr. Thorowgood's approval, to my old friend Spurgeon, proposing that he should come and fill it. He asked for a few days to decide definitely, and then wrote declining, chiefly on the ground that he was unwilling to renounce the evangelistic work which he combined with the position 'he then held. He stated, then, or in a subsequent letter, that he had preached more than three hundred times in the previous twelve months, and that the chapel at Waterbeach was not only full, but crowded with outside listeners at the open windows.")

Chapter Twenty-Three - Reminiscences as a Village Pastor.

My witness is, and I speak it for the honor of God, that He is a good Provider. I have been east upon the Providence of God ever since I left my father's house, and in all cases He has been my Shepherd, and I have known no lack. My first income as a Christian minister was small enough in all conscience, never exceeding forty-five pounds a year; yet I was as rich then as I am now, for I had enough; and I had no more cares, nay, not half as many then as I have now; and when I breathed my prayer to God then, as I do now, for all things temporal and spiritual, I found Him ready to answer me at every pinch, — and full many pinches I have had.

Many a pecuniary trial have I had in connection with the College work, which depends for funds upon the Lord's moving His people to liberality: my faith has been often tried, but God has always been faithful, and sent supplies in hours of need If any should tell me that prayer to God was a mere piece of excitement, and that the idea of God answering human cries is absurd, I should laugh the statement to scorn, for my experience is not that of one or two singular instances, but that of hundreds of cases, in which the Lord's interposition, for the necessities of His work, has been as manifest as if He had rent the clouds, and thrust forth His own naked arm and bounteous hand to supply the needs of His servant. — C. H. S.

WHEN I became Pastor at Waterbeach, the people could do very little for my support, and therefore I was an usher in a school at Cambridge at the same time. After awhile, I was obliged to give up the latter occupation, and was thrown on the generosity of the people. They gave me a salary of £45 a year, but as I had to pay 12s. a week for two rooms which I occupied, my income was not sufficient to support me; but the people, though they had not money, had produce, and I do not think there was a pig killed by any one of the congregation without my having some portion of it, and one or other of them, when coming to the market at Cambridge, would bring me bread, so that I had enough bread and meat to pay my rent with, and I often paid my landlady in that fashion.

There was one old man at Waterbeach who was a great miser. On one of my visits to the place, after I had removed to London, I heard that, in his last illness, he had a bed made up in the sitting-room downstairs, and ordered his grave to be dug just outside the window, so as to reduce the cost of his funeral as much as possible. One of the friends who was talking about him said, "*He* was never known to give anything to anybody."

"*Well,*" I replied, "*I* know better than that, for, one Sunday afternoon, he gave me three half-crowns and as I was wanting a new hat at the time, I got it with the money." "Well," rejoined the friend, "I am quite sure he never forgave himself for such extravagance as that, and that he must have wanted his three half-crowns back again." "Ah, but!" I answered, "*you* have not heard the whole of the story yet, for, the following Sunday, the old man came to me again, and asked me to pray for him that he might be saved from the sin of covetousness, "*for,*" said he, "the Lord told me to give you half-a-sovereign, but I kept back half-a-crown, and I can't rest of a night for thinking of it."

(Dr. D. A. Doudney, describing an interview with Mr. Spurgeon at "Westwood," wrote in *The Gospel Magazine* for March, 1892: —

"Among other subjects brought up was that of Dr. Gill's *Commentary.* I was asked by Mr. Spurgeon how it was that I was led to reproduce it. Its truthful character was urged as a reason, as well as its great price putting it beyond the power of ministers in general to possess it. My own copy simply bound in plain canvas boards had cost me f6 10s. Moreover, I was anxious to set up an Industrial School, and thus find occupation for the youths of the parish. 'In what volume,' asked Mr. Spurgeon, 'did the names of the subscribers appear?' I could not recollect, but, withdrawing for a moment to his study, he quickly reappeared with the fourth volume of the Old Testament, — the last issued upon the completion of the work, and, pointing to his own name, said, 'You published it in half-crown parts, or else I could not have taken it in.' Here was a fair specimen of Mr.

Spurgeon's character, — his proverbial simplicity and honesty. How few, in like manner, amid such surroundings, and having attained, as he had, to such a name, and such a popularity, would have made that frank statement,' You published it in half-crown parts, or I could not have taken it in.'"

The following inscriptions, in Mr. Spurgeon's handwriting, are in his set of volumes of Dr. Gill's *Commentary:* —

In Vol. 1. — "I subscribed for this, and took the monthly parts.

"C. H. SPURGEON, 1852.

"To this Author's Pulpit I was permitted to succeed in 1854.

"C. H. SPURGEON."

In Vol. V. — "I subscribed for these vols. of Gill in monthly parts, and had them bound. December, 1852.

"C. H. SPURGEON,

"living in Cambridge,

"Baptist Minister of Waterbeach.

"In April, 1854, unanimously elected Pastor of the same Church, which once met in Carter Lane, under Dr. Gill, and then Dr. Rippon, — now New Park Street, Southwark.

"In the year 186I, this Church migrated to the Metropolitan Tabernacle, Newington Butts, having far outgrown the space of New Park Street Chapel."

In Vol. V1. — "Many sneer at Gill, but he is not to be dispensed with. In some respects, he has no superior. He is always well worth consulting.

"C. H. S. 1886."

"There is *myself."* I stopped him at this point, with the query whether he was quite sure about the *first* one.

Since then, his character has gone I know not where, but certainly he will get on better without it than with it; yet he was the first on his own list, and a few others of the same black sort made up the five. There were, in the other places of worship to which he did not go, men, whose characters for integrity and up-rightness, ay, and for spirituality and prayerfulness, would have been degraded by being put into comparison with his; yet he set himself up as judge in Israel, and pretended to know exactly how many people of God were in the village. "The Lord knoweth them that are His."

I bless God that I have learned to have very little respect for the vision of *the man* with the measuring line. When I see an angel with it, I am glad enough; but when I see: *a man* with it, I tell him that he must give me a warrant from God, and show me how he is to know the elect by any other method than that laid down by our Lord Jesus Christ: "By their fruits shall ye know them."

I have sometimes been greatly obliged to a wicked world for what it has done to inconsistent professors of religion. While I was Pastor at Waterbeach, a cer-tain young man joined the church. We thought he was a changed character, but there used to be in the village, once a year, a great temptation in the form of a feast; and when the feast came round, this foolish fellow was there in very evil company. He was in the long room of a public house, in the evening, and when I heard what happened, I really felt intense gratitude to the landlady of that place. When she came in, and saw him there, she said, "Halloa, Jack So-and-so, are *you* here? Why, you are one of Spurgeon's lot, yet you are here; you ought to be ashamed of yourself. This is not fit company for you. Put him out of the window, boys." And they did put him out of the window on the Friday night, and we put him out of the door on the Sunday, for we removed his name from our church-book. Where was he to go to? The world would not have him, and the church would not have him; if he had been all for the world, the world would have made something of him; and if he had been all for Christ, Christ would have made something of him. But as he tried to be a little for each, and so nothing to either, his life became a wretched one; as he walked the streets, people pointed at him with scorn. The Christians turned away, thinking him a hypocrite, as I fear he was; and the worldlings called him one, and made: his name a by-word and a proverb.

In those early days, I had sometimes to contend with the Antinominian preachers as well as with their people. I once found myself in the midst of a com-pany of ministers and friends, who were disputing whether it was a sin in men that they did not believe the gospel. Whilst they were discussing, I said, "Gentle-men, am I in the presence of Christians? Are you believers in the Bible, or are you not?" They said, "We are Christians, of course."

"Then," said I, "does not the Scripture say, 'of sin, because they believe not on Me'? And is it not the damning sin' of men, that they do not believe on Christ?" I should not have imagined, if I had not myself heard them, that any persons would be so wicked as to venture to assert that "it is no sin for a sinner not to believe on Christ." I should have thought that, however far they might wish to push their sentiments, they would not tell a lie to uphold the truth; and, in my opinion, this is what such men really do. Truth is a strong tower, and never requires to be buttressed with error. God's Word will stand against all man's devices. I would never invent a sophism to prove that it is no sin on the part of the ungodly not to believe, for I am sure it is. When I am taught in the Scriptures that "this is the condemnation, that light is come into the world, and men loved darkness rather than light," and when I read, "*He* that believeth not is condemned already, because he hath not believed in the name of the only begotten Son of God," I affirm, and the Word declares it, *unbelief is a sin.* Surely, with rational and unprejudiced persons, it cannot require any reasoning to prove it. Is it not a sin for a creature to doubt the Word of its Maker? Is it not a crime and an insult to the Deity, for me, an atom, a particle of dust, to dare to deny His Words? Is it not the very summit of arrogance and the height of pride for a son of Adam to say, even in his heart, "God, I doubt Thy grace; God, I doubt Thy love; God, I doubt Thy power"? I feel that, could we roll all sins into one mass, — could we take murder, blasphemy, lust, adultery, fornication, and everything that is vile, and unite them all into one vast globe of black corruption, — they would not even then equal the sin of unbelief. This is the monarch sin, the quintessence of guilt, the mixture of the venom of all crimes, the dregs of the wine of Gomorrah; it is the A1 sin, the masterpiece of Satan, the chief work of the devil. Unbelief hardened the heart of Pharaoh, — it gave license to the tongue of blaspheming Rabshakeh, — yea, it became a deicide, and murdered' the Lord Jesus Christ. Unbelief! it has mixed many a cup of poison it has brought thousands to the gallows, and many to a shameful grave, who have murdered themselves, and rushed with bloody hands before their Creator's tribunal, because of unbelief. Give me an unbeliever, — let me know that he doubts 'God's Word, — let me know that he distrusts His promise and His threatening; and with that for a premise, I will conclude that the man shall, by-and-by, unless them is amazing restraining power exerted upon him, be guilty of the foulest and blackest crimes. Unbelief is a Beelzebub sin; like Beelzebub, it is the leader of all evil spirits. It is said of Jeroboam that he sinned, and made Israel to sin; and it may be said of unbelief that it not only itself sins, but it makes others sin; it is the egg of all crime, the seed of every offense; in fact, everything that is evil and vile lies couched in that one word unbelief.

In striking contrast to those apologists for sin, I met in my first pastorate, as I have often done since, a number of persons who professed to be perfect, and who said that they had lived so many months or years without sinning against God. One man, who told me that he was perfect, was hump-backed; and when I remarked that I thought, if he were a perfect man, he ought to have a perfect body, he became so angry that I said to him, "*Well,* my friend, if *you* are perfect, there are a great many' more as near perfection as you are." "*Oh!*" he exclaimed, "*I* shall feel it for having been betrayed into anger." He said that he had not been angry for many years; I had brought him back to his old state of infirmity, and painful as it might be for him, I have no doubt that it did him good to see himself as he really was. When a man thinks that he is a full-grown Christian, he reminds me of a poor boy whom I used to see. He had such a splendid head for his body that he had often to lay it on a pillow, for it was too weighty for his shoulders to carry, and his Mother told me that, when he tried to stand up, he often tumbled down, overbalanced by his heavy head. There are some people who appear to grow very fast, but they have water on the brain, and are out of due proportion; but he who truly grows in grace does not say,

"Dear me! I can feel that I am growing; bless the Lord! Let's sing a hymn,

'I'm a growing! I'm a growing!'" I have often felt that I was growing smaller; I think that is very probable, and a good thing, too. If we are very great in our own estimation, it is because we have a number of cancers, or foul gatherings, that need to be lanced, so as to let out the bad matter that causes us to boast of our bigness.

Our Wesleyan brethren have a notion that they are going to be perfect here on earth. I should be very glad to see them when they are perfect; and if

any of them happen to be in the position of servants, wanting situations, I would be happy to give them any amount of wages I could spare, for I should feel myself highly honored and greatly blessed in having perfect servants; and what is more, if any of them are masters, and need servants, I would undertake to come and serve them without any wages at all if I could but find a perfect master. I have had one perfect Master ever since I first knew the Lord, and if I could be sure that there is another perfect master, I should be greatly pleased to have him as an under-master, while the great Supreme must ever be chief of all. One man, who said he was perfect, called upon me once, and asked me to go and see him, for I should receive valuable instruction from him if I did. I said, "I have no doubt it would be so; but I should not like to go to your house, I think I should hardly be able to get into one of your rooms." "How is that?" he inquired.

"Well," I replied, "I suppose that your house would be so full of angels that there would be no room for me." He did not like that remark; and when I made one or two other playful observations, he went into a towering rage. "Well, friend," I said to him," I think, after all, I am as perfect as you are; but *perfect men* ever get angry?" He denied that he was angry, although there was a peculiar redness about his cheeks, and a fiery flash in his eyes, that is very common to persons when they are in a passion. At any rate, I think I rather spoiled his perfection, for he evidently went home much less satisfied with himself than when he came out. I met another man who considered himself perfect, but he was thoroughly mad; and I do not believe that any of the pretenders to perfection are better than good maniacs, a superior kind of Bedlamites; for, while a man has got a spark of reason left in him, he cannot, unless he is the most impudent of impostors, talk about being perfect. He who imagines such a thing must be insane; for any man who examines himself for five minutes, in the light of God's Word, will find enough in his own heart to drive from him any shadow of a thought about being perfect in this world. I have little patience with such willfully blind people, and when I hear of some who are said to be perfectly holy, and of others who are utterly foolish, I think the two classes are wonderfully alike. I have met with a few people who seemed to me almost perfect, but they have been the very ones who have groaned most over their own imperfections; while those with whom I have come into contact, who have professed to be holy and without blemish, have been the most imperfect individuals I have ever known.

My own experience is a daily struggle with the evil within. I wish I could find in myself something friendly to grace; but, hitherto, I have searched my nature through, and have found everything in rebellion against God. At one time, there comes the torpor of sloth, when one ought to be active every moment, having so much to do for God, and for the souls of men, and so little time in which to do it. At another time, there comes the quickness of passion; when one should be calm and cool, and play the Christian, bearing with patience whatever has to be endured, there come the unadvised word and the rash expression. Anon, I am troubled with conceit, the devilish whisper, — I can call it no less, — "How well thou hast done! How nobly thou hast played thy part!" Then crawls out distrust, — foul and faithless, — suggesting that God does not regard the affairs of men, and will not interpose on my behalf. Yet, what would I not give if I might but be perfect! Sometimes, I think that, if God's people mentioned in the Old and New Testaments had all been perfect, I should have despaired; but, because they seem to have had just the kind of faults I grieve over in myself, I do not feel any more lenient toward my faults, but I do rejoice that I also may say with each of them, "The Lord will *perfect* that which concerneth *me*." He will most assuredly, beyond a doubt, bring to perfection my faith, my love, my hope, and every grace. He will perfect His own purposes; He will perfect His promises, He will perfect my body, and perfect my soul. While I am fully persuaded that perfection is absolutely impossible to any man beneath the sky, I feel equally sure that, to every believer, future perfection is certain beyond a doubt. The day shall come when the Lord shall not only make us better, but shall make us perfectly pure and holy; when He shall not merely subdue our lusts, but when He shall cast the demons out altogether; when He shall make us holy, and unblameable, and unreprovable in His sight. That day, however, I believe, shall not come until we enter into the joy of our Lord, and are glorified together with Christ in Heaven. Then, but not till then, shall He present us "*faultless* before the presence of His glory with exceeding joy."

While I was going about the Cambridgeshire villages, preaching and visiting, it often saddened me to see, especially in the houses of the poor, Roman Catholic pictures hanging on the walls, — I suppose, because they happened to be rather pretty, and very cheap. Popish publishers have very cleverly managed to get up pictures of the Virgin Mary, and the lying fable of her assumption to Heaven, and all sorts of legends of saints and saintesses; and being brightly colored, and sold at a low price, these vile productions have been introduced into thousands of houses. I have seen, to my horror, a picture of God the Father represented as an old man, — a conception almost too hideous to mention, — yet the picture is hung up in the cottages of England; whereas the Lord has expressly commanded us not to make any likeness or image of Him, or to try to represent His appearance in any way, and any attempt to do so is disobedient and even blasphemous.

It was grievous also to find what gross ignorance prevailed among many of the villagers concerning the way of salvation. They seemed, somehow, to have got into their heads the notion that they could not be saved because they could not read, and did not know much. Frequently, when I asked anything about personal salvation, I received the answer, "Oh, sir, I never had any learning!" and that was supposed to be a sufficient excuse for not having repented of sin, and trusted in the Savior. Yet the unlearned need not stay away from Christ. It was said of an old Greek philosopher, that he wrote over his door, "None but the learned may enter here;" but Christ, on the contrary, writes over His door, "He that is simple, let him turn in hither." I can 'testify that great numbers of those humble country folk accepted the Savior's invitation, and it was delightful to see what a firm grip they afterwards had of the verities of the faith; many of them became perfect masters in divinity. I used to think, sometimes, that if they had degrees who deserved them, diplomas would often be transferred, and given to those who hold the plough-handle or work at the carpenter's bench; for there is often more divinity in the little finger of a ploughman than there is in the whole body of some of our modern divines. "Don't they understand divinity?" someone asks. Yes, in the letter of it; but as to the spirit and life of it, D.D. often means DOUBLY DESTITUTE.

An incident that I once witnessed at Waterbeach furnished me with an illustration concerning death. A company of villagers, the younger branches of a family, were about to emigrate to another land. The aged Mother, who had not for some years left her cottage fireside, came to the railway-station from which they must start. I stood among the sorrowful group as their friend and minister. I think I see the many embraces which the fond Mother gave to her son and daughter, and her little grandchildren; I can picture them folding their arms about her aged neck, and then saying farewell to all the friends in the village who had come to bid them adieu. A shrill sound is heard; it sends a pang through all hearts, as if it were the messenger of death to her who is about to lose the props of her household. In great haste, at the small village station, the passengers are hurried to their seats; they thrust their heads out of the carriage window; the aged parent stands on the very edge of the platform that she may take her last look at them.

There is a whistle: from the engine, and away goes the train. In an instant, the poor woman, jumping from the platform, rushes along the railway, with all her might crying, "My children! My children! My children! They are gone, and I shall never see them again." The illustration may not be classical; but, nevertheless, I have been reminded of it by many a death, when I have seen the godly suddenly snatched away. They have gone from us, swiftly as the wind itself could bear them, or as the hasty knaves of the sea could bury them out of our sight. It is our affliction and trouble that we must remain behind and weep, for they are gone beyond recall; yet there is something pleasant in the picture. It is but a departure; — they are not destroyed; they are not blown to atoms; they are not taken away to prison; — 'tis but a departure from one place to another. They still live; they still are blessed. While we weep, they are rejoicing; while we mourn, they are singing psalms of praise; and, by-and-by, in God's good time, we shall meet them again, to be parted no more for ever.

There was an amusing incident in my early Waterbeach ministry which I have never forgotten. One day, a gentleman, who was then mayor of Cambridge, and who had more than once tried to correct my youthful mistakes, asked me if I really had told my congregation that, if a thief got into Heaven, he would begin picking the angels' pockets. "Yes, sir," I replied, "I told them that, if it were possible for an ungodly man to go to Heaven without having his nature changed, he would be none the better for being there; and then, by way of illustration, I said that, were a thief to get in among the glorified, he would remain a thief still, and he would go round the place picking the angels' pockets!.... But, my dear young friend,' asked Mr. Brimley, very seriously, "don't you know that the angels haven't any pockets?...No, sir," I replied, with equal gravity, "I' did not know that; but I am glad to be assured of the fact from a gentleman who does know. I will take care to put it all right the first opportunity I get." The following Monday morning, I walked into Mr. Brimley's shop, and said to him, "I set that matter right yesterday, sir," "What matter?" he inquired.

"Why, about the angels' pockets!" "What *did* you say?" he asked, in a tone almost of despair at what he might hear next. "Oh, sir, I just told the people I was sorry to say that I had made a mistake the last time I preached to them, but that I had met a gentleman, the mayor of Cambridge, — who had assured me that the angels had no pockets, so I must correct what I had said, as I did not want anybody to go away with a false notion about Heaven. I would therefore say that, if a thief got among the angels without having his nature changed, he would try to steal the feathers out of their wings!.... Surely, you did not say that?" said Mr. Brimley. "I did, though,"

I replied. "*Then,*" he exclaimed, "I'll never try to set you right again," which was just exactly what I wanted him to say.

Once, while I was at Waterbeach, I had a sleepy congregation. It was on a Sabbath afternoon; — those afternoon services in our English villages are usually a doleful waste of effort. Roast beef and pudding lie heavy on the hearers' souls, and the preacher himself is deadened in his mental processes while digestion claims the mastery of the hour. The 'people had been eating too much dinner, so they came to chapel heavy and dull, and before long many of them were nodding. So I tried an old expedient to rouse them. I shouted with all my might, "Fire! Fire! Fire!" When, starting from their seats, some of my hearers asked where it was, I answered, as other preachers had done in similar circumstances, "In hell, for sinners who will not accept the Savior."

On another occasion, I had a trouble of quite a different character. I had preached on the Sunday morning, and gone home to dinner, as was my wont, with one of the congregation. The afternoon sermon came so close behind the morning one, that it was difficult to prepare the soul, especially as the dinner was a necessary but serious inconvenience where a clear brain was required. By a careful measuring of diet, I remained in an earnest, lively condition; but, to my dismay, I found that the pre-arranged line of thought was gone from me. I could not find the trail of my' prepared sermon; and press my forehead as I might, the missing topic would not come. Time was brief, the hour was striking, and in some alarm I told the honest farmer that I could not for the life of me recollect what I had intended to preach about. "Oh!" he said, "never mind; you will be sure to have a good word for us." Just at that moment, a blazing block of wood fell out of the fire upon the hearth at my feet, smoking into my eyes and nose at a great rate. "There," said the farmer, "there's a text for you, sir, — 'Is not this a brand plucked out of the fire?... No," I thought, "it was not plucked out, for it fell out of itself." Here, however, was a text, an illustration, and a leading thought as a nest-egg for more. Further light came, and the discourse was certainly not worse than my more prepared effusions; it was better in the best sense, for one or two came forward declaring themselves to have been aroused and converted through that afternoon's sermon. I have always considered that it was a happy circumstance that I had forgotten the text from which I had intended to preach.

(The following is a *facsimile* of Mr. Spurgeon's Outline of the discourse that came to him in this singular manner. In this instance, the notes must have been written out afterwards. The numbers at the foot of the Outline mean that the service at Waterbeach, that Sabbath afternoon, was the 412th time that Mr. Spurgeon had preached, — although he was then only eighteen years of age, — and that he took the same subject again at six other places.)

Chapter Twenty-Four - Memorable Services From Waterbeach

AFTER I had been preaching at Waterbeach for about a year or so, I was invited to conduct anniversary and other special services in various places.

On several occasions, I had very curious experiences. One eccentric individual, whose acquaintance I made in those early days, was Mr. Porto Brown, "the miller of Houghton." He asked me over to preach in his chapel, and from Saturday night to Monday morning I had the felicitous misery of being his guest, — I can use no other term to describe the strange mixture of emotions that I felt while under his roof. nothing of special interest occurred the first night, but when I came downstairs, the following morning, Mr. Brown said to me, "*We* always provide two eggs for the minister's breakfast on Sunday morning; the phosphorus in them feeds the brain, and it looks as though you will need plenty of mental nourishment to-day." I made no reply to this remark, thinking it was better to bide my time, and when I did open fire, to give him such a broadside as he did not expect. There were three services during the day; Mr. Brown preached in the morning, a neighboring minister in the afternoon, and myself at night. After we had returned to my host's house, and had taken supper, the good man leaned back in his easy chair, with his eyes closed and the fingertips of each hand touching, and began to soliloquize aloud: —

"O Lord, we thank Thee for a good day all through! In the morning, Lord, Thy unworthy servant was privileged to speak in Thy name, — with some degree of liberty, and he hopes also with some measure o! acceptance to the people. In the afternoon, a worth)' brother preached a good, sound, solid, gospel sermon; — nothing very brilliant; but, still, likely to be useful.

In the evening, Lord, we had a regular steam-engine, — ran over everything and everybody." Then, opening his eyes, and looking across at me, he began a dialogue which, as nearly as I can recollect it, ran as follows: —

Brown. — Young man, whoever persuaded you that you could preach?

Spurgeon. — I believe, sir, that the Lord called me to this work, and I have found a good many people who are of the same opinion. B. — How long have you been a minister?

Spurgeon — A little more than twelve months.

Brown — How many souls did you save, last year?

Spurgeon — None, sir.

Brown — None? You have been a minister twelve months, and yet there have been no souls saved. You ought to be ashamed to confess it; though, if you have preached the same doctrines as you gave us to-night, I am not surprised to hear that no souls have been saved.

Spurgeon — I did not say that souls had not been saved; I said that I did not save any. I am happy to know that the Lord *has* saved some through my instrumentality.

Brown — Most of your brethren would have said, "humble instrumentality," when, all the while, they were as proud as Lucifer. But that is only the common ministerial cant; you knew well enough what I meant. Well, how many were converted?

Spurgeon — Twenty-one, I believe, sir.

Brown — How often do you preach?

Spurgeon — Three times on the Sunday, and once in the week, at Waterbeach; and nearly every night in the week somewhere else.

Brown — We will only reckon the Sunday morning and evening sermons; afternoon services never save anybody, the people are too sleepy to listen after dinner. So, let us say, a hundred and four sermons, and twenty-one souls saved; that is eighty-three sermons wasted! Indeed, we might say, a hundred and three, for the whole twenty-one souls might just as well have been saved under one sermon. Do you live at Waterbeach?

Spurgeon — No, sir; I live at Cambridge, where I teach in a school.

Brown — Oh, then; you are only an apprentice boy at present, just trying your hand at preaching! Your ministry is a sort of off-hand farm, to be cultivated at odd times. What salary do your people give you?

Spurgeon — £45 a year.

Brown — Oh, that accounts for everything.! Souls can't be saved under £100 a year; that is, of course, where the people can afford to pay it, and that amount is little enough for any minister. Well, now, my young friend, let me give you a bit of good advice. You'll never make a preacher; so just give it up, and stick to your teaching.

When, in after years, I reminded him of his advice and prophecy, he used waggishly to say, "Ah! there's no knowing how much good a man may do by a little timely correction; no doubt my sharp speech put you on your mettle." That was really the case, though not in the sense he meant. I soon discovered that he was a rank Arminian, and when he attacked the Calvinism that was so dear to me. I denounced his system of doctrine as being worthless theology. I found that he used to give his money to different Missionary Societies according to the proportion of converts they reported as brought to the Lord at the lowest possible cost! He would take the various Annual Reports, divide the amount expended by the number of additions to the churches, and then subscribe the most where the amount per head was the least! There was a modicum of truth at the back of what he said; but I was really shocked by the way he talked about conversions being dependent upon the money contributed, so I spoke out my opinion as freely as he did his, and gave him a Roland for his Oliver without the slightest compunction. It was a battle royal, and both the old gentleman and the 'prentice boy grew sufficiently warm; but no scars remained on either combatant. On the

Monday morning, Mr. Brown walked to Huntingdon with me in loving conversation, and afterwards sent me Haldane's "*Life*" as a present, with his sincere regards; and I, whom he had horrified with his doctrinal statements, felt an inward drawing towards the bluff heretic. No doubt he purposely put forward his most *outer* views of doctrine on that occasion to draw out the youthful preacher, probably intending to set him right on many points; but he had an unpromising pupil to deal with, one who had no tear of Porto Brown, or Professor Finney, or any other Arminian, before his eyes, but held his own opinion with a firmness which interested and did not displease the good but eccentric miller, who had usually dealt with softer material when criticizing the young gentlemen who preached in his chapel on Sundays.

Another singular character with whom I became acquainted early in my ministry, was old Mr. Sutton, of Cottenham. He had never seen me, but he heard that I was a popular young minister, so he invited me over to preach his anniversary sermons. I was in the vestry of the chapel before the morning service, and when the aged man came in, and saw me, he seemed greatly surprised to find that I was so young. After gruffly exchanging the usual greetings, he remarked, "*I* shouldn't have asked you here, had I known you were such a bit of a boy. Why, the people have been pouring into the place all the morning in wagons, and dickey-carts, and all kinds of vehicles! More fools they!" he added. I said, "*Well,* sir, I suppose it will be so much the better for your anniversary; still, I can go back as easily as I came, and my people at Waterbeach will be very glad to see me." "*No, no,*" said the old pastor; "*now* you are here, you must do the best you can. There is a young fellow over from Cambridge, who will help you; and we shan't expect much from you;" and thereupon he paced the room, moaning out, "Oh, dear! what a pass the world is coming to when we get as preachers a parcel of boys who have not got their Mother's milk out of their mouths!"

I was in due time conducted to the pulpit, and the old minister sat upon the stairs, — I suppose, ready to go on with the service in case I should break down.

After prayer and singing, I read, from the Book of Proverbs, the chapter containing the words, "The hoary head is a crown of glory." When I had gone so far, I stopped, and remarked, "I doubt it, for, this very morning, I met with a man who has a hoary head, yet he has not learnt common civility to his fellow-men." Proceeding with the reading, I finished the verse, — "if it be found in the way of righteousness." "Ah!" I said, "that's another thing; a hoary head would then be a crown of glory, and, for the matter of that, so would a red head, or a head of any other color." I went on with the service, and preached as best I could, and as I came down from the pulpit, Mr. Sutton slapped me on the back, and exclaimed, "Bless your heart! I have been a minister nearly forty years, and I was never better pleased with a sermon in all my life; but you are the sauciest dog that ever barked in a pulpit." All the way home from the chapel, he kept on going across the road to speak to little groups of people who were discussing the service. I heard him say, "I never knew anything like it in all my life; and to think that I should have talked to him as I did!" We had a good time for the rest of the day, the Lord blessed the Word, and Mr. Sutton and I were ever afterwards the best of friends. [18]

never forget Mr. Sutton's description of a sermon he had preached; I had
⠂s of the discourse from his own lips, and I trust they will remain as notes,
⠂er be preached from again in this world. The text was, "The nighthawk,
and the cuckoo." That might not strike anyone as being exceedingly rich
in matter; it did not so strike me, and therefore I innocently inquired, "And what
were the heads?" He replied most archly, "Heads? why, wring the birds' necks,
and there are three directly, 'the night-hawk, the owl, and the cuckoo.'" He
showed that these birds were all unclean under the law, and were plain types of
unclean sinners. Night-hawks were persons who pilfered on the sly, also people
who adulterated their goods, and cheated their neighbors in an underhand way
without being suspected to be rogues. As for the owls, they typified drunkards,
who are always liveliest at night, while by day they will almost knock their heads
against a post because they are so sleepy. There were owls also among professors. The owl is a very small bird when he is plucked; he only looks big because
he wears so many feathers; so, many professors are all feathers, and if you could
take away their boastful professions, there would be very little left of them Then
the cuckoos were the church clergy, who always utter the same note v⠂   ⠂ r⠂
they open their mouths in the church, and live on other birds' egg
church-rates and tithes. The cuckoos were also, I think, the free⠂
were always saying, "Do-do-do-do." Was not this rather too mu⠂⠂
thing? Yet, from the man who delivered it, the discourse would
remarkable or odd.

The same venerable brother preached a sermon equally singu
original and useful; those who heard it will remember it to their dy⠂⠂⠂
from this text: "The slothful man roasteth not that which he took in hu   ⠂e
good old man leaned upon the top of the pulpit, and said, "Then, my bretnrc.⠂, he
was a lazy fellow!" That was the exordium; and then he went on to say, "He went
out a-hunting, and after much trouble he caught his hare, and then was too idle
to roast it. He was a lazy fellow indeed!" The preacher made us all feel how ridiculous such idleness was, and then he said, "But, then, you are very likely quite as
much to blame as this man, for you do just the same. You hear of a popular minister coming down from London, and you put the horse in the cart, and drive ten
or twenty miles to hear him; and, then, when you have heard the sermon, you
forget to profit by it. You catch the hare, and do not roast it; you go hunting after
the truth, and then you do not receive it." Then he went on to show that, just as
meat needs cooking to prepare it for assimilation in the bodily system, — I do
not think he used that word, though, — so the truth needs to go through a certain
process before it can be received into the mind, that we may feed thereon and
grow. He said he should show us how to cook a sermon, and he did so most in-
structively.

He began as the cookery books do, — "First, catch your hare." "So," he said,
"first, get a gospel sermon." Then he declared that a great many sermons were
not worth hunting for, and that good sermons were mournfully scarce, and it was
worth while to go any distance to hear a solid, old-fashioned, Calvinistic discourse. Then, after the sermon had been caught, there was much about it which
might be necessary because of the preacher's infirmity, but which was not profitable, and must be put away.

Here he enlarged upon discerning and judging what we heard, and not believing every word of any man. Then followed directions as to roasting a sermon; —
run the spit of memory through it from end to end, turn it round upon the roast-
ing-jack of meditation, before the fire of a really warm and earnest heart, and in
that way the sermon would be cooked, and ready to yield real spiritual nourishment. I am only giving just the outline of the discourse, and though it may look
somewhat laughable, it was not so esteemed by the hearers. It was full of allego-
ry, and kept up the attention of the people from the beginning to the end.

"Well, my dear sir, how are you?" was my salutation to him, one morning,
"I'm pleased to see you so well at your age." "Yes, I am in fine order for an old
man, and hardly feel myself failing at all." "I hope your good health will continue
for years to come, and that, like Moses, you will go down to your grave with your
eye undimmed, and your natural force unabated."

"All very fine," said the old gentleman, "*but,* in the first place, Moses never went
clown to his grave at all, he went up to it; and, in the next place, what is the
meaning of all you have been talking about? Why did not the eye of Moses wax
dim?.... I suppose, sir," said I, very meekly, "*that* his natural mode of life and quiet
spirit had helped to preserve his faculties, and make him a vigorous old man."
"*Very* likely," said he, "*but* that's not what I am driving at: what's the meaning, the
spiritual teaching of the whole matter?

Is it not just this? Moses is the law, and what a glorious end of the law the Lord
gave it on the Mount of His finished work; how sweetly its terrors were all laid to
sleep with a kiss from God's mouth! and, mark you, the reason why the law no
more condemns us is not because its eye is dim, so that it cannot see our sins, or
because its force, with which to curse and punish us, is abated; but Christ has
taken it up to the Mount, and gloriously made an end of it."

Such was Mr. Sutton's usual talk, and such was his ministry. Peace to his ashes.
He was a quaint old man, who, after being a shepherd of sheep for between thirty
and forty years, became a shepherd of men for a similar period; and he often told
me that his second flock was "*a* deal more sheepish than the first." The converts,
who found the road to Heaven under his preaching, were so many that, when we
remember them, we are like those who saw the lame man leaping after he heard
the word of Peter and John; they were disposed to criticize, but "*beholding* the
man that was healed standing with Peter and John, they could say nothing
against it."

In the beginning of my preaching experience, there was a dear good man who,
when I took the service for him, would persist in announcing the hymn commencing —

"Mighty God! while angels bless Thee,
May an infant *lisp Thy name?"*

That was to be sung with special reference to me, and at first it was all very
proper, for the veteran saint might well regard me as "*an* infant" in spiritual
things; but, ten years later, when I went down into the country to preach for him
again, there was still the same hymn to be sung before my sermon, —

"Mighty God! while angels bless Thee,
May an infant *lisp Thy name?"*

And when I was forty years of age, and the venerable man was near the close of his long life, and I went once more to help him by a sermon, I still had to join the congregation in singing —

"Mighty God! while angels bless Thee,
May an infant *lisp Thy name?"*

I thought that I was rather a largish infant, and felt that I would have preferred to choose my own hymns.

On another occasion, the minister of the place where I was preaching would give out the hymns, and the hymn-book in use was that one by Dr.

Watts in which there are first the Psalms, and then Books I., II., and III. of Hymns. I had selected a hymn out of one of the divisions, but by some mistake the minister had turned to the wrong part of the book, and before he had discovered his error, he was reading —

"When the Eternal bows the skies
To visit earthly things,
With scorn Divine He turns His eyes
From towers of haughty kings.
"He bids His awful chariot roll
Far downward from the skies,
To visit every humble soul
With pleasure in His eyes."

Those who are familiar with the hymns of Dr. Watts, know that the last verse begins —

'Just like His nature is His grace,
All sov'reign and all free;"

and when the minister had read these two lines, he said, "We won't sing this hymn." I felt that, under the circumstances, the hymn ought to be sung, so I said, "If you please, we *will* sing that hymn; or we will not have any at all if we do not have that one." So the minister shut up the book, and I went on with the sermon. I had fixed upon quite: a different subject for my discourse; but when such a challenge was given to me, I felt compelled to change my theme, so I announced as my text, "I will have mercy on whom I will have mercy, and I will have compassion on whom I will have compassion. So then it is not of him that willeth, nor of him that runneth, but of God that sheweth mercy," and I preached from those words a discourse full of good sound doctrine, — sixteen ounces to the pound, — which filled with delight the hearts of all the brethren and sisters who loved the marrow and fatness of the faith which some call Calvinism, but which we trace back to our Lord Himself and His apostles.

In my early ministerial days, I was invited to preach at Isleham, Cambridge-shire:, where I was baptized. I was to conduct the morning service; my brother Aldis, I think it was, preached in the afternoon; and then I was to take my turn again in the evening. The people at Isleham had such a belief that I should draw a congregation, that they went and borrowed the largest chapel in the place. I shall never forget it, because I preached that morning at eleven o'clock to seven persons! That was all the people I had; and I remember how I told them that they reminded me of the way ducks act when they go through a doorway, they always lower their heads; they will do it even when they are going in or out of a barn.

The entrance may be twenty feet high, but a duck never goes through it without putting his head down, for fear he might possibly hit the top of the door! So I said to the people, "You were so afraid of your place being overcrowded that you borrowed that big chapel for seven people!" Well, being there, I resolved that I would preach that morning at my very best, although the congregation was so small. The brother, who took the afternoon service, said to me, "I can't think how you did it; you were as earnest, and you preached as well as if you had had the place crowded."

"Yes," I replied, "I thought that was the only way to make sure of getting it full in the evening; so I determined that I would lay out all my guns, and make the greatest possible impression upon those few people." In the afternoon, we had a very decent audience of, perhaps, a hundred or a hundred and fifty; but when I preached at night, there was not standing room in the place. Though I did not compliment myself upon gathering the crowd, yet I could not help saying that, if I had not preached at my best to the seven people in the morning, I should not have had the large company at night, for those who were there at the first service went away, and talked about how well they had got on, and so induced many others to come out in the evening to hear for themselves.

Chapter Twenty-Five - Sermonettes

THERE are probably few, if any, detailed records of the services mentioned in the preceding chapters, and the number of persons, still living, who were among "the boy-preacher's" first hearers, must be continually diminishing.

Even their reminiscences of his preaching would be necessarily very incomplete after so great a lapse of time. It is, therefore, a happy circumstance that Mr. Spurgeon was moved first to write, and then to preserve, considerable portions of the discourses that, in those early days, were the means of winning so many souls for the Lord Jesus Christ. The manuscripts are by no means full reports of the young Pastor's utterances, — they are Sermonettes rather than Sermons, — but they tell what were the subjects brought before the notice of the villagers who crowded "the little thatched chapel" at Waterbeach, and they also show how the various topics were handled.

Following the arrangement adopted in Chapter 20., one Sermonette is given from each of the Volumes V., V1., and VII., with the inscriptions written at the beginning and end of the earlier books in the series.

Volume V. commences thus, —

Feb. 26, 1853.

"Jehovah Jireh," — "I am ever with you."
"It is better to trust in the Lord than to put confidence in man."
"It is better to trust in the Lord than to put confidence in princes."
Underneath thee are the everlasting arms.

Never have I sought in vain.

OUTLINE 243. — CHRIST OUR SURETY

"Be surely for Thy servant for good, let not the proud oppress me."
— Psalm 119:122.

The 22nd verse of Hebrews 7 supplies a comment on this text. These are the only two places in Scripture in which a surety between God and man is mentioned; but though spoken of sparingly, it is none the less important,

I. CONSIDER WHEREIN CHRIST IS A SURETY.
II. WHAT HE ENGAGED TO DO AS A SURETY.
III. WHAT BENEFITS FLOW TO US THROUGH HIS SURETYSHIP.

I. CONSIDER IN WHAT SENSE JESUS IS A SURETY.

1. Not for His Father, — to us, — for God is so true, His word and oath so firm, that we need not wish for a Surety; and, indeed, it would not be an assistance to our faith, since he who doubts the Father would doubt the Son.

2. Not as promising in our behalf. He is not bound to see that we perform our obligations, for He knows well enough that we could not pay a farthing of our debt to God, even if we would.

3. But He is our Surety by taking all our debts upon Himself, — standing in our stead, — promising to do what we ought to have done.

We will illustrate this subject from instances in the world. A son, about to set up in business, has little money; but his father says, "Charge the goods to my account; let him have them, but send me the bill, I will be surety for its payment."

A poor man is in prison for debt, and must continue to lie there unless someone pays 1.t for him. A philanthropist, like John Howard, comes in, and bids the creditor loose his prisoner, and accept himself as surety for the debtor.

Damon is in prison, condemned to die; but he wishes first to see his children. His friend, Pythias, is chained in his place, and engages to die in his stead if he does not return at the appointed time.

II. WHAT CHRIST ENGAGED TO DO AS A SURETY.

Not more than He could do, — for He is God.

Not more than He will do, — for He is faithful.

1. He has promised to render to the law perfect obedience. This was our debt; but He has taken it away, canceled it for ever.

2. He has promised to satisfy justice for our debt of punishment. Just as Paul wrote to Philemon, concerning Onesimus, "If he hath wronged thee, or oweth thee ought, put that on mine account I will repay it." This Christ has done for all believers.

3. He has engaged to bring all the elect home to glory. Judah said he would bear the blame if he did not bring Benjamin back. Jacob had to be responsible for the sheep of Laban. So Jesus is bound by covenant to save every believer.

III. WHAT BLESSINGS FLOW TO US THROUGH CHRIST'S SURETYSHIP.

1. Complete pardon, — for the punishment of our sin has been transferred from us to Him, and we are reckoned as if we had ourselves endured the full penalty of our guilt.

2. Complete justification. What Christ does for us is counted as done by ourselves, so that we are now considered as sinless, and acceptable unto God by Jesus Christ.

3. Freedom from fear, — a settled peace. We have no ground for despondency or terror; no bailiff can arrest us now, for our debt is fully paid.

4. Everlasting security. Our whole indebtedness is gone, and we are safe for ever.

How foolish not to seek this Surety! How dangerous to delay, for death may come, and God demand His due, and we shall have nothing with which to pay our debt! A life of holiness cannot pay it. Tears, groans, and prayers cannot pay it. An eternity of woe cannot pay it.

Faith looks to Jesus as Surety, and desires no other means of paying the debt. Trust Him, then, and you are free for ever.

Lord, aid me!

(Inscription at the end of Volume V: —)

The Lord is my Banner; why am I fearful when God furnishes me with all that is needful?

(Inscription at the beginning of Volume VI: —)

O Lord, I am entirely dependent on Thine aid! Do not cut off the supplies, but ever give me to drink of Thy fountain, and to guide others to the same Divine spring.

OUTLINE 311. — CHRIST IS PRECIOUS.

"Unto you therefore which believe He is precious." — 1 Peter 2:7.

This was the theme of the first sermon I ever preached; I hope it is my theme now, and ever shall be, — living, dying, and glorified.

This is one of the texts from which everyone imagines he could preach; but which, for that very reason, is all the more difficult to preach from to your satisfaction. However, if the Good Spirit will apply to your hearts my few homely thoughts, your being satisfied will not matter. Here we have, —

I. A PRECIOUS PEOPLE.
II. A PRECIOUS CHRIST.
III. A PRECIOUS EXPERIENCE.

I. A PRECIOUS PEOPLE.

Not so in themselves, but quite the reverse; yet they are so in the eyes of their Lord and Savior. They are His special favorites. They are His crown jewels.

They are all believers, whether they have great faith or little faith. They are not mere repeaters of creeds, but true, hearty believers in the Lord Jesus Christ.

It is only these precious people who are able to see the preciousness of Christ. Faith is indispensable to the enjoyment of Christ. Can a child know how precious is gold before he has been taught its value? Does the beggar in the street appreciate a picture by Raphael, or can the ignorant rightly estimate the value of learning?

Faith is the eyesight of the soul, whereby it discerns spiritual beauty. Faith is the mouth which relishes Heavenly sweetness.

God has made faith the mark of His precious people, because it is a grace which greatly exalts God, and, at the same time, abases the creature.

209

Precious are God's people, — elect, redeemed, guarded, fed, nurtured, and at last glorified.

II. A PRECIOUS CHRIST.

What need is there for me to enlarge here? We, who believe, know that Chris,: is precious.

1. My Christ is more precious to me than anything that my fellow-creatures have. I see some who live in palaces, sit on thrones, wear crowns, and feast on dainties. I have heard of Alexanders, Napoleons, and Caesars; but I envy them not, for *Christ is more precious to me than all earthly dominion.*

I see others with great riches; they are afraid of losing what they have, yet they are' groaning after more. They have many cares through their wealth, and they must leave it all one day; but Christ is better than all earthly riches. Shall I give up Christ for gold? No, for *Christ is more precious to me than wealth could ever be.*

Some men have noble minds; they long for knowledge, they toil that they may measure the earth, survey the heavens, read the lore of the ancients, dissolve minerals, etc., but *Christ is better to me than learning.*

Others pant for fame. I shall be forgotten, save by the few whose steps I guided in the path to Heaven; but I weep not at that, for *Christ is more precious to me than fame.*

2. He is more precious than anything I myself have.'.

If I have a home and a fireside, and feel a comfort in them, yet, if called to suffer banishment, I have a better home. *Christ is better lo me than home.*

If I have relatives, — Mother and father, — or faithful friends; these I value, and rightly, too. 'Tis a bitter pang to lose them, but *Christ is better than relatives or friends.* He is my Husband, my brother, my Lover.

I have health, and that is a precious jewel. Take it away, and pleasures lose their gloss; but my Jesus is mine still, and He *is heller than health; yea, life itself is valueless in comparison with Him.*

When I consider the glory of His nature, the excellence of His character, the greatness of His offices, the richness of His gifts, surely He is indeed precious.

III. A PRECIOUS EXPERIENCE.

Merely to say that Christ is precious, is nothing; but to know that He is precious, to feel it in truth, is everything.

1. The self-denials of missionaries, —

2. The sufferings of martyrs, —

3. The deathbeds of saints, — all attest the reality of the experience here spoken of.

Have *we* felt it? If so, may we once more feel it at His table! Oh, to live ever with the taste of this honey in our mouths, — to feast even on the name of our dear Redeemer! O precious One, help! Help! Help!

OUTLINE 327. — "PRAISE YE THE LORD."

"Praise ye the LORD. Praise ye the LORD from the heavens: praise Him in the heights." — Psalm 148:1.

Having once and again exhorted you to the most excellent work of praising God, it may seem unnecessary to mention it again. Yet it is most probable that some of you have neglected the duty; and if you have not, you ,.'ill find your soul still prepared to hear more on the subject, that you may rise to higher flights and more animated strains.

There are two places where we can praise God, — in Heaven and on earth.

There are two great ways of praising God, — by song and by service.

I. ON EARTH, WE HAVE TWO WAYS OF PRAISING GOD, — BY SONG AND BY SERVICE.

1. *By song.* Almost all great events have been celebrated in song; poets have employed their utmost ability in this way. One of the oldest books in the world, next to the Bible, sings of the ten years' siege of Troy. Virgil, the almost equal of the mighty Homer, sang, "Arms and the man." The taking of Jerusalem, the discovery of America, great battles, notable births, and even the sinking of ships, have found poets to celebrate them.

In early times, the wily priests called in music and poetry to aid in their false worship. Whether Jupiter or Baal, Bacchus or Moloch, Venus or Thammuz, Dagon or Neptune, was worshipped, hymns or paeans were chanted in their praise, making valleys and mountains ring with the heathen melodies.

Nor has true religion — offspring of Heaven, whose life-blood came from Christ upon the cross, — refused to employ poesy in the worship of the great Jehovah, who says, "I am God, and there is none else." In our days, the poet of the sanctuary puts into our mouths his simple yet harmonious strains. Sometimes, we sing, —

"Behold the glories of the Lamb!"

At other times, filled with holy rapture, we sing, —

"What equal honors shall we bring!"

or, though in lowlier notes, we —

"Join our cheerful songs
With angels round the throne;"

or, to a solemnly grand tune, we sing, —

'Keep silence, all created things.'

Our friends opposite (the Wesleyans) have the warm and fervent strains of Wesley, — *"Hark, the herald angels sing."*

"Jesu, lover of my soul."

"Oh, for a heart to praise my God!"

Then we have Doddridge singing, —

"Jesus, I love Thy charming name."

"Grace! 'tis a charming sound!"

Sometimes, —

"All hail the power of Jesus' name !"

rises loftily to a noble tune Then, John Newton, the African blasphemer, who was converted, while standing at the helm of the ship in a storm, as he recalled a text his Mother taught him, — leads us in singing, —

"How sweet the name of Jesus sounds !"
"Sweeter sounds than music knows,
Charm me in Immanuel's name."
"When any turn from Zion's way;"

or his companion, the amiable, tender, loving Cowper, sings, —

211

"There is a fountain fill'd with blood;"
or, —
"God *moves in a mysterious way*
His wonders to perform."
Toplady, strong in faith, sings, —
"A *debtor to mercy alone."*
"Jesus immutably the same;"
or, —
"Rock of ages, cleft for me,
Let me hide myself in Thee."

But why enumerate when we all have a large store of sacred poetry, dear to us even from childhood, and treasured in our memories? If we go back to the times of the second Reformation, we find the Covenanters in Scotland and the old Conventiclers of England, under such men as Baxter, Bunyan, Cameron, etc., etc., ever fond of hymning God's praises. In the first Reformation, Luther's hymns and ballads probably did more than his massive tomes to help forward the good cause. Look on yon Alpine steeps and vales, where but here and there a cottage can be seen. Wait awhile, and you shall hear the songs of praise ascending to the God of Heaven. In apostolic times, the prisoners of Philippi heard the voices of Paul and Silas praising God at midnight. Paul and James agree in advising us to sing; and our Lord Himself sometimes joined with His apostles in singing a hymn.

Mary and Elizabeth sang praises unto God.

Go back to the age of the prophets, and see how often their inspired writings are songs. Retreat still further till you come to the golden age of psalmody. Solomon and David especially are full of praise to Jehovah.

"Bless the Lord, O my soul!"
"Make *a joyful noise unto the Lord all ye lands;"*

Who can forget the song of Deborah, or the song of Moses? Who does not believe that, long ere their day, the sons of God, in their meetings at the throne of grace, sang praises unto God? I believe, with Milton, that in Eden's garden sublimer songs were heard than any that we fallen beings can even imagine. Let us, then, praise the Lord by singing.

2. *By service,* we may praise God as much as by song.

Our common duties should be done in such a manner that they may become spiritual worship. Then there is the temple worship of the Lord's house on the Sabbath and also on week-days.

Then, acts of charity, liberality, and holy labor for souls, performed by the tract-distributor, the Sunday-school teacher, the minister, the deacon; above all, by the missionary who risks his life for his Master's honor and service; — all these are praising the Lord as they minister unto Him in various ways. In some way or other, let all of us who believe in Jesus serve our God right heartily. Let us be like the woman who anointed Christ with the precious ointment, loving much, since we have had much forgiven.

II. IN HEAVEN, THE SAME TWO MODES OF PRAISING GOD ARE EMPLOYED.

1. *By song.* The angelic hosts praise Him now as they have ever done. We read that these sons of God shouted for joy on Creation's morning; and they still praise the Lord whenever a prodigal returns. The saints now add their notes, and sing what angels cannot sing, — how Immanuel, God with us, suffered and died for them. How sweet their voices, how matchless their tunes, how glorious the melody! How magnificent the Heavenly concert will be when all the ransomed throng at once shall sing unto Him who loved them, and washed them from their sins in His own blood!

2. *By service.* Even in the garden of Eden, Adam had to till the ground; and in Heaven no idlers are to be found, all there are employed. Some are ministering spirits, some attendant angels, some are studying the perfections of Deity, and others are framing music to His praise. They have, doubtless, far more to do with us than we wot of God, who makes all things work, and work together in harmony, and work together for the good of His chosen people, will not leave His noblest creatures unemployed.

Let us, then, begin *song* and *service* below, that soon we may continue our worship on high with a sweeter *song* and nobler *service.*

(The above was the 600th discourse delivered by Mr. Spurgeon. It was preached at Waterbeach in the course of his last year as Pastor there.)

Chapter Twenty-Six - Glimpses of Essex Cambridge-shire 1853.

It has been my privilege and joy, sometimes, to tarry for a little season amongst the lowly. I have had a seat given me in the chimney corner, and, by-and-by, as the time to retire for the night drew nigh, the good man of the house has said to me, "Now, sir, will you kindly read for us to-night, as you are here?" And I have noticed the faces of the little group around me, as I have read some portion like this, "Truly, God is good to Israel, even to such as are of a clean heart." Then I have said to the father of the family, "I will not lead you in prayer this time; you must be priest in your own house, and yourself pray." So the good man has prayed for his children, and when I have seen them rise up from their knees, and kiss their parent for the night, I have thought, "Well, if this is the kind of family that the religion of Jesus Christ makes, 'let the whole earth be filled with His glory.' For the present blessedness and for the eternal happiness of man, let God's Kingdom come, and let His will be done on earth even as it is done in Heaven." — C. H. S.

I WAS delighted, one Sabbath evening in the year 1853, when driving from the village where I had supplied for a minister, to see in one place a father, with four or five little ones about him, sitting on a small plot of grass before the cottage door. He had a large Bible on his knee, and the children also had their Bibles; and he in the midst was holding his finger up, with all solemnity and earnestness, in simple style endeavoring to enforce some sacred truth. It was a road but little frequented on the Sabbath-day, and I Should hope that scarcely a rumbling or rattling noise was heard there on the holy day of rest, saving the gig bearing the minister to and from the place of his labor, or other vehicles carrying devout worshippers to the house of God. It appeared almost a sacrilege to drive by, — although I was returning from a sacred errand, — it seemed a pity to break the spell even for a moment, and to take the eyes and the attention of the little ones for an instant from such sweet employment. A little further was a house which had a small workshop adjoining it. The door was open, so I could see that

no one was inside; but there stood a chest, and on it lay a Bible of the largest kind, and on the floor below was a cushion which still bore the impress of knees which, I trust, had been bent in wrestling prayer. Perhaps a Mother had there been begging at the Redeemer's hands the souls of her dearly-beloved children; or, possibly, some son, in answer' to that Mother's prayer, had been secretly pouring out his heart, and crying for mercy from the hands of God. Yet once more, I saw a little girl spelling over to her parents the words of the Book of Truth, and I felt constrained to pray that the daughter and the lowly pair might all be able to read their titles clear to mansions in the skies. I have seen hills and forests, vales and rivers, fine buildings and romantic ruins, but never, never have I seen a sight more simple, more beautiful, nor more sublime. Blest households, of which these things can be written! May you not be solitary instances, but may God raise up thousands like unto you!

Household piety is the very cream of piety. There is no place in which religion so sweetly opens all its charms as in the family gathered round the hearth. Who does not admire the house where, at the hour of prayer, all are assembled, and the head of the household reads from the sacred page the Word of Inspiration, and then all on bended knee seek for a blessing on themselves that day, or in joyful strains give thanks to Heaven for the manifold mercies so freely and so constantly dispensed? Who, on the other hand, can refrain from pitying the family where the day is a round of duties begun and ended without one prayer to God, — no place where all may come together in supplication, and feel as one, — no way for the parent to express his thoughts of love for the souls of his offspring? I know the sweetness of kneeling at eventide beneath the paternal roof, and hearing my father say, "Lord, we bless Thee that our son has again returned to us in health and strength; and, after an absence from each other, we praise Thee that we now meet an unbroken circle. Oh, our God, we beg most earnestly of Thee that we may all meet: around the throne in Heaven, not one being left behind!" The father's words are all but choked in their utterance whilst he weeps tears of joy to think that his first-born is walking in the ways of God, and the Mother sobs aloud, and her tears are falling, big with gratitude, that once more she is kneeling beside her son, the delight of her eyes, whilst the whole tribe are around her secure from death and ill.

I pity the wretch without a chair or bed on which to rest his weary limbs; I pity the miserable creature who shivers in the wintry blast, and finds no fire to give the needed heat; but I pity far more the homeless creature, for he is truly homeless, — who has no altar, no family prayer. Half the happiness is absent where this is neglected. I despise unmeaning formality, but this is no form. Spoiler, lay not thy ruthless hand on this most sacred thing! Rather let the queen of night forget to rise with all her train of stars than that family devotion should even begin to be neglected. The glory of Britain is her religion, and one of religion's choicest treasures is the Christian home.

Who is so foolishly alarmed as ever to suppose that an invading host will ravage our fair shores when the whole land is studded with castles, — not with turret towers, 'tis true, but yet with places where the God of Jacob dwells, residing as a fire around, a glory in the midst? Go invader, go, the prayer of households will blow thee adown the white cliffs of Albion like chaff before the wind! The flag of old England is nailed to the mast, not by our sailors, but by our God; and He has fastened it there with something stronger than iron, — He has nailed it with the prayers of His people, the fathers, Mothers, sons, and daughters, with whom He delights to dwell.

From' the tents of Jacob arise the fair-footed sons of Zion, who on the mountains stand declaring good tidings of great joy, and from these tabernacles there is gradually gathering a host, glittering and white, who continually praise God and the Lamb.

(The foregoing paragraphs and the two following letters show that Mr. Spurgeon was preaching in his native county of Essex twice, if not thrice, or even oftener, during the year 1853. He had treasured, among his most precious papers of those early days, evidently with a view to inclusion in his Autobiography, this characteristic epistle from his venerable grandfather: —

"Dear Charles,

"I just write to say that we hope nothing will occur to prevent our exchange on Sabbath, the 14th of August. Will you come by Broxted? If so, your Uncle will bring you to Stambourne. I have hardly made up my mind whether I shall drive through, or leave my pony at my son Obadiah's; but my intention is to be at Waterbeach on the Wednesday. As you ought to be on the way, and as so many want to see as well as hear you, don't you stay on my account. I had too much respect manifested to me the last time I was with your good people, so no doubt they will gladly receive me again. I am, and have been for some days, very poorly. I hope, by the blessing of God, I shall soon be all right once more. I must — I ought to expect pains and aches now; yet how natural it is to wish to be free from them! But if this was always the case, it would be bad for us, for we should become cold, careless, glued to the world, — pride and self-righteousness would arise within us. But our Savior's declaration has gone forth, and cannot be recalled, 'In the world ye shall have tribulation;... in Me, ye shall have peace.'

"With kind love to you, in which all here, if they knew I was writing, would unite,

"Believe me to be,

"Your affectionate grandfather,

"J. SPURGEON."
"Stambourne,
"July 27/53."

"N.B. — Some People Do Not Date Their Letters; I Do, And Think It Quite Right.")

(Two months later, Mr. Spurgeon wrote, to one of his uncles at Stambourne, the letter printed on the next page. This communication is interesting, not only because of its faithful reference to the ordinance of believers' baptism, but also from its revelation of the intense longing of the young preacher to be doing more for his Lord, either at home or abroad. Verily, the Holy Spirit, whose coming he so ardently desired, was preparing him for the wide sphere of service which was so soon after to open up for him.)

"9, Union Road,
"Cambridge,
"Sep. 27/53.

"My Dear Uncle,

"I have two or three reasons for writing to you just at this time. We are going to have a baptizing service on October 19, and I should be so glad to see my uncle following his Master in the water. I am almost afraid to mention the subject, lest people should charge me with giving it undue prominence; if they will do so, the? must. I can bear it for my Master's sake. I know you love my Jesus; and the mention of His name makes the tear rush to your eye, and run down your cheek. Better than wife or child is our Beloved; you can sing,

"Yes, Thou art precious to my soul,
My transport and my trust;
Jewels to Thee are gaudy toys
And gold is sordid dust.'

"You can lift your eye to Heaven, and, on your bended knee, before the presence of your Redeemer, exclaim, "Lord,   Thou knowest all things; Thou knowest that I love Thee.'

"Now, my beloved brother in Jesus, can you refuse to perform this one easy act for Him? 'No,'   you say,' I do not refuse; I would do it at once if I were sure He had commanded it. I love Him too well to keep back any part of my obedience.' Ah! but you ARE sure it is your duty, — or, permit me to hint that you may be sure, — for it is clearly revealed in the New Testament. Taking the lowest view of it, *suppose* it is your duty, only make a *supposition* of it, — now, can you go to bed happily with the bare *supposition* that you are refusing to practice an express command of your Redeemer?

Surely, a true lover of his Divine Master will never let even a supposed duty rest; he will want to be sure either that it is his duty, or that it is not; and knowing that, he will act accordingly.

"I charge you, by the debt — the infinite debt, you owe to Christ, — I charge you, by the solemnity of all our Savior's commands, — I charge you, by the shortness of time, and the near approach of the awful judgment, — not to trifle with convictions of the rightness of this ordinance, not to put off a serious, prayerful inquiry as to whether it is, or is not, enjoined upon all believers in Jesus, and then to carry out your conscientious conviction. If Christ commands me to hold up my little finger, and I do not obey Him, it looks like a coolness in my love to Him; and I feel assured that I should sustain loss by the neglect.

"I will not press the matter as one in authority; I only beg of you, as a friend, and a dear friend, as well as a loving relative, not to forget or trifle with the commands of One dearer still to me.

"Now with regard to coming for a week to preach at Stambourne and neighboring villages, I am yours to serve to the utmost; — not on the Sabbath, but all the week. I have a good sphere of labor here, but I want to do more, if possible. There is a great field, and the laborers must work with all their might. I often wish I were in China, India, or Africa, so that I might preach, preach, preach all day long. It would be sweet to die preaching. But I want more of the Holy Spirit; I do not feel enough — no, not half enough, — of His Divine energy. 'Come Holy Spirit, come!' Then men must be converted; then the wicked would repent, and the just grow in grace.

"If I come, I shall not mind preaching two evenings in Stambourne if you cannot get other convenient places; and I should love to have some good, thoroughly-hot prayer-meetings after the services. I wish it were possible to preach at two places in one evening, but I suppose time would hardly permit me to do that. Consult the friends, send me word, and I am your man.

"As to the books, you had better bring them yourself when you come to be baptized. Mr. Elven, of Bury, is going to preach the sermon for me; and, as we have not many candidates this time, we shall all the more value your presence.

"If you do not come, — I cross that out, because you MUST, — then send the books when you can. *I left some tracts in Mr. Howell's* gig. I should be obliged if you will see after them if you go to Hedingham. I should like to go there, too, if I come.

"You may show grandfather all I have written, if you like, for truth is truth, even if he cannot receive it; — still, I think you had much better not, for it is not at all likely he will ever change an opinion so long roofed in him, and it is never worth while for us to mention it if it will only irritate, and do no good. I wish to live in unity with every believer, whether Calvinist, Arminian (if not impossible), Churchman, Independent, or Wesleyan; and though I firmly believe some of them are tottering, I do not like them well enough to prop them up by my wrangling with them.

"My best respects and regards to Aunt, — Uncles and Aunts, — cousins, — grandfather, — Mr. Unwin, Will Richardson, and all the good people in Stambourne, not excepting yourself.

"I am,
"Yours most truly,

"C. H. SPURGEON."

(The "Will Richardson" here mentioned was a godly ploughman, at Stambourne, to whom C. H. Spurgeon, while living at his grandfather's, was devotedly attached; and the friendship between them was continued in after years. The first volume of *The New Park Street Pulpit* contains the following reference to him: — "I recollect walking with a ploughman, one day, — a man who was deeply taught, although he was a ploughman; and, really, ploughmen would make a great deal better preachers than many College gentlemen, — and he said to me, 'Depend upon it, my good brother, if you or I ever get one inch above the ground, we shall get just that inch too high.'" This was a favorite utterance of the good man, as appears from the brief sketch of him written by Pastor J. C. Houchin: —

"When I came to Stambourne, one of the old men who had overlived their former Pastor, and whose grey hairs adorned the table-pew of the old chapel, was William Richardson, a farm-laborer, and a man of clear and strong mind. He was able to read, so as to make fair use of his Bible and hymn-book, and he had a heartfelt knowledge of the gospel. It is said that 'Master Charles' was very fond of

Will, and that Will used to like to talk with the boy, and that the two have been seen walking up and down the field' together when Will was following the plough.

"Will Richardson had a reputation for what they call 'cramp' sayings, many of which used to be retailed in the village twenty years ago. On one occasion, when a young minister, just settled in the neighborhood, had occupied the pulpit for the day, in exchange with the present Pastor, he was met at the foot of the pulpit stairs by Will, who, shaking his hand, said, 'Ah, young man, you have got a good many stiles to get over before you get into Preaching Road!' Will spoke the truth, as it turned out, but it was pretty straight hitting.

"Visiting him, one day, and finding him full of faith, and giving glory to God, on my expressing a strong desire for fellowship with him in those experiences, he remarked that, when the sun shone, and the bees were at work, if there was honey in one skep, there was enough to fill another. Some friends had visited him, and had observed that, if they were blessed with his experiences, they should be beyond all doubt and fear; and he replied that God only gave these great things when His former gifts had been made good use of.

I quoted the parable of the talents, and he said, 'That is it.'

"Will was wont to say, 'Depend upon it, if we get one inch above the ground in our own estimation, we get just that inch too high.'

"On one occasion, I found him excessively weak, but quite sensible, and he said, 'Don't we read of one of old tried in the fire?' I quoted the passage, and he replied, 'That is gold indeed.' He then said that he had felt the two armies of the flesh and the spirit as lively in him now as when he was well and about in the world, and that he was disappointed and grieved to find it so, as it gave the enemy his chief advantage. So Satan had laid all his sins for years past before him, and insinuated that they must end in his destruction. 'But,' said Will, 'I was enabled to say to him, "God is a gracious and holy God, and what He has put into my heart, He will not take away any more; and He has put love into my heart; and if He were to send me to hell, I must love Him still." And I told him not to say any more to me about my sins, but to "go to the Lord about them; for He knows whether I be pardoned, and made His child, or whether I be a hypocrite."

He could not carry such a message. Then there seemed to come a strong voice, which said, "He shall die in the Lord." And oh, the peace and the joy, I cannot describe to you nor nobody! Oh, that His dear name was known and loved by every person all over the whole world!'

"My last visit, in July, 1870, four days before his death, showed the ruling passion for 'cramp' sayings to be strong in death. He was quite sensible, and after conversation, I took up the Bible, and, opening it at the seventeenth of John, I commenced reading, when he shouted aloud, 'Oh, that is my blood horse!' I said, 'What do you mean?' and he replied, 'I can ride higher on that chapter than on any other.' So I read it, and prayed with him for the last time.")

(The uncle, referred to in the following playful note, has kindly sent it for the Autobiography, with another and longer letter which appears in Chapter 30., so that, clearly, he was living at the time it was written, although he had not answered his nephew's previous communications: —)

"No. 60, Park Street,

"Cambridge,

"_____, 1853.

"My Dear Aunt,

"Can you kindly inform me whether Mr. James Spurgeon, Junr., of the parish of Stambourne, Essex, is yet alive? I have written two letters to the said gentleman, and, as he was a particular friend of mine, I begin to feel somewhat anxious seeing that I have had no reply. If you should find, among the papers he has left, any letter directed to me, I shall feel much obliged by your forwarding the same.

"When I was last at his house, he was extremely kind to me, and I flattered myself that, if I should ever have occasion to ask a favor, I should not be refused; or, if denied, it would be in so kind a manner that it would not look like neglect. If he is alive, and not gone beyond the seas, please to give him my kind love the first time you meet him, and tell him I suppose he must have gout in his hands, so that he cannot write. Should it turn out that it is so, keep all wines and spirits from him, as they are bad things for gouty folk; and be so good as to foment his hands with warm water boiled with the heads of poppies. By this treatment, the swelling will subside; and, as soon as he is able, if you find him at all tractable, put a pen in his hand, and make him write his name, and post it to me, so that I may be sure he is alive. Ah, 'tis a sad thing people will get gouty!

"But perhaps he is gone. Well, poor fellow, he was not the worst that ever lived; I felt sorry to part from him the last time, and, as the Irishman said, I hoped he would, at any rate, have let me know that he was dead. I thought you were the most likely person to know him, as I have seen you at his house several times when I have been there. I trust you will just send me a line to let me know how the poor fellow is, if alive at all.

"With best love to you and the little ones,

"I am,

"Yours truly,

"CHARLES H. SPURGEON."

Chapter Twenty-Seven - Last Dear at Waterbeach and Cambridge.

BRIGHT constellation of Jubilee celebrations has risen on our age; amongst them, as one star in the galaxy, too small to be recognized singly, was the Waterbeach Baptist Chapel Jubilee. The year 1853 beheld the grass of fifty years growing in the small spot surrounding the meeting-house where a crowd of willing worshippers often assembled in the memorable days of my first pastorate. The village should! not be unknown to fame, for the records of the Baptist Church prove that Rowland Hill first exercised in Waterbeach his gifts as a minister of Jesus, after riding over *from* Cambridge by stealth between the hours of College duty. The house still stands in which he is said to have commenced his labors as a preacher.

Long before that time, the sainted Holcroft, the apostle of Cambridgeshire, ejected by the Act of Uniformity front his living at Bassingbourne, had founded a church in this village, as in many others around. When confined in Cambridge Castle for the truth's sake, he obtained favor in the eyes of his jailer, who allowed him by night to visit Waterbeach, where he preached and administered the ordinances of our Lord to his little band of followers, returning always before morning light awoke his slumbering foes. Since then, the little vessel, launched in boisterous times, has been safely steered by its Captain even until, now. It has passed through rough waters and fierce storms; but it still lives, thanks to Him who sits at the helm.

(The following hymns, composed by the young Pastor, were sung at the Waterbeach Jubilee services on Lord's-day, June 26th, 1853: —)

THE ONE REQUEST.

If to my God I now may speak,
And make one short request;
If but one favor I might seek
Which I esteem the best, —
I would not choose this earth's poor wealth;
How soon it melts away!
I would not seek continued health;
A mortal must decay.
I would not crave a mighty name;
Fame is but empty breath.
Nor would I urge a royal claim;
For monarchs bow to death.
I would not beg for sinful sweets;
Such pleasures end in pain.
Nor should I ask fair learning's seats;
Love absent, these are vain.
My God, my heart would choose with joy,
Thy grace, Thy love, to share;
This is the sweet which cannot cloy,
And this my portion fair.

IMMANUEL.

When once I mourned a load of sin,
When conscience felt a wound within,
When all my works were thrown away,
When on my knees I knelt to pray,
Then, blissful hour, remembered well,
I learned Thy love, Immanuel!
When storms of sorrow toss my soul,
When waves of care around me roll,
When comforts sink, when joys shall flee,
When hopeless gulfs shall gape for me,
One word the tempest's rage shall quell,

That word, Thy name, Immanuel!
When for the truth I suffer shame,
When foes pour scandal on my name,
When cruel taunts and jeers abound,
When "bulls of Bashan" gird me round,
Secure within my tower I'll dwell,
That tower, Thy grace, immanuel!
When hell, enraged, lifts up her roar,
When Satan stops my path before,
When fiends rejoice, and wait my end,
When legion'd hosts their arrows send,
Fear not, my soul, but hurl at hell
Thy battle-cry, Immanuel!
When down the hill of life I go,
When o'er my feet death's waters flow,
When in the deep'ning flood I sink,
When friends stand weeping on the brink,
I'll mingle with my last farewell,
Thy lovely name, Immanuel!
When tears are banished from mine eye,
When fairer worlds than these are nigh,
When Heaven shall fill my ravish'd sight,
When I shall bathe in sweet delight,
One joy all joys shall far excel,
To see Thy face, Immanuel!

At our Waterbeach prayer-meetings, we used sometimes to have very quaint utterances from certain of the brethren who led the devotions of the assembly. I once heard a poor man offer this singular supplication: "Lord, watch over these young people during the feast time, for Thou knowest, Lord, how their enemies watch for them as a cat watches for mice." Some ridiculed the form of the petition, but it appeared to me to be natural and expressive, considering the person who presented it. When it was known that I was coming to London, I was made the subject of many remarkable requests. One queer old man offered a very extraordinary prayer for me. I did not understand it at the time, and I hardly think he ought to have prayed it in public in that shape. He pleaded that I might be able "to swallow bush-faggots cross-ways." It was a very strange prayer; but I have often done just what he asked that I might do, and it has cleared my throat wonderfully; and there is many a man, who cannot now speak out boldly for God, who will be obliged to have some of those bush-faggots thrust down his throat; and when those great troubles come, and he is compelled to swallow them, then he will grow to be a man in Christ Jesus, who will proclaim with power to others the truths he has tried and proved in his own experience.

Another of my country brethren prayed that I might be "delivered from the bleating of the sheep;" and, for the life of me, I could not make out what he meant. I am not sure that he understood it himself, but I quite understand it now. He meant to ask the Lord that I might live above the fear of man, so that, when some persons said to me, "How much we have been edified today!" I might not be puffed up; or if another said, "How dull the discourse was to-day!" I might not be depressed. There is no leader of the flock who will not occasionally wish to be delivered from the bleating of the sheep, for they bleat such different tunes sometimes. There is some old bellwether, perhaps, that is not bleating in the right style, and one is apt to be troubled about it; but it is a great thing to feel, "Now, I am not going to be influenced by the way these sheep bleat. I am set to lead them rather than to let them lead me, and I am going to be guided by something far more reliable than the bleating of the sheep, namely, the voice of the Great Shepherd." I soon found that the best way to be delivered from the bleating of the sheep was to seek to be filled with the spirit of the Good Shepherd.

(On page 229, there is the Outline of the *first* Sermon preached by Mr. Spurgeon at Waterbeach; the following are his notes of his *last* Sermon as Pastor of the little village church which had been so greatly increased under his ministry: —)

OUTLINE 365. — JESUS SAVES FROM SIN.

"Thou shall call His name JESUS:
for He shall save His people from their sins." — Matthew 1:21.

As this was. my first text in Waterbeach, so, by the help of God, it shall be the one with which I close my stated ministry among you, — in order that Jesus may be Alpha and Omega with us. Let us speak of —

I. THE GLORIOUS NAME.
II. THE WONDROUS SALVATION.
III. THE BLESSED PEOPLE.

I. THE GLORIOUS NAME: Jesus, or Joshua, "the Savior."

Two men, who had borne this name before, — Joshua the son of Nun, and Joshua the son of Jozadak, — were both types of Christ.

Joshua, the son of Nun, —
Fought for Israel, and overcame.
He led them through Jordan.
He divided their inheritance for them.
Joshua, the son of Jozadak, —
Restored the priesthood, and
Rebuilt the temple;
but how much greater is our Joshua, Jesus, the Son of God! All that these two men did, and far more, He has done in His glorious work of saving His people.

II. THE WONDROUS SALVATION.

The salvation Jesus wrought for His people is salvation from sin.

1. From the result of sin, — the anger of God, — death, — hell, — loss of Heaven. He who trusts in Jesus is pardoned for all his offenses against God.

2. From the guilt and charge of sin, so that we become innocent in the sight of God, yea, and even meritorious through the righteousness of Jesus. This justification is instantaneous, perfect, unalterable, and brings with it all the blessings which by right only belong to perfection.

3. From the very being of sin. There is in each of us our original depravity, and our acquired habits, but these the Lord graciously takes away; and puts in their place a new nature, and holy desires leading to holy acts.

This is a gradually progressive work. These three things pardon, justification, and sanctification, — must go together. God will not justify an unpardoned or unsanctified sinner at the last.

Oh, how glorious is this salvation! My soul, often muse thereon!

III. THE BLESSED PEOPLE.

Not known at first, but mingled with others; some of all countries, ranks, and characters, shall be brought in. The marks by which they are distinguished are —

1. A sincere desire after Heaven.

2. A devout seeking for God.

3. Diligent labor to find the way of salvation.

4. Great abhorrence of sin.

5. Sense of personal nothingness.

6. Humble reliance on Jesus.

And now, my Father, make Thy servant mighty at last to wrestle with sinners! Come, O Father, to mine assistance, by the ever-blessed Spirit, for JESUS CHRIST'S sake! Amen.

Before I left Cambridge, to come to London, I went: one day into the library of Trinity College, and there! noticed a very fine statue of Lord Byron. The librarian said to me, "Stand here, sir." I did as I was directed, and as I looked at it I said, "What a fine intellectual countenance! What a grand genius he was!.... Come here," said the librarian, "and look at the other side of the statue." I said, "Oh! what a demon! There stands the man who could defy the Deity." He seemed to have such a scowl and such a dreadful leer on his face, as Milton would have painted upon Satan when he said, "Better to reign in hell, than serve in Heaven." I turned away, and asked the librarian, "Do you think the artist designed this?.... Yes," he said,

"he wished to picture the two characters, — the great, the grand, the almost-superhuman genius that Byron possessed, and yet the enormous mass of sin that was in his soul." Was ever libertine more free in his vices?

Was ever sinner more wild in his blasphemy? Was ever poet more daring in his flights of fancy? Was ever any man more injurious to his fellows? Yet what did Byron say? There is a verse of his which just tells us what he felt in his heart; the man had all that he wanted of sinful pleasure, but here is his confession, —

"I fly, like a bird of the air,
In search of a home and a rest;
A balm for the sickness of care, —
A bliss for a bosom unblest."

Yet he found it not, for he had no rest in God. He tried pleasure till his eyes were red with it; he tried vice till his body was sick; and he descended into his grave a premature old man. In the year 1853, I was asked to give an address at the annual meeting of the Cambridge Sunday School Union, in the Guildhall of. that town. There were two other ministers to speak, both of them much older

223

than myself; and, as a natural consequence, I was called upon first. I do not now recollect anything that I said on that occasion, but I have no doubt that I spoke in my usual straightforward fashion I do not think there was anything in my remarks to cause the other speakers to turn upon me so savagely as they did when it came to their turn to address the large gathering. One of them, in particular, was very personal and also most insulting in his observations, specially referring to my youth, and then, in what he seemed to regard as a climax, saying that it was a pity that boys did not adopt the Scriptural practice of tarrying at Jericho till their beards were grown before they tried to instruct their seniors.

Having obtained the chairman's permission, I reminded the audience that those who were bidden to tarry at Jericho were not boys, but full-grown men, whose beards had been shaved off by their enemies as the greatest indignity they could be made to suffer, and who were, therefore, ashamed to return home until their beards had grown again. I added that, the true parallel to their case could be found in a minister who, through falling into open sin, had disgraced his sacred calling, and so needed to go into seclusion for a while until his character had been to some extent restored.

As it happened, I had given an exact description of the man who had attacked me so unjustly, and for that reason all who were present, and knew the circumstances, would be the more likely to remember the incident. There was in the hall, that evening, a gentleman from Essex, —

Mr. George Gould, of Loughton, — who felt so deeply sympathetic with me in the trying position in which I had been placed, through no fault of my own, and who also was so much impressed by what he had heard that, shortly afterwards, meeting in London old Mr. Thomas Olney, one of the deacons of the church worshipping in New Park Street Chapel, he pressed him to try to secure my services as a supply for the vacant pulpit, and thus became, in the hand of God, the means of my transference from Cambridgeshire to the metropolis.

(The night before he came to London, Mr. Spurgeon gave the following poem, which he had composed, to the ladies with whom he had lodged after leaving Mr. Leeding's school; it has probably never been published until now: —)

THE NOBLE ARMY OF MARTYRS.

Rouse thee, Music! Rouse thee, Song!
Noble themes await thee long.
not the warrior's thund'ring car,
not the battle heard afar,
not the garment rolled in blood,
not the river's redden'd flood;
Subjects more sublime I sing,
Soar thee, then, on highest wing!
Sing the white-robed hosts on high,
Who in splendor suns outvie;
Sing of them, the martyr'd band,

With the palm-branch in their hand:
Fairest of the sons of light,
Midst the bright ones doubly bright.
Who are these? Of noble birth?
Were they monarchs of the earth?
Kings of Babel's ancient state,
Lords of Persia, proud and great,
Grecian heroes, bold and brave,
Romans, making earth their slave?
No, — but hearken! Heav'n replies,
List the music from the skies: —
"These are they who dared to die,
Champions of our Lord on high.
At His name they bow'd the knee,
Sworn to worship none but He.

Fearless of the tyrant's frown,
Mindful of the promised crown;
Trampling on Satanic rage,
Conqu'ring still from age to age.
Come, the glorious host review,
March the glittering squadrons
through."
Some, from show'rs of deadly stones,
Some, from wheels, — with broken
bones,
Snatch'd by sweet seraphic might,
Borne above the tyrant's spite, —
Wondrous in their dying hour,
Rose above the demon's power.
Some by cruel racks were torn,
others were in sunder sawn.
Hunger, nakedness, and thirst,
Sword, and ax, and spear accurs'd,
Cross, and knife, and fiery dart,
All conspiring, join'd their smart:
Yet, unconquer'd e'en in death,
Triumph fill'd their latest breath.
Yonder rank in chariots came,
Blazing o'er with fiery flame;
Now, in burnish'd arms they shine,
Glorious in the gift Divine.
Some, from jaws of cruel beasts,
Rose to Heav'n's triumphal feasts;
Some, in dungeons long immured,
Saw in death their crown secured,

Writhing in their tortures dread,
Smiled as if on downy bed.
These, from Rome's dark dungeons
flew;
These, on Alps, the despot slew;
These, by Spanish priests were:
slain;
These, the Moslem curs'd in vain.
Yonder stands a gallant host,
Martyrs from the Gallic coast,
Heroes from Bartholomew,
Soldiers to their Master true.
These, again, in shining row,
Saw the fiery torments glow,
They in Smithfield kiss'd the stake,
Blest to die for Jesus' sake.
Those who, further in the plain,
Lift to Heav'n the lofty strain,
In the ocean found a grave,
Plung'd by force beneath the wave.
Some, by English prelates tried,
On the scaffold firmly died;
Scorn'd to own prelatic sway,
Nobly dared to disobey.
Covenanters bold are there,
Sons of Scotia's mountains bare,
Mingled with the valiant band,
Heroes of my fatherland.

Chapter Twenty-Eight - Dr. Rippon's Prayer and its Answer.

One of the best things that a church can do is to catch a minister young, and train him for themselves. Some of the happiest and longest pastorates in our denomination commenced with the invitation of a young man from the country to a post for which he was barely qualified. His mistakes were borne with, his efforts were encouraged, and he grew, and the church grew with him. His pastorate continued for many: a year, since he was under no temptation to leave for another position, because he felt at home, and could say, like one of old, "I dwell among mine own people."

I am told that my venerable predecessor, Dr. Rippon, used often, in his pulpit, to pray for somebody, of whom he knew nothing, who would follow him in the ministry of the church, and greatly increase it. He seemed to have in his mind's eye some young man, who, in after years, would greatly enlarge the number of the flock, and he often prayed for him. He died, and passed away to Heaven, a year or two after I was born. Older members of the church have told me that they have read the answer to Dr. Rippon's prayers in the blessing that has been given to us these many years. — C. H. S.

THE Christians commonly called Baptists are, according to my belief, the purest part of that sect which, of old, was "*everywhere* spoken against," and I am convinced that they have, beyond their brethren, preserved the ordinances of the Lord Jesus as they were delivered unto the saints. I care very little for the "*historical* church" argument; but if there be anything at all in it, the plea ought not to be filched by the clients of Rome, but should be left to that community which all along has held by "*one* Lord, one faith, and one baptism." This body of believers has not been exalted into temporal power, or decorated with worldly rank, but it has dwelt for the most part in dens and caves of the earth, — "destitute, afflicted, tormented," — and so has proved itself of the house and lineage of the Crucified. The church which most loudly claims the apostolical succession wears upon her brow more of the marks of Antichrist than of Christ; but the afflicted Anabaptists, in their past history, have had such fellowship with their suffering Lord, and have borne: so pure a testimony, both to truth and freedom, that they need in nothing to be ashamed. Their very existence under the calumnies and persecutions which they have endured is a standing marvel, while their unflinching fidelity to the Scriptures as their sole rule of faith, and their adherence to the simplicity of gospel Ordinances, is a sure index of their Lord's presence among them. It would not be impossible to show that the first Christians who dwelt in this land were of the same faith and order as the believers now called Baptists. The errors of the churches are all more or less modern, and those which have clustered around the ordinance of baptism are by no means so venerable for age as some would have us suppose. The evidence supplied by ancient monuments and baptisteries, which still remain, would be conclusive in our favor were it not that upon this point the minds of men are not very open to argument. Foregone conclusions and established ecclesiastical arrangements are not easily shaken. Few men care to follow truth when she leads them without the camp, and calls them to take up their cross, and endure to be thought singular even by their fellow-Christians.

The church now worshipping in the Metropolitan Tabernacle [19] took its rise front one of the many assemblies of immersed believers who met in the borough of Southwark. Crosby, in his *History of the Baptists,* says: —

"This people had formerly belonged to one of the most ancient congregations of the Baptists in London, but separated from them in the year 1652, for some practices which they judged disorderly, and kept together from that time as a distinct body." They appear to have met in private houses, or in such other buildings as were open to them. Their first Pastor was WILLIAM RIDER, whom Crosby mentions as a sufferer for conscience sake, but he is altogether unable to give: any further particulars of his life, except that he published a small tract in vindication of the practice of laying on of hands on the baptized believers. The people were few in number, but they had the reputation of being men of solid judgment, deep knowledge, and religious stability, and many of them were also in easy circumstances as to worldly goods. Oliver Cromwell was just at that time in the ascendant, and Blake's cannon were sweeping the Dutch from the seas, but the Presbyterian establishment ruled with a heavy hand, and Baptists were under a cloud. In the following year, Cromwell was made Protector, the old parliament was sent about its business, and England enjoyed a large measure of liberty of conscience. This seems to have been a period of much religious heart-searching, in which the ordinances of churches were tried by the Word of God, and men were determined to retain nothing which was not sanctioned by Divine authority; hence, there were many public disputes upon baptism, and, in Consequence, many became adherents of believers' immersion, and Baptist churches sprang up on all sides. Truth suffers nothing from free discussion; it is, indeed, the element in which it most freely exerts its power. I have personally known several instances in which sermons in defense of infant baptism have driven numbers to more Scriptural views, and I have felt that, if Paedo-Baptists will only preach upon the subject, Baptists; will have little to do but to remain quiet and reap the sure results. It is a dangerous subject for any ministers to handle who wish their people to abide by the popular opinion on this matter.

How long William Rider exercised the ministerial office, I am unable to tell; but the church's next record, bearing date 1668, says: — "The Pastor having been dead for some time, they unanimously chose MR. BENJAMIN KEACH to be their elder or pastor." Accordingly, he was solemnly ordained, with prayer and the laying on of hands, being then in the twenty-eighth year of his age. Previous to his coming to London, Keach was continually engaged in preaching in the towns of Buckinghamshire, making Winslow his headquarters; and so well did the good cause flourish under his zealous labors, and those of others, that the government quartered dragoons in the district in order to put down unlawful meetings, and stamp out Dissent. The amount of suffering which this involved, the readers of the story of the Covenanting times in Scotland can readily imagine. For publishing a little book, *The Childs Instructor,* Keach was fined, imprisoned, and put in the pillory at Aylesbury and Winslow; but he continued to labor in the country until 1668, when he came to London, and very speedily was chosen Pastor of the late Mr. Rider's congregation.

Benjamin Keach was one of the most useful preachers of his time, and for thirty-six years built up the Church of God with sound doctrine. Having been in his very earliest days an Arminian, and having soon advanced to Calvinistic views, he preserved the balance in his preaching, and was never a member of that exclusive school which deems it to be unsound to persuade men to repent and believe. He was by no means so highly Calvinistic as his great successor, Dr. Gill; but evidently held much the same views as are now advocated from the pulpit of the Tabernacle. Nor must it be supposed that he was incessantly preaching upon believers' baptism, and other points of denominational peculiarity; his teaching was sweetly spiritual, intensely Scriptural, and full of Christ. Whoever else kept back the fundamental truths of our holy gospel, Benjamin' Keach did not so. During the time of an indulgence issued by Charles II., the congregation erected a large meeting-house, capable of holding "*near* a thousand hearers," in Goat's 'Yard Passage, Fair Street, Horse-lie-down, Southwark, and this is the first house of prayer actually set apart for Divine worship which I find that our church possessed. The joy of being able to meet in quiet to worship God, the delight of all assembling as one church, must have been great indeed. I have tried to imagine the cheerful salutations with which the brethren-greeted each other when they all gathered in their meeting-house of timber, and worshipped without fear of molestation. The architecture was not gorgeous, nor were the fittings luxurious; but the Lord was there, and this made amends for all. In all probability, there were no seats, for at that time most congregations stood, and pews are mentioned, in after days, as extras which persons erected for themselves, and looked upon as their own property. Mr. Keach trained his church to labor in the service of the Lord. Several were by his means called into the Christian ministry, his own son, Elias Keach, among them. He was mighty at home and useful abroad. By his means, other churches were founded, and meeting-houses erected; he was, in fact, as a pillar and a brazen wall among the Baptist churches of his day, and was in consequence deservedly had in honor. He *"fell* on sleep," July 16, 1704, in the sixty-fourth year of his age, and was buried at the Baptists' burying-ground *in the Park, Southwark.* It was not a little singular that, in after years, the church over which he so ably presided should pitch its tent so near the place where his bones were laid, and that New Park Street should appear in her annals as a well-beloved name.

When Mr. Keach was upon his death-bed, he sent for his son-in-law, BENJAMIN STINTON, and solemnly charged him to care for the church which he was about to leave, and especially urged him to accept the pastoral office should it be offered to him by the brethren. Mr. Stinton had already for some years helped his father-in-law in many ways, and therefore he was no new and untried man. It is no small blessing when a church can find her pastors in her own midst; the rule is to look abroad; but, perhaps; if our home gifts were more encouraged, the Holy Spirit would cause our teachers to come forth more frequently from among our own brethren.

Still, we cannot forget the proverb about a prophet in his own country.

When the church gave Mr. Stinton a pressing invitation, he delayed a while, and gave himself space for serious consideration; but, at length, remembering the dying words of his father-in-law, and feeling himself directed by the Spirit of God, he gave himself up to the ministry, which he faithfully discharged for fourteen years, — namely, from 1704 to 1718. He had great natural gifts, but felt in need of more education, and set himself to work to obtain it as soon as he was settled over the church. To be thoroughly furnished for the great work before him, was his first endeavor.

Crosby says of him: — "He was a very painful and laborious minister of the gospel, and though he had not the advantage of an academical education, yet, by his own industry, under the assistance of the famous Mr.

Ainsworth (author of the Latin dictionary), after he had taken upon him the ministerial office, he acquired a good degree of knowledge in the languages, and other useful parts of literature, which added luster to those natural endowments which were very conspicuous in him." In his later days, as the lease of the meeting-house in Goat's Yard had nearly run out, preparation was made for erecting a new place of worship in Unicorn Yard. Spending himself in various works of usefulness, Mr. Stinton worked on till the 11th of February, 1718, when a close was put to his labors and his life. He was taken suddenly ill, and saying to his wife, "*I am going*," he laid himself down upon the bed, and expired in the forty-third year of his life. He smiled on death, for the Lord smiled on him. He was buried near his predecessor, in the Park, Southwark.

The loss of its Pastor is always a serious matter to a Baptist church, not only because it is deprived of the services of a well-tried and faithful guide, but because, in the process of selecting a successor, some of the worst points of human nature are apt to come to the front. All may unite in the former Pastor, but where will they find another rallying point? So many men, so many minds. All are not prepared to forego their own predilections, some are ready to be litigious, and a few seize the opportunity to thrust themselves into undue prominence. If they would all wait upon the Lord for His guidance, and consent to follow it when they have obtained it, the matter would move smoothly; but, alas! it is not always so. In the present instance, there came before the church an excellent young man, whose after life proved that he was well qualified for the pastorate, but either he was too young, being only twenty or one-and-twenty years of age, or there were certain points in his manner which were not pleasing to the older friends, and therefore he was earnestly opposed.

The deacons, with the exception of Mr. Thomas Crosby, schoolmaster, and son-in-law of Keach, were resolved that this young man, who was no other than JOHN GILL, from Kettering, should not become the Pastor. He found, however, warm and numerous supporters, and when the question came to a vote, his admirers claimed the majority, and in all probability their claim was correct, for the other party declined a scrutiny of the votes, and also raised the question of the women's voting, declaring, what was no doubt true, that apart from the female vote John Gill was in the minority. The end of the difference was that about half the church withdrew from the chapel in Goat Yard, and met in Mr. Crosby's school-room, claiming to be the old church, while another portion remained in the chapel, and also maintained that they were the original church. The question is now of small consequence, if it ever had any importance, for the company who rejected Gill, after selecting an excellent preacher, and prospering for many years, met with a checkered experience, and at length ceased to exist. In all probability, the division promoted the growth of the cause of Christ, and whatever unhappy circumstances marred it for a while, both parties acted conscientiously, and in a very short time were perfectly reconciled to each other. Mr. Gill's people did not long worship in Crosby's school-room, but, as the other friends were moving out and erecting another meeting-house in Unicorn Yard, they came back to the old building in Goat Yard, and found themselves very much at home.

Dr. Gill's pastorate extended over no less a period than fifty-one years, reaching from 1720 to 1771, and he proved himself to be a true master in Israel. His entire ministry' was crowned with more than ordinary success, and he was by far the greatest scholar the church had yet chosen; but he cannot be regarded as so great a soul-winner as Keach had been, neither was the church at any time so numerous under his ministry as under that of Keach. His method of address to sinners, in which for many years a large class of preachers followed him, was not likely to be largely useful. He cramped himself, and was therefore straitened where there was no Scriptural reason for being so. He does not appear to have had the public spirit of Stinton, though he had a far larger share of influence in the churches, and was indeed a sort of archbishop over a certain section. The ordination discourses and funeral sermons which he preached must have amounted to a very large number'; it seemed as if no Particular Baptist minister could be properly inducted or interred without Dr. Gill's officiating. In the beginning of the year 1719, the church at Horsleydown invited him to preach with a view to the pastorate, and he was ordained March 22, 1720. Little did the friends dream what sort of a man they had thus chosen to be their teacher; but had they known it, they would have rejoiced that a man of such vast erudition, such indefatigable industry, such sound judgment, and such sterling honesty, had come among them. He was to be more mighty with his pen than Keach, and to make a deeper impression upon his age, though perhaps with the tongue he was less powerful than his eminent predecessor. Early in his ministry, he had to take up the cudgels for Baptist views against a Paedo-Baptist preacher of Rowel, near Kettering, and he did so in a manner worthy of that eulogium which Toplady passed upon him in reference to other controversies, when he compared him to Marlborough, and declared that he never fought a battle without winning it. As a Pastor, he presided over the flock with dignity and affection. In the course of his ministry, he had some weak, some unworthy, and some very wicked he was an affectionate friend and father. He readily bore with their, weaknesses, failings, and infirmities, and particularly when he saw they were sincerely on the Lord's side. In 1757, the church under his care erected a new meeting-house for him in Carter Lane, St. Olave's Street, Southwark, near London Bridge; which he opened on October 9, preaching two sermons from Exodus 20:24.

In the Doctor's later years, the congregations were sparse, and the membership seriously declined. He was himself only able to preach once on the Sabbath, and living in a rural retreat in Camberwell, he could do but little in the way of overseeing the church. It was thought desirable that some younger minister should be found to act as co-pastor. To this, the Doctor gave a very decided answer in the negative, asserting "that Christ gives *pastors,* is certain; but that he gives *co-pastors,* is not so certain." He even went the length of comparing a church with a co-pastor to a woman who should marry another man while her first husband lived, and call him co-husband. Great men are not always wise. However, by his stern repudiation of any division of his authority, the old gentleman held the reins of power till the age of seventy-four, although the young people gradually dropped off, and the church barely numbered 150 members.

Soon, the venerable divine became too feeble for pulpit service, and confined himself to his study and the writing-desk, and by-and-by he found that he must lie down to rest, for his day's work was done. He died as he had lived, in a calm, quiet manner, resting on that rich sovereign grace which it had been his joy to preach. The last words he was heard to speak were, "O my Father, my Father!" He died at Camberwell, October 14, 1771, and was buried in Bunhill Fields. His eyesight had been preserved to him so that he could read small print by candle-light even to the last, and he never used glasses. His was a mind and frame of singular vigor, and he died before failing sight, either mental or physical, had rendered him unfit for service: in this as highly favored as he had been in most other respects. He was one of the most learned men that the Baptist denomination has ever produced. His great work, *The Exposition of the Old and New Testaments,* is still held in the highest esteem even by those whose sentiments widely differ from the author's. His *Body of Divinity* is also a masterly condensation of doctrinal and practical theology, and his *Cause of God and Truth* is high l y esteemed by many. The system of theology with which many identify his name has chilled many churches to their very soul, for it has led them to omit the free invitations of the gospel, and to deny that it is the duty of sinners to believe in Jesus: but for this, Dr. Gill must not be altogether held responsible, for a candid reader of his Commentary will soon perceive in it expressions altogether out of accord with such a narrow system; and it is well known that, when he was dealing with practical godliness, he was so bold in his utterances that the devotees of Hyper-Calvinism could not endure him. "Well, sir," said one of these, "if I had not been told that it was the great Dr. Gill who preached, I should have said I had heard an Arminian."

The mighty commentator having been followed to his grave "by his attached church and a numerous company of ministers and Christian people, among whom he had bee. n regarded as a great man and a prince in Israel, his church began to look around for a successor. This time, as in the case of Dr. Gill, there was trouble in store, for there was division of opinion. Some, no doubt, as true Gillites, looked only for a solid divine, sound in doctrine, who would supply the older saints with spiritual food, while another party had an eye to the growth of the church, and to the securing to the flock the younger members of their families. They were agreed that they would write to Bristol for a probationer, and MR. JOHN RIPPON was sent to them. He was a youth of some twenty summers, of a vivacious temperament, quick and bold. The older members judged him to be too young, and too flighty; they even accused him of having gone up the pulpit stairs two steps at a time on some occasion when he was hurried, — a grave offense for which the condemnation could hardly be too severe. He was only a young man, and came from an academy, and this alone was enough to make the sounder and older members afraid of him. He preached for a lengthened time on probation, and finally some forty persons withdrew because they could not agree with the enthusiastic vote by which the majority of the people elected him. John Rippon modestly expressed his wonder that even more had not been dissatisfied, and his surprise that so large a number were agreed to call him to the pastorate. In the spirit of forbearance and brotherly love, he proposed that, as these friends were seceding for conscience sake, and intended to form themselves into another church, they should be lovingly dismissed with prayer and God-speed, and that, as a token of fraternal affection, they should be assisted to build a meeting-house for their own convenience, and the sum of £300 should be voted to them when their church was formed and their meeting-house erected. The promise was redeemed, and Mr. Rippon took part in the ordination service of the first minister. This was well done. Such a course was sure to secure the blessing of God. The church in Dean Street thus became another offshoot from the parent stem, and with varying conditions it remains to this day as the church in Trinity Street, Borough. It is somewhat remarkable, as illustrating the perversity of human judgment, that the seceding friends, who objected to Rippon's youth, elected for their pastor Mr. William Button, who was younger still, being only nineteen years of age. His father, however, was a deacon under Dr. Gill, and therefore no doubt the worthy youth was regarded with all the more tenderness; nor did he disappoint the hopes of his friends, for he labored on for male than forty years with the utmost acceptance. The friends who remained with young John Rippon had no reason to regret their choice: the tide of prosperity set in, and continued for half a century, and the church again came to the front in denominational affairs. The chapel in Carter Lane was enlarged, and various agencies and societies set in notion; there was, in fact, a real revival of religion in the church, though it was of that quiet style which became a Baptist church of the straiter sort. Rippon was rather clever than profound; his talents were far inferior to those of Gill, but he had more tact, and so turned his gifts to the greatest possible account. He said many smart and witty things, and his preaching was always lively, affectionate, and impressive. He was popular in the best sense of the term, — beloved at home, respected abroad, and useful everywhere. Many souls were won to Jesus by his teaching, and out of these a remarkable number became themselves ministers of the gospel. The church-book abounds with records of brethren preaching before the church, as the custom was in those days.

In his later years, Dr. Rippon was evidently in very comfortable circumstances, for we have often heard mention of his carriage and pair, or rather, "glass coach and two horses." His congregation was one of the wealthiest within the pale of Nonconformity, and always ready to aid the various societies which sprang up, especially the Baptist Foreign Mission, and a certain Baptist Itinerant Society, which I suppose to have represented the Baptist Home Mission. The Pastor occupied no mean position in the church, but ruled with dignity and discretion, — perhaps;, ruled a little too much. "How is it, Doctor, that your church is always so peaceful?" said a much-tried brother minister. "Well, friend," said Rippon, "you see, we don't call a church-meeting to consult about buying a new broom every time we want one, and we don't entreat every noisy member to make a speech about the price of the soap the floors are scrubbed with."

In many of our smaller churches, a want of common sense is very manifest in the management, and trouble is invited by the foolish methods of procedure. Dr. Rippon once said that he had some of the best people in His Majesty's dominions in his church, and he used to add with a nod, — "*and some of the worst*" Some of the latter class seem to have got into office at one time, for they were evidently a hindrance rather than a help to the good man, though from his independent mode of doing things the hindrance did not much affect him. As well as I can remember it, the story of his founding the Almshouses and Schools, in 1803, runs as follows. The Doctor urges upon the deacons the necessity of such institutions; they do not see the urgency thereof; he pleads again, but, like the deaf adder, they are not to be charmed, charm he never so wisely. "The expense will be enormous, and the money cannot be raised;" this was the unceasing croak of the prudent officers. At length the Pastor says, "The money can be raised, and shall be. Why, if I don't go out next Monday, and collect £500 before the evening meeting, I'll drop the proposal; but: while I am sure the people will take up the matter heartily, I will not be held back by you."

Disputes in this case were urged in very plain language, but with no degree of bitterness, for the parties knew each other, and had too much mutual respect to make their relationships in the church depend upon a point of difference. All were agreed to put the Doctor to the test, and challenged him to produce the £500 next Monday, or cease to importune them about Almshouses. The worthy slow coaches were up to time on the appointed evening, and the Doctor soon arrived. "Well, brethren," said he, "I have succeeded in collecting £300; — that is most encouraging, is it not?...

But," said two or three of them at once in a hurry, "you said you would get £500, or drop the matter, and we mean to keep you to your word." "By all means," said he, "*and* I mean to keep my word, too, for there is £800 which the friends gave me almost without asking, and the rest is nearly all promised." The prudent officials were taken aback, but recovering themselves, they expressed their great pleasure, and would be ready to meet the Pastor at any time, to arrange for the expending of the funds.

"No, no, my brethren," said the Doctor, "I shall not need your services. You have opposed me all along, and now I have done the work without you, you want to have your say in it to hinder me still; but neither you nor any other deacons shall plague a minister about this business. So, brethren, you can attend to something else." Accordingly, the old trust deed of the Almshouses had a clause to the effect that the Pastor should elect the pensioners, "*no deacon interfering.*"

'When the time came for removing the Almshouses and Schools to the fine block of buildings erected by our friends in the Station Road, Walworth, near the Elephant and Castle Railway Station, I had great pleasure in inducing the Charity Commissioners to expunge this objectionable clause, and to give the Pastor and deacons unitedly the power to select the objects of the charity.

Dr. Rippon continued in the pastorate from 1773   to 1836, a period of sixty-three years. He outlived his usefulness, and it was a wonderful instance of Divine care over the church that the old gentleman did not do it serious injury. He retained the will to govern after the capacity was gone:, and he held his power over the pulpit though unable to occupy it to profit.

Supplies who came to preach for him were not always allowed to officiate; and when they did, the old minister's remarks from his pew were frequently more quaint than agreeable. It is not an unqualified blessing to live to be eighty-five. During the last few months, MR. CHARLES ROOM, with the Doctor's full. approbation, acted as his assistant, but he resigned upon the decease of Dr. Rippon. He left with the esteem and good wishes of the church, and afterwards exercised a useful ministry at Portsea. In 1830, six years before Dr. Rippon's death, the old sanctuary in Carter Lane was closed, to be pulled down for making the approaches to the present London Bridge. Due compensation was given, but a chapel could not be built in a day, and, therefore, for three years, the church was without a home, and had to be indebted to the hospitality of other congregations.

After so long a time for choice, the good deacons ought to have pitched upon a better site for the new edifice; but it is not judging them hardly when I say that they could not have discovered a worse position. If they had taken thirty years to look about them with the design of burying the church alive, they could not have succeeded better. New Park Street is a low-lying sort of lane close to the bank of the River Thames, near the enormous breweries of Messrs. Barclay and Perkins, the vinegar factories of Mr. Potts, and several large boiler works. The nearest way to it from the City was over Southwark Bridge, *with a toll to pay.* No cabs could be had within about half-a-mile of the place, and the region was dim, dirty, and destitute, and frequently flooded by the river at high tides. Here, however, the new chapel must be built because: the ground was a cheap freehold, and the authorities were destitute of enterprise, and would not spend a penny more than the amount in hand. That God, in infinite mercy, forbade the extinction of the church, is no mitigation of the shortsightedness which thrust a respectable community of Christians into an out-of-the-way position, far more suitable for a tallow-melter's business than for a meeting-house. The chapel, however, was a neat, handsome, commodious, well-built edifice, and was regarded as one of the best Baptist chapels in London. Dr. Rippon was present at the opening of the new house in 1833, but it was very evident that, having now found a place to meet in, the next step must be to find a minister to preside over the congregation. This was no easy task, for the old gentleman, though still revered and loved, was difficult to manage in such matters. Happily, however, the deacons were supremely judicious, and having kept the church out of all rash expenditure, they also preserved it from all hasty action, and tided over affairs till the worn-out Pastor passed away to his rest, and with due funereal honors was laid in that Campo Santo of Nonconformists, — the cemetery of Bunhill Fields, of which it had been his ambition to become the historian and chronicler. There are thousands in Heaven who were led first to love the Savior by his earnest exhortations. He quarried fresh stones, and built up the church. He molded its thought, and directed its energies.

Without being great, he was exceedingly useful, and the period in which he was one of the judges of our Israel was one of great prosperity in spiritual things. It was a good sixty-three years, and with the previous pastorate of Dr. Gill, enabled the church to say that, during one hundred and seventeen years, they had been presided over by two ministers only.

The next Pastor was Mr., now Doctor, Joseph Angus, a gentleman whose career since he left us to become secretary of the Baptist Missionary Society, and afterwards the tutor of Stepney Academy, now Regent's Park College, has rendered his name most honorable among living Baptists.

During Mr. Angus's pastorate, the privilege of communing at the Lord's table was extended to members of other churches, whether baptized or not, and this was done quietly and without division, though a considerable minority did not agree with it. The church remains a community of baptized believers, and its constitution will not admit any persons into its membership but those immersed upon personal profession of faith in the Lord Jesus;; but it does not attempt to judge the order and discipline of other churches, and has fellowship in the breaking of bread with all churches which form parts of the mystical body of Christ: thus it endeavors to fulfill at the same time the duties of purity and love. In December, 1839, the Baptist Missionary Society invited Mr. Angus to become its Home Secretary. a sense of the importance of the Missionary Society, and the fact that, after much deliberation, the Committee could not discover anyone else about whom they could be at all unanimous, were the motives which led him to leave the church, to the deep regret of all the members.

After the removal of Dr. Angus, the church was happily directed to hear MR. JAMES SMITH, whose ministry in Cheltenham was an abundant guarantee that he was likely to prove the right man to collect a congregation in New Park Street. He was Pastor for about eight years and a half, from 1841 to 1850, and then returned to Cheltenham, from which many of his best friends are of opinion that he ought never to have removed. He was a man of slender education, but of great natural ability, sound in the faith, intensely earnest, and a ready speaker. Few men have ever been more useful than he. In July, 1851, the church invited the REV. WILLIAM WALTERS, of Preston, to become the Pastor, but as he understood the deacons to intimate to him that his ministry was not acceptable, he tendered his resignation, and although requested to remain, he judged it more advisable to remove to Halifax in June, 1853, thus closing a ministry of two years. These changes sadly diminished the church, and marred its union. The clouds gathered heavily, and no sunlight appeared; but the Lord had not forgotten His people, and in due time He poured them out such a blessing that there was not room to receive it. Let me tell once more the pleasing story.

On the last Sabbath morning in November, 1853, I walked, according to my wont, from Cambridge to the village of Waterbeach, in order to occupy the pulpit of the little Baptist Chapel. It was a country road, and there were five or six honest miles of it, which I usually measured, each Sunday, foot by foot, unless I happened to be met by a certain little pony and cart which came half-way, but could not by any possibility venture further because of the enormous expense which would have been incurred by driving through the toll-gate at Milton! That winter's morning, I was all aglow with my walk, and ready for my pulpit exercises. Sitting down in the table-pew, a letter, bearing the postmark of London, was passed to me. It was an unusual missive, and was opened with curiosity. It contained an invitation to preach at New Park Street Chapel, Southwark, the pulpit of which had formerly been occupied by Dr. Rippon, — the very Dr. Rippon whose hymn-book was then before me upon the table, — the great Dr. Rippon, out of whose Selection I was about to choose the hymns for our worship.

The late Dr. Rippon seemed to hover over me as an immeasurably great man, the glory of whose name covered New Park Street Chapel and its pulpit with awe unspeakable. I quietly passed the letter across the table to the deacon who gave out the hymns, observing that there was some mistake, and that the letter must have been intended for a Mr. Spurgeon who preached somewhere clown in Norfolk. He shook his head, and remarked that he was afraid there was no mistake, as he always knew that his minister would be run away with by some large church or other, but that he was a little surprised that the Londoners should have heard of me quite so soon. "Had it been Cottenham, or St. Ives, or Huntingdon," said he, "I should not have wondered at all; but going to London is rather a great step from this little place." He shook his head very gravely; but the time had come for me to look out the hymns, therefore the letter was put away, and, as far as I can remember, was for the day quite forgotten.

The next day, this answer was sent to the letter from the London deacon: —
"No. 60, Park Street,

"My Dear Sir,

"I do not reside at Waterbeach, and therefore: your letter did not reach me till yesterday, although the friends ought to have forwarded it at once. My people at Waterbeach are hardly to be persuaded to let me come, but I am prepared to serve you on the 11th [December]. On the 4th, I could not leave them; and the impossibility of finding a supply at all agreeable to them, prevents me from leaving home two following Sabbaths. I have been wondering very much how you could have heard of me, and I think I ought to give some account of myself, lest I should come and be out of my right place. Although I have been more than two years minister of a church, which has in that time doubled, yet my last birthday was only my nineteenth. I have hardly ever known what the fear of man means, and have all but uniformly had large congregations, and frequently crowded ones; but if you think my years would unqualify me for your pulpit, then, by all means, I entreat you, do not let me come. The Great God, my Helper, will not leave me to myself. Almost every night, for two years, I have been aided to proclaim His truth. I am therefore able to promise you for the 11th, and should you accept the offer, I will come on Saturday afternoon, and return on Monday. As I shall have to procure a supply, an early answer will oblige —

"*Yours* most truly,

"C. H. SPURGEON."

In due time came another epistle, setting forth that the former letter had been written in perfect knowledge of the young preacher's age, and had been intended for him and him alone. The request of the former letter was repeated and pressed, a date mentioned for the journey to London, and the place appointed at which the preacher would find lodging. That invitation was accepted, and as the result thereof the boy-preacher of the Fens traveled to London. Though it is so long ago, yet it seems but yesterday that I lodged for the night at a boarding-house in Queen Square, Bloomsbury, to which the worthy deacon had directed me. As I wore a huge black satin stock, and used a blue handkerchief with white spots, the young gentlemen of that boarding-house marveled greatly at the youth from the country who had come up to preach in London, but who was evidently in the condition known as "verdant green." They were mainly of the Evangelical Church persuasion, and seemed greatly tickled that the country lad should be a preacher. They did not propose to go and hear the youth, but they seemed to tacitly agree to *encourage* me after their own fashion, and I was encouraged accordingly! What tales were narrated of the great divines of the metropolis, and their congregations! One, I remember, had a thousand *city* men to hear him; another had his church filled with *thoughtful* people, such as could hardly be matched all over England; while a third had an immense audience almost entirely composed of the *young' men* of London, who were spell-bound by his eloquence. The study which these men underwent in composing their sermons, their herculean toils in keeping up their congregations, and the matchless oratory which they exhibited on all occasions, were duly rehearsed in my hearing, and when I was shown to bed in a cupboard over the front door, I was not in an advantageous condition for pleasant dreams. New Park Street hospitality never sent the young minister to that far-away hired room again; but, assuredly, that Saturday evening in a London boarding-house was about the most depressing agency which could have been brought to bear upon my spirit. On the narrow bed I tossed in solitary misery, and found no pity. Pitiless was the grind of the cabs in the street, pitiless the recollection of the young city clerks, whose grim propriety had gazed upon my rusticity with such amusement, pitiless the spare room which scarcely afforded me space to kneel, pitiless even the gas-lamps which seemed to wink at me as they flickered amid the December darkness. I had no friend in all that city full of human beings, but felt myself to be among strangers and foreigners, and hoped to be helped through the scrape into which I had been brought, and to escape safely to the serene abodes of Cambridge and Waterbeach, which then seemed to be Eden itself. The Sabbath morning was clear and cold, and I wended my way along Holborn Hill towards Blackfriars and certain tortuous lanes and alleys at the foot of Southwark Bridge.

Wondering, praying, fearing, hoping, believing, — I felt all alone, and yet not alone. Expectant of Divine help, and inwardly borne down by my sense of the need of it, I traversed a dreary wilderness of brick to find the spot where my message was to be delivered. One text rose to my lips many times, I scarcely know why, — "He must needs go through Samaria." The necessity of bur Lord's journeying in a certain direction, is. no doubt repeated in His servants; and as my journey was not of my seeking, and had been by no means pleasing so far as it had gone, — the one thought of a "needs be" for it seemed to overtop every oth-er. At sight of New Park Street Chapel, I felt for a moment amazed at my own te-merity, for it seemed to my eyes to be a large, ornate, and imposing structure, suggesting an audience wealthy and critical, and far removed' from the humble folk to whom my ministry had been sweetness and light. It was early, so there were no persons entering; and when the set time was fully come, there were no signs to support the suggestion raised by the exterior of the building, and I felt that, by God's help, I was not yet out of my depth, and was not likely to be with so small an audience. The Lord helped me very' graciously, I had a happy Sabbath in the pulpit, and spent the interval with warm-hearted friends; and when, at night, I trudged back to the Queen Square narrow lodging, I was not alone, and I no longer looked on Londoners as flinty-hearted barbarians. My tone was altered; I wanted no pity of anyone, I did not care a penny for the young gentlemen lodgers and their miraculous ministers, nor for the grind of the cabs, nor for anything else under the sun. The lion had been looked at all round, and his majesty did not appear to be a tenth as majestic as when I had only heard his roar miles away.

(The friend who walked back with Mr. Spurgeon to his lodging in Queen Square, at the close o! the first Sabbath evening's service at New Park Street Chapel, was Mr. Joseph Passmore. That walk was the prelude to a life-long friendship and happy association in church work and in the publication of the beloved Pastor's many works. The following is the first letter ever written by Mr. Spurgeon to his friend, and is included in the Autobiography through the kind-ness of his eldest son and namesake, Mr. Joseph Passmore: —)

"May 17th, 1854.

"My Dear brother,

"I am extremely obliged to you for your kind present. I find that all the kind-ness is not in the country, some at least grows in town; and, if nowhere else, it is 'to be found in a house in Finsbury.

"It is sweet to find oneself remembered. I trust the harmony between us may never receive the slightest jar, but continue even in Heaven. We have, I trust, just commenced a new era; and, by God's blessing, we will strive to make it a glorious one to our Church. Oh, that our hopes may all be realized! I feel assured that your constant prayers are going up fervently to Heaven; let us continue wrestling, and the wished-for blessing must arrive.

"With Christian regards to you and Mrs. Passmore,

"I am,

"Yours most truly,

C. H. SPURGEON."

Chapter Twenty-Nine - First Sermons at Park Street Chapel

Let every man, called of God to preach the Word, be as his Maker has fashioned him. Neither Paul, nor Apollos, nor Cephas is to be 'imitated by John; nor are John's ways, habits, and modes of utterance to be the basis for a condemnation of any one or all of the other three. As God gives to every seed its own body as it rises from the soil, so to each man will He grant his own appropriate development, if he will but be content to let his inner self reveal itself in its true form. The good and the evil in men of eminence are both of them mischievous when they become objects of servile imitation; the good when slavishly copied is exaggerated into formality, and the evil becomes wholly intolerable. It each teacher of others went himself to the school of our one only Master, a thousand errors might be avoided. — C. H. S.

THE text of Mr. Spurgeon's first sermon in London has long been well known; but, until now, there does not appear to have been any printed record of the opening discourse in that marvelous Metropolitan ministry which was des-tined to exercise such a mighty influence, not only throughout London, and the United Kingdom, but "unto the uttermost part of the earth." Happily, the young preacher had written at considerable length the message he felt called to deliver on that occasion in his Master's name, and now, after a whole generation has passed away, his long-forgotten words will speak to a far larger audience than he addressed that winter's morning (December 18th, 1853,) in New Park Street Chapel. It may interest some readers to know that the sermon was the 673rd that Mr. Spurgeon had preached. The evening discourse appears to have been re-delivered at a later period, taken down in shorthand, and afterwards revised by Mr. Spurgeon for publication in *The Baptist Messenger*.

MORNING SERMON.

THE FATHER OF LIGHT.

"Every good gift and every perfect gift is from above, and cometh down from the Father of lights, with whom is no variableness, neither shadow of turning." — James 1:17.

Some sciences and subjects of study are to us inexhaustible. We might ever find in them fresh matter for instruction, wonder, and research. If we were to descend into the depths of the earth, with the geologist, and bring up the skeletons of extinct monsters, and note the signs of great convulsions, and study the old and new formations and strata; or if we were to soar aloft, with the astronomer, and attempt to measure the heavens, and count the stars; we should ever be lost in the new discoveries which we should make.

The same may be said of all the natural sciences. Whatever the subject of his study may be, it does not seem possible that man should ever be able to say, "I have nothing more to learn; I am master of it all."

But should it one day happen that our race has so progressed in knowledge, and become so well informed as to leave nothing unknown, — should nature be stript of all her mystery, and the heavens, the sea, and the earth be all perfectly understood, — there will yet remain one subject upon which the sons of men may meditate, dispute, and ponder; but it shall still be unknown. That subject is, — GOD, of whom, with humble reverence, I am now to speak. May it please the great Spirit of wisdom to enlarge our minds, and guide our hearts into an understanding of that portion of truth concerning Him which is revealed in the text! We have, here, —

I. A MAJESTIC FIGURE.
II. A GLORIOUS ATTRIBUTE.
III. A GRATEFUL ACKNOWLEDGMENT.

I. A MAJESTIC FIGURE.

God is here called "the Father of lights," — comparing Him to the sun. It is most true that this lower world is the reflection of the upper one. In it, once, the face of God might have been seen as on some glassy lake; but sin has ruffled the surface of the waters, so that the portrait is broken, and presented only in pieces. Yet there are the pieces, — the wrecks of the picture, — and we will not throw them aside. Let us lift up our eyes on high, and behold the only object which is worthy to be called an emblem of Deity. We think we can see several ideas couched in the figure used in our text by the apostle.

1. *Independence; or, Self-existence.*

God is the only self-existent Being. The sun is not really so; but he is far more independent than any other object we know of. All else of nature is continually borrowing; vegetables draw their nourishment from the soil, animals from them, or from one another, man from all; — he is the greatest beggar in the universe. The moon lights her nightly torch at the sun's lamp, the planets rekindle theirs in his bright storehouse. Mother Earth is greatly dependent on the sun; despite the pride of her children, what is she but a tiny globule dancing in the rays of that majestic orb? The sun gives, but takes not; bestows on all, receives from none, leans on none; but lives alone, in his own solemn grandeur and glory.

Such is God, the great I AM, who sits on no borrowed throne, and begs no leave to be. All things are of Him, and by Him. He needs them not; were they all annihilated, it would not injure Him. He could exist, as He has from eternity existed, alone. He has in Himself all that is worth having. On Him all things lean; He leans on none. But we can scarcely speak of Him, —

"Who, light Himself, in uncreated light,
Invested deep, dwells awfully retired
From mortal eye, or angel's purer ken.
Whose single smile has, from the first of time,
Fill'd overflowing all those lamps of heaven
That beam for ever through the boundless sky;
But should He hide His face, th' astonish'd sun
And all th' extinguish'd stars would loosening reel
Wide from their spheres, and chaos come again."

2. *Sublimity* is another idea suggested by the figure in the text. The sun is one of the most magnificent of created things; when he shows himself, the moon and stars conceal their blushing faces. Seen in any part of his course, he is a grand object. When first he tinges the Eastern sky with his rising beams, when he sits serenely in mid-heaven at noon, or when he retires in splendor at eventide, grandeur is always one of his characteristics. He is too bright for our eyes to gaze upon, although we are at such a vast distance from him.

Far more sublime is God. Who shall describe Him? His angelic servants are glorious, the starry floor of His throne is glorious; what must He Himself be?

"Imagination's utmost stretch
In wonder dies away."

Well may angels veil their faces, for even their eyes could not endure His brightness. No man can see Him. His train was all that Moses saw. Borrow the eagle's eye and wing, soar on and on until the glory overcomes you, and you fall reeling back to the earth; do it again and again, and you will find that man cannot see God. Clouds and darkness are round about Him, for He may truly have it said to Him, —

"Dark with' excessive bright Thy skirts appear."

3. *Power* also seems a prominent idea in this expression of the apostle: *"The Father' of lights."* The sun is as a giant coming out of his chamber; and, like a strong man, he rejoices to run a race. He drags the whole immense solar system along in his majestic course, nor can any oppose him. How mightily he still moves on in his appointed course!

So is our God glorious in His power. No one knows His might; it is like Himself, infinite. He speaketh, and His Word is with power. He willeth, and His will is omnipotent. Who can thwart His purposes? Shall nature?

No; the hills melted like wax at the presence of the Lord. They skipped before Him like rams. By His power, the waters are divided; fire singes not His servants; wild beasts are tamed. He lifteth His finger, and the flood ariseth; He droppeth it, and the waters assuage. In vain could mountains, torrents, stars, and all the elements war against Him. Who can conquer Him in battle? Shall man? No; He counteth all men but as a drop in a bucket. He that sitteth in Heaven hath His enemies in derision. Shall the devils in hell withstand Him? No; once have they fallen from the battlements of Heaven, and in vain is their loudest roar. Satan is chained, and led as a conquer'd monarch to grace God's victory over him. He is God's slave, and unwillingly doth his Master's will. O beloved, what a God is here revealed to us! Put this thought under thy pillow; and when troubles arise, still calmly sleep on, for His power protecteth thee from all evil!

4. But *Beneficence* seems even more the leading idea of the text. The sun is absolutely necessary to our being; there would be no light, no heat, no life, no rain, nothing without him. He is necessary also to our well-being; the sun is indeed the great philanthropist; he visits every land, he gives freely, and gives to all, to the peasant as well as to the prince. Curse him, or bless him, he is the same; he does not refuse his light even to the felon, but he visits the prisoner in his cell.

Such also is God, the good, the greatly-good. Should He withdraw His face, Heaven would not be Heaven. Without God, the whole universe would be a valley full of dry bones, a horrible charnel-house. Oh, how good is our God! He confines not His mercies to any one race; the Hottentots are as welcome to His love as are any of us. The sinful receive His grace, and lose their former evil nature. He gives to sinners, and to the unthankful; and if men were not by nature blind, they would see by His light; the defect is in them, and not in Him.

Yon sun has shone on my cradle, it will beam on my death-bed, and cast a gleam into my grave. So doth God, the Beneficent, gild our path with sunshine. Earth were a gloomy vault without Him; with Him, it is light and joyous, the porch of a still more blissful state.

II. A GLORIOUS ATTRIBUTE.

The apostle, having thus introduced the sun as a figure to represent the Father of lights, finding that it did not bear the full resemblance of the invisible God, seems; constrained to amend it by a remark that, *unlike the* sun, *our Father has no turning, or variableness.*

The sun has *parallax*, or, variation; he rises at a different time each day, and he sets at various hours in the course of the year. He'. moves into other parts of the heavens. He is clouded, eclipsed, and even suffers a diminution of light from some mysterious decrease of the luminiferous ether which surrounds him. He also has *tropic*, or, turning. He turns his chariot to the South, until, at the solstice, God bids him reverse his rein, and then he visits us once more. But God is superior to all figures or emblems. He is immutable. The sun changes, mountains crumble, the ocean shall be dried up, the stars shall wither from the vault of night; but God, and God alone, remains ever the same. Were I to enter into a full discourse on the subject of immutability, my time, if multiplied by a high number, would fail me. But reminding you that there is no change in His power, justice, knowledge, oath, threatening, or decree, I will confine myself to the fact that His love to us knows no variation. How often it is called *unchangeable*, everlasting love! He loves me now as much as He did when first: He inscribed my name in His eternal book of election. He has not repented of His choice. He has not blotted out one of His chosen; there are no erasures in that book; all whose names are written in it are safe for ever.

Nor does God love me less now than when He gave that grand proof of love, His Son, Jesus Christ, to (tie for me. Even now, He loves me with the same intensity as when He poured out the vials of justice on His darling to save rebel worms. We have all had times which we considered times of special love, when His candle shone round about us, and we basked in the light of His smiling face; but let us not suppose that He really loved us more then than now. Oh, no! He then discovered His love in a way pleasing to flesh and blood; but trials are equally proofs of His love. In the fight with Apollyon in the Valley of Humiliation, in the Valley of the Shadow of Death, or in 'Vanity Fair, He will be ever the same, and will love us neither more nor less than when we sing with seraphic voices the songs of Heaven.

Death, sometimes, in the prospect, is very trying to flesh and blood; but if this truth of God's unchanging love were well remembered, death would not be such a trial to us as it has been to many. We should know that He who helped Jacob to gather up his feet, and die, — that He who enabled David to say, "Although my house be not so with God; yet He hath made with me an everlasting covenant, ordered in all things,, and sure: for this is all my salvation, and all my desire, although He make it not to grow," —

and that He who permitted Stephen to fall asleep amid a shower of stones:, will be the Deliverer of all who trust in Him. Throughout eternity, there shall be no jars, not a breath of strife; but the same uninterrupted, blessed unity shall prevail for ever, and God will continue to bestow upon us His unchanging love. Thanks be unto Him for loving us so!

III. A GRATEFUL ACKNOWLEDGMENT.

The apostle, having introduced God as the Father of lights, and qualified the figure, now proceeds to ascribe all good gifts to Him alone: "Every good gift and every perfect gift is from above, and cometh down from the Father of lights, with whom is no variableness, neither shadow of turning."

If it seemed perfectly reasonable that, at the rising of the sun, nature should welcome it with song, is it not even more reasonable that, at the name of the Father' of lights, we should lift up a song? What is said here, is what angels can sing in Heaven; it is what Adam could have hymned in Paradise; it is what every Christian feels heartily willing to confess.

Ever since the Fall, this verse has had an added emphasis of meaning, since in us, by nature, there dwells no good thing, and by our sin we have forfeited every right to any favor from God. So that our *natural gifts,* such as beauty, eloquence, health, life, and happiness, all come from Him equally with our *graces.* We have nothing which we have not received. Earth, one day, shall make this song thrill through infinity; Heaven shall join the chorus; the region of chaos and old night shall shout aloud, and even hell's unwilling voice shall growl out an acknowledgment of the fact that *"Every good gift and every perfect gift is from above, and cometh down from the Father of lights, with whom is no variableness, neither shadow of turning."*

I have succeeded in my object if, with me, you can from your hearts say, at the contemplation of Jehovah, — "Glory be unto the Father, and to the Son, and to the Holy Ghost, as it was in the beginning, is now, and ever shall be, world without end! AMEN."

EVENING SERMON.

THE FAULTLESS ASSEMBLY.

"They are without fault before the throne of God."
— Revelation 14:5.

It is well, beloved, sometimes to get aside from the worry of business, to have a little conversation concerning that future world to which we are tending. We will, therefore, indulge in a brief contemplation of Heaven, and will speak concerning those things which, if we are the Lord's people, we are soon to realize when we shall be —

"Far from a world of grief and sin,
With God eternally shut in,"

to live with Him for ever.

There are three things in these words; first, *the character of the people in* Heaven: "they are *without fault;"* secondly, *who they are,* "they" are without fault;" and then, thirdly, *where they are'* "they" are without fault *before the throne of God."*

I. THE PEOPLE IN HEAVEN ARE OF A CERTAIN PECULIAR CHARACTER: "without fault."

I have never discovered such creatures living upon earth, and do not suppose I ever shall. I might travel many a weary journey before I could find a man in the three kingdoms that would be "without fault;" yea, if an angel were to be sent down to the world for this purpose, he might fly round it many a time, till his wings were weary, yet never find a man "without fault." I knew a man, once, who told me that he was perfect; but he soon got very cross when I began to speak, and I saw that he was perfect only in one thing, — he was perfect in weakness; that was the only perfection he had. It is only now and then that you meet with a man who has the impudence to tell you that he is perfect; but you can soon see, from the very look of him, that he is not perfect, for at any rate he is not perfect in humility; he seems to glory in his perfection, and all the while his very mouth betrayeth him. That eye of pride, and that lip of lust with which he speaks, as he lusteth for the praise of men, tell you that he is far from being perfect. A faultless creature, — where is there such a being on earth? Fly, Gabriel, fly I enter thou the loftiest palace, and then go to the humblest cottage, go to the most remote realm, to the most civilized, polite, and educated people, and thou shalt find no perfect being; nay, go into the church, go into the pulpit, thou wilt ne'er find a perfect man nor a perfect minister. Imperfection is stamped upon all things; and, save the completeness that is in Christ Jesus, and the perfection we have in Him, perfection is nowhere to be found beneath the skies; nor in Heaven itself could it be found unless God were there, for He alone can make a creature perfect. But there, beloved, is perfection; despite the faults of men on earth, when they shall have been fitted for the skies by God's most precious grace, they shall stand before God "without fault."

We will, first, look at our own faults, and then admire those glorious beings above, and the grace of God in them, that they are "without fault." I think there are three great faults in the Church of God at large, as a body, from which those who are in Heaven are entirely free. Those three are, — a want of love to one another; a want of love to souls; and a want of love to Jesus Christ.

I. We need not go far without seeing that there is, among Christians, *a want of love to one another.* There is not too much love in our churches; certainly, we have none to give away. We have heard that —

"Whatever brawls disturb the street,
There should be peace at home;"

but it is not always as it *should* be. We have known Churches where the members can scarcely sit down at the Lord's table without some disagreement. There are people who are always finding fault with the minister, and there are ministers finding fault with the people; there is among them "a spirit that lusteth to envy," and "where envying and strife is, there is confusion and every evil work." We have met with people among whom it would be misery to place ourselves, because we love not war; we love peace and charity. Alas! how continually do we hear accounts of disputings and variance in churches! O beloved, there is too little love in the 'churches! If Jesus were to come amongst us, might He not say to us, "This is My commandment, that ye love one another; but how have you kept it when you have been always finding fault with one another? and how ready you have been to turn your sword against your brother!"?

But, beloved, "they are without fault before the throne of God." Those who on earth could not agree, are sure to agree when they get to Heaven.

There are some who have crossed swords on earth, but who have held the faith, and have been numbered amongst the saints in glory everlasting.

There is no fighting amongst them now; "they are without fault before the throne of God." There are many, who would never sit at the same table with each other when they were upon earth, though they were the children of God; but now, side by side, they are standing and singing to the same tune, "Glory be to God and to the Lamb!" We discover, by reading the records of distinguished men, that there has scarcely been one eminent man who could walk side by side with his fellow. Like great mountains, they touch at their foundations; certainly, they unite nowhere else. But in Heaven all stand side by side, and there is no disunion amongst them. We know that, in many churches, some of the richer members will scarcely notice the poorer; but it will not be so above, there is true love there. We hear of church-members who have been sick for months, yet no brother or sister-member has ministered to them; but in Heaven it is not so, there is no neglect there. They cannot suffer there; but if it were possible that they could suffer, so sweet would be: the love displayed towards each other, that suffering would be removed in a moment. Ask the cherubim if they ever knew a jar in Christ's glorified Church above; and they would say,

"Nay." And if you could make all the blessed ones pass in review, and ask them if they love one another, "Yes," they would say, "*with* a pure heart, fervently; and though we had brawls and disputings on earth, they are all forgotten now, for the blood of Christ, that covers a multitude of sins, has ended all our disagreements; and that holy mantle of a Savior's love, that He casts over all our faults, has ended all our wars with one another. We are all one in Christ Jesus; would to God we had seen more of this oneness when below!" They are "without fault" in that respect, beloved, above.

There is no harshness there; there is no ill humor there; there is no bitterness there; there is no envy, no evil-speaking, no spite, no uncharitableness, there; "*they* are without fault before the throne of God."

244

Oh, how my wearied spirit longs to be there! I wish not to live with men of strife; the lions' den is not for me, nor the house of leopards. Give me the quiet place where the oil runneth down from the head even to the skirts of the garments. Let me live in peace with all Christ's Church; let me not find fault with anyone. Sooner will I allow them to sheath their daggers in my heart than I would draw mine in angry contest. Thank God! there are some of us who can say, "There is not a man living with whom we are at arm's length any more than the infant that is just born." There are some of us who can give our hand very readily to anyone in whom we see anything that is pleasing to the Spirit of God; but when we see anything that is contrary to the Spirit, we say, "Oh! that I had wings — not like an eagle to fly at my brother, — oh! that I had wings like a dove, that I might fly away, and be at rest." That happy time shall soon come, beloved, when we, like those above, shall be "without fault before the throne of God."

2. A second fault is, that there is *a great want of love to souls.* John Bunyan gives the portrait of a man whom God intended to be a guide to Heaven; have you ever noticed how beautiful that portrait is? He has a crown of life over his head, he has the earth beneath his feet, he stands as if he pleaded with men, and he has the Best of Books in his hand. Oh! I would that I were, for one moment, like that pattern preacher; that I could plead with men as John Bunyan describeth. We are all of us ambassadors for Christ, and we are told that, as ambassadors, we are to beseech men as though God besought them by us. How I do love to see a tearful preacher!

How I love to see the man who can weep over sinners; whose soul yearns over the ungodly, as if he would, by any means, and by all means, bring them to the Lord Jesus Christ! I cannot understand a man who stands up and delivers a discourse in a cold indifferent manner, as if he cared not for the souls of his hearers. I think the true gospel minister will have a real yearning after souls, something like Rachel when she cried, "Give me children, or else I die;" so will he cry to God, that He may have His elect born, and brought home to Him. And, methinks, every true Christian should be exceedingly earnest in prayer concerning the souls of the ungodly; and when they are so, how abundantly God blesses them, and how the church prospers! But, beloved, souls may be damned, yet how few of you care about them! Sinners may sink into the gulf of perdition, yet how few tears are shed over them! The whole world may be swept away by a torrent down the precipice of woe, yet how few really cry to God on its behalf! How few men say, "Oh that my head were waters, and mine eyes a fountain of tears, that I might weep day and night for the slain of the daughter of my people!" We do not lament before God the loss of men's souls, as it well becomes Christians to do.

Ah! but in Heaven, they love souls. Angels rejoice over one sinner that repenteth. As a good Puritan said, "Whenever a prodigal returns, they set all Heaven's bells ringing, because there is another sinner come back." O beloved, when you get a convert to bring to the church, you see some of the members look at him, through their spectacles, as if they would frighten the poor timid one! Many do not, like angels, rejoice over him; but they look at him as if they were afraid he was a hypocrite. The poor soul stands trembling before the church; the hand of the Lord is mighty upon him, but they sit by as coldly as if they were on a judgment seat, and have neither love nor mercy for him. I know that, when a church increases, there should be judgment and discretion shown, and I would rather have too much of what I am speaking against, than too little of it; but, sometimes, the members look at the converts, and say, "It cannot be possible; how should *they* be gathered in?" And when there is an addition to their numbers, they even go home with a heavy heart, as if the church were likely to come to harm by admitting them. Give me a church-meeting where they weep with joy over those who come in, and say, "Bless the Lord, there is another poor soul rescued from the world!" I think it is a sort of mark of the sheep, that they love to see,. the lambs; and I think it is a feature of the Lord's family, that they love to see another child born into it. When you see anyone brought to the Lord, do you not bless God for it? When you hear that such an one has received grace and mercy, do you not bless God for it? No, not half so much as you ought; we are not half thankful enough to our Father for it. But, up there, beloved, they are "without fault" in that matter, and they do rejoice:, every one of them, when they see souls brought in. Methinks, young man, your pious Mother will rejoice when God brings you to His feet; and those godly friends of yours shall lift up their notes high in Heaven, when they see those dear to them on earth united to the Church of God on high. Blessed be God's name for them, they are "without fault before the throne of God;" and especially in this matter of their love to souls.

3. The other fault I mentioned was, *want of love lo Jesus Christ.* Yes, how little there is among us of love to Jesus Christ! When I think of myself, sometimes, and think of the Lord Jesus, it does appear as if I did not love Him at all. When I think of that "love so amazing, so Divine," which led Him to give Himself for me; when I remember that in me was no good thing, yet He loved me when I was dead in trespasses and sins; loved me when I hated Him, loved me when I spurned Him, loved me when I despised and rejected Him, and hid, as it were, my face from Him; for "He was despised and rejected of men,... He was despised,... and we esteemed Him not;" — when I think of all this, I cannot but wonder in my heart that I do not consecrate myself more entirely to Him. Oh, if we did but love that sweet Lord Jesus with more ardor and devotedness! He has love enough for us, but how little is our love for Him!

Methinks there is nothing over which a Christian should groan so much as the littleness of his love to the Savior. When our faith is small, we often lament; but we should recollect that love is the flower of faith, and springs from frith; and when that is feeble, it is a sign that faith also is feeble.

Rutherford somewhere beautifully, says, "O Lord Jesus, let me love Thee, and that will be Heaven enough for me; for I find such sweetness in loving Thee that, if it were possible that Thou didst not love me, Thou canst not be so cruel as to prevent me loving Thee; and if Thou wouldst but let me have the presumption to love Thee, I think it would be Heaven enough."

Rutherford felt it was so sweet to love his Lord, he found it was so delightful to have his heart go out to the Savior, that so long as the Lord would let him love Him, he would be thankful for it, even though his Lord did not love him. Beloved, there is nought like the love of Jesus to make us happy! I love the doctrines of grace as well as any mortal living does, but I love Jesus better; I love Christ's people as much as anyone can, but I love Christ best. Oh, His sweet, glorious, exalted person! that is the object of our love; we look upon all else as the clothes of Jesus, the crown of Jesus.

And we love the Lord Jesus, for His own blessed name's sake; we love Him for what we know of Him; still, the fault is that we do not know enough of Him, and we do not love Him enough. But up there, beloved, "*they* are without fault before the throne of God." Ask those bright spirits whether they know Jesus, and love Jesus, and how would they answer you? Spirit immortal, dost thou love Jesus? Hear his answer! He stops not to tell you, but he repeats the song he sings in Heaven, "*Blessing,* and honor, and glory, and power, be unto Him that sitteth upon the throne, and unto the Lamb for ever and ever." Ask him whether he loves Christ, he does not stay to tell you, but sweeps his fingers across the golden strings of his harp, and again lifts up his thrice-glorious voice in praise of the name of Jesus.

> *"'Jesus! my Lord!' their harps employs;*
> *'Jesus! my Love!' they sing;*
> *'Jesus! the life of all my joys!'*
> *Sounds sweet from every string."*

If there were nothing else to expect in Heaven but that we should know Christ better and love Him more, that is all the Heaven that any of us need desire. To touch with our finger His wounded side, to grasp His nail-pierced hands, to gaze on His benignant face, to look on those compassionate eyes which once were cold and glazed in the tomb, — to know Him, and to love Him perfectly, — that were Heaven enough; and it shall be so, for "they are without fault before the throne of God," and so shall we be.

We have thus described, beloved, the people in Heaven without fault before the throne. We have been necessarily brief, and we might have enlarged considerably, by observing how they are without fault *in the opinion of others,* and *in their own opinion,* for now they cannot see any fault in themselves. But, best of all, they are without fault *in God's opinion,* for even the scrutinizing eye of Jehovah sees no fault in them. He looks upon them, and beholds not the shadow of a stain. That God, 'who sees every little insect in the air, and every creeping thing at the bottom of the sea, can perceive nothing wrong in His people in Heaven; no, nor even here, when He considers them in Christ. But more especially then, when we shall be completely sanctified by the Spirit, there shall be no indwelling corruption, no original sin, all that is sinful in us shall be gone; and God Himself upon His throne shall say, "They are without fault before Me." As He looks upon the living stones in the. Heavenly Temple, perfectly joined together with the vermilion cement of Christ's blood, He will say of them all, "They are without fault."

II. Now, let us inquire, WHO ARE THESE PEOPLE THAT ARE WITHOUT FAULT?

"Oh!" says one, "they are the apostles." Certainly, they are "without fault."

Another says, "They are some eminent saints such as Noah, Elijah, and Daniel." No; not them exclusively, beloved. Another friend says, "They are some faithful ministers who preach the truth very boldly; therefore they are without fault before the throne." No; they are not the only ones who are without fault; I will tell you who they are. "I looked, and, lo, a Lamb stood on the Mount Sion, and with

Him an hundred forty and four thousand, having His Father's name written in their foreheads." "After this I beheld, and, lo, a great multitude, which no man could number, of all nations, and kindreds, and people, and tongues, stood before the throne, and before the Lamb, clothed with white robes, and palms in their hands; and cried with a loud voice, saying, Salvation to our God which sitteth upon the throne:, and unto the Lamb." These are the faultless people; the chosen ones of God, the elect; these are they who have the Father's name written in their foreheads; those whom God selected out of the world to show forth His praise; the hundred and forty-four thousand, and the multitude which no man could number who were redeemed from among men. It does not matter whether they have been great sinners or little sinners, they are all "without fault before the throne" now; it matters not whether they have been swearers, drunkards, whoremongers, or what not, they are "without fault before the throne" if they are but amongst the number whom God hath chosen and sanctified. It matters not what they were; it matters not whether men despised them, or found fault with them; we care not whether they have been put in the pillory of scorn, and hoofed and hissed at by mankind, all 'the elect are "without fault" in the person of Jesus Christ; and they shall all be at the last bright and glorious day before the throne in person "without fault" in themselves, when God shall gather home His people, and glorify His ransomed ones. *They* are without fault; they are without fault before the throne; they are those whom God hath chosen, those who have their Father's name in their foreheads.

By reading the earlier part of this chapter, you will see that *they were all redeemed persons.* "The hundred and forty and four thousand, which were *redeemed front the earth.*" "These were *redeemed from among men,* being the firstfruits unto God and to the Lamb." All who were redeemed shall stand before God without speck or blemish. We will not go into the doctrinal part of this subject, but simply speak of it as a matter of experience. "They are without fault." Do you ask, beloved, "Am I one of the redeemed?" Canst thou say that the blood of the Lamb has been sprinkled upon thy lintel, and thy door post? Hast thou, by faith, sat down and fed on that Paschal Lamb? Is He thy rod, thy stay, thy all in all, thy very existence? Can thy faith lay her hand on that dear head of His, and there confess thy sin? Canst thou see traces of His blood on thy conscience? Hast thou marks of His blood on thy soul? Art thou blood-washed? Hast thou felt that Jesus Christ is thine? Canst thou say,

"I'm a poor sinner, and nothing at all,
But Jesus Christ is my all in all"?

Canst thou see the purchase price given for thee? Canst thou sing, —

"Oh! how sweet to feel the flowing
Of his sin-atoning blood!
With Divine assurance knowing
He hath made my peace with God"?

If so, though thou mayest be loaded with sin, though conscience may condemn thee, though Satan may bring all thy faults before thee, thou shalt be "without fault before the throne of God." Thou mayest have been a black and gross sinner, thou mayest have been a great backslider, thou mayest have been horribly wicked, almost as bad as the devil himself; thou mayest have had risings of corruption, so horrible that thou darest not reveal them to thy fellow-man; thou mayest be the subject of insinuations so vile and black that thou puttest thy hand to thy mouth to prevent their finding utterance; the flesh may be struggling so hard against the spirit that thou dost scarcely know which shall have the predominance, and thou art crying, "*If* it be so, why am I thus?" — it may be that thou art lying down, self-condemned and law-condemned, fearing that the sword of Justice will smite thy head from thy shoulders; and yet, with all this, thou shalt one day be "without fault before the throne of God," for thou hast been redeemed by Christ's atoning blood. O beloved, when I look back upon my past life, I am horrified at the thought of what I should have come to if God had left me to work out my own righteousness! I was the subject of black thoughts and sad feelings, I sinned against early warnings and pious training, against God, against my own soul and body; and yet I know that, notwithstanding all these sins, I shall one day be "*without* fault before the throne of God." Possibly I may be addressing some man who has been notoriously guilty of swearing, and drunkenness, and every filthy vice, yet he has come to be a believer in Christ; or perhaps he is saying, "I am condemned, there is nothing but hell for me; I know I cannot be pardoned." Nay, poor sinner, if thou art trusting in Jesus, God's law cannot condemn twice. If God's law has condemned thee, God's grace absolves thee, if thou tremblest at God's Word, and sayest, "*I* am a sinner, but I trust the Savior." Recollect the apostle's message, "*This* is a faithful saying, and worthy of all acceptation, that Christ Jesus came into the world to save sinners; of whom I am chief;" — as if Paul would say that you cannot go further in sin than the chief of sinners went. What sayest thou to this, O drunkard? One day, the Lord having mercy on thee, thou shalt stand, white as driven snow, before the Majesty on high. What sayest thou to this, O thou whose mouth has been stained with black oaths? If thou hast fled to Jesus to be saved, one day, unblemished and complete, thou shalt join in the hallelujahs of the glorified before the throne of God. O youth, though thou hast gone into the very kennel of sin, and raked up all that is vile and base; though thou hast gone down, down, down, till it seemed impossible for thee to take another step into the hell of sin; even thou shalt stand "*without* fault before the throne of God," if thou art a believer, trusting in the blood of Jesus, and hast that blood applied to thy soul. And thou, O woman, outcast, lost, ruined; though thou dost hide thy face, ashamed to bear the gaze of man, and comest with stealthy steps into God's house, as if afraid to be seen, for thou knowest what thou hast been; ay, but a woman, who was a sinner, once washed the Savior's feet with her tears, and why? Because He had washed her heart with blood; — and, O thou poor, guilty Magdalene, there is blood that can wash even thee! Though thou hast stains as black as hell upon thee, Christ's blood can wash them out; that precious blood can take away all thy sins. His blood availed for me, and, having availed for me, where shall I find another whose guilt shall go beyond the merit of His sacrifice, whose crimes shall exceed His power to save? Never shall I find such an one, for Christ has boundless grace. I always love that phrase of Hart's, —

"A *sinner is a sacred thing,*

The Holy Ghost hath made him so."

Ah! let me know that I am addressing such a sinner! I will preach the gospel to real, *bona-fide,* actual, positive sinners; and no flesh and blood shall stop me for evermore in all my sermons, as long as God gives me life and breath, breaching to those real sinners. As for your sham sinners, the people, who talk very daintily of being sinners, I have no good opinion of them. John Berridge said that he kept a rod for sham beggars, and I will keep one for these pretenders. I love to see one who feels himself to be a real sinner; not the one who says, just by way of compliment, that he is a sinner; not the one who can read the Ten Commandments all through, and say that he has not broken any of them; but the real sinner, the downright guilty man, the man who is a thorough sinner, and knows it, that is the man to whom I like to preach the gospel. O sinner, — you, *you,* you, — if you are trusting in Christ's name, and if His blood has been sprinkled on your conscience, shall yet stand before the throne of God "*without* fault." Or, as the good man in Yorkshire said, when he was dying, and someone told him he had been a great sinner, "Ah!" said he, "I have been a great sinner, but there is a crown in Heaven which Gabriel cannot wear; it will fit no head but mine, and I shall wear it, too, for I am bought and paid for by the blood of Christ; and I shall be with Him soon." Bought and paid for by the blood of Christ, thou also, believing soul, shalt be "*without* fault before the throne of God."

Beloved, there is one thought that will suggest itself to some of you, and that is, *there are some of your relatives that are "without fault! before the throne of God."* There is a dear, pious Mother, on whose knees you sat in childhood, over whose grave you wept: and she is "without fault before the throne." You loved her, but when you look back, you can see that there was a little fault of some kind in her; perhaps she loved her children too much, there was some fault or other that she had: but she has no fault now.

And there, husband, is your beloved wife, who cheered you on your way; you look back, and almost faultless as you in your fondness deemed her, yet you feel that she was not quite free from some little error: but she is "without fault before the throne" now. If you could behold her now, you would see her, — as the Interpreter described the pilgrims who had been washed, — "fair as the moon." Mother, there is your daughter; and there are our brothers and sisters who have crossed the flood. When speaking on this subject of re-union with departed friends, we can say, —

"E'en now, by faith, we join our hands
With those that went before;
And greet the blood-besprinkled bands,
On the eternal shore!"

The members of our churches have ascended up to our Father, and to their Father, and to Christ's Father, and now "they are without fault before the throne of God." Oh, to be "without fault"? If I might ask one thing of God, if it were not sinful to ask such a thing, methinks I would ask, "Let me die now, that I may go and be without fault before Thy throne!"

"O that the happy word were given, —
Loose me, and let me rise to Heaven,
And wrap myself in God!"

Why are we afraid to die? What are the pains, the groans, the dying struggle? It is the paying of a penny for a pound to go through them, that so we may get to Heaven.

"Oh I if my Lord would come and meet,
My soul should stretch her wings in haste,
Fly fearless through death's iron gate,
Nor feel the terrors as she passed.'

"They are without fault before the throne of God." Yes, they are there; and perhaps we, too, shall be there in a few days. I am no prophet, nor the son of a prophet; but it may be that one of us, who loves the Lord, will be with Him before long; but whether it be so or not, whichever one of us is to depart, we know that it is to be "without fault." So we are not afraid, whoever it may be; if we are of the Lord's family, we shall be "*without* fault before the throne of God."

III. We can only very briefly explain the third part of the subject, which is, to show where They ARE WHO ARE WITHOUT FAULT: "They are without fault before the throne of God." "Before the throne of God." We know what it is to lie *beneath the throne;* for we sometimes sing, —

"We would no longer lie
Like slaves beneath the throne."

We know what it is, at times, to be *far off from the throne.* Satan stands blocking up the way to the throne. It is as much as we can do to push past him, and get a word from the Master. Have you not sometimes thought that you were *behind the throne,* and that God could not look at you, — that He could look at all His servants, but not at you, for you were behind the throne? The proud infidel wants to get *on the throne,* but even if it were possible for him to be in Heaven, he could not do that, for he would neither be beneath the throne, nor behind the throne, nor on the throne, but he would have to stand *before* it to be condemned.

But the saints of God are all before the throne. Why? Because *they can then always look at God, and God can always look at them.* They stand before the throne. That is all I want here, to stand before the throne of God. If I could always be before it, if I could always see the light of His countenance, always feel the comforting assurance of being safe in Jesus, always taste His love, always receive of His grace, that were enough for me. And if that is' sweet here, how much sweeter shall it be to bow before the throne hereafter, and "unceasing sing His love"! At times, here, we are so far off the throne, that we can scarcely tell where it is; and if it were not a glorious high throne, being so far off, we should never be able to see it.

But it is one that you can see a long way off; yet there "they are" immediately "before the throne," drinking in bliss with their eyes and ears, with their whole soul lost in Jesus, standing perpetually before the throne!

That part of the verse needs so much illustration to explain it, that I am afraid, more briefly, to venture on it. I, therefore, must, for the present, leave it. "They are without fault before the throne of God." But, beloved, there is one serious question which I shall put to you, and that is, *Shall we be without fault before the throne hereafter?* The answer rests here; are we without fault before the throne of God now, through the justifying blood and righteousness of Christ? Are we able to say, —

"Jesus, thy blood and righteousness,
My beauty are, my glorious dress"?

If so, the Christian cannot change his position in God's sight. He is now justified, and shall be so hereafter; there is now no condemnation, and he never can be condemned. "Ah!" says someone, "I cannot say as much as that." Well, then, are you full of fault in your own eyes? Hath God the Spirit shown you your sin? Next to being shown the righteousness of Christ, one of the best evidences of His working is our being aware of our own sinfulness. Do you, then, see your own sinfulness? Have you been brought down till all that nature has set upon the throne has been cast in the dust, and that garment which you gloried in has been torn away, and you stand naked, and worse than naked; filthy, and worse than filthy; diseased, and worse than diseased; polluted in heart, worse than dead; worse than lying among the slain; like those that go down to the pit, those that have been long since dead; — nay, if possible, worse than that? Can you feel as if you have been brought down, down, down, till desperation seized you, and you had nothing to rest in? Can you feel that you have been stripped to the lowest degree, and all that you possessed and gloried in has been scattered to the winds? And can you now say, "Out of the depths have I cried unto Thee, O Lord"? Well, if you have plenty of faults here, and have known them, and been taught them, and feel that you cannot overcome them of yourself, you shall be "without fault before the throne of God" by-and-by, for the Lord will not bring you to that state of soul-distress, and self-despair, without bringing you also to peace and liberty. O sinner, is not this glorious news to thee? Thou knowest thy sinnership, thou canst understand that thou art a sinner; that is the first thing thou needest to know. We sometimes sing, —

"All the fitness He requireth,
Is to feel your need of Him."

But I love the next two lines of the verse, —

"This He gives you;
'Tis the Spirit's rising beam."

Good old Martin Luther used to say, "The devil comes to me, and says, 'Martin, thou art an exceeding sinner.' "....I know that very well," said Martin, "*and* I'll cut off thy head with thine own sword; for Christ died for sinners, and the more I feel I am a sinner, the more evidence I have that Christ died for me." Oh! to know our sinnership! to recognize it in our inmost soul! — that is blessed! And there is only one more step, and that God shall lead us to, — to put us in Christ Jesus in our own feelings; for we are already in Him in the eternal covenant, if so be we are out of ourselves. Oh! trust Him, *trust Him,* TRUST Him, TRUST HIM! He is a good Christ, and a great Christ. Ah, great sinner! trust thou to His blood and righteousness; and thou, even thou, the filthiest, the vilest, the off-cast, the unde-serving, the ill-deserving, and hell-deserving sinner, even thou shalt yet wear a blood-washed robe, spotless and white; even thou shalt sing the perfect song, and be perfect thyself, for thou shalt be "without fault before the throne', of God."

Chapter Thirty - Letters Concerning Settlement in London

I do not know whether all of you can go with me here; but I think you must, in some instance or other, be forced to see that God has indeed ordained your inher-itance for you. If you cannot, I can. I can see a thousand chances, as men would call them, all working together, like wheels in a great piece of machinery, to fix me just where I am; and I can look back to a hundred places where, if one of those little wheels had run awry, if one of those little atoms in the great whirlpool of my exist-ence had started aside, I might have been anywhere but here, and occupying a very different position. If you cannot say this, I know I can with emphasis; and [can trace God's hand back even to the period of my birth. Through every step I have taken, I can feel that indeed God has allotted my inheritance for me. If any of you are so willfully beclouded that you will not see the hand of God in your being, and will insist that all has been done by your own will without the control of Provi-dence, — that you have been left to steer your own course across the ocean of ex-istence, and that you are where you are because your own hand guided the tiller, and your own arm directed the rudder, — all I can say is, my experience, and the experience of many now in this place, would rise in testimony against you, and we should say. "Verily, it is not in man that walketh to direct his steps." "Man proposes, but God disposes;" and the God of Heaven is not unoccupied, but is engaged in over-ruling, arranging, ordering, altering, and working all things according to the good pleasure of His will. — C. H. S.

THE Church in New Park Street was sadly reduced in numbers, and from the position of its meeting-house there seemed no prospect before it but ultimate dissolution; but there were a few in its midst who never ceased to pray for a gra-cious revival. The congregation became Smaller and smaller; yet they hoped on, and hoped ever. Let it never be forgotten that, when they were at their worst, the Lord remembered them, and gave to them such a tide of prosperity that they have since had no mourning, or doubting, but many, many years of continued rejoicing.

('The following official record shows in what condition the New Park Street Church was at the time that Mr. Spurgeon preached his first sermon in London. Although there had not been any additions during the year, and the total income for 1853 had been less than £300, the members of the church and congregation were so concerned about the spiritual welfare of their neighbors that, without waiting for the election of a new Pastor, they had subscribed the amount needed to secure the services of a city missionary for five years: —

"Monthly church-meeting, 14th Dec., 1853.

"brother Low presided.

"The minutes of the last church-meeting were read, and the correctness of the entry confirmed.

"Agreed to grant the use of the chapel to the London Baptist Association for the holding of their annual meeting on Wednesday, the 11th of January, 1854.

"The letter proposed to be sent from this church to that meeting was read, approved, and ordered to be signed by brother Low as presiding deacon. It was as follows: — To the Ministers and Messengers composing the London Baptist Association, the baptized Church of Christ assembling in New Park Street, Southwark, sendeth Christian salutation.

"Dear Brethren,

"'We regret that, during the past year, we. have made no additions to our numbers in consequence of our being without a Pastor, and that we have nothing particular to communicate to the Association, except that a friend has presented the sum of one hundred pounds, on condition that our church and congregation would raise the like amount, with the view to securing the services of a missionary in our locality, with the aid of the London City Mission, for five years.

We have the pleasure to state that our friends have contributed the full sum required for the carrying out of this important object. We enclose our statistics. 'Brethren, pray for us.'

"Signed on behalf of the church, at our church-meeting, 14th Dec., 1853,

"'JAMES LOW, Presiding Deacon.'")

(Mr. Spurgeon wrote two letters to his father, recounting his first experiences in London. A considerable portion of the earlier one is missing, including the first sheet, and also the end of the epistle. Evidently, the young preacher had been relating what the deacons had told him concerning the falling-off in the congregations, for the part of his letter that has been preserved begins as follows: —)

"...me that the people would be back at the first blast of the trumpet which gives a certain sound....The people are Calvinistic, and they could not get on with anything else. They raised £100 last week for a city missionary, so that they have the sinews of war. The deacons told me that, if I were there three Sundays, there would be no room anywhere. They say that all the London popular ministers are gospel-men, and are plain, simple, and original. They have had most of the good preachers of our denomination out of the country; but they have never asked one of them twice, for they gave them such philosophical, or dry, learned sermons, that once was enough. I am the only one who has been asked twice, the only one who has been heard with pleasure by all. I told them they did not know what they were doing, nor whether they were in the body or out of the body; they were so starved, that a morsel of gospel was a treat to them.

The portraits of Gill and Rippon — large as life — hang in the vestry. Lots of them said I was Rippon over again.

"It is God's doing. I do not deserve it; — they are mistaken. I only mention facts. I have not exaggerated; nor am I very exalted by it, for to leave my own dear people makes it a painful pleasure. God wills it.

"The only thing which pleases me is, as you will guess, that I am right about College. I told the deacons that I was not a College man, and they said, 'That is to us a special recommendation, for you would not have: much savor or unction if you came from College.'

"As to a school, or writing to my deacons in case I do not go, I shall feel happiest if left to manage alone, for I am sure that any letter to my deacons would not do any good. A church is free to manage its own affairs. We are in loving unity now, and they will improve. But churches of the Baptist denomination would think it an infringement of their rules and liberties to be touched in the least by persons of other denominations in any matter which is their own concern. I should at once say, and you would not mind my saying so, 'I *had nothing to do with the hole; I never asked my father to write it; anti the deacons must do as they please about laying' it before the church.'*

"I feel pleasure in the thought that it will not now be necessary, and I feel that, if it had been, I should have been equally contented. Many other ministers have schools; it is a usual thing. It is not right to say, 'If you mean to be a minister;' for I *am* one, and have been for two years as much a minister as any man in England; and probably very much more so, since in that time I have preached more than 600 times.

"More soon."

(The allusions to a school refer to the following advertisement which Mr. Spurgeon had inserted in a Cambridge newspaper: —

"No. 60, Park Street, Cambridge. Mr. C. H. Spurgeon begs to inform his numerous friends that, after Christmas, he intends taking six or seven young gentlemen as day pupils. He will endeavor to the utmost to impart a good commercial Education. The ordinary routine will include Arithmetic, Algebra, Geometry, and Mensuration; Grammar and Composition; Ancient and Modern History; Geography, Natural History, Astronomy, Scripture, and Drawing. Latin and the elements of Greek and French, if required. Terms, £5 per annum.")

"No. 60, Park Street,
"Cambridge,
"December __, 1853.

"My Dear Father,

"I concluded rather abruptly before; — but you are often called out from your writing, and therefore can excuse it in me. I hardly know what I left unsaid. I hope *to* be at home three days. I think of running down from London on Tuesday (January) 3rd, and to go home by Bury on Friday, 6th. I hope it will be a sweet visit although a short one.

"Should I be settled in London, I will come and see you often. I do not anticipate going there with much pleasure. I am contented where I am; but if God has more for me to do, then let me go and trust in Him. The London people are rather higher in Calvinism than I am; but I have succeeded in bringing one church to my own views, and will trust, with Divine assistance, to do the same with another. I am a Calvinist; I love what someone called 'glorious Calvinism,' but 'Hyperism' is too hot-spiced for my palate.

"I found a relation in London; a daughter of Thomas Spurgeon, at Ballingdon. On the Monday, she came and brought the unmarried sister, who you will remember was at: home when we called last Christmas. I shall have no objection to preach for Mr. Langford on Wednesday, January 4th, if he wishes it.

"I spent the Monday in going about London, climbed to the top of St. Paul's, and left some money with the booksellers. [20]

"My people are very sad; some wept bitterly at the sight of me, although I made no allusion to the subject in the pulpit, as it is too uncertain to speak of publicly. It is Calvinism they want in London, and any Arminian preaching will not be en- dure, d. Several in the church are far before me in theological acumen; they would not admit that it is so, but they all expressed their belief that my originali- ty, or even eccentricity, was the very thing to draw a London audience. The chapel is one of the finest in the denomination; somewhat in the style of our Cambridge Museum. A Merry Christmas to you all; a Happy New Year; and the blessing of the God of Jacob!

"Yours affectionately,

"C. H. SPURGEON."

(At the laying of the foundation stone of the Metropolitan Tabernacle, Mr. Spurgeon's father made the following interesting reference to the College inci- dent and his son's coming to London: —

"My Lord Mayor, I am very happy to meet you to-night. We are Essex men; we come from Colchester. Colchester has something to boast of great men. The chief physician of London comes from Colchester; the Lord Mayor comes from Col- chester; and I need not tell you who else. I have never had the headache in my life, friends; but if I ever had it, it would have been to-day. I feel nervous and ex- cited. But I do feel very happy to-day to acknowledge my faults; and when a man confesses his faults, he has done a great deal towards amending them. I always thought my son did wrong in coming to London; now you see that I was wrong. I always thought he was wrong in not going to College; I tried three or four hours with him, one night, with a dear friend who loved him; but it was no use. He said 'No, I will never go to College, except in strict obedience to you as a father.' There I left the matter; and I see that God has been with him, though I thought it was a wrong step in him to go to London. And I thought it was a wrong step for me to come here to-night; but perhaps I may be mistaken again. I can tell you it is one of the happiest days of my life. I feel beyond myself when I think of the kind- ness that has been shown to my son when but a youth. I ascribe it all to God's goodness, and the earnest prayers of His people. He has been exposed to tempta- tion from every source, and even now, my friends, he is not free from it. You have prayed for him, and God has sustained him. Let me entreat you to continue your prayers. Every one here to-night, go home, and pray for your Pastor.

A meeting like this is enough to carry a man beyond himself, and fill his heart with pride; but the grace of God is all-sufficient. Several persons said to me — I do not know what their motive was, — 'Your son will never last in London six months; he has no education.' I said, 'You are terribly mistaken; he has the best education that can possibly be had; God has been his Teacher, and he has had earthly teachers, too.' I knew, as far as education went, he could manage London very well. Then they said his health would fail; but it has not failed him yet. He has had enough to shake his constitution, it is true; but God has been very merciful to him. I think, if there is one thing that would crown my happiness to-day, it would have been to see his grandfather here. I should have loved to see him with us. He said, 'Boy, don't ask me to go, I am too old; I am overcome with God's goodness and mercy to me.' He is always talking about you, Pastor. Old people like to have something to talk about, so he always talks about his grandson. And next to that, I should like, my dear friends, to have seen his Mother here. I believe, under God's grace, his Mother was the means of leading him to Christ.")

In *The Preachers' Annual* for 1877, in an article by Rev. G. T. Dowling on "Candidating," I read as follows: — "Charles Spurgeon was not even seriously thought of as a prospective pastor the first time he preached in London. Months passed by before he was again invited to spend a Sabbath; and even when a call was extended, it was by no means unanimous. Some families even left the church because 'that boy' was called."

This is given as a proof that successful preachers frequently produce a poor impression as candidates. This may be a general fact, but it was a pity to fabricate an instance. The truth is exactly the contrary. The moment after my first sermon was preached,. I was invited by the principal deacon to supply for six months, for he felt sure that, at a church-meeting, which would at once be held, such a resolution would be passed. I declined his offer, for I thought it too hast),; but I promised to preach on alternate Sabbaths during the next month, and this was done, and followed up immediately by a further invitation. No one person left the church to my knowledge, and the resolution inviting me was as nearly unanimous as possible, only one man and four women voting to the contrary, all of these becoming in after time most friendly to me. I only mention the incident as a specimen of the manner in which advocates of a theory too often manufacture their instances, and as a warning to friends to be slow in believing anything which they may hear or read about public persons.

(The three Sabbaths on which Mr. Spurgeon agreed to preach in London were January 1st, 15th, and 29th, 1854; but before the last-named date, the church had already taken definite action with a view to securing his services permanently. He had preserved, amongst his most treasured papers, the following letters, which are now published for the first time, together with a correct copy of his reply to the invitation to supply the pulpit at New Park Street Chapel for six months: —

"15, Creed Lane,
"Ludgate Hill,
"London,
"Jan. 25, 1854.

"My Dear Sir,

"It is with pleasure that I write these few lines to you hoping, through Divine grace, you are well and happy.

"You will remember that I gave you a hint of the intention of the members of the church to request the deacons to call a special church-meeting for the purpose of inviting you to preach for a certain period. That special meeting has taken place this evening, and I am most happy to tell you that, at the private request of Mr. W. Olney, I moved a resolution that you should be invited for six months. Old Mr. Olney was in the chair, — Mr. Low being unwell, but strongly in favor of your coming'. We had a full vestry, and there were only five against you; three out of the five rarely occupy their places with us. It was a happy meeting, and I hope that God, in His tender mercy, will send you to us, and that you will see your way clear to come; and should the Great Shepherd of the flock make you the instrument to revive this ancient church, we shall be glad indeed, and shall give God all the glory. For my own part, since I have been at Park Street, I never saw such a desire on the part of the brethren toward a minister as there is at the present time toward you. We are cast down, but not destroyed. It has been a trying' time to us; our church is scattered, but there is a goodly remnant filling their places constantly, and a band of young members growing up, requiring the watchful care of a good Pastor.

I know you are being persuaded not to come among us; but I will say, 'come and try us.' I hope next week to spend half a day with you, if possible, and then I will tell you more than I can write. I should have written before, but I thought I would wait for the result of this evening's meeting. We don't want an idle preacher; I know we shall not have *that* in you. As I have said before, we are cast down, but there is room to rise; and I believe God is about to answer our poor prayers, though they have been offered weak in faith. The different societies in connection with the chapel will be revived with an active Pastor as our leader. There may be a few against you, but I assure you it is only on the part of those who are as unstable as water, and seldom are at chapel. You will find a great many faithful friends; and should the Holy Spirit lead you to decide for New Park Street after you have received the request from the deacons, I hope and pray that you will prove a blessing to thousands, — that God will give you a great number of souls for your crown of rejoicing, that, like Rippon, and Cox, Collier, Bennet, and others, you will be a guide to thousands of ignorant travelers to conduct them to the cross of Jesus. I hope I shall soon see you, and if it shall please God that it shall add to His glory for you to come among us, I will thank Him, and do all I can so far as my influence is concerned, for your temporal and spiritual happiness.

"I have enclosed a copy of the resolution which I moved at the meeting, and which Mr. Ward seconded. I conclude with my Christian love to you, hoping you will be wisely directed in all your ways, and believe me to be,

"Your sincere friend and brother in Christ,

"WILLIAM CUTLER, Superintendent of the Sunday School."

"To The Rev. C. H. Spurgeon."

"Resolved, That the ministry of the Rev. Charles H. Spurgeon having been very generally appreciated, he be invited to supply the pulpit for six months; and that the deacons be requested to communicate this resolution to him, and to make the necessary arrangements with him."

"Market Street,
"Bermondsey,
"London,

258

"My Dear Sir,

"I cannot refrain from informing you of the very satisfactory result of our church-meeting last evening. It was called specially to confer as to giving you a further invitation. There was a very large attendance, and a most cordial and hearty enthusiasm on your behalf. I do trust God will incline your heart to come among us. He has already given both you and us clear indications that there is a great work for you to do among us. There is one consideration that makes me feel very deeply on this subject, and that is, my brother Henry. He has so repeatedly expressed his regard for your ministry, and his desire to attend it, that I do trust there are already some impressions for good on his heart. Oh, that the Holy Spirit may seal these good impressions, and make them abiding, and to end in his conversion to God! May you, my dear friend, be indeed his spiritual teacher, to lead him to Christ! I do most earnestly pray that it may be so. [21] Then, also, there are the young men at my father's. It is with great difficulty they can be induced to enter any place of worship, yet they will come and hear you, and I believe will continue to do so. I have most earnestly prayed that you may be directed aright in this matter, and I trust already your heart is turned towards us.

"I most heartily promise you sympathy and co-operation; and anything that lies in my power to promote your comfort and usefulness shall be done. This is, I am certain, the general feeling throughout the church; and if you come for six months, will, I believe, be the unanimous one. There is now but one family not prepared to vote for you, and I believe a short acquaintance with you will soon change their minds. Hoping you will have a happy Sabbath with us next Lord's-day, and give us then your affirmative reply to our invitation,

"I remain,

"Yours in Christian bonds,

"WILLIAM OLNEY."

MR. JOHN T. OLNEY wrote: —

"We had a very delightful church-meeting last evening. We met at 7, and closed at 9 o'clock; and, during the whole evening, not a word was spoken which did not consort with the Heavenly precept, 'Walk in love.' The vestry was well filled, great unanimity prevailed, and a delightful satisfaction beamed in the countenances of all the members. The special church-meeting then held was convened by a memorial requesting the deacons that it might be holden to invite your services for six months, subject to the approval of the majority of the church. The memorial was signed by most of the influential members of the church, so that the deacons cheerfully convened the meeting. There were a great many speeches made, because we were anxious all should speak out most fully and freely their opinions. The resolution may be said to have been carried almost unanimously, — only one hand and four small kid gloves having been held up in answer to the Chairman's inquiry, 'Any on the contrary?'

These five friends were quite friendly with the majority, and will continue to fill their places with us. They object to you on the ground that they consider you do not use sufficient reverence in prayer. This was very well answered by Mr. Carr, and some of the other brethren. Apart from this unimportant exception, the members were quite unanimous in giving you a cheerful, cordial, and loving invitation for six months. I never expected we could have been nearly so much united in sentiment respecting any man to occupy the pulpit of a church consisting of many belonging to the old church at Carter Lane under Dr. Rippon, and of many introduced by Dr. Angus and Mr. Smith. I am sure you will find the church render to you all that esteem and affection you will desire, and be ready to sustain you by their prayers and co-operation, and I am equally certain that you will not be lacking in your efforts to supply them with the Bread of Life, and the Good Wine of the Kingdom. I hope and pray that you may be led by what appears to my mind, and I trust will appear to yours also, to be the guiding of Providence, — to accept the invitation of the church. The church, the neighborhood, and the denomination in London, have, I think, need of the talents and order of preaching which God has, for good and gracious purposes, given you to possess.")

(Mr. Spurgeon's reply to the official letter from the deacons was. as follows: —)

"No. 60, Park Street,

"Cambridge,

"January 27th, 1854.

"To James Low, Esq.,

"My Dear Sir,

"I cannot help feeling intense gratification at the unanimity of the church at New Park Street in relation to their invitation to me. Had I been uncomfortable in my present situation, I should have felt unmixed pleasure at the prospect Providence seems to open up before me;. but having a devoted and loving people, I feel I know not how.

"One thing I know, namely, that I must soon be severed from them by necessity, for they do not raise sufficient to maintain me in comfort. Had they done so, I should have turned a deaf ear to any request to leave them, at least for the present. But now my Heavenly Father drives me forth from this little Garden of Eden; and whilst I see that I must go out, I leave it with reluctance, and tremble to tread the unknown land before me.

"When I first ventured to preach at Waterbeach, I only accepted an invitation for three months, on the condition that if, in that time, I should see good reason for leaving, or they on their part should wish for it, I should be at liberty to cease supplying, or they should have the same power to request me to do so before the expiration of the time.

"Now, with regard to a six months' invitation from you, I have no objection to the length of time, but rather approve of the prudence of the church in wishing to have one so young as myself on an extended period of probation. But I write, after well weighing the matter, to say positively that I cannot, I *dare not*, accept an unqualified invitation for so long a time. My objection is not to the length of the time of probation, but it ill becomes a youth to promise to preach to a London congregation so long, until he knows *them* and they know *him*. I would engage to supply for three months of that time, and then, should the congregation fail, or the church disagree, I would reserve to myself liberty, without breach of engagement, to retire; and you could, on your part, have the right to dismiss me without seeming to treat me ill. Should I see no reason for so doing, and the church still retain their wish for me, I can remain the other three months, either with or without the formality of a further invitation; but even during that time

260

(the second three months), I should not like to regard myself as a fixture, in case of ill-success, but would only be a supply, liable to a fortnight's dismissal or resignation.

"Perhaps this is not business-like, — I do not know; but this is the course I should prefer, if it would be agreeable to the church.

Enthusiasm and popularity are often the crackling of thorns, and soon expire. I do not wish to be a hindrance if I cannot be a help.

"*With* regard to coming *at once,* I think I must: not. My own deacons just hint that I ought to finish the quarter here; though, by *ought,* they mean simply, 'Pray do so, if you can.' This would be too long a delay. I wish to help them until they can get supplies, which is only to be done with great difficulty; and as I have given you four Sabbaths, I hope you will allow me to give them four in return. I would give them the first and second Sabbaths in February, and two more in a month or six weeks' time. I owe them much for their kindness, although they insist that the debt lies on their side. Some of them hope, and almost pray, that you may be tired in three months, so that I may be again sent back to them.

"*Thus,* my dear sir, I have honestly poured out my heart to you.

You are too kind. You will excuse me if I err, for I wish to do right to you, to my people, and to all, as; being not mine own, but bought with a price.

"*I* respect the honesty and boldness of the small minority, and only wonder that the number was not greater. I pray God that, if He does not see fit that I should remain with you, the majority may be quite as much the other way at the end of six months, so that I may never divide you into parties.

"Pecuniary matters I am well satisfied with. And now one thing is due to every minister, and I pray you to remind the church of it, namely, that in private, as well as in public, they must all earnestly wrestle in prayer to the God of our Lord Jesus Christ, that I may be sustained in the great work.

"I am, with the best wishes for your health, and the greatest respect,

"Yours truly,

"C. H. SPURGEON."

(The following letter was written to the Uncle mentioned in Chapter 26.

The swift transition from innocent mirth to deep solemnity was characteristic of Mr. Spurgeon to the end of his days.)

"75, Dover Road,
"Borough,
"March 2, 1854.

"Dear Uncle,

"I shall be extremely obliged if you will, at the earliest opportunity, forward to my address, as above, by rail or otherwise, the books I purchased of you. I have been expecting them for many months; but thought that, perhaps, you had no means of sending them. Send them to any station, carriage I will pay.

"Of course, I shall not look for an answer to my note; I never shall again expect to see your handwriting to me. 'Hope deferred maketh' — never mind, — let Solomon finish the sentence. I have a birch in pickle for you; and when I come to your house, I shall use it with but little mercy, so you had need have on your very thickest skin. I might say some sharp things about the matter, but I will save them until I sit in your easy chair, or you are seated in mine. When you are in London, you will be in for a sound scolding if you do not come to see me. I do not think you dare come, and I am sure you will not venture to stay away. I promise you a hearty welcome.

"75, Dover Road,
"Borough of Southwark,
"London.

"Can you see my address? I send my very best respects to your good wife; she is certainly worth more than you, if I am to value her by the number of letters I have received.

"But, to joke no more, you have heard that I am now a Londoner, and a little bit of a celebrity. No College could have put me in a higher situation. Our place is one of the pinnacles of the denomination. But I have a great work to do, and have: need of all the prayers the sons of God can offer for me.

"I shall be glad to hear of your temporal and spiritual prosperity.

Do not, for a moment, imagine that I am cold towards you. My Master's one aim was to spread the spirit of love among His disciples; and I trust little things will never chill my love to the brethren. Permit me, most respectfully and lovingly, to inquire, '

How does the cause of God prosper?' 'How does your soul prosper?' 'How is your love to the precious name of Jesus?' I wish for myself and you much soul-prosperity. We cannot afford to live a useless life; the sands of time are too valuable to be allowed to run on unheeded. We have a work before us, and woe be unto us if we are idle or unfaithful servants! Blessed is the man who often talks with his God alone, and comes forth from his closet, like Moses from the mountain top, with a celestial glory on his brow!

Let us seek that blessing, and may God be ever with us!

Do not forget the books, and believe me to be —

"Yours truly,

"C. H. SPURGEON."

(The following letter was written by Mr. Spurgeon to the ladies with whom he had lodged at Cambridge: —)

"75, Dover Road,
"Borough,
"March, 1854.

"To the Misses Blunson,
"My Dear 'Friends,

"I have not forgotten you, although I have been silent so long. I have thought of your trials, and have requested of my Master that He would comfort and sustain you. If you have a portion in Him, your troubles will be blessings, and every grief will be turned into a mercy.

"I am very well, and everything goes on even better than I could have hoped. My chapel, though large, is crowded; the aisles are blocked up, and every niche is packed as full as possible. I expect to come and see you in about a month. I hope to be at Waterbeach the fourth Sabbath in April. I get on very well in my present lodgings; — but not better than with you, for that would be impossible. I had nothing to wish for better than I had, for your attention to me was beyond all praise. I cannot but feel very much for you, and only wish that I knew how I could serve you.

"I hope you will not give way to doubts and despondency; but do what you can, and leave the rest to God. Blessed is the man who has the God of Jacob for his Helper; he need not fear either want, or pain, or death. The more you can realize this, the happier will you become; and the only means for so doing is to hold frequent communion with God in prayer. Get alone with Jesus, and He will comfort your hearts, and restore your weary souls. I hope you have let your rooms. I think I shall stop at Mrs. Warricker's; but I will be sure to come and see you, and leave something to remember me by.

Trust in God, and be glad, and —

"Believe me to be,

"Yours truly,

"**C. H. SPURGEON.**"

The six months' probation was never fulfilled, for there was no need. The place was filled, the prayer-meetings were full of power, and the work of conversion was going on. A requisition for a special church-meeting, signed by fifty of the male members, was sent in to the deacons on April 12, the meeting was held on April I9, with the result mentioned in the following letter: —

"30, Gracechurch Street,
"April 20th, 1854.

"My Dear Young brother,

"I annex a copy of a resolution passed last evening at a numerously-attended special church-meeting held at New Park Street Chapel.

"If you feel it your duty to accept the invitation of the Church to become its Pastor, it will be desirable that you should obtain your dismission from the Church at Waterbeach to our Church as early as you can, in order that you may be in a position as a member to attend our church-meetings.

"I remain,

"My dear young brother,

"Yours affectionately,

"JAMES LOW, Chairman."

"**Rev, C. H. Spurgeon.**"

(*Copy of Resolution.*)

"At a special church-meeting, held on Wednesday evening, April 19th, 1854, at New Park Street Chapel, after prayer by two of the brethren, it was resolved unanimously, That while, as members of this Church, we desire to record with devout and fervent gratitude to God our estimation of the Rev. C. H. Spurgeon's services, during the period of his labors amongst us, we regard the extraordinary increase in the attendance upon the means of grace', both on Lord's-days and week-evenings, combined with the manifest fact that his ministry has secured the general approbation of the members, as an encouraging token that our Heavenly Father has directed his way towards us, in answer to the many prayers we have offered up for a suitable Pastor, — and as there are several inquirers desir-

263

ous of joining our fellowship, we consider it prudent to secure as early as possible his permanent settlement with us; — we, therefore, beg to tender our brother, the Rev. C. H. Spurgeon, a most cordial and affectionate invitation forthwith to become Pastor of this Church, and we pray that his services may be owned of God with an outpouring of the Holy Spirit, and a revival of religion in our midst, and that his ministry may be fruitful in the conversion of sinners, and the edification of those that believe."

(Mr. Spurgeon's letter, accepting the invitation to the pastorate, was as follows: —)

"75, Dover Road,
"Borough,
"April 28th, 1854.

"To the Baptist Church of Christ worshipping in New Park Street Chapel, Southwark,

"Dearly Beloved in Christ Jesus,

"I have received your unanimous invitation, 'as contained in a resolution passed by you on the 19th instant, desiring me to accept the pastorate among you. No lengthened reply is required; there is but one answer to so loving and cordial an invitation. I ACCEPT IT. I have not been perplexed as to what my reply should be, for many things constrain me thus to answer.

"I sought not to come to you, for I was the minister of an obscure but affectionate people; I never solicited advancement. The first note of invitation from your deacons came quite unlooked-for, and I trembled at the idea of preaching in London. I could not understand how it had come about, and even now I am filled with astonishment at the wondrous Providence. I would wish to give myself into the hands of our covenant God, whose wisdom directs all things. He shall choose for me: and so far as I can judge, this *is* His choice.

"I feel it to be a high honor to be the Pastor of a people who can mention glorious names as my predecessors, and I entreat of you to remember me in prayer, that I may realize the solemn responsibility of my trust.

Remember my youth and inexperience, and pray that these may not hinder my usefulness. I trust also that the remembrance of these will lead you to forgive mistakes I may make, or unguarded words I may utter.

"Blessed be the name of the Most High, if He has called me to this office, He will support me in it, — otherwise, how should a child, a youth, have the presumption thus to attempt the work which filled the heart and hands of Jesus?

"Your kindness to me has been very great, and my heart is knit unto you. I fear not *your* steadfastness, I fear my own. The gospel, I believe, enables me to venture great things, and by faith I venture this.

"I ask your co-operation in every good work; in visiting the sick, in bringing in inquirers, and in mutual edification.

"Oh, that I may be no injury to you, but a lasting benefit! I have no more to say, saving this, that if I have expressed myself in these few words in a manner unbecoming my youth and inexperience, you will not impute it to arrogance, but forgive my mistake.

"And now, commending you to our covenant God, the Triune Jehovah,
"I am,

"Yours to serve in the gospel,

"C. H. SPURGEON."

(Professor Everett says, concerning this period in Mr. Spurgeon's life: —
"He gave me prompt intimation of his call to New Park Street Chapel; and soon after his settlement there, I called upon him by appointment. I spent half a day with him, and he poured forth to me, without reserve, the full tale of his successes, telling me of the distinguished men who continually came to hear him, and of the encomiums pronounced on his delivery by elocutionists like Sheridan Knowles."

Pastor G. H. Davies, of Lisbon, North Dakota, thus records Sheridan Knowles' remarkable prophecy: —

"I was a student at Stepney, now Regent's Park College. Sheridan Knowles, the celebrated actor and play-writer, had just been baptized by Dr. Brock, and appointed our tutor in elocution. We had collected funds to give the grand old man a handsome Bible. The presentation was made one Wednesday afternoon. It was an occasion never to be forgotten, not only for the sake of Sheridan Knowles himself, but because of his prophecy concerning one of whom till then we knew nothing.

Immediately on entering, Mr. Knowles exclaimed, 'Boys, have you heard the Cambridgeshire lad?' None of us had heard him. 'Then, boys,' he continued, 'go and hear him at once.' This was after Mr., Spurgeon had been preaching at New Park: Street Chapel two Sundays. 'Go and hear him at once if you want to know how to preach. His name is Charles Spurgeon. He is only a boy, but he is the most wonderful preacher in the world. He is absolutely perfect in his oratory; and, beside that, a master in the art of acting. He has nothing to learn from me, or anyone else. He is simply perfect. He knows everything. He can do anything. I was once lessee of Drury Lane Theater; and were I still in that position, I would offer him a fortune to play for one season on the boards of that house. Why, boys, he can do anything he pleases with his audience! He can make them laugh, and cry, and laugh again, in five minutes. His power was never equaled. Now, mark my word, boys, *that young man will live lo be the greatest preacher of this or any other age. He will bring more souls to Christ than any man who ever proclaimed the gospel, not excepting the apostle Paul. His name will be known everywhere, and his Sermons will be translated into many of the languages of the world.*'"

Mr. Sheridan Knowles lived until 1862, and was able, therefore, to witness in great part the fulfillment of his own prophecy. His widow long survived him, and for some years was one of Mr. Spurgeon's company of faithful friends who gathered at Mentone; and when she also was "called home," she showed her appreciation of his work by leaving generous legacies to the Pastors' College and the Stockwell Orphanage.)

Chapter Thirty-One - Divine and Ordination

THERE is good reason for asking, concerning many practices, — Are these Scriptural, or are they only traditions of the fathers? A little Ritualism in one generation may develop into downright Popery in a few years; therefore it is well to take these things as they arise, and crush them in the bud. I do not believe that, among our Nonconformist churches, there is more than a fly or two of the priestly system in the pot of ointment, but even those flies should be purged out. Great evils have small beginnings; the little foxes are to be dreaded among the vines. Where so much is admirable, it is a pity that the specks and spots should be suffered to remain. We have a stern fight before us against Ritualistic Popery, and it is well to clear our decks of all lumber, and go into the controversy with clean hands. It is a tar more popular thing to find fault with other denominations: than to point out follies and failings among ourselves; but this consideration should never occur to the right-minded, except to be repulsed with a "Get thee behind me, Satan."

Confining myself to one branch of the subject, I ask, — *Whence comes the whole paraphernalia of* "ordination" *as observed among some Dissenters?*

Since there is no special gift to bestow, why in any case the laying on of empty hands? Since we cannot pretend to that mystic succession so much vaunted by Ritualists, why are men styled "regularly-ordained ministers"?

A man who has preached for years is Mr. Brown; but after his ordination, or recognition, he develops into the Rev. Mr. Brown, what important change has he undergone? This matter comes before me in the form of addresses upon letters, — "Rev. Titus Smith, Mr. Spurgeon's College, or sometimes, "Rev. Timothy Jones, Spurgeon's Tabernacle." Rather odd, this! Here are reverend students of an un-reverend preacher, the title being given to one out of courtesy, and withheld from the other for the same reason. The Reverend Titus has met with a church which will insist upon an ordination, and he is ordained; but the President of his College, having; never- undergone such a process, nor even that imitation of it called a *recognition,* remains an unordained, unrecognized person to this day, and has not yet discovered the peculiar loss which he has sustained thereby. I do not object to a recognition of the choice of the church by its neighbors and their ministers; on the contrary, I believe it to be a fraternal act, sanctioned by the very spirit of Christianity; but where it is supposed to be essential, is regarded as a ceremony, and is thought to be *the* crowning feature of the settlement, I demur. "The Reverend Theophilus Robinson offered up *the ordination prayer,"* has a Babylonish sound in my ears, and it is not much improved when it takes the form of "the *recognition prayer."* Is there, then, a ritual? Are we as much bound by an unwritten extempore liturgy as others by the Book of Common Prayer? Must there always be "usual questions"? And why "usual"? Is there some legendary rule for *the* address to the church, and *the* address to the pastor? I do not object to any one of these things, but I do question the propriety of stereotyping them, and speaking o! the whole affair as if it were a matter robe gone about according to a certain pattern seen in the holy mount, or an order given forth in trust to the saints. I see germs of evil in the usual parlance, and therefore meet it with a *Quo warranto?* Is not the Divine call the real ordination to preach, and the call of the church the only ordination to the pastorate? The church is competent, under the guidance of the Holy Spirit, to do her own work; and if she calls in her sister-churches, let her tell them what she has done, in such terms that they 'will never infer that they are called upon to complete the work. The ordination prayer should be prayed in the church-meeting, and there and then the work should be done; for other churches to recognize the act, is well and fitting, but not if it be viewed as needful to the completion of the act itself. I have noticed many signs of an error in this direction.

(The following letter shows how Mr. Spurgeon regarded the question of an "ordination" or "recognition" service at the beginning of his London pastorate:)

"75, Dover Road,
"Borough,
"May 2nd, 1854.

"To James Low, Esq.,

"My Dear Sir,

"I sit down to communicate to you my thoughts and feelings with regard to a public recognition. I am sure I need not request your notice of my sentiments, for your usual good judgment is to me a rock of reliance. I can trust any matter with you, knowing that your kindness and wisdom will decide rightly.

"I have a decided objection to any public ordination or recognition.

I have, scores; of times, most warmly expressed from the pulpit my abhorrence of such things, and have been not a little notorious as the opponent of a custom which has become a kind of iron law in the country. I am willing to retrace my steps if in error; but if I have been right, it will be no very honorable thing to be-lie my former loud outcries by submitting to it myself.

"*I object to ordinations and recognitions, as such,* (1.) Because I am a minister, and will never receive authority and commission from man; nor do I like that which has the shadow of such a thing about it. I detest the dogma of apostolic succession, and dislike the revival of the doctrine by delegating power from minister to minister.

"(2.) I believe in the glorious principle of Independency. Every church has a right to choose its own minister; and if so, certainly it needs no assistance from others in appointing him to the office.

You, yourselves, have chosen me; and what matters it if the whole world dislikes the choice? They cannot invalidate it; nor can they give it more force. It seems to me that other ministers have no more to do with me, as your minister, than the crown of Prance has with the crown of Britain. We are allies, but we have no authority in each other's territories. They are my superiors in piety, and other personal matters; but, *ex officio,* no man is my superior. We have no apostles to send Titus to ordain. Prelatic power is gone. All we are brethren.

"(3.) If there be no authority inferred, what is the meaning of the ceremony? 'It is customary.' Granted; — but we are not all Ecclesiastical Conservatives; and, moreover, I know several instances where there has been none. Rev. W. Robinson, of Cambridge, agrees with me, I believe; and has not: endured it himself. Rev. J. Smith had nothing of it, nor had Rev. Burton, of Cambridge, nor Rev. Wooster, of Sandbeach, etc., etc.

"Furthermore, I have seldom heard of an ordination service in which there was not something objectionable. There are dinners, and toasts, and things in that line. There is foolish and needless advice, or, if wise advice, unfit for public mention. I am ready to be advised by anyone, on any subject, in private; but I do not know how I could sit in public to be told, as Mr. C was told by Mr. S___, that I must not spend more than my income; and (if married), that I must be a good husband, and not let the wife say that, being a minister, had lessened my affection, with all the absurd remarks on family and household matters. I do not know what sort of a homily! should get; but if I am to have it, let it be in my study; or if it be not a very good one, I cannot promise to sit and hear it.

"I trust, my dear sir, that you will not imagine that I write warmly, for I am willing to submit; but it will be *submission.* I shall endure it as a *self-mortification,* in order that you may all be pleased. I would rather' please you than myself; but, still, I would have it understood by all the church that I endure it as a penance for their sake. I find the friends do not care much about it, and others have, like myself, a decided aversion. I am your servant; and whatever is for the good of the church, let it be done. My knowledge is little; I simply express my feelings, and leave it entirely with you.

"A tea-meeting of members, with handbills, and notices in the papers, will be a real recognition; and if my God will make me useful, I am not afraid of being recognized by all good men. I write now to you as a kind and wise friend. You can use my communication as you think best; and believe me to be —

"Yours, with the profoundest respect,

"**C. H. SPURGEON.**"

(Shortly after writing the above letter, Mr. Spurgeon preached the following sermon at New Park Street Chapel: —)

THE MINISTER'S TRUE ORDINATION.

"Son of man, I have made thee a watchman unto the house of Israel' therefore hear the word at My mouth, and give them warning from Me." — Ezekiel 3:17.

The office of a gospel minister in some respects resembles that of the ancient prophets. Though we cannot, like Elisha, raise the dead; nor, like Isaiah, pour forth eloquent predictions; nor, as Ezekiel, foretell certain coming and immediate judgments; yet, like them, we are commanded to teach, to warn, and to encourage. So much are we like Ezekiel, that his commission will suit any gospel minister even of our day. Let us consider, —

I. THE MINISTER'S COMMISSION.

Here is a scrap of ancient writing worthy of a place in the museum. It ought to be in every minister's study. It is the ultimatum of the King of Heaven to us in our doubts as to our calling. It is our Emperor's protocol to all His legions. It is *the minister's true ordination*, a real installation, worth more than a thousand Papal bulls from Rome bearing the mark of the fisherman's ring; yea, worth more than all the charters of universities, or the appointments of archbishops. notice, —

1. *The wording of this ancient commission.* It is worded in the Court language of Heaven, and each letter is Divine. "Son *of man.*" Here is the title by which Ezekiel is addressed; — not Right Reverend, nor the Very Venerable; but he has given to him a graciously-humbling title. Ezekiel is called "son of man" no less than ninety times. This is the name Jesus often took to Himself when He was on earth, and therefore it is a truly glorious one. The gracious and all-wise Father saw that too lofty an eminence might tempt Ezekiel to pride. He therefore styles him son of man, as much as to say, — "Your visions, rank, talents, and office, must not exalt you, for you are, after all, only man. You must not lean on sell:, for you are utter weakness, being only the 'son of man.' You must sympathize with each of your fellow-creatures, and deal with him, not as if you were a prince, or a master, but as being, like him, a 'son of man.'"

"*I have made thee a watchman.*" Here we read, on this ancient manuscript, a true account of the making of a minister. God alone can do it. Two things are absolutely requisite to make a man a preacher, viz., — (1.) *Special gifts*, — such as perception of truth, simplicity, aptness to impart instruction, some degree of eloquence, and intense earnestness. (2.) *Special call.* Every man who is rightly in the ministry must have been moved thereto of the Holy Ghost. He must feel an irresistible desire to spend his whole life in his Master's cause. No college, no bishop, no human ordination, can make a man a minister; but he who can feel, as did Bunyan, Whitefield, Berridge, or Rowland Hill, the strugglings of an impassioned longing to win the souls of men, may hear in the air the voice of God saying, "Son of man, I have made *thee* a watchman."

"*Unto the house of Israel.*" Ezekiel's was a limited commission; but ours is not, it is as wide as the earth, and as long as time. The world is our parish.

We are not ordered to cast the net alone in the pools of Heshbon, or the streams of Jordan, or the Lake of Gennesaret; but we may cover all seas and rivers with the gospel fishing-boats, — the navy of Jesus. Yet, still, it is for the sake of the true Israel that we go.

"*Therefore hear the word at My mouth.*" The ancient seers spoke not at random; but they declared what they had been taught of God. Sometimes, in dreams, they heard Heaven's message; sometimes, by a. voice from on high; but, most commonly, by vision, did the Word of the Lord come unto them. The soul, inspired by God, seems at times to leave the body, and that narrow tube of vision which we call eyesight, and, with its own eagle eye, to pierce the thick cloud, and to mount into that remote region which the ordinary eye cannot see.

The prophets heard the spoken Word, but we have the written Word; and this we must devoutly read. It becomes a minister diligently to study the Scriptures, with all the assistance he can gain from holy men who have gone before, but chiefly from the most excellent of all instructors, the true Interpreter, the Holy Ghost.

"*And give them warning front Me.*" There are other duties; but as this is the most arduous, it is specially mentioned. We are to warn the Christian if he is found backsliding, or sinning; and to warn the sinner of the consequences of his sin. of the strict justice of God, and of the tearful hell in which the ungodly shall suffer.

2. *The high office conferred by this commission.* It is that of "watchman."

Every soldier of the Cross is bound to watch; but the minister is in a double sense a watchman. He is so called because —

(1) The ministry requires great vigilance. We must not sleep: we must watch against false doctrine and false brethren; we must be ready to help benighted

travelers, and to give alarm to any who may be in danger. The true minister is to sit like the shepherd in the wilderness by night, or like the whisper-hearing sentinel.

(2.) The ministry involves toil and trouble. Few think of the watchman who tramps by their door. Hark! there is a scuffle, a fight! Who is sure to be in it? The watchman. How the wind blows! The snow must be a foot deep; pray put list on the doors, and stir the fire. Surely no one is out of doors to-night, — except the watchman! His bare face is cut by the driving sleet, his fingers are numbed with the cold, his eye-lids are almost frozen. "Well, well," someone says, "never mind about the watchman and his trials; that's his work, and he is used to it." Some of you come here, and sit, and smile, and enjoy the sermon; but there are some who criticize, and find fault, and slander, and calumniate. The minister must bear it all, for he is the watchman. He had need be a very tough veteran, who has swallowed many "Nor-westers" and I know not what to fit him for the task he has in hand.

(3.) The ministry should be arousing. If there be a fire, or a thief, or a door or shutter unfastened, the watchman must not spare, but cry aloud. We must cry out with all our might, — not being afraid to disturb, or alarm, or hurt the feelings of the sleepers. We may as well be asleep as be mumblers, or speak in such a way that none can really make Out what we mean; we must preach the truth in plain, blunt, honest language which none can mistake. Every man, who labors in Word and Doctrine, should ponder over this commission, and wear it next his heart, and on his brow. It is to be feared that many, who profess to preach the gospel, are not alive to a sense of their position; but, having the next presentation to a living, or having purchased a benefice, they rush in where angels if. like them, uncalled, would tear to venture.

II. THE MINISTER'S RESPONSIBILITY.

The watchman holds a responsible office. If the sentinel, by sleeping, causes the death of a single person, he is a murderer. It the prisoner escapes from his charge, he shall be required to answer for his neglect. So, if the ungodly man is not warned, he shall suffer for his own guilt, but my unfaithfulness will lie as a crime on me. If the professing Christian falls, his fall is his own; but if I have not warned him, I also am guilty. If I do not utter the whole truth, — the threatenings, the promises, and the invitations of God, — I shall be a sleeping sentinel, a careless captain, a negligent railway guard, and I shall be the slaughterer of my fellow creatures, Or if, to the professor, I give wine instead of medicine, a plaster instead of a lancet, or a stone for bread, — I shall be a guilty wretch, and God help me, then, for no one more requires help than an unfaithful minister!

III. THE MINISTER'S COMFORT.

1. The Lord's call to the office: "Son of man, I have made thee a watchman."

2. The promises peculiar to that call, for every call from God hath the strength to perform it enclosed within itself.

3. The blessed brow-hardening Spirit, who makes us despise alike the frown or the smile of man, and thus keeps us from unfaithfulness.

4. The fact that success is not required of us, — but faithfulness.

O my Father, keep me clear of the blood of all men! Amen.

Chapter Thirty-Two - The Long Pastorate Commenced, 1854.

Here and there we meet with one to whom it is given to believe in God with mighty faith. As soon as such a man strikes out a project, or sets about a work which none but men of his mold would venture upon, straightway there arises a clamor: — "The man is over-zealous," or he will be charged with an innovating spirit, rashness, fanaticism, or absurdity. Should the work go on, the opposers whisper together, "Wait a little while, and you'll see the end of all this wild-fire." What said the sober semi-faith of men to Luther? The monk had read in the Scriptures this passage, "We are justified by faith, and not by the works of the law." He went to a venerable divine to ask him about it, and at the same time he complained of the enormities of Rome. What was the good but weak brother's reply? "Go thou to thy cell, and pray and study for thyself, and leave these weighty matters alone." Here it would have ended had the brave Reformer continued to consult with flesh and blood; but his faith enabled him to go forward alone, if none would accompany him. lie nailed up his theses on the church door, and showed that one man at least had faith in the gospel and in its God.

Then trouble came, but Luther minded it not, because the Father was with him. We also must be prepared, if God gives us strong faith, to ride far ahead, like spiritual Uhlans, who bravely pioneer the way for the rank and file of the army. It were well if the Church of God had more of the fleet-footed sons of Asahel, — bolder than lions, swifter than eagles, in their Lord's service, — men who can do and dare alone, till laggards take courage, and follow in their track. These Valiant-for-truths will pursue a solitary path full often, but let: them console themselves with this thought, "Yet I am not alone, because the Father is with me." If we can believe in God, He will never be behindhand with us; if we can dare, God will do; if we can trust, God will never suffer us to be confounded, world without end. It is sweet beyond expression to climb where only God can lead, and to plant the standard on the highest towers of the foe. —C. H. S.

WHEN I came to New Park' Street Chapel, it was but a mere handful Of people to whom I first preached; yet I can never forget how earnestly they prayed. Sometimes, they seemed to plead as though they could really see the Angel of the covenant present with them, and as if they must have a blessing from Him. More than once, we were all so awe-struck with the solemnity of the meeting, that we sat silent for some moments while the Lord's power appeared to overshadow us; and all I could do on such occasions was to pronounce the Benediction, arid say, "*Dear* friends, we have had the Spirit of God here very manifestly to-night; let us go home, and take care not to lose His gracious influences." Then down came the blessing; the house was filled with hearers, and many souls were saved. I always give all the glory to God, but I do not forget that He gave me the privilege of ministering from the first to a praying people. We had prayer-meetings in New Park Street that moved our very souls. Every man seemed like a crusader besieging the New Jerusalem, each one appeared determined to storm the Celestial City by the might of intercession; and soon the blessing came upon us in such abundance that we had not room to receive it.

There is a confidence in one's own powers which must ever be of service to those who are called to eminent positions, provided the confidence is well-grounded, seasoned with humility, and attended with that holy gratitude which refers all honor and glory to the Giver of every good and perfect gift. But, at the same time, there is nothing more true than the fact that the self-confident are near a fall, that those who lean on themselves must be overthrown, and that carnal security has but a baseless fabric in which to dwell. When I first became a Pastor in London, my success appalled me; and the thought of the career which it seemed to open up, so far from elating me, cast me into the lowest depth, out of which I uttered my *miserere,* and found no room for a *gloria in excelsis.* Who was I that I should continue to lead so great a multitude? I would betake me to my village obscurity, or emigrate to America, and find a solitary nest in the back-woods, where I might be sufficient for the things which would be demanded of me. It was just then that the curtain was rising upon my life-work, and I dreaded what it might reveal. I hope I was not faithless; but I was timorous, and filled with a sense of my own unfitness. I dreaded the work which a gracious Providence had prepared for me. I felt myself a mere child, and trembled as I heard the voice which said, "Arise, and thresh the mountains, and make them as chaff." This depression comes over me whenever the Lord is preparing a larger blessing for my ministry; the cloud is black before it breaks, and overshadows before it yields its deluge of mercy. Depression has now become to me as a prophet in rough clothing, a John the Baptist, heralding the nearer coming of my Lord's richer benison.

So have far better men found it. The scouring of the vessel has fitted it for the Master's use. Immersion in suffering has preceded the baptism of the Holy Ghost. Fasting gives an appetite for the banquet. The Lord is revealed in the backside of the desert, while His servant keepeth the sheep, and waits in solitary awe. The wilderness is the way to Canaan. The low valley leads to the towering mountain.' Defeat prepares for victory'. The raven is sent forth before the dove. The darkest hour of the night precedes the day-dawn. The marine, go down to the depths, but the next wave makes them mount towards the heavens; and their soul is melted because of trouble before the Lord bringeth them to their desired haven.

Not long after I was chosen Pastor at Park Street, I was interviewed by a goodman who had left the church, having been, as he said, "*treated* shamefully." He mentioned the names of half-a-dozen persons, all prominent members of the church, who had behaved in a very unchristian manner to him, — he, poor innocent sufferer, having been a model of patience and holiness! I learned his character at once from what he said about others (a mode of judging which has never misled me), and I made up my mind how to act. I told him that the Church had been in a sadly unsettled state, and that the only way out of the snarl was for every one to forget the past, and begin again. He said that the lapse of years did not alter facts: and I replied that it would alter a man's view of them if in that time he had become a wiser and a better man. I added that all the past had gone away with my predecessors, that he must follow them to their new spheres, and settle matters with *them,* for I would not touch the affair with a pair of tongs. He waxed somewhat warm; but I allowed him to radiate until he was cool again, and we shook hands, and parted. He was a good man, but constructed upon an uncomfortable principle, so that, at times, he crossed the path of other people in a very awkward manner; and if I had gone into his case, and taken his side, there would have been no end to the strife. I am quite certain that, for my own success, and for the prosperity of the church, I took the wisest course by applying my blind eye to all disputes which dated previously to my advent. It is the extremity of unwisdom for a young man, fresh from College, or from another charge, to suffer himself to be earwigged by a clique, and to be bribed by kindness and flattery to become a partisan, and so to ruin himself with one-half of his people.

I do not find, at the present time, nearly so much advice being given to young men as when I first came to London. Dear me, what quantities I had! I believe I had as much as that American humorist, who said he found enough advice lying loose round about him to ruin three worlds at least; I am sure I had quite enough to have: done that. But now, instead of advising our young brethren, and hinting at their indiscretions, we rather rejoice in their impetuosity and earnestness. We like to see much freshness and vigor about them: and if they do kick over the traces now and then, we feel that time will moderate their zeal, and probably a very few years will add to them the prudence which they now lack.

I could tell many stories of the remarkable conversions that were wrought in those early days. Once, when I was in the vestry, an Irishman came to see me. Pat began by making a low bow, and saying, "Now, your *Riverence,* I have come to ax you a question." "Oh!" said I, "Pat, I am not a *Riverence;* it is not a title I care for; but what is your question, and how is it you have not been to your priest about it?" He said, "I have been to him; but I don't like his answer." "Well, what is your question?" Said he, "God is just; and if God be just, He must punish my sins. I deserve to be punished. If He is a just God, He ought to punish me; yet you say God is merciful, and will forgive sins. I cannot see how that is right; He has no right to do that. He ought to be just, and punish those who deserve it. Tell me how God can be just, and yet be merciful." I replied, "That is through the blood of Christ." "Yes," said he, "that is what my priest said, you are very much alike there; but he said a good deal besides, that I did not understand; and that short answer does not satisfy me. I want to know how it is that the blood of Jesus Christ enables God to be just, and yet to be merciful."

Then I saw what he wanted to know, and explained the plan of salvation thus: — "Now, Pat, suppose you had been killing a man, and the judge had said, 'That Irishman must be hanged.'" He said quickly, "And I should have richly deserved to be hanged." "But, Pat, suppose I was very fond of you, can you see any way by which I could save you from being hanged?...

No, sir, I cannot." "Then, suppose I went to the Queen, and said, 'Please your Majesty, I am very fond of this Irishman; I think the judge was quite right in saying that he must be hanged; but let me be hanged instead, and you will then carry out the law.' Now, the Queen could not agree to my proposal; but suppose she could, — and God can, for He has power greater than all kings and queens, — and suppose the Queen should have me hanged instead of you, do you think the policemen would take you up afterwards?" He at once said, "No, I should think not; they would not meddle with me; but if they did, I should say, 'What are you doing? Did not that gentleman condescend to be hung for me? Let me alone; shure, you don't want to hang two people for the same thing, do ye?'" I replied to the Irishman, "Ah, my friend, you have hit it; that is the way whereby we are saved! God must punish sin. Christ said, 'My Father, punish Me instead of the sinner;' and His Father did. God laid on His beloved Son, Jesus Christ, the whole burden of our sins, and all their punishment and chastisement; and now that Christ is punished instead of us, God would not be just if He were to punish any sinner who believes on the Lord Jesus Christ. If thou believest in Jesus Christ, the well-beloved and only-begotten Son of God, thou art saved, and thou mayest go on thy way rejoicing."

"Faith," said the man, clapping his hands, "that's the gospel. Pat is safe now; with all his sins about him, he'll trust in the Man that died for him, and so he shall be saved."

Another singular conversion, wrought at New Park Street, was that of a man who had been accustomed to go to a gin-palace to fetch in gin for his Sunday evening's drinking. He saw a crowd round the door of the chapel, so he looked in, and forced his way to the top of the gallery stairs. Just then, I turned in the direction where: he stood; I do not know why I did so, but I remarked that there might be a man in the gallery who had come in with no very good motive, for even then he had a gin-bottle in his pocket.

The singularity of the expression struck the man. and being startled because the preacher so exactly described him, he listened attentively to the warnings which followed, the Word reached his heart, the grace of God met with him, he became converted, and soon was walking humbly in the fear of God. On another occasion, a poor harlot found the Savior in the same building. She had determined to go and take her own life on Blackfriars Bridge; but, passing the chapel on a Sunday evening, she thought she would step in, and for the last time hear something that might prepare her to stand before her Maker. She forced her way into the aisle; and being once in, she could not get out even it she had wanted to do so.

The text that night was, "Seest thou this woman?" I described the woman in the city who was a notorious public sinner, and pictured her washing her Savior's feet with her tears, and wiping them with the hair of her head, loving much because she had been forgiven much. While I was preaching, the wretched woman was melted to tears by the thought that her own evil life was being depicted to the congregation. It was, first, my great joy to be the means of saving the poor creature from death by suicide, and, then, to be the instrument of saving her soul from destruction.

Deeds of grace have been wrought in the Tabernacle after the same fashion. Men and women have come in, simply out of curiosity, — a curiosity often created by some unfounded story, or malicious slander of prejudiced minds; yet Jesus Christ has called them, and they have become both *His* disciples and *our* warm-hearted friends. Some of the most unlikely recruits have been, in after days, our most valuable soldiers. They began with aversion, and ended with enthusiasm. They came to scoff, but remained to pray. Such cases are not at all uncommon. They were not unusual in the days of Whitefield and Wesley. They tell us 'in their Journals of persons who came with stones in their pockets to throw at the Meth-

274

odists, but whose enmity was slain by a stone from the sling of the Son of David. others came to create disturbances, but a disturbance was created in their hearts which could never be quelled till they came to Jesus Christ, and found peace in Him. The history of the Church of God is studded with the remarkable conversions of persons who did not wish to be converted, who were not looking for grace, but were even opposed to it, and yet, by the interposing arm of eternal mercy, were struck down and transformed into earnest and devoted followers of the Lamb.

Ever since I have been in London, in order to get into the habit of speaking extemporaneously, I have never studied or prepared anything for the Monday evening prayer-meeting. I have all along selected that occasion as the opportunity for off-hand exhortation; but I do not on such occasions select difficult expository topics, or abstruse themes, but restrict myself to simple, homely talk about the elements of our faith. When standing up, on such occasions, my mind makes a review, and inquires, "What subject has already occupied my thought during the day? What have I met with in my reading during the past week? What is most laid upon my heart at this hour? What is suggested by the hymns or the prayers?" It is of no use to rise before an assembly, and hope to be inspired upon subjects of which one knows nothing; if anyone is so unwise, the result will be that, as he knows nothing, he will probably say it, and the people will not be edified.

But I do not see why a man cannot speak extemporaneously upon a subject which he fully understands. Any tradesman, well versed in his line of business, could explain it without needing to retire for meditation; and surely I ought to be equally familiar with the first principles of our holy faith; I ought not to feel at a loss when called upon to speak: upon topics which constitute the daily bread of my soul. I do not see what benefit is gained, in such a case, by the mere manual labor of writing before speaking; because, in so doing, a man would write extemporaneously, and extemporaneous writing is likely to be even feebler than extemporaneous speech. The gain of the writing lies in the opportunity of careful revision; but, as thoroughly able writers can express their thoughts correctly at the first, so also may able speakers. The thought of a man who finds himself upon his legs, dilating upon a theme with which he is familiar, may be very far from being his first thought;; it may be the cream of his meditations warmed by the glow of his heart. He having studied the subject well before, though not at that moment, may deliver himself most powerfully; whereas another man, sitting down to write, may only be penning his first ideas, which may be vague and vapid.

I once had a very singular experience while preaching at New Park Street Chapel. I had passed happily through all the early parts of Divine service on the Sabbath evening, and was giving out the hymn before the sermon. I opened the Bible to find the text, which I had carefully studied as the topic of discourse, when, on the opposite page, another passage of Scripture sprang upon me, like a lion from a thicket, with vastly more power than I had felt when considering the text which I had chosen. The people were singing, and I was sighing. I was in a strait betwixt two, and my mind hung as in the balances. I was naturally desirous to run in the track which I had carefully planned, but the other text would take no refusal, and seemed to tug at my skirts, crying, "No, no, you must preach from me! God would have you follow me." I deliberated within myself as to my duty, for I would neither be fanatical nor unbelieving, and at last I thought within myself,

"Well, I should like to preach the sermon which I have prepared, and it is a great risk to run to strike out a new line of thought; but, still, as this text constrains me, it may be of the Lord, and therefore I will venture upon it, come what may." I almost always announce my divisions very soon after the exordium; but, on this occasion, contrary to my usual custom, I did not do so, for a very good reason. I passed through the first head with considerable liberty, speaking perfectly extemporaneously both as to thought and word. The second point was dwelt upon with a consciousness of unusual quiet efficient power, but I had no idea what the third would or could be, for the text yielded no more matter just then; nor can I tell even now what I could have done had not an event occurred upon which I had never calculated. I had brought myself into great difficulty by obeying what I thought to be a Divine impulse, and I felt comparatively easy about it, believing that God would help me, and knowing that I could at least close the service should there be nothing more to be said. I had no need to deliberate, for in one moment we: were in total darkness, — the gas had gone out; and, as the aisles were choked with people, and the place was crowded everywhere, it was a great peril, but a great blessing. What was I to do then? The people were a little frightened, but I quieted them instantly by telling them not to be at all alarmed, though the gas was out, for it would soon be re-lighted; and as for myself, having no manuscript, I could speak just as well in the dark as in the light, if they would be so good as to sit or stand still, and listen. Had my discourse been ever so elaborate, it would have been absurd to have continued it; and, as my plight was, I was all the less embarrassed. I turned at once mentally to the well-known text which speaks of the child of light walking in darkness, and of the child of darkness walking in the light, and found appropriate remarks, and illustrations pouring in upon me; and when the lamps were again lit, I saw before me an audience as rapt and subdued as ever a man beheld in his life.

The odd thing of all was that, some few church-meetings afterwards, two persons came forward to make confession of their faith, who professed to have been converted that evening; but the first owed her conversion to the former part of the discourse, which was on the new text that came to me, and the other traced his awakening to the latter part, which was occasioned by the sudden darkness. Thus, Providence befriended me. I cast myself upon God, and His arrangements quenched the light at the proper time for me. Some may ridicule, but I adore; others may even censure, but I rejoice.

This illustration represents the pulpit stairs used by me at New Park Street Chapel after the enlargement. When that building was sold, I removed them to my garden at Nightingale Lane, and fixed them to a huge willow tree. I remember reading, with some amusement, of Lorenzo Dow, who is reported, many years ago, to have slipped down a tree in the backwoods, in order to illustrate the easiness of backsliding. He had previously pulled himself up, with extreme difficulty, in order to show how hard a thing it is to regain lost ground. I was all the more diverted by (the story because it has so happened that this pretty piece of nonsense has been imputed to myself. I was represented as sliding down the banisters of my pulpit, and that at a time when the pulpit was fixed in the wall, and was entered from behind. I never gave even the remotest occasion for that falsehood; and yet it is daily repeated, and I have even heard of persons who have declared that they were present when I did so, and, with their own eyes, saw me perform the silly trick. [22]

It is possible for a person to repeat a falsehood so many that he at length imposes upon himself, and believes that he is stating the truth. When men mean to say what is untrue and unkind, they are not very careful as to the back upon which they stick the slander. For my own part, I have so long lived under a glass case that, like the bees which I have seen at the Crystal Palace, I go on with my work, and try to be indifferent to spectators; and when my personal habits are truthfully, reported, though they really are not the concern of anybody but myself, I feel utterly indifferent about it, except in times of depression, when I sigh "for a lodge in some vast wilderness, where rumors of newspaper train anti interviewers might never reach me more. I am quite willing to take my lair share of the current criticism allotted to public men; but I cannot help saying that I very seldom read in print any story connected with myself which has a shade of truth in it. Old Joe Millers, anecdotes of Rowland Hill, Sydney Smith, and John Berridge, and tales of remotest and fustiest antiquity, are imputed to me as they have been to men who went: before, and will be to men who follow after. Many of the tales told about me, even to this day, are not only without a shadow of truth, but some of them border on blasphemy, or are positively profane.

On the whole, I am inclined to believe that the trade in falsehood is rather brisk, or so many untruths would not be manufactured. Why, I actually heard, not long since, of a minister, who said that a certain thing occurred to him, the other day; yet I told the original story twenty years ago! When I related it, I said it had been my experience, the other day, and I believed it was so; but after hearing that this man says that it happened to him, it makes me question whether it really did occur to me at all. I think it is a great pity for a preacher, or any speaker, to try to make a story appear interesting by saying that the incident related happened to him, when it really did not. Scrupulous truthfulness should always characterize everyone who stands up to proclaim the truth of God.

I mentioned to my New Park Street deacons, several times, my opinion that the upper panes of the iron-framed windows had better be taken out, as the windows were not made to open; yet nothing came of my remarks; but it providentially happened, one Monday, that somebody removed most of those panes in a masterly manner', almost as well as if they had been taken out by a glazier. There was considerable consternation, and much conjecture, as to who had committed the crime; and I proposed that a reward of five pounds should be offered for the discovery of the offender, who when found should receive, the amount as a present. The reward was not forthcoming, and therefore I have not felt it to be my duty to inform against the individual. I trust none will suspect me,' but if they do, I shall have to confess that I have walked with the stick which let the oxygen into that stifling structure. In a very short time after I began to preach in London, the congregation so multiplied as to make the chapel, in the evening, when the gas was burning, like the Black Hole of Calcutta. One night, in 1854, while preaching there, I exclaimed, "By faith, the walls of Jericho fell down; and by faith, this wall at the back shall come down, too."

An aged and prudent deacon, in somewhat domineering terms, observed to me, at the close of the sermon, "Let us never hear of that again." "What do you mean?" I inquired; "you will hear no more about it *when it is done,* and therefore the sooner you set about doing it, the better." The following extract from the church-book shows that the members did set about doing it in real earnest: —

"Church-meeting, 30th August, 1854.

"Resolved, — That we desire, as a church, to record our devout and grateful acknowledgments to our Heavenly Father for the success that has attended the ministry of our esteemed Pastor, and we consider it important, at as early a period as possible, that increased accommodation should be provided for the numbers that flock to the chapel on Lord's-days; and we would affectionately request our respected deacons to give the subject their full and careful consideration, and to favor us with their report at the church-meeting in October."

A considerable, but unavoidable delay, took place, in consequence of the vestry and school-rooms being held on a different Trust from that of the chapel, so that it became necessary to apply to the Charity Commissioners before including those rooms in the main building. After fully investigating the circumstances, they did not interpose any obstacle, so the alterations were commenced, early in 1855, and in due course the chapel was enlarged as proposed, and a new school-room was erected along the side of the chapel, with windows which could be let down, to allow those who were seated in the school to hear the preacher.

Chapter Thirty-Three - The Cholera Year in London

Whether we gather in the harvest or not, there is a reaper who is silently gathering it every hour. Just now, it is whispered that he is sharpening his sickle. That reaper is DEATH! You may look upon this great city as the harvest-field, and every week the bills of mortality tell us how steadily and how surely the scythe of death moves to and fro, and how a lane is made through our population, and those who were once living men are taken, like sheaves to the garner, carried to the graveyard, and laid aside. You cannot stop their dying; but, oh, that God might help you to stop their being damned! You cannot stop the breath from going out of their bodies; but, oh, that the gospel might stop their souls from going down to destruction! It can do it, and nothing else can take its place. Just now, the cholera has come again. There can be little doubt, I suppose, about it being here already in some considerable force, and probably it may be worse. The Christian need not dread it, for he has nothing to lose, but everything to gain, by death. Still, for the sake of others, he may well pray that God would avert His hand, and not let His anger burn. But, since it is here, I think it ought to be a motive for active exertion. If there ever be a time when the mind is Sensitive, it is when death is abroad. I re collect, when first I came to London, how anxiously people listened to the gospel, for the cholera was raging terribly. There was little scoffing then. All day, and sometimes all night long, I went about from house to house, and. saw men and women dying, and, oh, how glad they were to see my face! When many were afraid to enter their houses lest they should catch the deadly disease, we who had no fear about such things found ourselves most gladly listened to when we spoke of Christ and of things Divine. And now, again, is the minister's time; and now is the time for all of you who love souls.

You may see men more alarmed than they are already; and if they should be, mind that you avail yourselves of the opportunity of doing them good. You have the Balm of Gilead; when their wounds smart, pour it in. You know of Him who died to save; tell them of Him. Lift high the cross before their eyes. Tell them that God became man that man might be lifted to God. Tell them of Calvary, and its groans, and cries, and sweat of blood. Tell them of Jesus hanging on the cross to save sinners. Tell them that —

"There is life for a look at the Crucified One."

Tell them that He is able to save to the uttermost all them that come unto God by Him. Tell them that He is able to save even at the eleventh hour, and to say to the dying thief, "to-day shalt thou be with Me in Paradise." — C. H. S., *in Sermon preached at the Metropolitan Tabernacle,* July 29, 1866.

IN the year 1854, when I had scarcely been in London twelve months, the neighborhood in which I labored was visited by Asiatic cholera, and my congregation suffered from its inroads. Family after family summoned me to the bedside of the smitten, and almost every day I was called to visit the grave. At first, I gave myself up with youthful ardor to the visitation of the sick, and was sent for from all corners of the district by persons of all ranks and religions; but, soon, I became weary in body, and sick at heart. My friends seemed falling one by one, and I felt or fancied that I was sickening like those around me. A little more work and weeping would have laid me low among the rest; I felt that my burden was heavier than I could bear, and I was ready to sink under it.

I was returning mournfully home from a funeral, when, as God would have it, my curiosity led me to read a paper which was wafered up in a shoemaker's window in the Great Dover Road. It did not look like a trade: announcement, nor was it, for it bore, in a good bold handwriting, these words: —

"Because thou hast made the Lord, which is my refuge, even the Most High, thy habitation; there shall no evil befall thee, neither shall any plague come nigh thy dwelling."

The effect upon my heart was immediate. Faith appropriated the passage as her own. I felt secure, refreshed, girt with immortality. I went on with my visitation of the dying, in a calm and peaceful spirit; I felt no fear of evil, and I suffered no harm. The Providence which moved the tradesman to place those verses in his window, I gratefully acknowledge; and in the remembrance of its marvelous power, I adore the Lord my God.

(In a pamphlet entitled, "The Best Refuge in Times of Trouble," published about the time of Mr. Spurgeon's "home-going," Mr. W. Ford, of 19H, Peabody Buildings, Orchard Street, Westminster, wrote: — "In the year 1854, the first year of Mr. Spurgeon in London, the cholera raged in the locality of his church, and the neighborhood where he resided. The parochial authorities were very thoughtful for the poor, and caused bills to be placed at the corners of the streets, headed CHOLERA, — in large type, — informing the public where advice and medicines would be supplied gratis. At that time, I lived in the Great Dover Road, and Mr. Spurgeon lived a little further towards Greenwich, in Virginia Terrace. Seeing the bills above-named at every turning, I was forcibly impressed that they were very much calculated to terrify the people. With the concurrence of a friend, I procured one, and wrote in the center these words: — 'Because thou hast made the Lord, which is my refuge, even the Most High, thy habitation; there shall no evil befall thee, neither shall any plague come nigh thy dwelling.' This bill I placed in my shop-window, hundreds read it, and I am not aware of one jeer or improper remark, — so subdued and solemnized were the people by the awful visitation. Among the readers of the bill, was Mr. Spurgeon.")

During that epidemic of cholera, though I had many engagements in the country, I gave them up that I might remain in London to visit the sick and the dying. I felt that it was my duty to be on the spot in such a time of disease and death and sorrow. One Monday morning, I was awakened, about three o'clock, by a sharp ring of the door-bell. I was urged, without delay, to visit a house not very far from London Bridge. I went; and up two pairs of stairs I was shown into a room, the only occupants of which were a nurse and a dying man. "Oh, sir!" exclaimed the nurse, as I entered, "about half-an-hour ago, Mr. So-and-so begged me to send for you."

"What does he want?" I asked. "He is dying, sir," she replied. I said, "Yes, I see that he is; what sort of a man was he?" The nurse answered, "He came home from Brighton, last night, sir; he had been out all day. I looked for a Bible, sir, but there is not one in the house; I hope you have brought one with you." "Oh!" I said, "a Bible would be of no use to him now. If he could understand me, I could tell him the way of salvation in the very words' of Scripture." I stood by his side, and spoke to him, but he gave me no answer. I spoke again; but the only consciousness he had was a foreboding of terror, mingled with the stupor of approaching death. Soon, even that was gone, for sense had fled, and I stood there.', a few minutes, sighing with the poor woman who had watched over him, and altogether hopeless about his soul. Gazing at his face, I perceived that he was dead, and that his soul had departed.

That man, in his lifetime, had been wont to jeer at me. In strong language, he had often denounced me as a hypocrite. Yet he was no sooner smitten by the darts of death than he sought my presence and counsel, no doubt feeling in his heart that I was a servant of God, though he did not care to own it with his lips. There I stood, unable to help him. Promptly as I had responded to his call, what could I do but look at his corpse, and mourn over a lost soul? He had, when in health, wickedly refused Christ, yet in his death-agony he had superstitiously sent for me. Too late, he sighed for the ministry of reconciliation, and sought to enter in at the closed door, but he was not able. There was no space left him then for repentance, for he had wasted the opportunities which God had long granted to him. I went home, and was soon called away again; 'that time, to see a young woman. She also was in the last extremity, but it was a fair, fair sight. She was singing, — though she knew she was dying, — and talking to those round about her, telling her brothers and sisters to follow her to Heaven, bidding good-bye to her father, and all the while smiling as if it had been her marriage day. She was happy and blessed. I never saw more conspicuously in my life, than I did that morning, the difference there is between one who feareth God and one who feareth Him not.

Notes

[1] *The Huguenots: their Settlements, Churches, and Industries in England and Ireland. By SAMUEL SMILES. John Murray.*

[2] *Those who heard it sung in the Metropolitan Tabernacle, June 4th, 1889, on the occasion of Mr. Spurgeon's address on "Old Fugal Tunes," are never likely to forget the enthusiasm evoked by the beloved Pastor's solo, which was rapturously encored.*

[3] *Extract from The Essex Telegraph, February 8th, 1881: —*
Interments at Colchester Cemetery for the week ended February 7th, 1881: —
February 2nd. — Emily Florence Norman, St. Mary, 7 weeks.
February 2nd. — Ruthford Dickerson, St. Botolph, 4 months.
February 3rd. — Elizabeth Bantock, St. Giles, 91 years.
February 5th. — Esther Pearson, (Esther Pearson is the old lady at whose shop I had trust for a farthing. — C. H. S.) St. Leonard, 96 years.

[4] *(Copy of memorial card.)*
JOHN SWINDELL,
Died at Jeffries Road, Clapham,
18th September, 1882,
Aged 81 years.
This is the person with whom I lived as usher at Newmarket.

C. H. SPURGEON.

[5] *It is remarkable that no less than three persons claimed to have been the preacher on this occasion, but Mr. Spurgeon did not recognize any one of them as the man to whom he then listened.*

[6] *It is definitely known that the date of Mr. Spurgeon's conversion was January 6th, 1850, for preaching at New Park Street Chapel, on Lord's-day morning, January 6th, 1856, from Isaiah 45:22, he said that, six years before, that very day, and at that very hour, he had been led to look to Christ, by a sermon from that text.*

[7] *On one of the foundation stones of the School-Chapel erected at Bexhill-on-Sea in ever-loving memory of Mr. Spurgeon, the following inscription has been cut, in the hope that passers-by may find salvation through reading the passage of Scripture which was blessed to his conversion: —*

HOW C. H. SPURGEON FOUND CHRIST.
"I looked to Him;
He looked on me;
And we were one for ever." — C. H. S.
"Look unto Me, and be ye saved, all the ends of the earth; for I am God, and there is none else." — Isaiah 45:22.

[15] *(Copy of memorial card,)*
IN LOVING REMEMBRANCE
OF
ROBERT BROWN,
BORN, JULY 5TH, 1805; DIED, MARCH 23RD, 1881.
Inferred in Newmarket Cemetery.

Mr. Robert Brown was a great friend of mine when I lived at Newmarket. He was superintendent of the Sunday-school, and found me opportunities for speaking. He was a fishmonger in business, and a genuine Christian in his life. — C. H. SPURGEON.

[16] See Chapter 22., — "The Lord's Hand behind the Maid's Mistake."

[17] Mr. Elven delighted to tell the story of this visit. In his Diary, that evening, he wrote: — "Have preached to-day at Waterbeach for C. H.

Spurgeon. He is a rising star. He will one day make his mark upon the denomination." Mr. Elven used to say: — "That day, I preached for Mr. Spurgeon, and he gave out the hynms for me; I should be very glad to give out the hymns for him if he would preach for me." This service Mr. Spurgeon very cheerfully rendered to Mr. Elven at Bury St.

Edmund's on more than one occasion.

[18] In Mr. Spurgeon's second volume of Outlines, there is the following note evidently referring to this day's services: — "Three joined the church at Cottenham through the sermons on Sabbath 179."

[19] Readers who desire more detailed information concerning the Tabernacle Church, can find it in The Metropolitan Tabernacle: its History and Work. By C. H. SPURGEON. Passmore and Alabaster. 1s.

and 2s.

[20] Mr. Spurgeon's volume, Commenting and Commentaries, explains this allusion: — Among entire commentators of modern date, a high place is usually awarded to THOMAS Scott, and I shall not dispute his right to it. He is the expositor of Evangelical Episcopalians, even as Adam Clarke is the prophet of the Wesleyans; but to me he has seldom given a thought, and I have almost discontinued consulting him. The very first money I ever received for pulpit services in London was invested in Thomas Scott, and I neither regretted the investment, nor became exhilarated thereby. His work has always been popular, is very judicious, thoroughly sound and gracious; but for suggestiveness and pith is not comparable to Matthew Henry. I know I am talking heresy; but I cannot help saying that, for a minister's use, Scott is mere milk and water; — good and trustworthy, but not solid enough in matter for full-grown men. In the family, Scott will hold his place; but in the study, you want condensed thought, and this you must look for elsewhere.

[21] This wish was in due time happily realized, for Mr. Henry Olney was converted, and joined the church under Mr. Spurgeon's pastoral charge. In 1854, Mr. William Olney was not a deacon, but he was a very active Christian worker.

[22] As recently as 1897, a professed minister of the gospel, lecturing in the United States, affirmed that he was present at New Park Street Chapel, and saw Mr. Spurgeon slide down the pulpit banisters! Of course, the lie was contradicted on the highest authority, yet probably he and others will still continue to tell it.

Made in the USA
Coppell, TX
27 February 2025

46474934R00157